USING COMPUTERS IN THE
LAW OFFICE

SIXTH EDITION

DELMAR CENGAGE Learning

Options.

Over 300 products in every area of the law: textbooks, online courses, CD-ROMs, reference books, companion websites, and more – helping you succeed in the classroom and on the job.

Support.

We offer unparalleled, practical support: robust instructor and student supplements to ensure the best learning experience, custom publishing to meet your unique needs, and other benefits such as Delmar Cengage Learning's Student Achievement Award. And our sales representatives are always ready to provide you with dependable service.

Feedback.

As always, we want to hear from you! Your feedback is our best resource for improving the quality of our products. Contact your sales representative or write us at the address below if you have any comments about our materials or if you have a product proposal.

Accounting and Financials for the Law Office • Administrative Law • Alternative Dispute Resolution • Bankruptcy Business Organizations/Corporations • Careers and Employment • Civil Litigation and Procedure • CLA Exam Preparation • Computer Applications in the Law Office • Constitutional Law • Contract Law • Court Reporting Criminal Law and Procedure • Document Preparation • Elder Law • Employment Law • Environmental Law • Ethics Evidence Law • Family Law • Health Care Law • Immigration Law • Intellectual Property • Internships Interviewing and Investigation • Introduction to Law • Introduction to Paralegalism • Juvenile Law • Law Office Management • Law Office Procedures • Legal Nurse Consulting • Legal Research, Writing, and Analysis • Legal Terminology • Legal Transcription • Media and Entertainment Law • Medical Malpractice Law Product Liability • Real Estate Law • Reference Materials • Social Security • Sports Law • Torts and Personal Injury Law • Wills, Trusts, and Estate Administration • Workers' Compensation Law

DELMAR CENGAGE Learning
5 Maxwell Drive
Clifton Park, New York 12065-2919

For additional information, find us online at:
www.delmar.cengage.com

USING COMPUTERS IN THE
LAW OFFICE

SIXTH EDITION

Matthew S. Cornick, J.D.
Clayton State University

DELMAR
CENGAGE Learning™

Australia • Brazil • Japan • Korea • Mexico • Singapore • Spain • United Kingdom • United States

Using Computers in the Law Office, Sixth Edition
Matthew S. Cornick

Vice President, Career and Professional Editorial: Dave Garza

Director of Learning Solutions: Sandy Clark

Senior Acquisitions Editor: Shelley Esposito

Managing Editor: Larry Main

Senior Product Manager: Melissa Riveglia

Editorial Assistant: Danielle Klahr

Vice President, Career and Professional Marketing: Jennifer Baker

Marketing Director: Deborah Yarnell

Marketing Manager: Erin Brennan

Marketing Coordinator: Erin DeAngelo

Production Director: Wendy Troeger

Production Manager: Mark Bernard

Content Project Manager: Christopher Chien

Senior Art Director: Joy Kocsis

Senior Technology Product Manager: Joe Pliss

For product information and technology assistance, contact us at
Cengage Learning Customer & Sales Support, 1-800-354-9706

For permission to use material from this text or product,
submit all requests online at **www.cengage.com/permissions**
Further permissions questions can be e-mailed to
permissionrequest@cengage.com

Library of Congress Control Number: 2010938512

ISBN-13: 978-1-4390-5691-2

ISBN-10: 1-4390-5691-9

Delmar
5 Maxwell Drive
Clifton Park, NY 12065-2919
USA

Cengage Learning is a leading provider of customized learning solutions with office locations around the globe, including Singapore, the United Kingdom, Australia, Mexico, Brazil, and Japan. Locate your local office at:
international.cengage.com/region

Cengage Learning products are represented in Canada by Nelson Education, Ltd.

To learn more about Delmar, visit **www.cengage.com/delmar**

Purchase any of our products at your local college store or at our preferred online store **www.ichapters.com**

Notice to the Reader

Publisher does not warrant or guarantee any of the products described herein or perform any independent analysis in connection with any of the product information contained herein. Publisher does not assume, and expressly disclaims, any obligation to obtain and include information other than that provided to it by the manufacturer. The reader is expressly warned to consider and adopt all safety precautions that might be indicated by the activities described herein and to avoid all potential hazards. By following the instructions contained herein, the reader willingly assumes all risks in connection with such instructions. The reader is notified that this text is an educational tool, not a practice book. Sine the law is in constant change, no rule or statement of law I this book should be relied upon for any service to any client. The reader should always refer to standard legal sources for the current rule or law. If legal advice or other expert assistance is required, the services of the appropriate professional should be sought. The publisher makes no representations or warranties of any kind, including but not limited to, the warranties of fitness for particular purpose or merchantability, nor are any such representations implied with respect to the material set forth herein, and the publisher takes no responsibility with respect to such material. The publisher shall not be liable for any special, consequential, or exemplary damages resulting, in whole or part, from the readers' use of, or reliance upon, this material.

Printed in the United States of America
1 2 3 4 5 6 7 15 14 13 12 11

For Renda, Peter, and Julia

BRIEF CONTENTS

CONTENTS

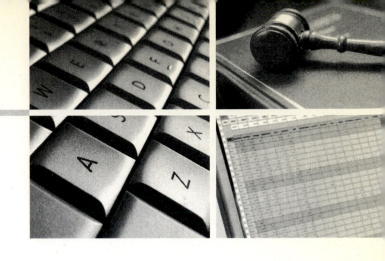

CHAPTER 3

Spreadsheet Software | 58

CHAPTER 4

Legal Timekeeping and Billing Software | 89

CHAPTER 5

Databases, Case Management, and Docket Control Software | 125

CHAPTER 6

Electronic Discovery | 148

CHAPTER 7

Litigation Support Software | 168

PREFACE

I should make a confession. There was a time (many years ago) when I believed that I could be successful in the law office without knowing much about computers. That was then. This is now. Let me state this as plainly as I can: a successful legal professional *must* know how to use a computer and the applications commonly used in a law office. With the advent of all things "e"—e-mail, e-discovery, e-filing, and so on—it is essential that you gain the skills this text seeks to impart. The 21st century is well under way and computer literacy is a basic competency in law offices. *Using Computers in the Law Office*, Sixth Edition, is designed to give students both theoretical understanding and practical experience with common law-office computer applications. These include both widely used applications, such as Microsoft Word, Excel, PowerPoint, Adobe Acrobat, and HotDocs; and programs specific to the law office, such as Tabs3, AbacusLaw, Summation iBlaze, CaseMap, TimeMap, Westlaw, LexisNexis, and TrialDirector. I hope that students will learn not only the specific uses of these programs, but also that they should not doubt their abilities or fear the prospect of working with computers.

TO THE STUDENT

If I could give you only one piece of advice, it would be this: *be patient*. Do not rush through the Hands-On Exercises. I can tell you from personal experience that haste is a sure path to mistakes and frustration. If you are a novice to these applications, I hope (and expect) that you will find you can do far more than you ever thought possible.

If I could give you a second piece of advice, it would be to *keep learning*. Technology is always evolving. Never more so than today, knowledge is power. For years, I have been telling my students that the surest way to make themselves invaluable to their employers is to know how to do something the employer does not know. Learn the skills emphasized throughout this text and then keep learning, and your success is almost a certainty.

ORGANIZATION OF THE TEXT

This textbook is organized into nine chapters. The first chapter introduces students to computers with a discussion of the importance of computers to the legal field and a review of computer hardware and software terms. The objective is to give students a rudimentary understanding of basic computer terminology and systems on which the rest of the book can build.

The next eight chapters represent the heart of the book. They cover word processing, spreadsheets, timekeeping and billing, case management/docket control, electronic discovery, litigation support, the Internet and electronic mail, computer-assisted research, and the electronic courthouse/automated courtroom and presentation graphics. Each topic is presented in a clear and organized manner and includes many examples of how the relevant software is actually used by paralegals in legal organizations.

CHANGES TO THE SIXTH EDITION

Technology in the legal field continues to grow at an astounding rate. This edition represents a substantial rewrite of much of the book and a complete overhaul of significant portions. Some of the changes include:

- Three new software applications have been added to the text:
  - Adobe Acrobat
  - HotDocs
  - TrialDirector
- Each of these new applications is accompanied by new Hands-On Exercises designed to impart the practical skills required in a modern law office.
- For the first time, most of the software applications can be installed directly from downloadable links via the Premium Website.
- The Hands-On Exercises are now contained in a separate Student Workbook.
- Almost every set of Hands-On Exercises includes a basic, intermediate, and advanced section. The exercises have been revised and updated.
- All of the screen shots have been updated.

- There are almost 500 screen shots in this edition; more than ever before.
- Expanded discussion of electronic discovery, metadata, and electronically stored information has been added.
- New, expanded sections on PDF files and document assembly were added to Chapter 2.
- A new, expanded section on law-office-specific presentation software has been added.
- A new section, entitled Ethics Question, is included in each chapter.
- All charts, graphs, surveys, terminology, and research in the book have been completely updated.
- The chapters have been reorganized and completely updated to make the information as current and applicable as possible.
- The latest developments in computer-assisted legal research (Google Scholar and Westlaw-Next) are introduced.

LEARNING FEATURES

Chapter features include the following:

- **Chapter objectives** open each chapter to focus the student's attention on the main elements of the chapter.
- **Internet sites** are referenced, and useful and relevant ones are listed near the end of each chapter.
- **Key terms** are boldfaced in the body of the text, and definitions appear in the margin for easy review and reference. (A comprehensive glossary appears at the end of the book.)
- **Numerous illustrations,** including screen shots, legal documents, tables, and other graphics, are included throughout the text.
- **Test your Knowledge exercises** are included in each chapter.
- **On the Web exercises** are included in each chapter.
- **Questions and Exercises** are included in each chapter to challenge students to apply the information learned in the chapter.
- An **Ethics Question** is included for each chapter.
- **Hands-On Exercises** are included for most chapters to give students actual experience on a computer.

HANDS-ON EXERCISES

With this new edition, the Hands-On Exercises have been collected in a separate Student Workbook. This will allow students to easily refer to the information contained in the main text while completing the exercises. Hands-On Exercises are included for 16 different applications; there are almost 120 exercises in all. These exercises assume that the student has access to a computer and to application software, but no prior computer experience is necessary to complete the tutorials.

The Hands-On Exercises include step-by-step instructions that guide the student through the application. There are literally hundreds of screen shots to guide the student and act as reference points. All of the Hands-On Exercises are completely interactive, allowing the student to gain hands-on experience with the software. In addition, all of the Hands-On Exercises are specifically related to legal organizations and legal applications, so the student not only learns how to operate the computer and software, but also learns how to use them in the legal environment.

Full tutorials are included for the following applications:

- Microsoft Word 2007
- Microsoft Word 2003
- Adobe Acrobat Professional (v.9) (NEW)
- HotDocs (v.10) (NEW)
- Microsoft Excel 2007
- Microsoft Excel 2003
- Tabs3 (v.15) (ON THE DISK)
- AbacusLaw (v.19)
- Summation iBlaze (v.3.1)
- LexisNexis CaseMap (v.8.5)
- LexisNexis TimeMap (v.5)
- Westlaw
- LexisNexis
- Microsoft PowerPoint 2007
- Microsoft PowerPoint 2003
- TrialDirector (v.6.1) (NEW)

To help students complete some of the Hands-On Exercises, data files are provided on the disk included with the text:

- Adobe Acrobat
- Excel
- HotDocs
- PowerPoint
- Tabs3
- Word Processing

EDUCATIONAL SOFTWARE

Access to the following demonstration software is included with the text via the Premium Website. Use the Access Code included on the Premium Website card included with your text to activate your free online access. Please visit http://www.CengageBrain.com to create your account, log in, and access the Premium Website.

Please note that many of the programs time out, and will not work after a certain number of days elapse from when the program was first loaded; other limitations may also apply to certain demonstration software.

- **Adobe Acrobat Professional** is a registered trademark of Adobe Systems Incorporated. Adobe Acrobat Professional times out 30 days after it is first installed.
- **HotDocs.** HotDocs 10 is a registered trademark of HotDocs, Ltd. HotDocs times out 120 days after it is first installed.
- **Tabs3.** Tabs3 is a registered trademark of Software Technology, Inc. Tabs3 does not time out, however the following features are disabled: run data file integrity check, run reindex data files, run advance current reporting month, run credit card authorization.
- **AbacusLaw.** AbacusLaw is a registered trademark of Abacus Data Systems, Inc. AbacusLaw times out 30 days after it is first installed.
- **Summation iBlaze.** Summation iBlaze is a registered trademark of the AccessData Group. Summation iBlaze times out 180 days after it is first installed.
- **LexisNexis CaseMap.** CaseMap is a registered trademark of CaseSoft, a division of LexisNexis. CaseMap times out 120 days after it is first installed.
- **LexisNexis TimeMap.** TimeMap is a registered trademark of CaseSoft, a division of LexisNexis. TimeMap times out 120 days after it is first installed.
- **TrialDirector.** TrialDirector is a registered trademark of inData Corporation. TrialDirector times out 140 days after it is first installed.

NOTE:

- Access to Microsoft Office applications (Word; Excel; PPT) is not included with the text.
- Access to the Westlaw and LexisNexis research databases (described in Chapter 8, with hands-on exercises) is not included with the text.

SUPPLEMENTAL TEACHING AND LEARNING MATERIALS

Paralegal CourseMate

Using Computers in the Law Office, Sixth Edition, includes Paralegal CourseMate, a complement to your textbook.

Paralegal CourseMate includes:

- an interactive eBook, with highlighting, note-taking, and search capabilities
- interactive teaching and learning tools, including:
  - Quizzing
  - Case studies
  - Chapter objectives
  - Chapter resources
  - Flashcards
  - Web links
  - Crossword puzzles
  - PowerPoint® presentations
  - And more!
- Engagement Tracker, a first-of-its-kind tool that monitors student engagement in the course

Go to login.cengagebrain.com to access these resources, and look for this icon **Course**Mate which denotes a resource available within CourseMate.

Premium Website

The Premium Website includes resources for instructors and students. The card in the main text includes an access code for this book's Premium Website. Go to login.cengagebrain.com to access the downloadable software demos and updates to the text.

Instructor's Manual

The Instructor's Manual has been revised to incorporate changes in the text and to provide comprehensive teaching support. The Instructor's Manual contains the following:

- Chapter Objectives
- Teaching suggestions and class discussion ideas
- Answers to exercises in the text
- Testbank and answer key
- Sample grading rubrics

Instructor Resources

Spend less time planning and more time teaching. With Delmar Cengage Learning's Instructor Resources to Accompany Using Computers in the Law Office, preparing for class and evaluating students have never been easier!

This invaluable instructor CD-ROM allows you "anywhere, anytime" access to all of your resources.

- The **Instructor's Manual** contains various resources for each chapter of the book.
- The **Computerized Testbank** in ExamView makes generating tests and quizzes a snap. With many questions and different styles to choose from, you can create customized assessments for your students with the click of a button. Add your own unique questions and print rationales for easy class preparation.
- Customizable **PowerPoint® Presentations** focus on key points for each chapter. (PowerPoint® is a registered trademark of the Microsoft Corporation.)

To access additional course materials (including Course-Mate), please go to login.cengage.com, then use your SSO (single sign on) login to access the materials.

All of these instructor materials are also posted on our Website (http://www.paralegal.delmar.cengage.com/) in the Online Resources section.

WebTutor™

The WebTutor™ supplement allows you, as the instructor, to take learning beyond the classroom. This online courseware is designed to complement the text and benefit students and instructors alike by helping to better manage your time, prepare for exams, organize your notes, and more. WebTutor™ allows you to extend your reach beyond the classroom.

WebPage

Come visit our Website at http://www.paralegal.delmar.cengage.com/, where you will find valuable information such as hot links and sample materials to download, as well as other Delmar Cengage Learning products.

Supplements At-A-Glance

Supplement:	What it is:	What's in it:
Paralegal CourseMate **CourseMate**	Online interactive teaching and learning tools and an interactive eBook. Go to login.cengage.com to access.	Interactive teaching and learning tools, including: • Quizzing • Case Studies • Chapter Objectives • Chapter Resources • Flashcards • Weblinks • Crossword Puzzles • PowerPoint® Presentations • Interactive eBook • Engagement Tracker
Premium Website	Resources for instructor and students. Access card included with textbook. Go to login.cengage.com.	• Downloadable software demo links • Updates to the text
Online Instructor's Manual	Resources for the instructor, posted online at www.paralegal.delmar.cengage.com in the Online Resources section and via Cengage Single Sign On	• Instructor's Manual with chapter objectives, teaching suggestions, answers to text questions, testbank, answer key, and grading rubrics. • PowerPoint® presentations
Instructor Resources CD-ROM **INSTRUCTOR RESOURCES**	Resources for the instructor, available on CD-ROM	• Instructor's Manual with chapter objectives, teaching suggestions, answers to text questions, testbank, and answer key. • Computerized Testbank in ExamView, with many questions and styles to choose from to create customized assessments for your students • PowerPoint® presentations
WebTUTOR™ **WebTUTOR™** WebTUTOR	WebTUTOR™ supplemental courseware is the best way to use the Internet to turn everyone in your class into a front-row student. It complements Cengage Learning paralegal textbooks by providing interactive reinforcement that helps students grasp complex concepts. WebTUTOR™ allows you to know quickly what concepts your students are or aren't grasping.	• Automatic and immediate feedback from quizzes and exams • Online exercises that reinforce what students have learned • Flashcards • Greater interaction and involvement through online discussion forums

ACKNOWLEDGMENTS

This book was made possible by many individuals. This book required an enormous amount of work from a superb team of talented professionals. To all of you, many thanks.

REVIEWERS

Special thanks go to the reviewers of the text for their ideas and suggestions:

Sally Bisson
College of St. Mary
Omaha, NE

Anne Murphy Brown
Ursuline College
Pepper Pike, OH

Katherine Currier
Elms College
Chicopee, MA

Darren Defoe
Andover College
South Portland, ME

Donna Donathan
Marshall University
Huntington, WV

Barry Goodson
Columbia Southern University
Orange Beach, AL

Jonathan Kaiser
Tacoma Community College
Tacoma, WA

Wesley Marion
Ivy Tech Community College of Indiana
Lafayette, IN

Susan McCabe
Kellogg Community College
Battle Creek, MI

Elizabeth McCowan
Pellissippi State Technical Community College
Knoxville, TN

Tonya Morse
Institute of Business and Medical Careers, Inc.
Fort Collins, CO

Mary Mullin
Cerritos College
Norwalk, CA

Jessica Neilson
Highline College
Des Moines, WA

Mary Carol Parker
Maryville University
St. Louis, MO

Beth Pless
NE Wisconsin Technical College
Green Bay, WI

Donna Schoebel
Capital University Law School
Columbus, OH

Marc Vallen
University of Hartford
West Hartford, CT

Delmar Cengage Learning

I am deeply indebted to my editors at Cengage Delmar Learning. Shelley Esposito is my Acquisitions Editor; she asked me to take on this project and was always there when I needed her. Melissa Riveglia, the Senior Product Manager, had the unenviable task of making sure all the T's were crossed and the I's dotted. So many other folks had the responsibility of double-checking the accuracy of the text and the Hands-On Exercises. This project would not have been possible without their support and encouragement.

My Family

I am so grateful to my family. By necessity, writing is a solitary task and there have been more than a few missed dinners and vacations not taken in the past two years. I love you all very much and appreciate your patience and encouragement. This is for you.

Please note that the Internet resources are of a time-sensitive nature and
URL addresses may often change or be deleted.

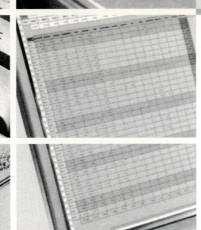

CHAPTER 1

Overview of Computers in the Law Office

CHAPTER OBJECTIVES

After completing this chapter, you should be able to do the following:

1. Identify how computers are being used in legal organizations.
2. Identify the various computer-system components.
3. Distinguish among the various forms of computer software.
4. Understand the concept of metadata.
5. Recognize the ethical issues raised by the use of computers in the law office.

Computers are an important part of our society. They are used in nearly every facet of our lives, including our jobs, to automate services and products; our health, to enhance medical treatment; our government, to maintain, organize, and analyze information; our education, to help children read and write; our financial institutions, to track and maintain our banking, credit, and investment-related information; our entertainment, including the Internet, movies, music, and the arts; and our transportation, to control the electronic systems in cars and public transportation systems such as subways.

Just as the use of computers in our society has grown, so has the use of computers in the practice of law. The application of computers in large, medium, and small law firms, corporate law departments, and government offices has increased dramatically over the past few decades. It is imperative for paralegals entering the job market to have an understanding of computers, because computers and computer skills (1) allow a paralegal to be more productive and efficient, (2) can give an attorney and paralegal a competitive advantage in court, (3) simplify complicated tasks, and (4) allow the user to stay competitive in the job market.

INTRODUCTION TO COMPUTERS AND THE LAW

Prior to the early 1980s, computers had little effect on the practice of law. A few extremely large firms used them for "back-office" functions such as accounting or billing, but other than that, computers were not used much in legal organizations. A legal professional's tools of the trade were pen, legal pad, law books, typewriter, and copy machine. After the introduction of personal computers in the mid-1980s, all of that began to change. Now computers are involved in nearly every facet of the legal professional's job. Virtually all legal professionals use a desktop, laptop, and/or handheld computer with DVD drives, Internet and email access, and a printer. It is now possible—indeed, often required—to stay in contact with colleagues no matter where they are.

A computer revolution has taken place in the legal industry. An industry that started out rejecting technology has now embraced it. Much of the rise in computer use in legal organizations is due to the increased power, decreased cost, and increased ease of use and efficiency of computers, all of which contribute to the competitive advantage that they give the user. Computers are being used for everything from word processing, timekeeping, and billing to legal research on the Internet to website management. This holds true for all types and sizes of law firms, whether a solo practitioner, a thousand-attorney global law firm, or a corporate or government legal department. In prior years, solo practitioners and small law offices lagged far behind larger law offices when it came to technology. This is generally no longer true. Technology is no longer a tool just for the large law firm. The cost of technology has decreased so much that even solo practitioners, small law offices, and legal aid offices can afford state-of-the-art computers.

Computers are used to organize documents, not just in large cases involving tens of thousands of documents, but in smaller cases as well. Computers are used to communicate with clients, often via email, and to exchange documents. Attorneys take depositions of witnesses by using videoconferencing. Laptop computers are used in the courtroom to search for documents, track exhibits, and make presentations to juries. Laptop or handheld computers are used in the courtroom to conduct legal research right at the counsel table. Later in this chapter, we will discuss some more recent and emerging technologies.

Internet
One of the world's largest computer networks; actually a "network of networks." It allows hundreds of millions of users around the world to share information.

The Internet has had a profound impact on the practice of law and on how paralegals perform their jobs. The **Internet** is one of the world's largest computer networks; actually, it is a "network of networks." It connects hundreds of millions of computers around the world and allows them to share information. Legal organizations and paralegals in particular can send and receive electronic messages, research both legal and nonlegal information, send documents, and do much more. The pervasive use of the Internet is clearly driving some of the need for paralegals to have good computer skills.

Computers are also being used by courts in a variety of ways. Many courts allow parties to file documents electronically, using the Internet, and allow attorneys and paralegals online access to the courts' computer systems. Courts use computers to track currently pending cases. Such systems can automatically set scheduling deadlines for each case and alert judges to scheduling concerns or problems, particularly for criminal cases in which defendants have the right to a speedy trial. In some courts, court reporters can store information electronically, within seconds of it being presented, so that it can be displayed immediately for jurors, judges, and parties to view the information.

In short, all types of legal organizations and legal professionals, including paralegals, are using computers on a daily basis in a variety of ways. Given this overwhelming move toward technology use and computerization, all types of legal organizations are looking for legal professionals who not only have good legal skills, but also have the skills to use the organization's computer systems with little additional training.

ELEMENTARY COMPUTER CONCEPTS

This text is not concerned with imparting technical and scientific information on how a computer operates; rather, its focus is on how paralegals can use computers in a practical way to carry out their duties. Nevertheless, it is necessary to cover some basic computer concepts as background for users. The following sections introduce most of the terms and concepts that the paralegal will encounter on the job.

SYSTEM COMPONENTS

A **computer** is an electronic device that accepts, processes, outputs, and stores information. Information that is entered into a computer is called **input**. Information that comes out of a computer is called **output**. **Hardware** is the actual physical components of a computer system. **Software** refers to instructions that make the computer hardware function. A computer system works together with peripheral devices, such as auxiliary storage and input, output, and communication devices (hardware), to accomplish the information-handling tasks. The system contains a central processing unit and a main memory.

Central Processing Unit

The **central processing unit (CPU)** organizes and processes information. It is the "brain" of the computer. It performs logical operations—in accordance with the operating system software—and coordinates and communicates with auxiliary storage devices and input, output, and communication devices (see Exhibit 1–1).

At the heart of the CPU is the **processor chip** (see Exhibit 1–1). One or more processor chips perform the actual arithmetic computations and logic functions. The speed of the processor, and thus of the computer, is determined by how many bits or bytes of information the chip can process at a time and how fast it acts to process the information. The more bits that can be processed in one cycle, the faster the computer will be. For example, a processor that processes 64 bits at a time is considerably faster than one that processes only 16 bits. How fast a computer works to process information is also characterized in **gigahertz (GHz)**, which refers to the "clock speed" of a computer. The faster the clock speed is, the faster the computer processes information.

EXHIBIT 1–1

Central processing unit (CPU)

© Cengage Learning 2012

computer
An electronic device that accepts input data, processes data, outputs data, and stores data electronically; types include desktop, laptop, handheld, tablet, and file server.

input
Data or information that is entered or transferred into a computer (including by keyboard, mouse, scanner, voice, etc.).

output
Information or computer results that are produced or transmitted from a computer to a user as a result of the computer's operations (including to monitor, printer, etc.).

hardware
The physical equipment of a computer system, as opposed to programs or software.

software
Computer programs that instruct the computer hardware how to function and perform tasks.

central processing unit (CPU)
The part of a computer that contains the processor chip and main memory. The CPU organizes and manipulates information, in addition to coordinating with peripheral devices.

processor chip
The part of the computer that performs the actual arithmetic computations and logic functions.

gigahertz (GHz)
Measure of the clock speed of a computer.

Main Memory

The function of the **main memory** is to hold or store information that the computer is processing. This is accomplished through memory chips. **Memory chips**, like processor chips, are made up of tiny electronic circuits, but instead of processing information, they store or hold information. Main memory comes in one of two types: read-only and random-access.

Read-Only Memory **Read-only memory (ROM)** is permanent, unchanging memory that a computer uses internally to operate itself. It is permanently installed by the manufacturer and cannot be changed or altered; hence the name "read-only." A computer reads ROM, but you cannot enter information into ROM or change the data in it. The data contained in ROM is not lost when the computer is turned off. Practically speaking, you never even become aware that ROM exists.

Random-Access Memory **Random-access memory (RAM)** is temporary memory that is used when the computer is turned on. Unlike ROM, it is erased when the computer is turned off. RAM is used to temporarily store programs "on the computer screen" when the programs are loaded. For example, when a person is using a word-processing program, that program is in RAM. As words are typed into the word processor, the words are also stored in RAM. To save the information when the computer is turned off, the user must save the information from RAM to an auxiliary storage device such as a hard disk. An auxiliary storage device stores data so it can be retrieved later. One of the most frustrating experiences in computer use occurs when one is working with information in RAM and power is interrupted, such as when the lights flicker from an interruption in power transmission. When power to the computer is lost, even if just for a fraction of a second, the computer turns off and any information in RAM is lost. (This quickly teaches users the value of frequent saves, which transfer information from RAM to more permanent **storage**.)

The number of bytes of information a computer can hold is measured in kilobytes (K), megabytes (MB), gigabytes (GB), terabytes (TB), or petabytes (PB) (see Exhibit 1–2).

PERIPHERAL DEVICES

Peripheral devices are pieces of equipment that are connected to a computer to perform specific functions. They include auxiliary storage devices, input devices, output devices, and communication devices.

Kilobyte(K)	=	One thousand bytes	(1,000)
Megabyte(MB)	=	One million bytes	(1,000,000)
Gigabyte(GB)	=	One billion bytes	(1,000,000,000)
Terabyte(TB)	=	One trillion bytes	(1,000,000,000,000)
Petabyte(PB)	=	One quadrillion bytes	(1,000,000,000,000,000)

EXHIBIT 1–2

Storage capacities

---

main memory
The part of the CPU that stores information that the computer is processing. Main memory consists of read-only memory and random-access memory.

memory chips
Parts of a computer that store or hold information.

read-only memory (ROM)
A part of main memory that contains permanent information a computer uses to operate itself. ROM can be read, but cannot be written to.

random-access memory (RAM)
A part of main memory that is temporary and volatile in nature; it is erased every time the computer's power is turned off. Application programs and data are loaded into RAM when the computer is processing the data.

storage
Retention of electronic information for future use (using storage devices such as hard disks, CD-ROMs, DVDs, flash drives, and other media).

peripheral devices
Pieces of equipment that are connected to a computer to perform specific functions, such as storing information (auxiliary storage devices), inputting information (input devices), outputting information (output devices), and communicating with other computers (communication devices).

Auxiliary Storage Devices

An **auxiliary storage device** is used to permanently store information. Auxiliary storage devices and RAM are sometimes confused with one another, because they both use megabytes and gigabytes to refer to their respective **storage capacities**, and they both store information, albeit for different purposes. RAM is where information is stored temporarily, while the user is working with it, and is erased every time the computer is turned off. In contrast, an auxiliary storage device stores information permanently.

Hard Disk For permanent storage, most personal computers contain a rigid magnetic disk or **hard disk drive**. Hard disks are very reliable and have fast **access times**. They can also read and write data. It is possible, however, for them to crash if they are handled roughly (e.g., if the computer is dropped) or if they are defective or old. When a crash occurs, some or all of the information on the hard disk is lost or destroyed. Crashing often causes physical damage to the surface of the disk, making data retrieval difficult even for experts. Sometimes, it seems that hard drives crash for no reason at all. This alone is a good reason to get in the habit of backing up your data on a regular basis.

At least one hard disk drive is usually mounted inside the computer; usually a small light turns on when information is either accessed from or saved to the drive. Most hard disks are permanently sealed and are fixed inside the drive; thus, they cannot be removed. Large-capacity hard disks are standard equipment on most computers produced today. Many people use external hard drives for backup purposes; these auxiliary devices are literally freestanding hard disk drive units.

Removable Drives A large amount of data can be stored using **removable drives**. Removable drives include zip drives and flash drives. Zip drives are about the size of an audio cassette and are relatively slow; they are a somewhat dated technology. Flash drives have largely replaced them. Flash drives, thumb drives (so called because they are about the size of a human thumb), or sticks are extremely small and portable, and are also fairly fast. A flash drive simply plugs into a computer's USB port and is immediately accessible by the computer once it has been loaded. Flash drives are typically used to move large files from one system to another. Many MP3 players also use this technology.

Magnetic Tape In a **magnetic tape system**, data is written to and stored on a spool of magnetic tape. The magnetic tape can be stored either on large tape reels or in tape cartridges.

Magnetic tape systems store data sequentially. (This is similar to a VHS tape: if you want to access a particular section of the tape, you typically have to fast-forward or rewind the tape to the desired section.) For this reason, access times are quite slow. This is why magnetic tape is usually used only for making backup copies of information residing on other storage devices. However, although their access times are slow, they have large capacities, up to a terabyte or more.

Optical Storage Devices Using laser beams, **optical storage devices** can record data on and retrieve data from small plastic disks, such as CDs and DVDs. Optical storage devices can store hundreds of megabytes of data on a single disk. This has allowed manufacturers to store everything from music and video/multimedia presentations to large software programs on a single disk. The space savings made possible by these technologies has been immensely beneficial to law offices, which often must keep large numbers of records for long periods of time.

---

auxiliary storage device
A device that stores information so that it can be retrieved for later use. Auxiliary storage devices retain data after power to the computer has been turned off. Auxiliary storage devices include flash drives, hard disk drives, and others.

storage capacity
The maximum amount of data that can be stored on a device.

hard disk drive
A reliable and fast auxiliary storage device that stores data on a rigid magnetic disk; may be built into the computer (internal) or a freestanding peripheral device (external).

access time
The amount of time it takes to transfer data between a storage device and RAM.

removable drive
A small portable device that stores a large amount of data; often used to transfer information between computers.

magnetic tape system
Storage device that records data on magnetic tape.

optical storage devices
Devices that use laser beams to write data onto small plastic disks. Optical storage devices can record hundreds of megabytes of data on a single disk.

Input Devices

Input devices are used to enter information into a computer. Input devices include the mouse, keyboards, scanners (including bar code and imaging scanners), voice recognition devices, digital cameras, and others.

Computer Keyboard Most computer keyboards are similar to the keyboard of an ordinary typewriter, with a few additions. They are made up of alphanumeric keys, function keys, cursor movement keys, special keys, and a numeric keypad. Keyboards are inexpensive and come in a variety of types and styles.

Scanners A scanner has the ability to bring hard-copy documents into a computer. Many scanners look like small office copiers. Scanners shine light on the document and translate the reflected light into digital signals that a computer can recognize and store. The scanner allows the image of a document, such as a photograph or a microfilm frame, to be put into a computer; this is called imaging.

More specifically, **imaging** refers to the ability to scan a document into a computer so the user can see the exact image of the original document on the computer. Imaging is similar to taking a photograph of a document: you can see the image of the document, but you cannot change it or edit the text. To edit the text of a document, you would need optical character recognition software (see below).

With document imaging, the paper is handled only once, when it is scanned into the computer. Document images can be reviewed, copied, sorted, and filed electronically. Document imaging gives users immediate access to documents, saves storage space, and keeps originals from being lost or damaged. Imaging software allows law offices to track and manage scanned images. Imaging and OCR technology are used quite frequently in litigation support, discussed in Chapter 7, to track and search for documents in litigation.

Scanners can also translate the text of a document into an electronic format so that the text can then be electronically searched or manipulated with a word processor. This is called **optical character recognition (OCR)**. Using a scanner and OCR software, users can "read" printed material into a computer so the text of the document can be searched (like searching in Westlaw or LexisNexis databases) or brought into a word processor for text editing. In OCR, the scanner reflects light onto the printed text, compares the shapes of the letters in the text to the letters in the scanner/computer memory, and writes the information into the computer. Through the use of OCR technology, it is possible to scan printed information into a computer much faster than a keyboard operator could enter the information. Large OCR scanners can scan thousands of pages of text into a computer in a relatively short time.

However, if the printed text that is being scanned does not exactly match the letters in the scanner's memory, an error will occur, and the right letter will not be entered. This potential for inaccuracy can be a problem. Even if a document is scanned in with 99 percent accuracy, that can still leave plenty of errors in the scanned version of the document. For example, if a user scans in a 10,000-word document, that would leave 100 errors in the document. The accuracy rating drops dramatically if a document is not clear or has nonstandard type. OCR scanners can be very useful, but accuracy must be checked carefully.

Imaging and optical character recognition are similar yet different. Imaging allows the user to see the document in its original state, but the user cannot search for words using imaging. Optical character recognition allows the user to search for words and word patterns, but not to see the exact image of the original document, only the text it contained.

---

input device
Devices used to enter information into a computer; include the mouse, keyboards, scanners, voice recognition devices, digital cameras, and others.

imaging
Scanning a document into a computer so the user can see an exact picture of the document on the computer.

optical character recognition (OCR)
A technology that allows the text of documents to be read or scanned into a computer so the text of the document can be searched or brought into a word processor to be edited.

Some law firms use **bar code scanner** systems to track documents in litigation. This is the same technology used in nearly all retail stores. Once a bar code is applied to a document, the bar code scanner or reader can read the special lines on the bar codes and recognize which document it identifies.

Many multifunction devices are currently on the market that combine OCR scanning, imaging, faxing, copying, and printing. The prices of all of these technologies have decreased significantly in recent years, making these useful devices extremely popular.

Mouse   The cursor on a monitor is moved with a **mouse**. It is approximately the same size as the palm of your hand. As the mouse is moved, it transmits to the computer a signal that correspondingly moves the cursor in the same direction. For example, if the mouse is moved to the right, the cursor moves to the right, and so on. There are a variety of other devices that perform functions similar to those of a mouse. These include trackballs, trackpoints, and touch pads.

Speech Recognition   The ability of a computer to understand spoken words is called **speech recognition**. The user speaks into a microphone that is connected to the computer. Using sophisticated software, the computer is able to interpret the speech and translate it into computer commands and into text for use with word processors, email, and other software. Most speech recognition software leads the user through exercises that are designed to teach the software the nuances of that particular person's voice.

Voice input systems have a number of advantages. Most people can speak faster and more naturally than they can write or type, and they need little or no training to use such a system. It also frees the hands to perform other tasks. Speech recognition systems are very popular in offices where they augment or take the place of some secretarial functions such as transcribing dictation. Some users also prefer to use speech recognition instead of typing, as it increases their productivity.

Although speech recognition accuracy is quite good—typically greater than 95 percent—it is still absolutely necessary to proofread the text created by the software. For this reason, among others, many legal organizations do not make much use of speech recognition technology.

Digital Cameras and Camcorders   Digital cameras and camcorders allow the user to take photographs or full-motion video and sound and download or transfer them directly into a computer. The software accompanying these devices also allows the user to easily edit, enhance, and view the information. Many legal organizations are using these devices to cut and paste data directly into presentation graphics programs for displaying evidence to juries. Many legal organizations are rediscovering the old adage that "a picture is worth a thousand words." Video evidence can be extremely persuasive to juries and factfinders.

Output Devices

Output devices provide a user with the data that a computer has generated or stored. Like input devices, they come in many different types. The type you select depends on the application you are using.

Computer output is displayed on a **monitor**. It is important to recognize that the quality of the picture on the monitor is in part determined by the **video adapter card**, which acts as an interface between the monitor and the computer. The number of colors that a color monitor can display also depends on the video adapter card. Because of the graphical nature of the Internet and the rise in multimedia and video, manufacturers now produce graphics accelerators, video card memory, and other hardware to make graphics appear on the monitor faster.

---

bar code scanner
Device that reads the special lines of bar codes. Can be used to track documents in litigation, or physical objects such as office furniture and equipment.

mouse
An input device used to move the cursor on the monitor. The cursor moves in the same direction as the mouse is moved.

speech recognition
The ability of a computer to understand spoken words.

output device
Peripheral device that provides a user with the data a computer has generated, accessed, or manipulated.

monitor
Screen that displays computer output.

video adapter card
Piece of hardware that acts as an interface between the monitor and the computer.

Much data is still output on paper (sometimes called hard copy) with a printer. Nearly all computers now come with a sound card and speakers. A **sound card** enhances the sounds that come out of the computer and/or enables speakers attached to a computer to function.

A portable projector allows a user to display the image from a computer to an audience. Portable projectors are often used in trials in conjunction with laptop computers to display presentations and computer-generated evidence to juries.

Communication Devices

A communication device, such as a modem, allows computers to exchange information. Such a device is technically both an input and an output device, as it can receive data from other computers (input) and also send data to other computers (output).

A **modem** allows computers in different locations to communicate using a telephone line. Although a modem acting through a dial-up connection allows users to exchange information with each other over long distances, this type of connection is very slow compared to other types of technology. This is particularly true regarding most World Wide Web sites on the Internet, which are graphically based. Cable, T1, and DSL are alternatives to standard analog phone lines and modems, and are increasingly popular because of the much speedier communication they enable. These and other technologies are making standard modems obsolete. The main advantages that dial-up connections have over cable, T1, and DSL are their much lower cost and almost universal availability. However, these advantages seldom compensate for the extended time required for information transfer via dial-up.

A **cable modem** is a data modem that is designed to work over cable television lines (increasingly, these lines are fiber-optic). The primary advantage of cable modems over dial-up modems is their much faster data-transmission speed, made possible by cable's far greater bandwidth.

DSL (Digital Subscriber Line) is a type of digital phone line that is hundreds of times faster than a dial-up connection. This type of connection also allows data and voice to be transmitted on the same line.

Wireless Modem Many mobile phones and handheld computers now use **wireless modems** to connect to the Internet. A wireless modem typically is either built into the device or slides into an open slot on a laptop or handheld computer; in either case, it allows the user to access email, the Internet, and other mobile devices without hardwired connections.

Videoconferencing **Videoconferencing** is a private broadcast between two or more remote locations, with live image transmission, display, and sound. This technology uses data communications to conduct long-distance, face-to-face meetings. Because of the huge amounts of sound and image data transferred with this technology, it requires audiovisual equipment and special communication lines. Videoconferencing is very useful in a legal organization for meeting with clients, interviewing job candidates, meeting with co-counsel, taking depositions, and other applications.

Voice over Internet Protocol **Voice over Internet Protocol (VoIP)** allows users to make telephone calls using a broadband Internet connection instead of a regular (analog) phone line. Most VoIP service providers allow the user to call anyone who has a telephone number, including local, long-distance, mobile, and international numbers. VoIP allows a user to make a call directly from a computer, a special VoIP phone, or a traditional telephone using an adapter. Cost savings over long-distance telephone charges can be substantial, because most VoIP providers charge a flat fee

---

sound card
A device that enhances the sounds that come out of a computer and/or enables speakers attached to a computer to function. Nearly all computers now come with a sound card.

modem
A device that allows computers in different locations to communicate using a telephone line.

cable modem
A data modem that is designed to work over cable TV lines.

DSL (Digital Subscriber Line)
A type of digital phone line that allows both data and voice to be transmitted on the same line, simultaneously if desired. Transmission speed is fairly fast.

wireless modem
Modems that many mobile phones and handheld computers now use to connect to the Internet.

videoconferencing
A private broadcast between two or more remote locations, with live image transmission, display, and sound. Uses data communications to conduct long-distance, face-to-face meetings.

Voice over Internet Protocol (VoIP)
Functionality that allows users to make telephone calls using a broadband Internet connection instead of a regular phone line.

for unlimited call time. Some systems can support multiparty conference calls, and can integrate voice mail and faxes with email.

A major disadvantage is VoIP's dependence on electrical power: if the power goes out, so do the phones, unless there is a backup system. VoIP is also dependent on proper operation of both the broadband connection and the network; if they go down, so do the phones.

Communication Devices in Legal Organizations Most legal organizations have long since moved from slower, dial-up modems to faster communication technologies such as cable, DSL, and T1. This is primarily due to the overwhelming use of the Internet in law offices and the need for fast connections to email.

LOCAL AND WIDE AREA NETWORKS

Networks connect a multitude of computers and allow them to work together. Law offices may use local area and/or wide area networks.

Local Area Networks

Computers started as single-user systems. A **single-user system** can accommodate only one person at a time and is not linked to other systems or computers. A **local area network (LAN)** is a multiuser system that links computers that are in close proximity for the purpose of communication. Two primary reasons for installing a LAN are to share data and software among multiple computers and to share peripheral devices such as printers, optical storage devices and communication devices (see Exhibit 1–3).

Consider how a LAN could be used in a law office. Suppose a law office has 20 staff members who need access to each other's word-processing files, docket control data, and time and billing information, and who also need to communicate via email with one another. Using stand-alone computers, the staff members would not be able to share information effectively. However, using a LAN, each staff member has access to all the information residing on any computer in the network. Another advantage is that different types of computers (e.g., IBM-compatible machines, Apple Macintosh machines, and others) can be linked together to share data in many LAN configurations.

Nearly all legal organizations now have a LAN, and most software that is purchased for legal organizations is a networked version of a single-user program. Primary network software used in a legal organization typically includes word processing, database management, spreadsheets, timekeeping and billing, accounting, calendar/docket control/case management, electronic mail, document management, litigation support, client files/records, and specialized legal-specific programs. With a network, attorneys and paralegals who are traveling can connect to the network and exchange messages, access files, and do other tasks.

There are different types of LANs, including client/server and peer-to-peer networks.

Client/Server Networks **Client/server networks** use a server or servers to enhance the functionality of the other computers on the network. Network servers are computers that meet the needs of the other computers on the network, which are called workstations or clients (see Exhibit 1–3). The server stores program files and data files, and hosts email and remote access platforms used by the workstations, among other possible applications. Some servers are dedicated, meaning that they

single-user system
A computer that can accommodate only one person at a time and is not linked to other systems or computers.

local area network (LAN)
A multiuser system linking computers that are in close proximity for the purpose of communication.

client/server network
A network that uses a server (or servers) to enhance the function and meet the needs of the other computers on the network.

EXHIBIT 1–3

A local area network (LAN) allows users to share hardware and software.

cannot be used for any other purpose. Other servers, depending on how the LAN is configured, are nondedicated, meaning that they can also be used as workstations. Most LANs in legal organizations are the client/server type.

Servers are generally high-powered machines with large memories that can support or even perform some of the computing functions of many workstations. Servers can be devoted to specific network operating functions and can be connected together on the network. For example, a legal organization could have separate electronic mail servers, file servers, print servers, web servers, and remote access servers (for giving staff access to the office network from remote locations such as a staff member's house, hotel room, or a courtroom).

In years past, most networks were hardwired. Today, an alternative to hardwired networks that require cables is **wireless networking.** Wireless networks are extremely popular in law offices, because they nearly eliminate the necessity to install long cable runs throughout an office.

Peer-to-Peer Networks   **Peer-to-peer networks** do not use a server; instead, each computer on the network acts as both a server and a client. Because the computers are

wireless networking
System that allows computers on the network to communicate with each other using wireless antennas coordinated through a wired access point.

peer-to-peer network
A computer network in which each computer acts as both a server and a client.

performing two tasks—running an application program, such as a word processor, and acting as a server—they are not as fast as the workstations on a client/server network. However, they still offer the ability to share printers, files, and other resources. Peer-to-peer networks are less expensive, because they do not require a separate server.

Web-Based Networks: Internet, Intranet, and Extranet

Many legal organizations have expanded their networks to include intranets and extranets. An **intranet** is an internal network designed to provide and disseminate information to internal staff; most such systems use a web browser and mimic the look and feel of the World Wide Web. In much the same way as the Internet provides information to the public, an intranet provides information to internal users. An intranet can be walled off from the Internet to provide security from Internet users. An intranet is part of a legal organization's networked computer system and in some cases the organization has a server dedicated to supporting the intranet. Information that a legal organization typically places on an intranet includes office policies and procedures, links to law-related websites, training materials, contact lists, and access to the firm's extranet. The use of intranets is growing substantially in legal organizations.

An **extranet** is a network designed to provide, disseminate, and share confidential information with clients. A client with a web browser can tap into the legal organization's extranet, after going through security and identification/password protections, to access his or her case plans, documents, case strategies, billing information, and other information. This is also extremely helpful when a law office must communicate with multiple clients or co-counsel on one case. Exhibit 1–4 notes the similarities and differences between intranets and extranets.

Wide Area Networks

Wide area networks take up where LANs stop. A **wide area network (WAN)** is a multiuser system linking computers that may be located thousands of miles apart. Large law firms that have offices located across the country or across the world can use WANs to allow their offices to communicate with each other as if they were next door. LANs and WANs can also be used together. A law firm's offices located in New York and Los Angeles may each have a LAN, but be connected to each other using a WAN. LANs and WANs allow law offices to share information in the same location, across town, or across the globe.

Networks in Legal Organizations

LANs, WANs, intranets, and extranets are now commonly found in legal organizations. As technology continues to expand, so will the use of all types of networks in the legal industry. Although it is not necessary for a paralegal to have detailed knowledge of the ins and outs of office networks, it is helpful to have a general overview of how they function, because of the importance of networks to the practice of law in the twenty-first century.

INTRODUCTION TO COMPUTER SOFTWARE

Computer hardware is useless without computer software to make it operate. Computer software (i.e., a computer program) is a set of step-by-step instructions that direct a computer how to function and perform tasks. Three basic types of software are available: operating system software, utility software, and application software.

The **operating system software (program)** instructs the computer hardware how to operate its internal circuitry and how to communicate with input, output,

intranet
An internal network designed to provide and disseminate information to internal staff; most mimic the look and feel of the World Wide Web.

extranet
A secure web-based site that allows clients to access information about their cases and collaborate with the legal professionals who are providing legal services to them.

wide area network (WAN)
A multiuser system linking computers that may be located thousands of miles apart.

operating system software (program)
A set of instructions that tell the computer how to operate its own circuitry and manage its components; also controls how the computer communicates with input, output, and auxiliary storage devices. Allows the user to manage the computer.

EXHIBIT 1–4

Extranet and intranet

and auxiliary storage devices; this program also allows the user to manage the computer. Operating system software ties the computer hardware and software together. Using operating system software, users can delete old or unwanted files, obtain a directory of the files on a disk, and manage the resources of a computer. Some type of operating system software comes free with nearly all computers.

Utility software helps users with the housekeeping and maintenance tasks that a computer requires. Thousands of utility programs are available. Utility programs can back up a hard disk, recover data that has been accidentally deleted, protect computers from viruses, and carry out many other tasks.

Application software instructs the computer to perform a specific function or task, such as word processing. Practically speaking, when people use the word software, they are usually referring to application software. A word-processing program, a spreadsheet program, and a database program are all examples of application software, because they each tell the computer how to perform a specific task or set of tasks.

Relax, You've Done This Before: Specific Law Office Uses of Computer Software

Take comfort in the fact that most paralegal students are already competent in and comfortable with performing basic computer functions. You may have used a software

utility software
Instructions that help users with the housekeeping and maintenance tasks a computer requires; helps manage either the hardware or software aspects of a computer.

application software
Instructions (programs) that tell the computer to perform a specific function or task, such as word processing.

program to "clean" your computer by removing unwanted files. That is an example of a utility program. It is likely that you have prepared documents (e.g., a term paper) using a word-processing program. That is an example of application software. It follows, then, that you probably already have many of the essential skills required to use a computer in a modern law office.

Software Licensing

Most software is purchased subject to a **license agreement**. The license agreement sets out the terms under which the person or group is allowed to use the software; it specifies the purchaser's rights to and restrictions on use of the software. Some license agreements are based on the number of computers that the software can be loaded on, whereas others are based on the number of people who can use the software. Use of software in a manner that violates the license agreement, such as loading software onto additional computers beyond the number of licenses that have been purchased, can constitute copyright infringement. The licensor may revoke a violator's license(s) and/or may bring a civil suit against the violator.

Operating System Software

When the computer is turned on, or "booted up," the operating system is loaded into RAM. The operating system is necessary to the basic functioning of a computer; the computer cannot even turn itself on properly without such a system.

Operating systems are usually unique to each type of computer. For example, an Apple Macintosh computer uses a different operating system than do IBM-compatible computers. The manufacturer of a computer usually supplies the operating system, though this is not always the case. Some computer manufacturers now offer a choice of the operating system to be used.

Duties of the Operating System The operating system is a cross between a traffic officer who directs the flow of data between the computer and different input, output, and auxiliary storage devices and a housekeeper who organizes and maintains the system. Operating systems manage main memory; control input, output, and auxiliary storage devices (including addition of new devices and deletion of old ones); manage the CPU; give the user tools with which to perform maintenance on the computer; and manage the computer's files. From a user's viewpoint, file management is one of the most important things the operating system software does. File management includes copying files, deleting files, and renaming files, as well as maintaining and accessing stored files.

The Windows Operating System **Windows** is a graphical operating system developed by Microsoft for IBM-compatible computers. Every few years Microsoft updates Windows to add more features.

All versions of Windows use a graphical user interface (GUI). The graphical interface allows users to enter commands and work with programs using a mouse, pull-down menus, and icons (pictures that appear on the screen to represent applications or documents) instead of requiring users to learn a complicated and exacting command structure. Windows is also a multitasking environment that allows users to run several programs at the same time.

Tens of thousands of programs are currently available for the Windows operating system. It is the predominant operating system for IBM-compatible computers, and it commands most of the computer software market share in the United States. Windows applications have similar menus and appearances, and

license agreement
Contract setting out the user's rights and restrictions on how a piece of software can be used.

Windows
A graphical operating system developed by Microsoft for IBM-compatible computers. Various versions of Windows include Windows XP, Windows Vista, and Windows 7.

can share information quite easily. This similarity among programs allows users to learn programs more quickly than if they had to learn a new command structure for each program. More than 95 percent of all legal organizations use some version of the Windows operating system. Microsoft Windows, in its various versions, dominates the legal market for computer operating systems.

Network Operating Systems   Local area networks require special **network operating systems** to handle communications among the computers on a network. Regular operating systems such as Windows XP and Windows 7 may work with file server networks. However, more complex client/server networks require network operating systems such as Windows NT or Novell Netware.

Utility Software

Utility software helps manage either the hardware or the software aspects of a computer. Some utility programs come as part of the operating system; others are separate programs. There is a huge amount of utility software, including utilities that compress files, back up files, and protect a computer from viruses or other "malware."

Compression Utilities   **Compression utilities**, such as WinZip, reconfigure (compress) a file so that it takes up less room when it is saved or transmitted. This is particularly important when one is sending or receiving extremely large files (files containing graphics or video are often huge, and can take a long time to download or upload). Many large files that are downloaded from the Internet are routinely compressed.

Backup Utilities   **Backup utility** programs create a copy of a user's hard disk or other storage device. The backup copy can be restored if the hard disk is damaged or lost. Some backup utilities allow users to schedule specific times to back up their files (for example, every Wednesday and Friday, or every morning at 2:00 a.m.).

Antivirus and Antispyware Utilities   **Antivirus and antispyware utilities** attempt to prevent viruses and spyware programs from getting into a computer system, and also locate and remove any viruses that do manage to get into the computer. Because new viruses and spyware appear almost daily, many antivirus software manufactures allow users to update their software from the Internet. Exhibit 1–5 lists some important things that users can do to prevent or lessen the chance of getting a computer virus or spyware. Once a virus or spyware gets onto a user's computer system, it can be extremely difficult to completely remove it (depending on the program). The best solution is to prevent it from attaching to or "infecting" the computer in the first place.

Application Software

Thousands of different kinds of application software (applications or apps) have been developed. This text focuses on the application programs that are widely used in legal organizations, including word processing, PDF creation and document assembly (Chapter 2), spreadsheets (Chapter 3), timekeeping and billing (Chapter 4), databases, case management and docket control (Chapter 5), electronic discovery (Chapter 6), litigation support (Chapter 7), computer-assisted legal research and electronic mail (Chapter 8), and presentation graphics/trial software (Chapter 9). Following is a brief description of several other types of application software used in legal organizations.

---

network operating system
System that handles communication tasks between the computers on a network.

compression utility
Program that reorganizes a file so that the file takes up less room when it is saved. Many large files that are downloaded from the Internet are routinely compressed to reduce the time needed for the download.

backup utility
Program that creates a copy of a user's hard disk or other storage device. The backup copy can be restored if the hard disk is damaged or lost.

antivirus and antispyware utilities
Programs that attempt to prevent virus and spyware programs from getting into the computer system; most also function to locate and remove any viruses or spyware that do manage to get into the computer.

- Make backup copies of data on a regular schedule.

- Do not borrow DVDs or CD-ROMs from others; buy and use your own.

- Use passwords on your computer system.

- Turn your computer off when you are not using it.

- Do not let other people install programs on your computer or use your computer without expressly telling you how they will use it.

- Avoid downloading games, shareware, and other information from the Internet or other sources if you are not certain that the site is reputable and virus-free.

- Do not loan or pass your software programs on to others.

- Install antivirus and antispyware programs and run them frequently.

- Update your antivirus and antispyware programs regularly.

- Do not open files that are attached to emails unless you know the sender of the email and that the attached file is safe. An email scanner, which may be part of your antivirus/ antispyware program package, is an excellent first line of defense.

- Read license agreements and installation instructions carefully to avoid installing spyware.

- Try to restrict your Internet surfing to known, reputable sites.

© Cengage Learning 2012

EXHIBIT 1–5

How to protect your electronic data from a computer virus

Project Management **Project management software** uses the computer to track the sequence and timing of the separate activities of a larger project or task. Complex projects or jobs consist of many smaller activities that must be completed before the overall project is finished. Some activities must be performed in a certain sequence, whereas others must be completed concurrently. Project management software tracks all of this information. For example, a paralegal might use a project manager to track all the tasks that must be completed before a case is ready for trial.

> **project management software**
> Application program that allows the user to track the sequence and timing of the separate activities of a larger project or task.

Accounting Accounting software uses a computer to track and maintain the financial data and records of a business. Accounting information is crucial to any business or organization. It is required for income tax purposes, to obtain loans, to help in the operation and control of an organization, and more. Computerized accounting programs are often less time-consuming to use, introduce fewer errors, and usually produce final reports better and faster than manual methods. Accounting software used by a legal organization might include a general ledger, accounts payable, accounts receivable, payroll, and trust accounting.

Document Management **Document management software** organizes, controls, distributes, and allows for extensive searching of electronic documents, typically in a networked environment. Document management software allows a legal organization to file documents electronically so that they can be found by anyone in the organization, even when there are hundreds of users spread across offices located throughout the country. Document management software goes far beyond the file management capabilities built into operating system software. It is the electronic equivalent of a file room with rows and rows of filing cabinets. As the legal community moves to the "paperless office," each legal organization will most likely have to use a document management program to manage

> **document management software**
> Program that organizes, controls, distributes, and allows for extensive searching of electronic documents, typically in a networked environment.

electronic files. Document management software also provides extensive searching capabilities and allows users to add a profile of every document, which can be easily searched on later.

Application Service Providers and Internet-Based Programs

application service provider (ASP)
A company that provides software or a service application through the Internet directly to the user's computer.

An **application service provider (ASP)** is a company that supplies software or a service application through the Internet directly to the user's computer. The software is not retained on the user's computer, but instead resides on the software company's computer/server at a remote location and is "rented" to the user as needed. This is sometimes referred to as hosted software. The advantages of ASPs are that the user does not have to purchase the software, install the software, upgrade the software, or maintain the software in any way. The user still has access to the software 24 hours a day, 7 days a week, globally, wherever there is an Internet connection.

Two of the best known ASPs in the legal industry are Westlaw and LexisNexis. Other common law-office ASP applications include timekeeping and billing, document management, and litigation support.

HOW COMPUTERS CAN HELP THE PARALEGAL

A paralegal's job is information intensive. A paralegal using a computer can both gather and organize data many times faster than one using manual methods.

The Internet

The availability of the Internet has had a profound impact on how legal professionals practice law and how paralegals do their jobs. The Internet is used in countless ways by paralegals: sending and receiving electronic mail (email); sending instant messages; conducting factual and legal research; accessing listservs, blogs, and newsgroups to gather information and communicate with groups of people; maintaining a legal organization's website; purchasing legal-related services; and gaining continuing education.

Electronic Mail Paralegals use email to exchange information and documents via the Internet with clients, attorneys, other paralegals, courts, co-counsel, vendors, and many others in a manner that is quick, convenient, and cost-effective. Many courts now accept electronic filing of documents in lieu of hard copy, so email is used to submit documents to many court clerks.

Instant Messaging Instant messaging allows users who are connected to the Internet to communicate immediately with one another. Using instant messaging, paralegals or attorneys in court can communicate in real time with colleagues at their office for assistance, legal research, or other needs that may affect the outcome of a case or a hearing.

General and Factual Research Paralegals use the Internet for a wide variety of research, including:
- Conducting background information research on parties to cases
- Locating expert witnesses throughout the world
- Finding newspaper, online, and technical articles related to cases
- Locating the current whereabouts of people for service of process
- Researching information about witnesses

- Discovering financial information about corporations, including accessing Securities and Exchange Commission filings
- Finding public records about people or businesses
- Finding co-counsel in another jurisdiction

Legal Research Many paralegals perform legal research. In the past, the only option for legal research was the law library with its law books, periodicals, statutes, indexes, and digests. Nowadays, legal research can be conducted for free using the Internet. Sites such as www.findlaw.com and hundreds of others provide access to federal and state cases and statutes, provide a portal to other legal research sites on the Internet, and generally offer a wealth of free legal-related information. Fee-based computer-assisted legal research sites, including Westlaw and LexisNexis, allow users to electronically search the full text of cases, statutes, and documents.

Listservs and Electronic Mailing Lists Listservs are like electronic mailing lists. They send email messages to people whose names are on a list. They are a simple way for groups of people to communicate with one another through email. There are thousands of listservs on the Internet. Paralegals use these to communicate with other paralegals, to communicate with other legal professionals who practice in their legal specialty, and to communicate with others who have similar interests in other areas. Examples include:

> *LawTech*—for legal professionals who want to discuss legal technology issues (see www.abanet.org)
>
> *Legal Assistant Today*—specifically for paralegals who want to share information about paralegal issues, ideas, and experiences or who have questions about practice issues (see www.legalassistanttoday.com)

To find more listservs about the practice of law or the paralegal profession, you can use an Internet browser and a general search engine to search for "legal assistant listservs," "paralegal listservs," or whatever specific topic you are interested in.

Blogs A blog (originally short for "weblog") is a website with information contained in posts that are arranged in reverse chronological order. Blogs resemble diary or journal entries, and they may contain links to other websites or articles. There are many law-related blogs (sometimes referred to as "blawgs") on the Internet, including blogs on specific areas of law, such as immigration or tax.

Litigation Support Software

Many paralegals are involved in litigation support tasks. This means that they help attorneys organize, store, retrieve, and summarize the information that is gathered for the conduct of a lawsuit. During the course of any lawsuit, numerous documents and pieces of information are gathered, and must be organized for use at the time of trial or in support of settlement negotiations. For example, suppose your case has 10,000 documents associated with it, and you are requested to find all the documents that refer to a person named John Doe. Manual methods, such as looking through all 10,000 documents, could take weeks. Computerized litigation support software automates this process so that you can do such a search in seconds. In addition, using the Internet or an extranet, your firm can make litigation support databases available to staff, clients, or co-counsel, so that they can access the information from remote locations such as other offices, a courthouse, or a client's office. Litigation support software is crucial in large cases, but even small cases can benefit from this technology. This is covered in detail in Chapter 7.

Collecting and Organizing Data: Database Management Software

Paralegals are often required to collect and organize data. For example, a paralegal might be asked to prepare a list of the names of witnesses and their probable testimony in a case; generate a list of all the documents in a case; prepare a chronological listing of major events in a case; or put together a current list of all the cases being handled by the firm, including name of client, adverse party, case number, court, and name of the presiding judge.

A database management system is a computer program that stores, searches, sorts, and organizes data. Database management systems allow users to manipulate information in many different formats. For example, a paralegal can easily create a current case list database that shows all active cases for the firm in alphabetical order. Once the data is entered, users can produce many different types of reports in many different formats without having to reenter the data. In our example, the paralegal could then use the same current-case database to produce a list of all the firm's cases in a specific court or before a particular judge or to produce a numerical listing by case number of all the firm's cases. Databases are covered in detail in Chapter 5.

Performing Mathematical Calculations: Spreadsheet Software

Paralegals may be required to perform mathematical calculations as part of their jobs. The calculations might be relatively simple, such as adding up the amount of damages a party has asked for in a case or preparing a case budget for a client; or more complicated, such as calculating principal and interest payments in a real estate transaction, analyzing statistics for trends, or calculating lost wages in a workers' compensation case.

A spreadsheet program calculates and manipulates numbers. Spreadsheet programs allow numerical data to be added, subtracted, multiplied, and divided automatically. They also allow users to edit, copy, and move numerical data; perform complex calculations quickly and accurately; graph numerical data automatically; save and retrieve information; and recalculate totals if any numbers in the spreadsheet change. Spreadsheet programs are easy to use and can greatly expedite work with numerical data. This is covered in detail in Chapter 3.

Performing Timekeeping and Billing Functions: Timekeeping and Billing Software

In some law firms, paralegals record and track attorney and paralegal time and then send out bills to clients based on the amount of time spent on a case. Using a word processor for timekeeping and billing functions is tedious and time-consuming. Manual billing methods are so slow, in fact, that billings done manually tend to be generated infrequently, and in many cases bills are late getting to clients. Both of these consequences hurt the cash flow of a law office. In addition, bills prepared manually are more likely to contain errors, as numerous calculations must be performed for many bills.

When set up correctly, computerized legal timekeeping and billing programs are simple and easy to use. Information, such as the client's name, address, and billing rates, is entered into the system once. Then, as an attorney or paralegal spends time on a case, the time is entered into the system. If all entries are accurate, at the end of a billing period—one week, two weeks, one month, etc.—the computer automatically calculates and generates invoices, so they are produced and mailed on time with no calculation errors. This is covered in detail in Chapter 4.

Tracking Appointments and Deadlines: Computerized Docket Control and Case Management Software

Some paralegals must track appointments, deadlines, hearings, and other important dates to ensure that events get scheduled and then are not forgotten. This function is referred to as docket control, or sometimes as case management.

Although scheduling and tracking appointments and deadlines in a legal organization may seem at first glance like unimportant or merely clerical tasks, controlling an attorney's schedule and legal docket is, in fact, critical to his or her practice. Every year, thousands of ethical complaints are filed against attorneys. A primary reason clients file ethical complaints against their attorneys is the attorneys' failure to properly follow up on client matters. Many legal malpractice claims are also filed every year for the same reason. The importance of an effective docket control system in a legal organization should not be underestimated.

Although the terms docket control and case management are sometimes used interchangeably, there is a difference. Docket control software is fairly limited in nature, and primarily tracks appointments and deadlines in legal matters. Case management programs typically control the docketing of a case, but they usually also help the legal professional track and control the entire case, not just the scheduling aspects. Many case management programs include the ability to track a client's name, address, and telephone numbers; make notes about each phone conversation a legal professional has with the client; track appointments and deadlines by case; automatically schedule deadlines by type of case (typically where court rules mandate deadlines); perform conflict-of-interest searches when new cases are entered; produce letters and notices depending on the type of case; and more. This is covered in detail in Chapter 5.

Presentation Graphics/Trial Software

High-quality, professional presentations can be created using presentation graphics software. Paralegals use presentation graphics programs to prepare charts, tables, video clips, evidence, and other information for juries and factfinders; to present information to clients; and to present information to colleagues, such as an in-house training program, a marketing plan for the law office, a proposed budget, or a new initiative. Each page of a presentation can contain many elements, including color, images of documents, text, charts, shapes, video, clip art, photos, and sound. Presentation graphics programs can produce the information on paper, overhead transparencies, 35-mm slides, or electronic on-screen presentations. This is covered in detail in Chapter 9.

LEGAL TECHNOLOGY TRENDS

Legal technology is continuing to move forward. Following are some general technology trends that are significantly changing how legal professionals will be performing their jobs in the future.

Mobile Computing, Instant Wireless Access, and Remote Access

Laptop, tablet, netbook, and handheld computers (also called personal digital assistants or PDAs), along with mobile phones and other wireless technologies, are changing the way legal professionals communicate. All of these technologies are being merged in small, extremely powerful, fully connected mobile machines. These machines, no matter what you call them, operate as mobile phones, allow the user to send and receive email, have instant messaging features, act as pagers, access the Internet, act as PDAs (including calendaring, note-taking, and address book functions), send and receive faxes, allow the user to edit and send documents, and synchronize with a user's desktop system. Small laptops or netbooks can store millions of pages of documents electronically, fully access online legal databases such as Westlaw and LexisNexis on the go, and can remotely access law firm and service provider databases nearly globally. Mobile printers, mobile scanners, and wireless hotspots where users can connect to networks and the Internet allow legal professionals to access nearly all the same information and tools as if they were sitting at a desk in the office. This kind of mobile and immediate access to information will continue to change and drive the way legal professionals practice law.

Electronic Discovery

Electronic discovery is the process of producing litigation documents in an electronic format. The Federal Rules of Civil Procedure and many state court rules now require electronic discovery. This fact is forcing legal organizations to develop internal systems that can produce, store, search, and handle the production of electronic information in a variety of formats and across multiple computing platforms (desktops, servers, laptops, PDAs, etc.). Electronic discovery will continue to have a profound impact on the practice of law for many years to come, especially as more and more courts and legal professionals make effective use of it. This is covered in detail in Chapter 6.

Electronic Filing

electronic filing
Supplying electronic versions of legal documents to a court, via the Internet or other electronic means, when the court does not require the hard copy of the document.

With **electronic filing**, courts accept (and may even require) electronic versions of legal documents to be submitted, via the Internet or other electronic means, instead of requiring a hard copy of the document. Although this might sound easy, in reality it can be quite complicated. Issues concerning standardization, control, security, and the establishment of hardware and software systems to support electronic filing have all had to be overcome. Nevertheless, many states, courts, federal agencies, and other regulatory bodies have successfully implemented electronic filing, and many others are currently entering the implementation stage.

The Paperless Office

paperless office
Firm in which all hard-copy documents are converted into electronic form(s) for storage, processing, and distribution.

Just as courts have been working to implement electronic filing and require electronic discovery, many law offices have begun to implement the **paperless office**. This refers to converting all information into an electronic form for storage, processing, distribution, and use. Typically, this is done by scanning all hard-copy documents that come into the office and saving all computer-generated documents electronically without a hard copy. Some advantages of the paperless office include: (1) significant reduction in paper usage and copying costs, (2) reduction of storage and lease space (the cost of office lease space now far exceeds the cost of electronic storage space), (3) increased portability, (4) increased collaboration (because digital information can be shared by multiple users via a network or the Internet), and (5) quicker search and retrieval of documents than with manual methods. As with electronic filing, there are implementation issues regarding the paperless office, including putting the hardware and software systems in place to support it, training staff, and other issues. Some law offices have fully implemented this concept and many others are taking steps toward this goal.

The Automated Courtroom

Many courts have installed sophisticated electronic equipment in their courtrooms, including evidence display systems and real-time court reporting. An evidence display system is a computerized system that shows evidence, via monitors, to the judge, jurors, counsel, and the public simultaneously. It also displays this information to the court reporter and clerks.

The master controls are located at the judge's bench so that he or she can control all monitors, sound systems, and cameras in the courtroom. The attorneys and/or judge can use the evidence display system to display properly admitted evidence in the courtroom, whether by means of video images, animation, photographic images, hard copy, or other media.

Many evidence display systems also support videoconferencing. For example, with the judge's approval, an out-of-state witness can testify at a trial without actually being present in the courtroom. It may also be possible to receive real-time text of the transcript in addition to the audio and video feeds.

Another type of courtroom technology is real-time court reporting. A witness's testimony is transcribed by a court reporter within a few seconds and can be displayed on the courtroom monitors or given to the judge, jurors, or attorneys on a real-time basis. This gives parties instant written and electronic access to witness testimony and can eliminate the need to read back a witness's testimony when there is a question.

LEGAL ETHICS AND COMPUTER TECHNOLOGY

At first it may appear that legal ethics and computers have little to do with one another. In fact, the opposite is true. In addition to known, existing ethical issues (which do not disappear with computerization), many legal ethical issues arise specifically from the proliferation of computers and computer use in legal organizations. Many of these ethical concerns revolve around two key issues: competence or negligence of a legal professional and client confidentiality.

Attorney Competence

Attorneys have a duty to perform legal services in a competent manner. Computers, though incredibly helpful, can also be a vehicle for incompetence and legal malpractice. Computer-related legal malpractice and ethical breaches can take place in a variety of ways:

- Legal research performed with a computer may be inadequate and less than thorough.
- New documents are prepared using previously saved word-processing documents, but are inadequately proofread and contain old information (from the previous client).
- Typographical errors are made (especially when the person preparing the document relies on a spell checker rather than intelligent proofreading).
- Improper computerized forms or templates are used.
- A user generally fails to understand how a computer or a piece of software works, and thus fails to anticipate or discover an error.
- Automated legal or spreadsheet software is used with formula errors, logic errors, or lack of oversight or proofreading/review by the supervising attorney or other legal professionals.

Attorneys are responsible for their work product. It does not matter whether it was prepared by or with the assistance of a computer: If the end product has errors in it or is incompetently prepared, the attorney is still ultimately responsible for the work product. If the error or incompetent work product causes harm to the client, the attorney may be subject to attorney discipline charges and a legal malpractice claim.

Client Confidentiality

Attorneys have a duty to safeguard and keep confidential all client-related information, including information that is contained on computers. Every state has rules requiring attorneys to maintain the confidentiality of client information, no matter where that information resides.

This represents an enormous responsibility, given the technological advances in society generally and in legal organizations in particular. Although computers yield tremendous benefits to legal organizations in terms of efficiency, productivity, and delivery of high-quality legal services to clients, they also create substantial ethical and security issues. The threat of confidential client information being released either by mistake or by intrusion is very real, and can happen in a wide variety of ways, including:

- Interception of electronic mail by a third party (whether inadvertent or intentional)
- Interception of word-processing documents and other attachments to electronic mail by outsiders
- A breach of legal organization computer security, such as:
  - passwords not being appropriately maintained
  - computer hackers gaining access to confidential legal organization computers via the Internet or other online means
  - computer viruses deleting, accessing, or corrupting confidential client information
  - laptop and handheld computers holding confidential client information being stolen or inadvertently left for third parties to find
  - computer disks holding confidential client information being left or misplaced for third parties to find
  - computer hardware and storage devices not being sufficiently cleaned, so that client data is not destroyed before outdated equipment is disposed of

General Law Office Security

Law office computer systems in general are vulnerable to ordinary security threats, such as theft, sabotage, and natural disasters. It is important for all legal organizations to maintain adequate security measures, including having security and alarm systems to protect computer equipment from being stolen or damaged.

password
Code entered into a computer system or software that acts as a key, allowing the user to access the system and the information it contains.

Passwords **Passwords** are codes entered into a computer system or software that act as a key and allow the user to access the system and the information it contains. Passwords are very important and are usually a good first line of defense against intrusion into a computer system, but they are not invulnerable.

It is important to choose strong passwords. Hacker software programs on the Internet contain tens of thousands of common passwords that can be used to break into a computer system. Here are some rules for selecting and using strong passwords:

- Passwords should be a minimum of eight characters.
- They should be non-dictionary words.
- They should combine uppercase and lowercase characters.
- They should use at least one symbol (e.g., $ or :).
- They should use at least one number.

- They should be changed every 90 days.
- They should not contain or be based on personal information such as birthdates, names of family members, or other easily attainable pieces of information.

An example of a strong password would be something such as: RD10$Tk# or XP358LIN!.

Access Rights All network operating systems for LANs and WANs and even some sophisticated application programs allow an administrator to limit the access rights of users. **Access rights** determine which computer directories, programs, or functions a user can get to and use, and are usually granted on a need-to-know basis. Users should be given only the access rights they absolutely need to have—never more than they need. For example, if John needed to use only general word-processing and litigation support files, his access rights could be limited to only those files and directories; he would thus not be able to access other directories and programs.

Limiting users' access rights limits the number of people who can access computer files, information, and programs, so the exposure of the legal organization is less than it would be if everyone were given access to everything. It is important that access rights be closely controlled and monitored regularly.

access rights
Network security measure that limits a user's access to only those directories and programs that the user is authorized to use.

Backing Up **Backing up** refers to making a copy of a computer file or program. Backups are absolutely necessary in the event the legal organization's file server or other storage device crashes; files are accidentally deleted; files become corrupted; the computer system becomes infected with a virus or other malware; or fire, theft, or a natural disaster occurs. If a legal organization has a good plan for regular, timely backup of its data, and a disaster does happen, the data can be restored with no loss of information.

Backing up data is easier than ever before. A number of hardware tools are available for performing backups, including high-capacity, highly reliable data backup units; secondary servers that back up data throughout the day or at the end of the day; and DVDs or CDs that duplicate information (typically used in smaller offices). Also, there are Internet-based companies that will back up a legal organization's data automatically at predetermined times.

Whatever method is chosen, it is important that the information be maintained securely offsite, that backup be done regularly, and that the backup be reliable and usable. Legal organizations should verify on a regular basis that their backups are actually working; a good way to do this is by restoring some of the saved data to make sure it is usable.

backing up
Making a copy of a user's computer files.

The Dangers of Metadata **Metadata** is electronically stored information that may identify the origin, date, author, usage, comments, or other information about an electronic file. Metadata is often described as "data about data." For example, in Microsoft Office files (such as Word or Excel files), you can see metadata that identifies the original author of a document, company name, subject, previous authors, date created, date last modified, editing time, and other information. You can see this for yourself by simply loading a file and clicking on File Properties. Metadata is usually not visible when a document is printed, but if one knows where to look it is often easy to find.

Other, more dangerous metadata includes things like the comments and tracked changes in a Word document. In several instances, Word files were produced and tracked changes or comments were enabled to show the various stages of revisions of the document, including who saw the document and when and exactly what changes

metadata
Electronically stored information that may identify the origin, date, author, usage, comments, or other information about a file; "data about data."

were made to the document. This kind of metadata allows subsequent users to infer things about the thinking of original creators.

Subsequent chapters will detail the specific dangers posed by metadata for specific law office computer applications and how best to mitigate those dangers.

Electronic Mail

Electronic mail is an incredibly popular means of communication. Millions of Americans use email and collectively we send hundreds of millions of messages each day. Although it is extremely convenient, email can pose a large security risk due to a lack of privacy and security. The problem is that email sent over the Internet is not secure; it may pass through many other networks before it gets to the intended recipient. As it passes through the networks, others have the potential to see or read the message. Email can be encrypted to ensure that no one except the intended recipient can read the contents of the message while it is in transit. **Encryption** runs the message through an encoder that uses an encrypting key to alter the characters in the message. Unless a person has the correct encryption (decryption) key needed to decode it, the message appears unreadable.

encryption
Process of running a message through an encoder that uses an encrypting key to alter the characters in the message. Unless the person wanting to read the message has the encryption key needed to decode it, the message appears unreadable.

There are many other security issues with email, including sending email to the wrong person, sending email to distribution lists (many email recipients) by mistake, and much more. These problems can become quite acute and complicated when the message contains confidential client information. Unless encryption or similar methods are used, it is safest not to send confidential client information via email, given the potential for abuse. These issues are discussed further later in this text.

Viruses Email also presents a threat because computer viruses can be attached to emails. A **computer virus** is a computer program that is destructive in nature. When the attachment containing the virus is opened, the virus is brought or allowed into the receiver's computer system. Users should never open an attachment from an unknown source. Most legal organizations run antivirus programs that prevent or at least alert users to potential viruses. However, because hackers are constantly updating their technology, legal organizations must regularly update their antivirus programs at least weekly (preferably daily), using the Internet. Most software suppliers issue patches and updates to their programs to respond to new threats. In addition to updating virus definitions regularly, many software companies update their programs to include new security measures. Users should regularly update their operating systems and application programs and take advantage of the latest security measures they provide.

computer virus
A destructive computer program that may be designed to delete data, corrupt files, or do other damage; may also be self-replicating, using an "infected" computer to transmit itself to other computers.

spyware
A general term for software that tracks a user's movement on the Internet for advertising and marketing purposes, collects personal information about the user, or changes the configuration of the user's computer without the user's consent.

Spyware **Spyware** is a general term used for software that tracks your movement on the Internet for advertising and marketing purposes, collects personal information about the user, or changes the configuration of the user's computer without the user's consent. Spyware commonly gets onto a user's computer when the user downloads or installs a program. Spyware may be included with the program software, although that information may be buried in the licensing agreement—or the user may not be warned about it at all. Whenever you install programs on your computer, it is important to carefully read the disclosures, the license agreement, and the privacy statement. A number of antispyware programs are available that can detect and remove installed spyware.

Computer Hackers and Firewalls Nearly all legal organizations now provide access to the Internet for their staff. Many of these organizations use DSL, T1, cable modems, or other communication technologies that are "always connected" to the Internet. Computer hackers can use such connections to access the office computer system unless there is a firewall that cuts off this access. A **firewall** allows users from inside an organization to access the Internet but keeps outside users from entering a computer or the organization's LAN.

Mobile Computing and Wi-Fi Dangers   The security threats associated with mobile computers and wireless networks are substantial. Because laptop computers now rival the power and versatility of desktop computers, they can contain literally tens of thousands of client records. The potential for harm to a client cannot be exaggerated. One way to protect data on laptops and handheld computers is to install a power-on password. With a **power-on password**, the computer immediately prompts the user to enter a password after the machine has been turned on, but before the computer has completely booted the operating system software. If the user does not know the password, the system will not start and the computer will be unusable. Nearly all laptops and handhelds have this feature, but it must be activated. This type of system is very effective in the event a computer is stolen.

Encryption software can also be loaded onto a laptop. If the user loses the laptop or it is stolen, the data on the laptop remains safe because it cannot be accessed without the encryption key.

Wi-Fi computing allows users to access wireless LANs. A Wi-Fi–enabled device allows a user to connect to the Internet when in proximity to an access point (sometimes referred to as hotspots). The problem is that in crowded and public spaces, there are increased security risks, including easier anonymous hacking, inadvertent transmission diversion, and intentional hijacking of signals and access points. For example, using a Wi-Fi connection in a hotel may let the person in the next room hack into your computer through its own wireless connection. It would be better, in these circumstances, to use an ethernet or other hardwired system.

"Delete" Is Not Permanent   Many users mistakenly believe that when a file is "deleted," it is permanently deleted. This is usually not the case. Simply erasing or deleting does not permanently delete files even if you have emptied the recycle bin. In many instances, files can be retrieved by hackers and others from hard drives, flash drives, and CD-ROMs even after the files have been deleted. It is critical to physically destroy a storage device such as a flash drive or CD-ROM to ensure that the data on it cannot be retrieved. In addition, in Windows, deleted files are typically not deleted at all, but are sent to the recycle bin, so it is important to empty that utility from time to time.

Disaster Recovery Plans

A **disaster recovery plan** is a plan of action that can be followed in case a disaster (whether of natural or human origin) befalls the legal organization. For example, what would happen if a legal organization suffered a total loss to its computer systems from a fire, hurricane, flood, earthquake, tornado, bomb, power failure, theft, hard disk crash, or virus? Disaster recovery plans are prepared in advance of a disaster (typically multiple plans are prepared for different types of disasters) when there is plenty of time to think through alternative courses of action, anticipate problems, and design appropriate solutions.

Disaster recovery plans include a wide variety of information, such as who will be in charge, what services are the most vital, what steps will be taken first, what each department will require in terms of resources (computers, software, data, etc.), how to contact vendors, and how to contact employees. Many organizations make offsite data and backup storage an integral part of disaster recovery planning.

firewall
Security measure that allows users from inside an organization to access the Internet but keeps outside users from entering the computer or LAN.

power-on password
Password that the computer immediately prompts the user to enter after the machine has been turned on, but before the computer has completely booted the operating system software. If the user does not know the password, the system will not start and the computer will be unusable.

disaster recovery plan
A prewritten plan of action to be followed if a disaster befalls the legal organization.

SUMMARY

A few years ago, it was important that the paralegal entering the competitive job market have computer skills. Now it is imperative. Computer use in law offices has grown substantially and will continue to grow in the future. Computers are currently used in the legal field for a wide variety of purposes.

A computer is an electronic device that accepts, processes, outputs, and stores information. Information that is entered into a computer is called input. Information that comes out of a computer is called output. Hardware is the actual, physical components of a computer system. Software refers to instructions to the computer hardware that make the computer function. Computers can be used to help paralegals perform many of their functions, including communicating with clients and other legal professionals using electronic mail; drafting documents using word-processing software; collecting and organizing data using database management software; performing mathematical calculations using spreadsheet software; performing timekeeping and billing functions using timekeeping and billing software; tracking appointments and deadlines using docket control and case management software; providing litigation support using litigation support software; preparing electronic discovery requests using electronic discovery software; conducting legal and factual research using the Internet and fee-based, online services; and creating presentations with presentation graphics software.

Every computer has a system unit, which contains the CPU and main memory. The CPU, which is the "brain" of the computer, organizes and processes information in addition to coordinating functions of peripheral devices. The main memory is made up of ROM, which is permanent memory, and RAM, which is volatile memory.

Auxiliary storage devices, such as hard disks and optical storage devices, store information so that it can be retrieved later. Removable drives such as flash or "thumb" drives are small and portable, but can still hold up to several gigabytes of information.

Input devices enter information into a computer. Scanning and imaging both refer to importing a picture of a hard-copy document into a computer. Making an image of a document is similar to taking a photograph of the document. A related functionality is optical character recognition. When a user scans a document into a computer using OCR, the result is a file that contains the text of the document, which can be edited or manipulated with a word processor or other application.

Output devices provide the user with the data that the computer has generated or received. They include monitors, printers, portable projectors, and soundboards.

Communication devices allow computers to exchange information with other users via the Internet and other channels. Communication technology uses dial-up modems, cable modems, DSL and T1 lines, wireless modems, VoIP, and videoconferencing, among others.

A local area network is a multiuser system that links mainframes or computers that are in close proximity for the purpose of communication. LANs can be either client/server or peer-to-peer networks. A wide area network is a multiuser system that links computers that may be located thousands of miles apart.

Operating system software instructs the computer hardware how to operate its circuitry and how to communicate with input, output, and auxiliary storage devices. It allows the user to manage the computer. Microsoft Windows is the most common operating system in the legal environment.

Utility software helps to manage the hardware and software of a computer. Popular utility programs including antivirus and antispyware programs.

Legal organizations use many types of application programs, and the list grows longer every day. Document management software organizes, controls, distributes, and allows for extensive searching of electronic documents, typically in a networked environment. An application service provider is a company that provides software or a service application through the Internet directly to the user's computer.

Current and future technology trends that will affect the way legal professionals provide services to clients include mobile computing and instant wireless access, automated courtrooms, electronic filing of court documents, the paperless office, and heightened security and confidentiality concerns.

Many security and ethical issues surround the use of technology in legal organizations. The underlying principle is that legal professionals must safeguard and keep client information confidential. Current security concerns include passwords, access rights to files, data backup, release of client information, security surrounding electronic mail, viruses, spyware, fire-walls, mobile computing problems with lost or stolen laptops or handhelds, disaster recovery, and metadata.

Metadata is electronically stored information that may identify the origin, date, author, usage, comments, or other information about a file.

KEY TERMS

access rights	hardware	peripheral devices
access time	imaging	power-on password
antivirus and antispyware utilities	input	processor chip
application service provider (ASP)	input device	project management software
application software	Internet	random-access memory (RAM)
auxiliary storage device	intranet	read-only memory (ROM)
backing up	license agreement	removable drive
backup utility	local area network (LAN)	single-user system
bar code scanner	magnetic tape system	software
cable modem	main memory	sound card
central processing unit (CPU)	memory chips	speech recognition
client/server network	metadata	spyware
compression utility	modem	storage
computer	monitor	storage capacity
computer virus	mouse	utility software
disaster recovery plan	network operating system	video adapter card
document management software	operating system software (program)	videoconferencing
DSL (Digital Subscriber Line)	optical character recognition (OCR)	Voice over Internet Protocol (VoIP)
electronic filing	optical storage devices	wide area network (WAN)
encryption	output	Windows
extranet	output device	wireless modem
firewall	paperless office	wireless networking
gigahertz (GHz)	password	
hard disk drive	peer-to-peer network	

INTERNET SITES

Internet sites for this chapter include:

GENERAL LEGAL ASSISTANT/LEGAL SITES ON THE INTERNET

ORGANIZATION	PRODUCT/SERVICE	WORLD WIDE WEB ADDRESS
American Bar Association	Products/services for legal professionals	www.abanet.org
National Federation of Paralegal Associations	Products/information for paralegals	www.paralegals.org
National Association of Legal Assistants	Products/information for paralegals	www.nala.org

International Paralegal Management Association	Products/information for paralegals	www.ipma.org
Legal Assistant Today magazine	Magazine for paralegals	www.legalassistanttoday.com
Technolawyer.com	Email newsletter re: legal technology issues	www.technolawyer.com
American Bar Association, Legal Technology Resource Center	Legal technology issues	www.lawtechnology.org
Findlaw's Legal Technology Center	Legal technology issues	www.technology.findlaw.com

COMPUTER HARDWARE

ORGANIZATION	PRODUCT/SERVICE	WORLD WIDE WEB ADDRESS
AMD	Microprocessors	www.amd.com
Apple	Hardware/software for Apple computers	www.apple.com
Blackberry	PDAs and smartphones	www.rim.net
Cisco	Network operating system peripherals	www.cisco.com
Dell Computers	Computer hardware/software	www.dell.com
Hewlett-Packard	Computer hardware/peripherals	www.hp.com
Iomega Corp.	Removable drives/storage devices	www.iomega.com
Intel	Microprocessors	www.intel.com
Lenovo	Computer hardware	www.lenovo.com
NEC	Computer hardware/software	www.nec.com
Toshiba	Computer hardware/peripherals	www.toshiba.com

COMPUTER SOFTWARE

ORGANIZATION	PRODUCT/SERVICE	WORLD WIDE WEB ADDRESS
Business Software Alliance	Antipiracy information	www.bsa.org
LexisNexis	Research databases and document assembly software	www.lexisnexis.com
Microsoft	Computer software	www.microsoft.com
Mozilla	Browser software	www.mozilla.com
Network Associates	Antivirus/spyware software	www.mcafee.com
Novell	Network operating systems	www.novell.com
Software and Information Industry	Antipiracy information	www.siia.com
Symantec Corp.	Antivirus and other application programs	www.symantec.com
Worldox	Document management software	www.worldox.com

TEST YOUR KNOWLEDGE

1. Why is it imperative for paralegals to have an understanding of computers?

2. True or False: The Internet has only had a mild impact on practicing paralegals, because many of their day-to-day activities have not changed.

3. Distinguish between intranets, extranets, and the Internet.

4. True or False: Manual billing systems are typically slow and impede a legal organization's cash flow.

5. In the legal field, another name for a calendaring system software is _____.

6. Name two ways in which computer technology affects an attorney's ethical duty.

7. True or False: The central processing unit is the "brain" of a computer.

8. The memory that is cleared when a user turns the machine off is called _____.

9. Name three auxiliary storage devices.

10. Differentiate between imaging and optical character recognition.

11. What is VoIP?

12. Why are software access rights important?

13. What is an alternative to backing up software using hardware components such as tape backup and secondary servers?

14. Define metadata.

15. What are some of the ethical dangers of mobile computing?

ON THE WEB EXERCISES

1. Using the Internet and a general search engine, such as www.yahoo.com or www.google.com, or using one or more of the websites listed at the end of this chapter, research one of the following topics and write a one- to two-page paper on the topic. Update the information contained in this chapter and give a general overview of the topic.
   - Automated courtroom
   - Videoconferencing
   - Electronic filing
   - The paperless office

2. Using the Internet and a general search engine, such as www.yahoo.com or www.google.com, identify at least one free source of online access to your state's statutes.

3. Identify a minimum of five potential security threats that could affect a law office. For each, identify ways in which a legal organization can mitigate the threat.

4. Using a general search engine on the Internet, such as www.google.com or www.yahoo.com, write a one-page summary of what metadata is. If possible, list examples of how mistakes or problems arise from the use of metadata for unintended purposes.

5. As a paralegal in a small law office, you have been asked for your input regarding replacing your current IBM-compatible computer, which is now outdated. Go to www.pcmagazine.com, www.pcworld.com, www.practice.findlaw.com, www.dell.com, www.gateway.com, www.toshiba.com, and www.compaq.com and research the following:
   a. What common microprocessors are being used
   b. How much RAM is usually included with the machines
   c. How much hard disk storage is typically being included
   d. What types and sizes of monitors are common
   e. What common peripherals (such as CD-ROM or DVD burners) are sold with the computers
   f. What choices you have among handheld, laptop, tablet, or desktop machines.

   What would you choose, and why?

6. Using the Internet, determine what is the largest-capacity flash drive you can find and what it costs. Approximately how many hard-copy pages of documents could be stored on the flash drive by an employee who decided to steal documents from your law firm?

7. As a paralegal in a corporate legal department, you are responsible for tracking hundreds of real estate transactions throughout the United States every year. Keeping the paperwork organized and on track is beginning to overwhelm you. Because you work with attorneys and corporate staff all over the country, it would be nice to be able to

forward electronic versions of real estate records, title searches, and other records. Because many of the documents are in hard-copy format, you would have to convert the documents to images. Using www.lawofficecomputing.com, www.lawtechnology.org, www.technolawyer.com, and www.practice.findlaw.com, write a short paper on imaging. Answer the following questions:

a. How much do high-speed scanners cost?

b. How accurate is imaging?

c. Do many legal organizations use imaging?

d. In the end, would you recommend the move to imaging?

8. As a paralegal in a solo practitioner's office, you have approached the attorney about purchasing handheld computers for both of you so that you can communicate more easily with each other and with clients. The attorney is concerned about security regarding handheld computers. He would like to know answers to the following questions:

a. If the device gets lost, can just anyone pick it up and have access to the information (and if so, are there any precautions that can be taken to reduce this risk)?

b. How secure is information when using wireless services such as wireless email?

c. Assuming that the security issues can be solved, what are the latest features being offered in these devices?

9. Microsoft is continually updating its Windows operating system software and Office application programs. Go to its website at www.microsoft.com and comment on the latest version(s) of the program that it is releasing.

QUESTIONS AND EXERCISES

1. Are you surprised to see the extent to which paralegals use computers in their jobs? What conclusions can you draw regarding the paralegal computer user?

2. Knowing that some legal research can be done free of charge on the Internet, and that other information is best found using a fee-based system, what approach would you use in conducting legal research?

3. You work as a paralegal for a small law firm that handles collection matters. The firm is currently representing a furniture store that loaned money to a number of customers who now have disappeared. Unless you find the whereabouts of the customers, the furniture store will not be able to collect its money. What computer resource would you use to try to find the customers, and why?

4. What policies and procedures could be put in place to limit an employee's ability to download and subsequently successfully use large amounts of client data when the employee leaves a law firm to practice elsewhere?

5. Write a two-page memorandum regarding the ethical rules in your state regarding a law firm's duty to safeguard client information that is stored electronically. What are the rules that might apply? Are there any exceptions for accidental disclosure?

ETHICS QUESTION

A client of your firm is engaged in complex litigation. She has just purchased the latest must-have mobile Wi-Fi device. The client plans on using this device for email and voice communication. What ethical issues are raised by this scenario?

Access an interactive eBook, chapter-specific interactive learning tools, including flash cards, quizzes, and more in your Paralegal CourseMate, accessed through CengageBrain.com.

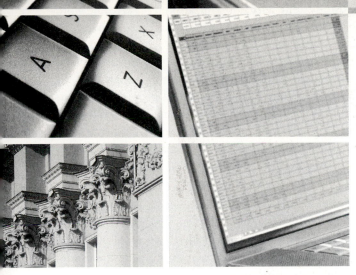

CHAPTER 2

Word Processing, PDF File Creation, and Document Assembly

CHAPTER OBJECTIVES

After completing this chapter, you should be able to do the following:

1. Explain how legal organizations and paralegals use word processors.
2. Describe major features found in word-processing programs.
3. Identify what a PDF file is and how PDF files are created.
4. Explain what document assembly is and how it works.
5. Discuss ethical problems related to word processing.

INTRODUCTION

This chapter introduces the fundamentals of word processing, Portable Document Format (PDF) file creation, and document assembly. **Word-processing software** is used to edit, manipulate, and revise text to create documents. It is one of the most widely used types of application software in legal organizations. Paralegals use word processors to prepare memos, correspondence, form letters, discovery documents, and many other legal documents.

Portable Document Format (PDF) is a file format developed by Adobe Systems for sharing files; it works independently of the application that was used to create the file or the operating system of the computer on which the file was created. The PDF file format is the de facto standard for digital document distribution, including for filing documents electronically with courts.

Document assembly software creates powerful standardized templates and forms. Once a template or form has been set up, users respond to a series of questions and prompts to fill in data. The document assembly program then merges the form or template with the answers and builds a new, completed document. Many legal organizations incorporate document assembly into their practices, particularly in areas for which well-structured forms and templates have been created and are routinely used.

CENTRALIZED AND DECENTRALIZED WORD PROCESSING

Legal organizations use various approaches to word processing, including centralized, decentralized, or a combination of both.

word-processing software
Program used to edit, manipulate, and revise text to create documents.

Portable Document Format (PDF)
A file format developed by Adobe Systems, Inc., for sharing files independently of the application that created the file or the computer's operating system.

document assembly software
Powerful computer program that creates standardized templates and forms.

Centralized Word Processing

centralized word-processing system

A system in which all the word-processing documents for an organization are input or typed in a single location or by one department (i.e., a word processing department).

With a **centralized word-processing system**, a legal organization has a separate word-processing department where correspondence, memorandums, and other documents in the office are input (typed). For example, a large firm with a centralized word-processing system might require its litigation, tax, and corporate law departments to send all their major word-processing projects to the word-processing department.

Most word-processing departments, sometimes called word processing centers, have trained staff that do nothing but type in documents and data. Usually, the firm uses a standardized form for requesting services from this department. When a document has been input and printed, it is then sent back to the originating party for correction and for distribution. Such centralized word-processing departments are most often found in large firms.

Decentralized Word Processing

decentralized word-processing system

A system in which individuals or separate departments in an organization perform their own word processing.

With a **decentralized word-processing system**, individuals perform word processing for themselves, for another person, or for a small group. For example, it is common for paralegals, law clerks, legal secretaries, and attorneys to perform some or all of their own word processing. Many law firms are now able to place relatively inexpensive personal computers on the desks of most staff, thus creating a decentralized system. In the past, attorneys rarely, if ever, did their own typing or word processing. Now it is very common.

Today, many small law firms use a decentralized word-processing system. Even large firms, which have traditionally used centralized word processing, may now use a combination of the two systems. It is common for large firms to maintain a word-processing center while still allowing legal professionals to do some of their own word processing.

LEGAL WORD-PROCESSING PROGRAMS: MICROSOFT WORD VS. COREL WORDPERFECT

The leading word-processing program for legal organizations is Microsoft Word, but some firms prefer to use Corel WordPerfect. Microsoft offers several versions of Word, which are all popular in the legal field: Word 2010, Word 2007 and Word 2003. Word 2007 implemented a major change in the Word interface. Word 2007 uses a "ribbon" (see Exhibit 2–1) packed with tools that the user can change based on what the user is doing. Seven different ribbon selections are available (see Exhibit 2–1). Word 2007 also includes a "quick access toolbar" that the user can customize (see Exhibit 2–1). One of the major differences between Word 2007 and earlier versions of Word is that the drop-down menus that have been a staple of Word were eliminated. Word 2003, like earlier versions of Word, uses an interface that includes drop-down menus and a static toolbar (see Exhibit 2–1A).

Another major change in Word 2007 is that the file format in which documents are saved was revised. The default file format in Word 2007 is ".docx" (e.g., "letter.docx"). For many years, Word saved documents with the ".doc" file extension (e.g., "letter.doc"). Word 2007 offers users the option of saving documents in the older ".doc" file format, but at the cost of sacrificing some Word 2007 options that are not available or do not work in the older file format. Extensive hands-on exercises, which can be done in Word 2007 or Word 2003, appear in Chapter 2 of the Student Workbook.

See Exhibits 2–2 and 2–2A for quick reference guides to Word.

LEGAL WORD-PROCESSING FUNDAMENTALS

Legal organizations use a variety of basic and advanced word-processing features and techniques. These include basic editing functions, such as copying, pasting, deleting,

Quick Access Toolbar   Ribbon Tabs

Office button

Help

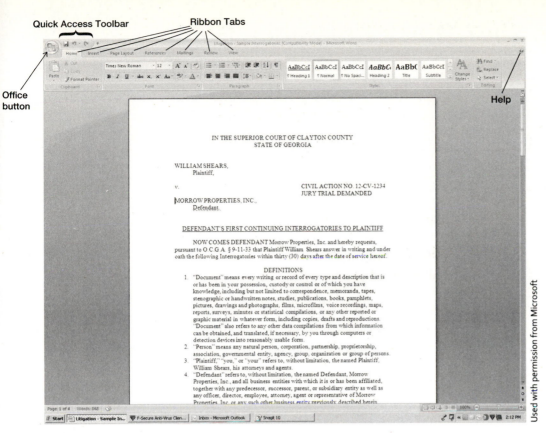

EXHIBIT 2–1
Microsoft Word 2007

Menu Selections

Drop-down menu

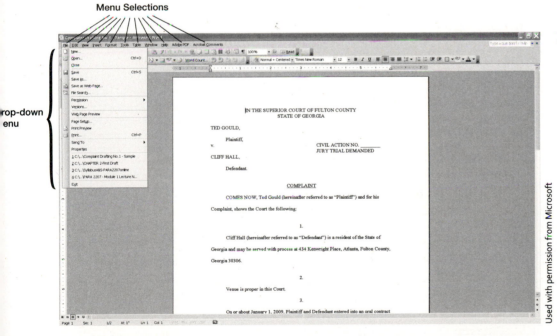

EXHIBIT 2–1A
Microsoft Word 2003

inserting, formatting text, and printing, among others. Legal organizations also make great use of some basic functions such as page numbering, footnoting, and tables. It is not uncommon for legal documents to be in the hundreds of pages, for a single footnote to run across several pages in a document, or for a table to be extremely complex. Legal organizations also use advanced word-processing features such as tables of authorities, macros, and merges. A number of these features are covered in this chapter.

Word 2007 Quick Reference Guide

HOME RIBBON

Office button

Cut, Copy, Paste

Dialog box launchs

Help

Font format · Paragraph format · Styles · Find/Replace

NAVIGATION

UP 1 SCREEN	[Page Up]	BEGINNING OF DOCUMENT	[CTRL]+[HOME]
DOWN 1 SCREEN	[Page Down]	END OF DOCUMENT	[CTRL]+[END]
BEGINNING OF A LINE	[Home]	GO TO	[F5]
END OF A LINE	[End]		

KEYBOARD SHORTCUTS

COPY TEXT	[Ctrl]+[C]	UNDO A COMMAND	[Ctrl]+[Z]
PASTE TEXT	[Ctrl]+[V]	REDO / REPEAT	[Ctrl]+[Y]
CUT TEXT	[Ctrl]+[X]	PRINT A DOCUMENT	[Ctrl]+[P]
BOLD TEXT	[Ctrl]+[B]	SAVE A DOCUMENT	[Ctrl]+[S]
UNDERLINE TEXT	[Ctrl]+[U]	SELECT EVERYTHING	[Ctrl]+[A]
ITALICS TEXT	[Ctrl]+[I]	OPEN FILE	[Ctrl]+[O]
FIND / REPLACE	[Ctrl]+[F]	NEW FILE	[Ctrl]+[N]
GO TO	[Ctrl]+[G]	REVEAL FORMATTING	[Shift]+[F1]
SPELL, GRAMMAR CHECK	[F7]	HIDE RIBBON	[Ctrl]+[F1]

WORD FEATURE — COMMAND STRUCTURE

WORD FEATURE	COMMAND STRUCTURE
ATTACH DOCUMENT TO AN EMAIL	Office Button, Send, Email
CHANGE CASE OF TEXT	Home, Font, Change Case
CLEAR ALL FORMATTING OF TEXT	Home, Font, Clear Formatting
CLIP ART FROM INTERNET (INSERTING)	Insert, Illustrations, Clip Art, Clip Art on Office Online
CLIP ART / FILES / CHARTS, SHAPES (INSERTING)	Insert, Illustrations
COMPARE DOCUMENTS	Review, Compare
FIND / REPLACE	Home, Editing, Find / Replace
FONT CONTROL	Home, Font
FOOTNOTES / ENDNOTES	References, Footnotes, Insert Footnotes
HEADER / FOOTER	Insert, Header & Footer, Header or Footer
INDENT TEXT	Home, Paragraph, Dialog Box Launcher
LINE SPACING CHANGES	Home, Paragraph, Line Spacing
MACROS	View, Macros
MAIL MERGE	Mailings, Start Mail Merge
MARGINS, PAPER ORIENTATION	Page Layout, Page Setup, Margins
SHADING	Home, Paragraph, Shading
STYLES	Home, Styles
TABLES (INSERTING)	Home, Insert, Tables
TABS	Home, Paragraph, Dialog Box Launcher, Indents and spacing, Tabs
TRACK CHANGES	Review, Tracking, Track Changes
NEW DOCUMENT	Office Button, New
OPEN (EXISTING) DOCUMENT	Office Button, Open
SAVE A DOCUMENT	Office Button, Save
PRINT AND PRINT PREVIEW	Office Button, Print
TABLE OF AUTHORITIES	References, Table of Authorities

© Cengage Learning 2012

EXHIBIT 2–2

Word 2007 Quick Reference Guide

Word 2003 Quick Reference Guide

STANDARD TOOLBAR

NAVIGATION

Up 1 Screen	[Page Up]	Beginning of Document	[Ctrl]+[Home]
Down 1 Screen	[Page Down]	End of Document	[Ctrl]+[End]
Beginning of a Line	[Home]	Go To	[F5]
End of a Line	[End]		

KEYBOARD SHORTCUTS

Copy Text	[Ctrl]+[C]	Undo a Command	[Ctrl]+[Z]
Paste Text	[Ctrl]+[V]	Redo / Repeat	[Ctrl]+[Y]
Cut Text	[Ctrl]+[X]	Print a Document	[Ctrl]+[P]
Bold Text	[Ctrl]+[B]	Save a Document	[Ctrl]+[S]
Underline Text	[Ctrl]+[U]	Select Everything	[Ctrl]+[A]
Italics Text	[Ctrl]+[I]	Open (Existing) File	[Ctrl]+[O]
Find / Replace	[Ctrl]+[F]	New File	[Ctrl]+[N]
Go To	[Ctrl]+[G]	Reveal Formatting	[Shift]+[F1]
Spell, Grammar Check	[F7]	Task Pane	[Ctrl]+[F1]

WORD FEATURE	COMMAND STRUCTURE
Attach Document to an Email	File, Send to, Mail Recipient (as Attachment)
Change Case of Text	Format, Change Case
Character Spacing	Format, Font, Character Spacing
Clear All Formatting of Text	Edit, Clear, Formats
Clip Art from Internet (Inserting)	Insert, Picture, Clip Art, Clip Art on Office Online
Clip Art / Files / Charts (Inserting)	Insert, Picture
Compare Documents	Tools, Compare and Merge Documents
Find / Replace	Edit, Find or Replace
Font Control	Format, Font
Footnotes / Endnotes	Insert, Reference, Footnote
Header / Footer	View, Header / Footer
Indent Text	Format, Paragraph, Indent
Line Spacing Changes	Format, Paragraph, Spacing
Macros	Tools, Macro
Mail Merge	Tools, Letters and Mailings, Mail Merge
Margins, Paper Orientation	File, Page Setup
Shading	Format, Borders and Shading, Shading
Styles	Format, Styles and Formatting
Tables (Inserting)	Tables, Insert
Tabs	Format, Tabs
Text Effects (Blinking, Las Vegas, etc.)	Format, Font, Text Effects
Toolbar Selection	View, Toolbars
Track Changes	Tools, Track Changes
Widow Control, Orphan Control, Keeping Lines Together	Format, Paragraph, Line and Page Breaks, Widow / Orphan Control or Keep Lines Together

EXHIBIT 2–2A

Word 2003 Quick Reference Guide

Whole-Paragraph Functions

Automatic Paragraph Numbering Most word processors have an automatic paragraph numbering feature that allows users to have paragraphs and lists of information numbered automatically by the software. This feature is used extensively in legal organizations because information is routinely presented in a hierarchical format (e.g., 1, 2, 3 or A, B, C). With the automatic paragraph numbering feature, the program will automatically renumber a list when you add or delete material. If you had not used the numbering function, you would have had to renumber the whole list manually each time you added information to or deleted material from the list. For example, notice in Exhibit 2–3 that the headings "A. Introduction" and "B. Jurisdiction" are in a hierarchical format, as is the list with items "1)," "2)," and "3)." If, for example after "A. Introduction," you created a new topic, "B. Venue," the program would automatically renumber "Jurisdiction" to be "C. Jurisdiction."

In addition to improving accuracy, this feature saves huge amounts of time for legal organizations, because motions and briefs can be extremely long and complex and have many levels of hierarchical information. Users can even set up custom paragraph numbering schemes, including setting custom margins to comply with local court rules and employing a variety of numbering formats and sublevels (including numeric, alphanumeric, alphabetical, and others).

style
A named set of formatting characteristics that users can apply to text.

Styles A **style** is a named set of formatting characteristics that users apply to text. Using styles, users can quickly apply multiple formatting to text. For example, notice the different styles used in Exhibit 2–3. The style applied to "A. Introduction" and "B. Jurisdiction" is titled "Heading 2." Any material styled "Heading 2" is bolded, underlined, set in small caps, and automatically numbered. Instead of having to go to

EXHIBIT 2–3

Word processing: Header, footer, Styles, footnotes, Auto Number, Automatic Page Numbering in Word 2007

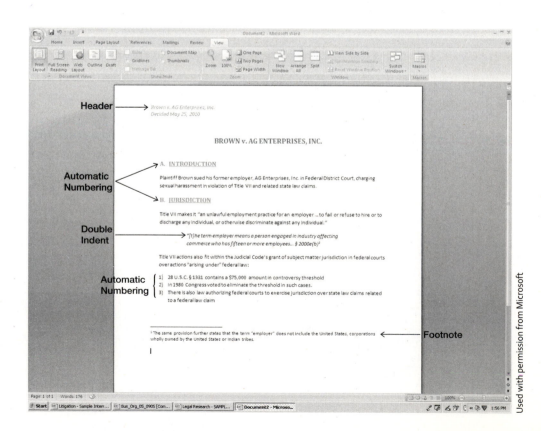

Used with permission from Microsoft

each section heading and then enter the font command and the automatic numbering command, you can simply use the Style command to have all the formatting automatically applied, all at once.

Styles can also be automatically changed and updated. Suppose that the user who created Exhibit 2–3 has 40 section headings and now needs to change the format of all of these headings so that they are not underlined. If the user had not used the Style feature, he or she would have had to go to each of the 40 headings and manually make the desired changes. Using the Style feature, the user can simply invoke the Style command, click on "Heading 2," use the Select All feature to automatically select all text with the "Heading 2" style, and then make the desired changes. All "Heading 2" text is then automatically updated.

The Style feature is particularly helpful in long and complex documents that have recurring elements and where consistency is important. Styles are covered in detail in Lesson 6 of the Hands-On Exercises for Word 2007 and Word 2003 in the Student Workbook.

Headers and Footers   A **header** is a title or heading that appears at the top of each page of a document. A **footer** is text that appears at the bottom of each page of a document. For example, a footer may indicate the current page number and the total number of pages of the document. The program can automatically calculate both the current page number and the total number of pages using an automatic page numbering feature.

Automatic Page Numbering   An **automatic page numbering** feature automatically calculates the appropriate page number for each page of a document. In most word processors, you can specify where the page number should be placed on the page (e.g., centered at the bottom of the page in a footer or in the upper right corner of the header). With the automatic page numbering feature, new page numbers are automatically recalculated and inserted when text is added to, moved or reformatted, or deleted from a page.

Double Indenting   Text is indented an equal distance from the left and right margins by using **double indenting**. Paralegals and attorneys use the double-indent feature frequently when including quotations from primary authorities. To use the double-indent feature, go to where the double indent should start, enter the Double Indent command, and type in the appropriate text. The text is automatically indented the same distance from the left and right margins.

Footnotes and Endnotes   A **footnote** is material that is printed at the bottom of a page on which a numbered reference appears in text. An **endnote**, like a footnote, has a numbered reference in the text, but instead of appearing at the bottom of a page, the note material appears at the end of a chapter or document. Footnotes and endnotes are easy to produce with a word processor. Most word processors have an automatic footnote feature that tracks the current footnote number and formats the page(s) so that the note text is printed (or at least started) at the bottom of the page on which the reference number appears. To enter a footnote, simply go to the place in the text that is to be referenced and execute the Insert Footnote command (within the References tab/ribbon in Word 2007). This command automatically enters the correct footnote number and brings up a special footnote screen in which the user types the text of the footnote. Word processors automatically number the notes, and renumber them as necessary when notes are added or deleted.

---

header
A title or heading that appears at the top of each page of a document.

footer
Text that appears at the bottom of each page of a document.

automatic page numbering
Word-processor feature that automatically numbers the pages of a document for the user; also renumbers pages as material is moved, added, or deleted.

double indenting
Word-processor feature (also found in other types of programs) that indents text an equal distance from the left and right margins.

footnote
Material that is printed at the bottom of a page; marked in text by a numbered referent.

endnote
Material that is printed at the end of a chapter or document; marked in text by a numbered referent.

Footnotes and endnotes are heavily used in law-office word processing, especially in legal briefs. Because lawyers and legal assistants must cite the law when making an argument, footnotes and endnotes containing citations are common—and may be quite lengthy.

Electronic Distribution of Documents

Any modern law office must be able to distribute documents, including word processing documents, in electronic form. For example, it is commonplace in many legal organizations to attach Microsoft Word documents to emails sent to corporate clients. This allows clients to see and make revisions to legal work. Most legal organizations are also now filing documents electronically with court clerks. Most courts use the Portable Document Format as the standard format for documents filed electronically. PDF can be a secure format when recipients are prohibited from editing the document. As long as the recipient has a PDF viewer, the recipient can view the file on a different type or version of computer than the one the document was created on. Some word processors can export to a PDF file from within the word-processing program. Users can also purchase a separate program to convert word-processing and other documents to PDF files using a separate program, such as Adobe Acrobat. PDF file creation is covered in more detail later in this chapter.

Printing

Even with the prevalence of electronic document distribution, the ability to print hard copies of documents is still important. Word processors are extremely flexible when it comes to printing documents. Users can print single pages, whole documents, specific pages (e.g., pages 67 to 74), color, one- or two-sided pages, and much more. Many legal organizations have moved to digital printing, using multifunction printers that can print, copy, scan, add tabs, collate, and staple. Most word processors also have a "print layout" view or a Print Preview command that allows the user to see exactly how the document will look when printed.

Tables

The table feature in a word processor allows you to create a table of information using rows and columns. You can then quickly organize information into columns and rows without using tabs. Exhibit 2–4 shows a basic table. Grid lines divide the table into rows and columns (although you can adjust the settings so the lines are not displayed). Tables can include text, numbers, and even formulas.

Tables are very easy to set up in most word processors. You simply enter the Table command and tell the program how many rows and columns to start with. You can also change the size of the columns or rows, add and delete columns or rows, split columns or rows, add color, add graphics, and include calculations. Tables are frequently used in legal word processing for many purposes. Tables are covered in detail in Lesson 4 of the Hands-On Exercises for Word 2007 and Word 2003, included in the Student Workbook.

macro
Word-processor feature that records the user's keystrokes, saves those keystrokes, and then allows the user to play those keystrokes back.

Macros

A **macro** records a user's keystrokes, saves those keystrokes, and then allows the user to play those keystrokes back. For example, you might create a macro for the legal organization's name or to close a letter. Notice in the first screen of Exhibit 2–5 that the user has created a macro entitled "PleadSignBlock." When it was created,

EXHIBIT 2–4

A table in Word 2007

the macro recorded the keystrokes that produce the standard signature block for a pleading. From then on, you never have to retype that signature block. At the end of a pleading, such as the second screen of Exhibit 2–5, you simply run the macro: the macro does the rest by quickly and sequentially replaying the recorded keystrokes.

Macros can also be created to perform word-processing commands or even series of commands (e.g., applying a style, then applying a double indent). Macros increase productivity, efficiency, and accuracy, because users do not have to keep

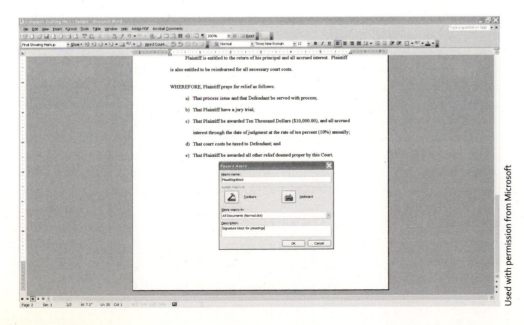

EXHIBIT 2–5

Macro in Word 2003

EXHIBIT 2–5

(*continued*)

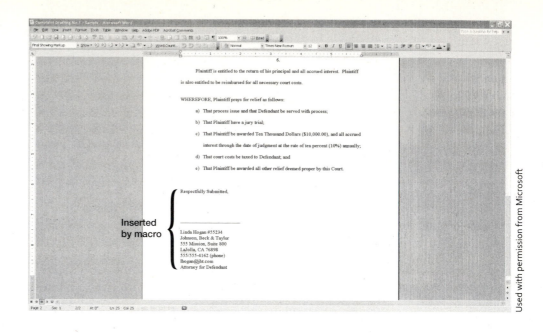

keying in repetitive material or going through long sequences of commands. Macros can be created by invoking the New Macro command; with the recording feature, the user's keystrokes and commands are recorded in the order in which they are executed, and then saved under whatever file name the user has assigned to the macro. To play the macro, the user simply invokes the Play Macro command and enters the name of the macro or clicks on the name in a list. (For even quicker access, macros that are used frequently can be assigned to a keyboard stroke combination, such as Ctrl-Alt-P; this means the user need not even go to the Macros menu or take hands off the keyboard.)

Macros are an extremely handy and time-saving feature. Macros are covered in detail in Lesson 12 of the Hands-On Exercises for Word 2007 and Word 2003 in the Student Workbook.

Comments, Comparing Documents, and Track Changes

comment

Word-processor feature that allows a user to annotate and create notes in a document without changing the text of the document.

Word processors allow groups of people to collaborate effectively using a number of features and tools, including comments, compare documents, and track changes. The **comment** feature allows a user to annotate and make notes or comments in a document without actually changing it. Notice in Exhibit 2–6 that the reviewer has inserted a comment, which includes questions, in the user's document. The original user can then make changes and delete the comment or respond to the reviewer by editing the comment with his or her own opinion.

compare documents

Word-processor feature that allows a user to compare and contrast two documents, either side by side or by blacklining (usually through the creation of a third document showing differences).

A **compare documents** feature allows you to compare two separate word-processing files. Most word processors can do this in a couple of ways, including allowing simultaneous viewing of the two files or by producing a third document that shows the differences between the two versions. Notice in the first screen in Exhibit 2–7 that two similar but different documents are being viewed. The second document adds some verbiage to paragraph 1 (Term of Employment), but other than that it is substantially similar to the first. Using this method, you can view two documents at the same time to find the differences. You can also set the word processor to synchronize the documents so that they scroll side by side as you move through the documents.

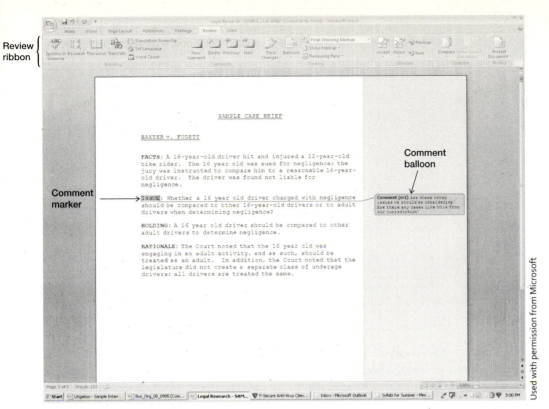

EXHIBIT 2–6

Adding a comment to a document in Word 2007

Another way to compare documents is to have the word processor "blackline" the documents. Notice in the second screen of Exhibit 2–7 that the two documents have been compared, but this time the word processor has created a new document showing what the second document added to or deleted from the first document.

Legal organizations find the Compare Documents feature to be very useful in many situations. The Compare Document feature is covered in detail in Lesson 8 of the Hands-On Exercises for Word 2007 and Word 2003 in the Student Workbook.

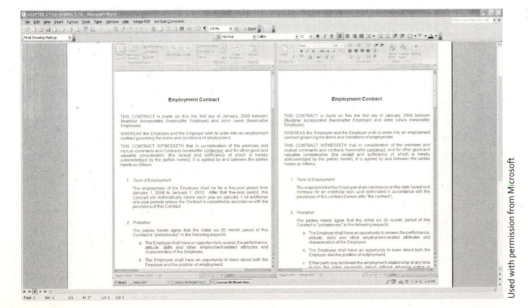

EXHIBIT 2–7

Comparing documents: Simultaneous viewing and blacklining in Word 2003

EXHIBIT 2–7

(*continued*)

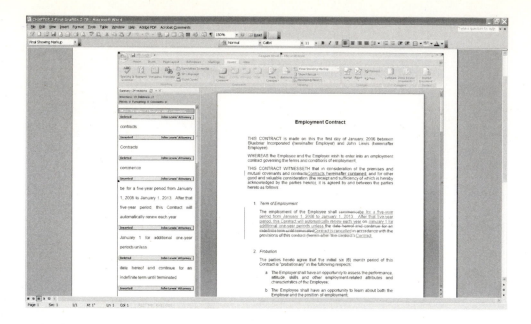

track changes

Word-processor feature that allows reviewers to make or recommend changes to a document; these changes can later be either accepted or rejected by the original author.

Another way for users to use word processors collaboratively is to use the Track Changes feature. **Track changes** allows reviewers to make changes to a document that later can be either accepted or rejected by the user. For example, suppose an attorney asks a paralegal to write a draft of a pleading. The paralegal drafts the pleading; then the attorney turns on the Track Changes feature and makes changes right in the document itself (see Exhibit 2–8). Notice in Exhibit 2–8 that you can see all the changes that the attorney made, with inserted and deleted material flagged. You could accept all of the changes at once, reject all of the changes at once, or go through the changes one by one and accept or reject them separately.

In some instances documents are reviewed by multiple people, including attorneys, co-counsel, and clients. Most word processors can accommodate reviews by multiple parties by assigning different colors to each reviewer. The user can then easily determine who made each change. Track changes is covered in detail in Lesson 9 of the Hands-On Exercises for Word 2007 and Word 2003 in the Student Workbook.

EXHIBIT 2–8

Track Changes in Word 2003

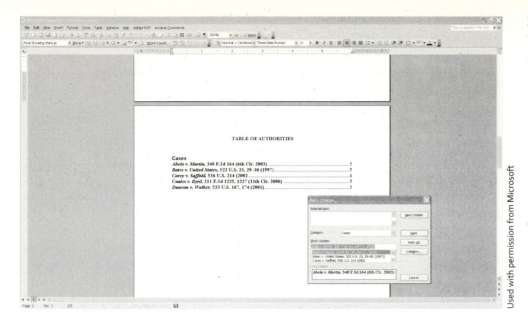

Used with permission from Microsoft

EXHIBIT 2–9
Table of authorities
in Word 2003

Table of Authorities

Most word processors have automated features for creating a table of authorities (commonly referred to as a TOA or TA). A **table of authorities** is a section in a legal document or brief that lists the cases, statutes, and other authorities referenced in that legal document or brief. A table of authorities is similar to a table of contents except that it lists cases and other reference materials, along with the page numbers on which they appear in the document. Tables of authorities are typically created by marking all of the case citations and other authorities and then generating the table itself near the beginning of the document (see Exhibit 2–9).

The Table of Authorities feature in a word processor is very important because manual creation of a TOA is an extremely time-consuming process, particularly if revisions are made after the table has been generated. With the automated feature, even if changes are made to a document after a table of authorities has been created, the user can regenerate the table; that is, the program will automatically recreate the table with all of the new items and page numbers. Tables of authorities are covered in detail in Lesson 11 of the Hands-On Exercises for Word 2007 and Word 2003 in the Student Workbook.

table of authorities
Automated word-processor feature that allows the program to generate an accurate list of case and statute citations (authorities), along with the page number(s) on which each cite appears.

Revealing Hidden Codes

When text is typed into a word processor, all the user sees on the screen is the actual text. However, most word processors have a command that allows the user to see the "invisible" codes that indicate things such as word spaces, boldfacing, and margin changes.

Revealing the hidden codes makes it easier to delete, edit, or change the formatting of a document (see Exhibit 2–10). For example, in Exhibit 2–10, when the Reveal Formatting feature is turned on, you can plainly see that the word "COMPLAINT" has formatting codes of "Font: Times New Roman, 12 pt., and Underline." If you wanted to delete one of these formatting codes, you could use a reveal codes command to go to the spot in the document where the code is and then delete it in the Reveal Formatting view. Reveal codes commands are helpful when trying to determine what formatting codes were previously entered in a document. (It can be the quickest and easiest way to discover why the word processor keeps doing something to a document other than what you thought you told it to do!)

EXHIBIT 2–10

Styles and formatting
revealed in Word 2003

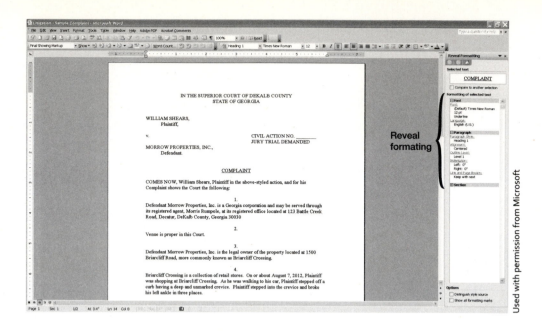

Microsoft Word calls this feature "Reveal Formatting." Revealing hidden codes and formatting is included in Lesson 5 of the Hands-On Exercises for Word 2007 and Word 2003 in the Student Workbook.

Legal Templates and Pleading Wizard

Pleading Wizard

Feature in some word
processors that helps legal
professionals quickly and
easily create a legal pleading
by providing a standard form
or forms having users answer
questions about the pleading
to be created.

A variety of legal word-processing templates are available for many different legal specialties and applications. In addition, some word processors come with a **Pleading Wizard** that helps legal professionals create new pleading templates. For example, Exhibit 2–11 shows a Pleading Wizard that presents the user with a number of questions to answer, including things like the name of the court, what the layout of the page should be, and whether there should be line numbers on the document. Once the general template has been created, the Pleading Wizard then asks the user about the specific document to be created, such as what the names of the parties are, the case number, and the attorneys involved. Based on the answers to these questions, the Pleading Wizard then generates the document template (see Exhibit 2–11). Obviously, a Pleading Wizard feature can greatly speed up the creation of legal templates and forms, and improve accuracy and thoroughness through its interactive questions.

In Microsoft Word 2003, the feature is accessed by selecting File > New > Templates on my computer > Legal Pleadings > Pleading Wizard. The Pleading Wizard is covered in detail in Lesson 14 of the Hands-On Exercises for Word 2007 and Word 2003 in the Student Workbook.

MERGING AND DOCUMENT ASSEMBLY IN WORD PROCESSORS

merging

The process of combining a
form with a list of variables
to automatically produce a
document; sometimes called
document generation.

Merging, sometimes called document generation or document assembly, is the process of combining an existing form with a list of variables to automatically produce a new document. For instance, if you want to send the same letter to a number of clients, but you want each letter to be personalized, you can use the Merge feature found in most word processors to do this quickly. The body of each letter remains the same; the only information that changes is the name and address of the client. The information that remains the same in each letter (in this

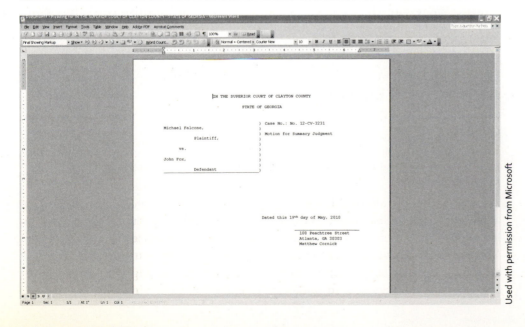

EXHIBIT 2–11

Legal Pleading Wizard
in Word 2003

primary file

A file that contains the information that remains the same (the constant) in a document that is used more than once; usually referred to as a form or template in a merge document.

secondary file

The file that contains the information that varies (the variable) in a merge document.

example, the body of the text) is called a constant. The information that changes in each letter (here, the name and address of the client) is called a variable.

The first step in the merge process is to create the primary file. The **primary file** (also called a main document) contains the constant information and is usually referred to as a form or template in a merge document. The second step is to create the list of names and addresses. This is called the secondary file. The **secondary file** (also called a data file) contains the variable information in a merge document. In this example, the secondary file contains the names and addresses of the clients. The third step is to merge or combine the primary file with the secondary file, thus creating a separate letter for each client, using the Merge command. The final step is to print the document(s).

Another way to use a merge file is to create a primary file or template and then enter information into the form as you go along, without using a secondary file at all. This is helpful for creating short, mundane forms such as letters, memos, and so forth. Once the primary file is created, use the merge command to retrieve it. Then, as you go along, fill in each variable that changes. Finally, when the document has been filled in, print it. Merge files greatly reduce the time it takes to perform repetitive tasks.

Many of the letters, pleadings, and other documents that law offices produce are essentially forms. In many instances, although the client names change from case to case, the letters and documents produced are generally the same. Merge files allow you to save these forms, so that later you can simply retrieve them and quickly fill in the blanks. Merging is covered in detail in Lessons 7 and 10 of the Hands-On Exercises for Word 2007 and Word 2003 in the Student Workbook.

In addition to word processors with merge/document assembly capabilities, there are also separate document assembly programs that work together with a word processor to perform this function. Document assembly programs typically have more features and capabilities than word processors. Many legal organizations use document assembly programs to further automate production of correspondence, pleadings, contracts, and other legal documents. These programs are covered later in this chapter.

WORD-PROCESSING FILE FORMATS

Most word processors, including Microsoft Word, can save documents in multiple file formats. Word 2007, for example, can save files in several formats, including Word 2007, Word 97–2003, plain text, Rich Text Format, Web Page, and others.

MICROSOFT WORD ONLINE TRAINING AND WORD TEMPLATES

Microsoft provides free online training courses for Microsoft Word on its website. More than 20 courses are available for each version. To find the online training courses, use a general search engine (such as www.google.com or www.yahoo.com) and use the search terms "Microsoft Word 2003 Courses" or "Microsoft Word 2007 Courses."

The Microsoft website also provides a wide variety of free Word templates. In Word 2007, the online templates can be accessed by selecting the Office button, selecting New, and then clicking on any of the categories to the left of the screen under Microsoft Office Online. In Word 2003, the online templates can be accessed by selecting File, selecting New, and then selecting Templates on Office Online under the Templates heading.

PDF FILE CREATION

As noted earlier, many courts now allow—and in fact require—legal organizations to file documents electronically. Most courts use PDF as the standard for filing documents electronically. The federal courts in particular have standardized filing around the PDF format. Thousands of attorneys have filed documents for millions of cases using the federal courts' Case Management and Electronic Case File system.

The PDF standard was created by Adobe Systems. PDF can be made a secure format, meaning that recipients cannot edit the document and that the look and format of the document are locked. For electronic filing of documents with a court, this is crucial.

Another advantage of PDF is that as long as the recipient has a PDF viewer (which is free), the recipient can view the file on a different type of computer than the one the document was created on. Thus, if a court system used a UNIX-based operating system and an attorney used an Apple Macintosh computer, it would not matter. As long as the attorney saved the document to be filed as a PDF, the court could still use and access the document, even though it was created on a computer with a completely different operating system.

Adobe Acrobat

Adobe Acrobat is a PDF conversion utility. Acrobat can convert many types of files to PDF. Adobe Acrobat has several versions, which may be confusing. Acrobat has a Reader program that can be downloaded for free from the Internet. However, to create PDF files, you need either the Standard or Professional version of Adobe Acrobat.

Adobe Acrobat is an output program; it is essentially a glorified digital printer. As a matter of fact, when Acrobat is downloaded, it adds an option to your list of available printers; images may now be sent to the PDF printer. This can be useful for saving images from web pages (receipts, travel information, etc.). Also, even though Acrobat is essentially a print utility, you can "print" a copy of something as a PDF without actually creating a hard copy; instead, you can just save a copy of a document as a PDF.

Acrobat is not used to create documents. That task is left to programs such as Word and Excel. However, Acrobat may be used to convert a digital photograph or other image to a PDF file. When you download Acrobat, it automatically installs (depending on the version of Windows on the computer) a new toolbar, or new buttons on your existing toolbars, that enable you to easily convert documents, pictures, and other images to PDFs.

Creating a PDF from a Microsoft Word File

There are a number of ways to convert documents and other images to PDFs. For example, suppose that you have a file in Word that you would like to convert to a PDF file. Notice in Exhibit 2–12 that when Adobe Acrobat was installed it created a new menu item in Word, entitled "Adobe PDF." The first step in converting the Word document to PDF is to select "Convert to Adobe PDF" from the Adobe PDF menu items on the Word menu line (see Exhibit 2–12, screen 1). Acrobat asks you to enter the name of the new PDF file that is being created. Acrobat then converts the file and opens it in the Adobe Acrobat program (see Exhibit 2–12, screen 2). Alternatively, you can load Acrobat first and identify the file to be converted, in this case the Word file; then Acrobat will convert it and load the converted file into Acrobat. Acrobat can also convert multiple files into one PDF file. The conversion progress is typically easy and straightforward.

EXHIBIT 2–12

Converting a Word file to a
PDF in Adobe Acrobat

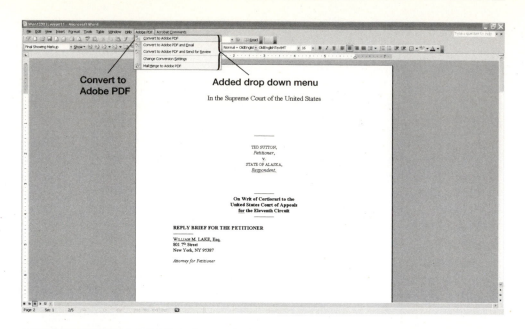

Convert to
Adobe PDF

Added drop down menu

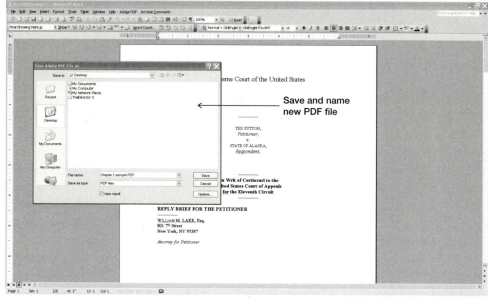

Save and name
new PDF file

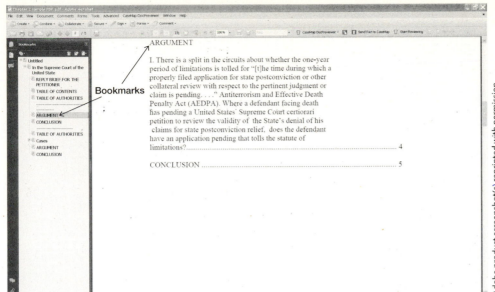

Adobe product screenshot(s) reprinted with permission from Adobe Systems Incorporated

EXHIBIT 2–13

Bookmarks in Adobe Acrobat

Creating a PDF from Internet Content

Adobe Acrobat can be used to capture—and, if desired, print—web pages. Without Acrobat, you would have to use a "screen shot" captured by clicking the Print Screen key. However, this often results in a less-than-satisfactory image. Acrobat provides a far better and more useful end product.

To create a PDF from a web page, you have several options. Perhaps the easiest is to "print" a PDF. To do this, all that is required is to click on the Print button and choose "PDF Printer"; then save the document as a PDF. Another option is to use the Acrobat buttons now embedded on the toolbar.

Acrobat has a number of features, including the Bookmark feature. A bookmark is a navigation link to a specific location in the PDF file. Notice in Exhibit 2–13 that to the left of the page, under the "Bookmarks" tab, there is a series of bookmarks, including "Table of Authorities," "Argument," "Conclusion," and so on. When the user clicks on the Argument bookmark, the user is immediately taken to that section of the document. This is a quick and convenient way to navigate in PDF files. Interestingly, if Microsoft Word users use the Style feature to create their documents, including using Headings in the Style feature, Acrobat can convert all of these headings directly to bookmarks.

Using Acrobat, users have tremendous control over how a PDF file will look. Users can assign custom page numbers, include headers or footers, insert multimedia links, create fill-in electronic forms, and much more.

Adobe Acrobat has many features, including the ability to create and insert notes and comments (see Exhibit 2–14). Using this feature, people can collaborate using Acrobat even if they do not all use the same word processor. Notice also in Exhibit 2–14 that the user has clicked on the Pages tab and that page views of the document are being displayed to the left.

Adobe Acrobat allows users to attach a digital signature to a PDF file. A digital signature not only validates the PDF file, but also validates with Acrobat the identity of the person signing it. Using digital signatures is another security feature: once a document is digitally signed, the recipient cannot alter the PDF file. Some courts require all PDF files to have a digital signature.

By default, new PDF files are *not* secure. This means that anyone receiving the PDF file can open, view, print, or make changes to that file. However, Acrobat offers a number

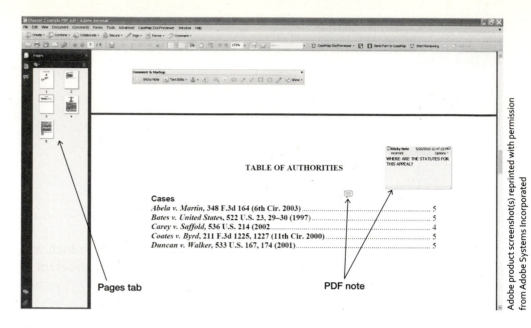

of security features that allow the creator to completely lock down a PDF file. For example, Exhibit 2–15 shows that the user has the option to restrict printing and editing of the documents and to choose its security settings. This enables the user to "lock" the PDF file so that unless the recipient has the password, the recipient cannot print or change the PDF file. However, Adobe Acrobat can export a PDF file to Microsoft Word as long as the user who created the original PDF file allows it by turning this feature on.

With all these features, and the considerable security protections it provides, Adobe Acrobat is an incredibly powerful tool for information sharing. It will most likely remain an important part of word processing and document distribution, for legal organizations, courts, and clients, for the foreseeable future.

DOCUMENT ASSEMBLY PROGRAMS

Document assembly software creates powerful standardized templates and forms. Users create forms and templates and then respond to a series of questions and prompts. The document assembly program then merges the selected template or form with the answers and builds a completed document. Document assembly programs work best, and are most useful, when the user has well-structured templates and forms that must be completed often and in a routine manner.

Word processors have some document assembly functions, but stand-alone document assembly programs are much more powerful. Text templates are based on text documents (e.g., a simple will or articles of incorporation) and are initially created with the user's word-processing program. Form templates create forms (e.g., an IRS tax form or credit application). At most law firms, text templates are much more common than form templates.

Suppose that a law firm routinely drafts employment contracts for a large client. Instead of using a word processor to slowly edit the document for every new employee the client hires, the law firm would like to use a document assembly program to automate the process.

Exhibit 2–16 shows a template for an employment agreement, which was built in a document assembly program. The document assembly program is running inside of the user's word processor; notice the special document assembly toolbar in Exhibit 2–16. Notice also that a number of variables are listed in Exhibit 2–16, including <Employee Name>, <Agreement Date>, <Job Title>, and others.

A variable is something that will change in the document. Notice that the variable <Employee Name> in Exhibit 2–16 is included more than once in the document. The beauty of a document assembly program is that once the text for the variable <Employee Name> has been entered (e.g., "Cynthia Jones"), the computer automatically fills it in anywhere the variable <Employee Name> appears. This software also allows the form to correctly enter "he" or "she" depending on the gender of the employee.

Once a template has been built, the user executes the template in the document assembly program (creates a custom document from a generic form). The document assembly program takes the answers the user gives and opens a new word-processing document. The next step is for the user to answer the questions the template asks. When all of the questions have been answered, the finished template document is displayed in the user's word-processing program so that the finished document can be edited as needed.

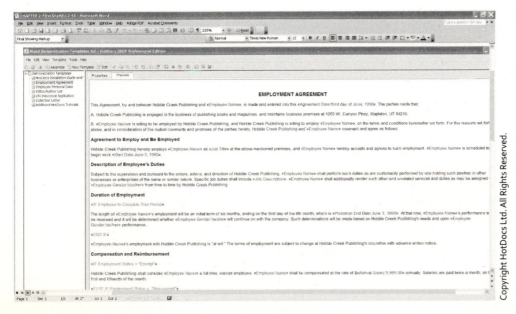

EXHIBIT 2–16

Document assembly program: Employment agreement—Completed template

Document assembly programs are extremely powerful and have many advanced features that make them great time-savers in many legal organizations. You will have the opportunity to assemble a text template and create a new text template in the HotDocs Hands-On Exercises in the Student Workbook (HotDocs 10).

ETHICAL CONSIDERATIONS

Although word processing has done wonders for the legal profession in terms of efficiency and ease of use, it has a downside that raises important ethical issues. Word processors can make users lazy. For instance, users may misspell words because they assume that the spell checker will catch them. Users can use poor grammar because the grammar checker will fix it. Users do not have to start from scratch to prepare a will or other legal document because form wills, templates, and other documents that can easily be modified are available on the computer or on the Internet. Users do not have to go back and do legal research over and over again every time a new legal document is filed, because they can copy legal research from one client's documents to another's.

Finally, even if a document's content is poor, users can make it look pretty with fancy fonts, justified margins, tables, and many other features. And that is the problem—potential lack of content. An attorney has an ethical duty to provide competent representation. Lawyers and paralegals must make sure that their word-processing documents are competently and thoroughly prepared. That is, they should not only look good, but also be proofread well, contain up-to-date and accurate cites, and be the best documents the attorney or paralegal can produce.

The following are a few common ethical issues related to the use of word processors.

Leaving Metadata in Documents

As you may recall from Chapter 1, metadata is electronically stored information that may identify the origin, date, author, usage, comments, or other information about a file. It is important that a legal organization delete or remove the metadata from any document before that document leaves the firm.

In Word 2007, a user can inspect all parts of a document for metadata. If metadata is discovered in the document, the user can choose to remove it. In addition, Adobe Acrobat now has strong security enhancements that can remove metadata from PDF files and permanently delete the redacted information.

It should be noted that while legal organizations do not want documents going out of the office with metadata still present in them, some courts have held that in the context of discovery (production of documents during the discovery stage of a lawsuit), opposing parties are entitled to metadata. Note here the major difference between documents prepared by attorneys for their clients (e.g., word-processing documents), where security is of the utmost importance, and discovery documents produced by clients for the opposing parties in a case. In the latter, some courts have said that the parties have the right to see the metadata, including the origin of documents and other information. This is another reason to make sure, as an important matter of practice, that a word-processing document has no metadata attached to it before it leaves the legal organization.

Old Client Data Left in New Document

It is common, when preparing a new document, to retrieve an old document and use it as the basis of the new one. For instance, when preparing a new real estate contract, the user might pull up an old real estate contract from a few months ago as a place to start. The trouble is that it is easy to leave the old data (i.e., old property description, old client names, old prices, wrong pronouns) in the new document. This problem is a strong argument for both excellent proofreading and the creation and use of fill-in templates or forms.

Typographical Errors That Spell Checkers Will Not Catch

Some typographical errors will not be caught by a spell checker; they can be picked up only by careful proofreading of the document. Common errors of this sort include insertion or retention of the wrong case facts, and misuse of a correctly spelled word. For example, a complaint should demand a jury *trial*, not a jury *trail*. In one well-publicized case, a paralegal mistakenly left out the last three zeros on a mortgage used to secure a $92,885,000 loan to a company that eventually went into bankruptcy. Because of the mistake, the company the paralegal worked for had only a $92,885 lien. Going by the provisions of the mortgage, that left $92,792,115 unsecured.

It is absolutely critical that all documents be carefully proofread even if the user is using a word processor, and a spell checker, and a grammar checker. Some mistakes can be caught only by the user. Supervising attorneys cannot afford to become careless about these matters, no matter how good or trustworthy the paralegal is.

Improper Form Selected; Leaving in or Deleting Wrong Paragraphs

It is very easy to select the wrong form when creating new documents. Unfortunately, this can have a devastating impact. Another very common error is to either leave in inappropriate material or delete a wrong paragraph from the form. If you are using a form, it is important to know and understand every paragraph in the form so you can make appropriate decisions about what stays and what goes.

Not Following Court Rules

Many courts have document preparation rules, especially regarding the kind of font or typeface to be used, the font size, margin widths, and paper sizes. It is important that these rules be followed exactly. In one case, a corporate legal department repeatedly filed appellate briefs using a 10-point Times New Roman font instead of the 12-point Courier required by court rules. The law department did this because another court rule limited briefs to 30 pages, and they could get in 50 percent more verbiage using the smaller font. The court finally dismissed the appeal because the law office did not follow the court's rules.

Preparing Legal Documents without the Supervision of an Attorney (Unauthorized Practice of Law)

Most states have a criminal statute that prohibits a layperson from practicing law. In addition to criminal laws, there are also ethical prohibitions that proscribe a nonlawyer from practicing law. Simply put, paralegals cannot draft legal documents, such as wills, briefs, motions, pleadings, or contracts, without the supervision of an attorney. Paralegals routinely draft these types of documents; the distinction is that they do so properly, under the direction and supervision of a member of the bar. The attorney is ultimately responsible for the legal documents.

What happens if an attorney does not look at a document a paralegal has prepared using a word processor or document assembly program? Assume that the paralegal has been working hard on a motion and has taken cases and arguments from past documents prepared by the supervising attorney, but the document is due by 5:00 p.m. and there is no time for the attorney to review it. This is how unauthorized practice of law issues regarding word processing and drafting documents arise in real life.

The reason for the rule is that legal documents affect the legal rights of clients and parties and therefore require the attention of an attorney. As long as a paralegal is actively working under the supervision of an attorney, and the attorney maintains a relationship with the client, the paralegal may interview witnesses or prospective clients, perform legal research, draft pleadings and briefs, and investigate the facts of cases without being accused of the unauthorized practice of law. However, the moment the paralegal prepares a legal document on her own, without the review of an attorney, a breach of the rule has most likely occurred.

No matter how routine the legal document is, always have an attorney review it. Never let an attorney approve your work without reading it. If the attorney says, "I don't have time to review it; I'll sign it and you just send it out, I trust you," bring the document back at another time or find a tactful way to suggest to the attorney that the document must be approved in the correct way.

Overlooking Prudent Practices

Competent representation of a client requires more than just competence regarding knowledge of the law and the quality of the legal services provided. It requires competence in all aspects of the law office, including the following areas.

Use Full-Function Spell and Grammar Checkers
Certainly, you should not rely on the spell checker/grammar checker to do your only review of documents. However, you should by all means use these functions on every document you prepare. There is nothing more embarrassing than finding obvious typographical or grammatical errors in a document that has gone out—particularly when it has been sent out under the signature of your supervising attorney. Never assume that the automatic spell/grammar checking that occurs as you type your document (where problems are flagged by being underlined with colored squiggly lines) is enough. *It is not.* It is extremely easy to fail to see these errors when drafting. Always go back and run the full-function spell/grammar checker to make sure you have not missed any obvious mistakes.

Always Validate Cases/Citations and Factual References
Before a paralegal cites a case or references a fact in a legal document that he is unsure about, it is imperative that he double-check and validate the case or fact to make sure it is still good law or that the "fact" actually happened. Never throw something into a word processor with the thought that you will get back to it and verify it—what happens if you forget? The answer is that the client can be harmed, the attorney's reputation can be harmed, your reputation certainly will be harmed, and serious ethical ramifications could arise for your supervising attorney or the law office. Do not take the chance; always double-check your work.

Password-Protect Confidential Word-Processing Documents That Will Be Emailed
It is always a good idea, out of an abundance of caution, to password-protect confidential documents that will be emailed through an Internet provider or sent over large networks. Most word-processing programs have the capability to do this; for example, Microsoft Word can password-protect word processing files. It is very easy to do and does not cost anything. It is just one more layer of protection to maintain the confidentiality of client or case-related data.

SUMMARY

Word processors are computer programs that are used to edit, manipulate, and revise text to create documents. A law office with a centralized word-processing system has a separate word-processing department that inputs all documents for an organization, as opposed to a decentralized word-processing system in which individuals perform word processing for themselves or a small group. The primary word-processing program in law offices is Microsoft Word, though some still use Corel WordPerfect.

Modern legal organizations use a variety of word-processing functions and features, including, among others, automatic paragraph numbering, styles, footnotes and endnotes, tables, macros, comments, multiple-document comparisons, change tracking, creation of tables of authorities, and document merging.

Creating Portable Document Format (PDF) files is an important part of document generation for many legal organizations because many jurisdictions require word processing documents to be filed electronically in this format. Adobe Acrobat is the most popular program used for converting files into PDFs.

Document assembly software creates powerful templates for form documents. Once the user answers the questions in the template, the answers are then merged with the template and a new, final document is output. Document assembly software is extremely sophisticated and serves many functions in legal organizations.

When preparing legal documents, it is important for users to carefully review their work to ensure that old information is not left in documents, metadata is deleted, research is updated and current, and there are no typographical errors.

KEY TERMS

automatic page numbering	endnote	Portable Document Format (PDF)
centralized word-processing system	footer	primary file
comment	footnote	secondary file
compare documents	header	style
decentralized word-processing system	macro	table of authorities
document assembly software	merging	track changes
double indenting	Pleading Wizard	word-processing software

INTERNET SITES

Internet sites for this chapter include:

ORGANIZATION	PRODUCT/SERVICE	INTERNET ADDRESS
LexisNexis	HotDocs document assembly program	www.hotdocs.com
Corel Corporation	WordPerfect	www.corel.com
Findlaw.com	Online legal forms	www.findlaw.com
Microsoft	Microsoft Word	www.microsoft.com/word
ProDoc	ProDoc document assembly program	www.prodoc.com
Adobe Systems, Inc.	Adobe Acrobat PDF file creation	www.adobe.com
Nitro PDF, Inc.	Free PDF creator software	www.primopdf.com

TEST YOUR KNOWLEDGE

1. What does "PDF" stand for?
2. Compare and contrast centralized and decentralized word processing.
3. True or False: The automatic paragraph numbering feature numbers the pages in a document.
4. True or False: A style is a named set of formatting characteristics that users apply to text.
5. Text that is indented an equal distance from the left and right margin is called _____.
6. True or False: A word-processing feature that combines a primary and secondary file is called a macro.

7. A word-processing feature that allows the reviewer to make annotations in the document without actually changing the document is called a _____.
8. Distinguish between primary and secondary merge files.
9. What standard document type do most courts use to allow attorneys to file documents electronically?
10. True or False: Word-processing merge files have exactly the same features as stand-alone document assembly programs.

ON THE WEB EXERCISES

1. Using the "Internet Sites" listed in this chapter and a general Internet search engine (such as www.google.com or www.yahoo.com), research the current versions of Microsoft Word. Prepare a summary of the differences, similarities, and reviews of the products. Which product would you rather use in the legal environment and why?
2. Using the "Internet Sites" listed in this chapter and a general Internet search engine (such as www.google.com or www.yahoo.com), research the Case Management and Electronic Filing System for the U.S. federal courts. Write a two-page summary of your findings, including how it works, what the standard is, and other relevant information about the system.
3. Using the "Internet Sites" listed in this chapter and a general Internet search engine (such as www.google.com or www.yahoo.com), find a word-processing template for a simple last will and testament for your state. How hard or easy was it to find? Were you able to find fee-based forms, free forms, or both?

4. Using http://forms.lp.findlaw.com, find a recent United States Supreme Court opinion under "Cases and Codes." Copy and paste the opinion into your word processor. How easy was this to do? Can you manipulate and edit the document? Describe why using the Internet and your word processor in this way might be an important feature for a legal organization.
5. Using the "Internet Sites" listed in this chapter and a general Internet search engine (such as www.google.com or www.yahoo.com), research document assembly programs. What programs did you find? What features do they have? What are their advantages? How are they different from the merge capabilities in word processors? Do they have any disadvantages?
6. Using the "Internet Sites" listed in this chapter and a general Internet search engine (such as www.google.com or www.yahoo.com), research what a PDF file is and what advantages PDFs have over other file formats.

QUESTIONS AND EXERCISES

1. Contact a law office, legal organization, paralegal, or attorney you know and ask what word processor they use and why. Ask what features they like about it, what features they wish they had, whether the program is fulfilling their basic needs, and whether they are looking to change word processors. Also, ask who does word processing at the firm, and if there is a centralized or decentralized system. Type a one-page summary of your conversations.

2. Word processors have developed over time to include hundreds of features and functions. Write a short paper on the top 10 functions or features that you use when you do word processing. Explain what each function is and why you use it.

3. On your own computer, open any word-processing document in your word processor. Point and click on File and then on Properties. What metadata was included in the "Properties" section of the document?

4. In Microsoft Word, open a new document and do the following:
   a. Type the following phrases: This is secret text no one should see. This is text that is open to the public.
   b. Turn on Track Changes by going to "Tools" on the menu bar and then clicking on "Track Changes."

   c. Now, using the delete key, delete the sentence "This is secret text no one should see." Notice that to the right it now shows the text is deleted.
   d. Point and click with your mouse on the down arrow next to "Final Showing Markup" in the "Tracking" item on the Review toolbar. Then click on "Final." Notice that you cannot see "This is secret text no one should see." Assume for the purposes of this exercise that you sent this document to the opposing party in a case.
   e. Now, assume that you are the opposing party in the case. Select the down arrow next to "Final" in the "Tracking" item on the Review toolbar and select "Original." Notice that you can perfectly see "This is secret text no one should see." Point and click with your mouse on the down arrow next to "Original" in the "Final Showing Markup" item on the Review toolbar and select "Original Showing Markup." You can now see all of the changes in the document.

   What confidentiality issues might arise with use of the Track Changes feature? Suggest some ways to avoid these problems.

ETHICS QUESTION

Your firm represents a wife in a divorce case. She wants to know what issues are covered in a separation agreement, so she asks you for a sample of a separation agreement. You do not have a "blank" separation agreement, but your computer contains dozens of examples. What ethical issues are raised by this scenario?

Go to the Workbook to complete the Hands-On Exercises. There are exercises for Word 2003, Word 2007, Adobe Acrobat, and HotDocs 10 (document assembly software).

 Access an interactive eBook, chapter-specific interactive learning tools, including flash cards, quizzes, and more in your Paralegal CourseMate, accessed through CengageBrain.com.

CHAPTER 3

Spreadsheet Software

CHAPTER OBJECTIVES

After completing this chapter, you should be able to do the following:

1. Explain what a spreadsheet is.
2. Describe how rows and columns make up the structure of a spreadsheet.
3. Explain what text, values, and formulas are.
4. Describe the types of graphs commonly found in spreadsheet programs.
5. Explain how copying formulas can simplify the use of a spreadsheet.
6. List and describe the ways in which paralegals can use spreadsheets.

INTRODUCTION

spreadsheet software
Programs that calculate and manipulate numbers using labels, values, and formulas.

Spreadsheet software calculates and manipulates numbers using labels, values, and formulas. Legal organizations use spreadsheets to create department and firm budgets; to calculate child support and alimony payments in domestic relations cases; to prepare amortization schedules, Truth-in-Lending statements, and loan calculations in real estate matters; and to estimate taxes and help prepare tax returns for tax matters. These are just a few of the many uses of spreadsheets for law offices of all types. Spreadsheet software can automate all of these tasks.

As word processors manipulate words, spreadsheets manipulate numbers. Instead of performing word processing, spreadsheets perform number processing. This chapter describes what a spreadsheet is and discusses "what if" analysis, the structure of spreadsheet programs, the fundamentals of spreadsheets, how to plan or create a spreadsheet, and how spreadsheets are used in the legal environment.

WHAT IS A SPREADSHEET?

spreadsheet
A computerized version of an accountant's worksheet or ledger page.

A **spreadsheet** is a computerized version of an accountant's worksheet or ledger page. Spreadsheet software is used to create a spreadsheet, sometimes called a worksheet. In the past, accounting professionals primarily used ledger pages, also sometimes called worksheets, to track financial information. They would enter financial transactions across the rows and down the columns of the ledger paper. Each column was then added up using a calculator or an adding machine. This process was cumbersome and time-consuming if changes were needed or if errors were found.

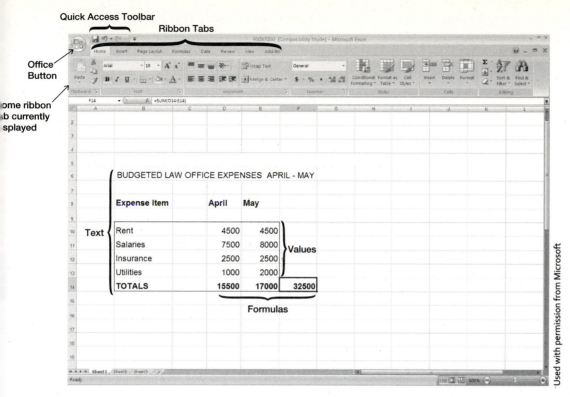

Quick Access Toolbar

Ribbon Tabs

Office Button

ome ribbon b currently splayed

Text

Values

Formulas

BUDGETED LAW OFFICE EXPENSES APRIL - MAY

Expense Item	April	May
Rent	4500	4500
Salaries	7500	8000
Insurance	2500	2500
Utilities	1000	2000
TOTALS	15500	17000	32500

EXHIBIT 3–1

A simple spreadsheet using Microsoft Excel 2007

Spreadsheets, in contrast, are flexible and easy to use. Exhibit 3–1 is a simple spreadsheet showing a small law firm's budgeted expenses for a two-month period. This example introduces basic spreadsheet concepts. More sophisticated and more useful spreadsheets for the legal environment are introduced later in this chapter.

Spreadsheet programs were among the first general business application programs designed to run on personal computers. Spreadsheets are easier to use than manual worksheets, because the data in a spreadsheet can easily be edited and changed. In addition, spreadsheets can calculate totals and perform other mathematical functions automatically. When data are changed in a spreadsheet, the resulting totals are automatically recalculated to reflect the changes made. (Note that data is often a plural word, as shown here.) Spreadsheets have greatly altered the way businesses and legal organizations track and keep numerical data. Reports and computations that once took hours or days now take minutes.

Law firms also enjoy the benefits of spreadsheets. Numerical data are critical in almost all areas of the law. Remember, if it involves money, it involves numbers. For example, many complaints and cases include claims for damages; that is, the people filing the suits often ask for money or some type of monetary relief. Damages calculations can be complex and are often well-suited to spreadsheets; spreadsheets are used extensively in bankruptcy law, tax law, estate law, real estate law, and other areas. Law firms also use spreadsheets administratively to track income and expenses, create budgets, produce financial and accounting records, produce statistical reports about the business, and so on.

Spreadsheet software is easy and flexible to use because it:

1. allows all entries to be edited, moved, or copied to other places in the spreadsheet.
2. makes it easy to insert additional columns and rows, even after the spreadsheet has been created.

3. multiplies, divides, adds, and subtracts one entry or many entries.
4. performs complex calculations (e.g., statistical functions, such as standard deviations, averages, and square roots; and financial calculations, such as present value, future value, and internal rate of return).
5. automatically recalculates totals and other calculations when information in a column or a row changes.
6. allows numerical information to be presented in several kinds of graphs and charts.
7. allows information to be saved and retrieved for future use.
8. allows information to be sorted or organized automatically.
9. allows the information in the spreadsheet to be printed.

Microsoft Excel is the spreadsheet program overwhelmingly used by most legal organizations. Versions of Excel that are widely used in the legal environment include Excel 2010, Excel 2007, and Excel 2003. The programs are largely similar except that Excel 2007 and 2010 uses a ribbon interface (see Exhibit 3–1) and Excel 2003 uses a largely menu-driven interface. Screen shots from Excel 2007 and Excel 2003 are used throughout this chapter.

"WHAT IF" ANALYSIS

"what if" analysis
A feature of spreadsheets that allows the user to build a spreadsheet and then change the data to reflect alternative planning assumptions or scenarios.

Spreadsheets can also be used for "what if" analysis. **"What if" analysis** refers to the ability to build a spreadsheet and then to change it to reflect alternative planning assumptions or scenarios. As mentioned before, when numerical data are entered into a spreadsheet and later changed, the totals are automatically recalculated. Thus, it is possible to evaluate the effects of a change simply by changing a number. This allows users to hypothesize and evaluate the effects of potential changes easily. For example, in Exhibit 3–1, if the small law firm wanted to evaluate what would happen if rent doubled for the two-month period shown, it could simply change the "4500" rent figure to "9000" and the spreadsheet would automatically recalculate the total. Most businesses are in a state of change at all times, so this feature allows users to prepare for unexpected events.

SPREADSHEET STRUCTURE AND ORGANIZATION

An electronic spreadsheet has many of the same components as its paper ancestor, such as rows and columns. However, it also has many features unique to the electronic format, such as formulas that automatically compute and display the desired information.

Rows and Columns

row
An area that extends across a page horizontally.

column
An area that extends down a page vertically.

Like an accountant's worksheet, a spreadsheet has rows and columns. A **row** is an area that extends across a page horizontally, and a **column** is an area that extends down a page vertically. For example, in Exhibit 3–2, rows are designated by a number (row 1, row 2, etc.), and columns are designated by a capital letter (column A, column B, etc.). Although only 21 rows and 10 columns are shown on the screen in Exhibit 3–2, the spreadsheet actually extends all the way down several thousand rows and all the way across several hundred columns. The exact length of a spreadsheet depends on the spreadsheet program. When the columns go past column Z, the column letters double up (column AA, column AB, etc.).

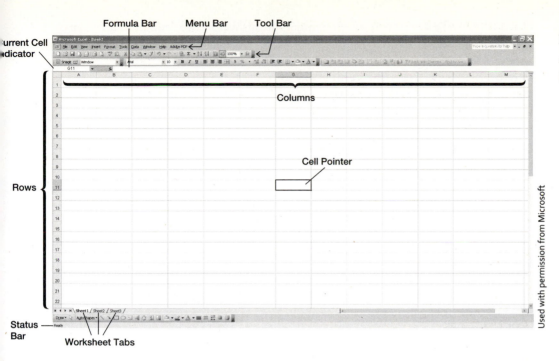

Used with permission from Microsoft

EXHIBIT 3–2

A simple spreadsheet using Microsoft Excel 2003

Cells and Cell Addresses

A **cell** is an intersection between a row and a column (see Exhibit 3–2). Every cell has a **cell address**. A cell address is the row and column location of a cell. The cell address is usually represented by the letter of the column and then the number of the row, such as cell G11 in Exhibit 3–2. Every cell in a spreadsheet has a cell address. Cells hold information such as values (numbers), formulas (mathematical calculations), and text.

The Elements of a Spreadsheet

Most spreadsheet programs have a user interface similar to the one in Exhibit 3–2. After a user loads a spreadsheet program, a blank spreadsheet is displayed. Exhibit 3–2 shows the various elements of a spreadsheet.

Cell Pointer All spreadsheets have a **cell pointer**, or cursor, that indicates which cell is currently selected. The cell pointer is moved by using the arrow or direction keys and can also be moved up and down pages or screens by using the [PAGE UP], [PAGE DOWN], and other keys, depending on the spreadsheet. Most spreadsheet programs also allow the cell pointer to be moved with a mouse. Finally, the cell pointer can be moved using the GO TO command. The GO TO command instructs the spreadsheet to "go to" a certain cell address. In Microsoft Excel 2003 and 2007, the [F5] key is the GO TO command.

Current Cell Indicator and Formula Bar The current cell indicator, sometimes called the name box, shows the address of the cell pointer (see Exhibit 3–2). The formula bar, which is just to the right of the current cell indicator, shows the contents of the current cell. Notice in Exhibit 3–2 that the current cell indicator shows "G11" and that there is nothing in the formula bar, because cell G11 is empty. When the cell pointer is on a cell containing text, a value, or a formula, the information in the cell will be shown in the formula bar. The text, value, or formula can be edited by placing the cursor in the formula bar. When the cell pointer is moved, the current cell indicator automatically displays the current cell address.

cell
An intersection between a row and a column in a spreadsheet.

cell address
The row and column location of a cell, usually expressed with column identifier first and row identifier second.

cell pointer
The cursor in a spreadsheet program.

Data Input Area Data are entered into a spreadsheet in the data input area, which is made up of cells.

Status Bar The status bar signifies the current status of the spreadsheet. For example, in Exhibit 3–2, the spreadsheet is in the ready mode, which means that it is ready to accept instructions from a user.

Menus, Toolbars, and Ribbons

Excel 2007 (see Exhibit 3–1) uses a changing ribbon as the interface with the user instead of menus. In Exhibit 3–1 the Home ribbon tab is shown. Available ribbons include: Home, Insert, Page Layout, Formulas, Data, Review, and View. The tools on the ribbon change depending on what tab is selected. Excel 2007 also has a small Quick Access toolbar that does not change and that is customizable by the user (see Exhibit 3–1). In contrast, Excel 2003 (see Exhibit 3–2) uses a static toolbar and a series of drop-down menus (File, Edit, View, Insert, Format, Tools, Data, Window, and Help) as the interface with the user. Most of the other elements in Excel 2007 and 2003 operate in the same way.

Horizontal and Vertical Scroll Bars To bring other parts of the spreadsheet into view, use the horizontal and vertical scroll bars.

Worksheets Most spreadsheet programs allow multiple worksheets in one spreadsheet file. Notice in Exhibit 3–2 that three sheets are available (Sheet 1, Sheet 2, and Sheet 3). Many users find it convenient to have separate worksheets in one file. For example, if your law office had three locations, you could have one spreadsheet file called "budget" with a separate worksheet for each location. The worksheets (Sheet 1, Sheet 2, etc.) can be renamed however you wish, such as Location 1, 2, and 3.

Spreadsheets with WYSIWYG

Most spreadsheets offer a WYSIWYG ("what you see is what you get"; pronounced "wizzy-wig") screen. Exhibits 3–1 and 3–2 are examples of Windows spreadsheet programs with WYSIWYG. The WYSIWYG format allows users to add different fonts or type styles to the spreadsheets and enables application of boxes and other formatting options that can make a spreadsheet easier to read. In addition, all of the formatting appears on the screen exactly as it will print out.

SPREADSHEET FUNDAMENTALS

In this section, you will learn about spreadsheet menus and about inputting text, values, and formulas. Exhibits 3–3A and 3–3B show Quick Reference guides for Excel 2007 and Excel 2003.

Data Input

Data are usually entered into a spreadsheet using a keyboard. Data can be entered more easily and faster if the keyboard has a separate numeric keypad in addition to the direction and cursor keys. This allows you to move the cell pointer with the cursor keys and to enter values and formulas using the numeric keypad.

Three types of data can be entered into a spreadsheet: text, values, and formulas.

text
Descriptive data, such as headings and titles, used for reference purposes in a spreadsheet.

Text Descriptive data, called **text**, are entered into a cell. This type of data cannot be used in making calculations. It includes headings, titles, and so forth. For example,

Excel 2007 Quick Reference Guide

HOME RIBBON

Home Button · Quick Access Toolbar · Font · Fill color · Font color · Font orientation · Wrap Text · Ribbon Tabs · Number Format · Insert cells · Autofill · Sum · Sort · Help

Cut · Paste · Copy · Find/Select

Format Painter · Bold · Italic · Underline · Borders · Format Cells · Dialog Box Launcher · Left · Center · Right · Merge Center · Increase decimal · Decrease decimal · Delete cells · Format Rows/Columns · Clear

NAVIGATION

UP ONE SCREEN	[Page Up]	TO CELL A1	[CTRL]+[HOME]
DOWN ONE SCREEN	[Page Down]	TO LAST CELL WITH DATA	[CTRL]+[END]
BEGINNING OF A ROW	[Home]	GO TO	[F5]
CELL BELOW CURRENT CELL	[Enter]		

KEYBOARD SHORTCUTS

COPY TEXT	[Ctrl]+[C]	UNDO A COMMAND	[Ctrl]+[Z]
PASTE TEXT	[Ctrl]+[V]	REDO/REPEAT	[Ctrl]+[Y]
CUT TEXT	[Ctrl]+[X]	PRINT A WORKBOOK	[Ctrl]+[P]
BOLD TEXT	[Ctrl]+[B]	SAVE A WORKBOOK	[Ctrl]+[S]
UNDERLINE TEXT	[Ctrl]+[U]	OPEN A WORKBOOK	[Ctrl]+[O]
ITALICS TEXT	[Ctrl]+[I]	FIND/REPLACE	[Ctrl]+[F]
EDIT A CELL	[F2]	ABSOLUTE CELL REFERENCE	F4

EXCEL FEATURES / COMMAND STRUCTURE

EXCEL FEATURES	COMMAND STRUCTURE
ABSOLUTE CELL REFERENCE	(=B10*a1); $ signs represent an absolute cell reference, the F4 key will insert the $ signs in a formula.
ADJUSTING COLUMN WIDTH OR ROW HEIGHT	Drag the right border of the column header or the bottom border of the row header. Double-click to Auto Fit the column/row. Or **Home>Cells>Format>Cell Size**
AUTOFILL	Point to the fill handle of the bottom corner of the cell(s), then drag to the destination cells(s).
CHART	**Insert>Charts>**
CLEAR CELL CONTENTS	DEL key or **Home>Editing** group>**Clear, Clear Contents**
CLEAR FORMAT	**Home>Editing>Clear>Clear Formats**
DELETE ROW/COLUMN	**Home>Cells>Delete**
EDIT A CELL	Select the cell and click the Formula Bar to edit the contents or press F2
FIND AND REPLACE	**Home>Editing>Find & Select>Find or Replace**
FIT TO ONE PAGE	**Page Layout> Scale to Fit Dialog Box Launcher>Fit To**
FORMAT CELLS	**Home>Font>Font Dialog Box Launcher>**or Right-click **Format Cells**
FORMULA	Select the cell where you want the formula, press = (equal), enter the formula, and press [enter] when done (e.g., =a1+a2; =a1*10). Excel performs operations in this order: ( ), :, %, ^, * and /, + and -.
FREEZE PANE	**View>Window>Freeze Panes**
FUNCTIONS	Click **Insert Function** icon next to the Formula Bar; or **Formulas> Function Library>Insert function**
HIDE/UNHIDE A COLUMN	Right-click **Column Header>Hide**; right-click **Header>Unhide;** or **View>Window>Hide**
INSERT ROW/COLUMN	**Home>Cells>insert**
MACRO	**View>Macros>Macros**
PAGE BREAKS FOR PRINTING	**Page Layout>Page Setup>Breaks** or **View>Workbook Views> Page Break Preview;** Drag page break Indicator line to where you want the page break to occur.
PASSWORD PROTECT	**Office Button, Save>Tools>General Options>Password to Open**
TOTAL A CELL RANGE	Click the cell where you want the total inserted, click the autosum icon (**Home, Editing, Sum** icon), verify the range, and press [Enter].
WORKSHEET TAB NAME	Click Sheet1 name and type over it to rename
WRAP TEXT	**Format>Cells>Alignment>Wrap Text**

EXHIBIT 3–3A

Excel 2007 Quick Reference Guide

Excel 2003 Quick Reference Guide

STANDARD TOOLBAR

New doc — Save doc — Email — Preview — Research — Copy — Format Painter — Redo — Autosum — Sort Z-A — Drawing — Font — Bold — Underline — Center — Merge Center — Percentage — Increase decimal — Decrease decimal

Open doc — Permission — Print — Spell — Cut — Paste — Undo — Hyperlink — Sort A-Z — Chart — Zoom — Font size — Italics — Left — Right — Currency — Comma style

Decrease indent — Increase indent — Borders — Fill color — Font color

NAVIGATION

Up 1 Screen	[Page Up]	To Cell A1	[Ctrl]+[Home]
Down 1 Screen	[Page Down]	To Last Cell With Data	[Ctrl]+[End]
Beginning of a Row	[Home]	Go To	[F5]
Cell Below Current Cell	[Enter]	1 Screen To The Left	[Alt]+[Page Up]
		1 Screen To The Right	[Alt]+[Page Down]

KEYBOARD SHORTCUTS

Copy Text	[Ctrl]+[C]	Undo a Command	[Ctrl]+[Z]
Paste Text	[Ctrl]+[V]	Redo/Repeat	[Ctrl]+[Y]
Cut Text	[Ctrl]+[X]	Print a Workbook	[Ctrl]+[P]
Bold Text	[Ctrl]+[B]	Save a Workbook	[Ctrl]+[S]
Underline Text	[Ctrl]+[U]	Open a Workbook	[Ctrl]+[O]
Italics Text	[Ctrl]+[I]	Find/Replace	[Ctrl]+[F]
Edit a Cell	[F2]	Absolute Cell Reference	F4

EXCEL FEATURES	COMMAND STRUCTURE
Absolute Cell Reference	(=B10*$A$1); $ signs represent an absolute cell reference; the [F4] key will insert the $ signs in a formula.
Adjusting Column Width or Row Height	Drag the right border of the column header or the bottom border of the row header. Double-click to auto fit the column/row.
Autofill	Point at the fill handle of the bottom corner of the cell(s), then drag it to the destination cells(s).
Chart	**Insert>Chart**
Clear Cell Contents	**[DEL]** or **Edit>Clear>Contents Del**
Clear Format	**Edit>Clear>Format**
Delete Row/Column	**Edit>Delete**
Edit a Cell	Select the cell and click the Formula Bar to edit the contents.
Find and Replace	**Edit>Find** or **Edit>Replace**
Fit to One Page	**File>Page Setup>Fit to 1 page**
Format Cells	**Format>Cells>(Number, Alignment, Font**, etc.)
Formula	Select the cell where you want the formula, press = (equal), and enter the formula, and press [Enter] when done (e.g., =A1+A2; =A1*10). Excel performs operations in this order: ( ), :, %, ^, * and /, + and -.
Freeze Pane	**Window>Freeze Pane**
Functions	**Insert>Function**
Hide/Unhide a Column	Right-click **Column Header>Hide**; right-click **Header>Unhide**
Insert a Row/Column	**Insert>Row** or **Insert>Column**
Macro	**Tools>Macro**
Page Breaks for Printing	**View>Page Break Preview>** drag page break indicator line to where you want the page break to occur. **View>Normal** when completed.
Password Protect	**File>Save>Tools>General Options>Password to Open**
Total a Cell Range	Click the cell where you want the total inserted, click the autosum icon on the toolbar, verify the range and press [Enter].
Worksheet Tab Name	Right-click on **Tab Name>Rename**
Wrap Text	**Format>Cells>Alignment>Wrap Text**

EXHIBIT 3–3B

Excel 2003 Quick Reference Guide

in Exhibit 3–1, the title "BUDGETED LAW OFFICE EXPENSES APRIL - MAY"; the column headings "Expense Item", "April," and "May"; and the row headings "Rent," "Salaries," "Insurance," "Utilities," and "TOTALS" are all text.

Text is usually entered as a series of words and/or abbreviations, but numbers can also be included, although no calculations can be performed on a number entered as text. For example, instead of writing out May for the column heading in Exhibit 3–1, the number 5 could be substituted, showing that May is the fifth month of the year. The numbers could be entered as text since no calculations will be performed using these cells, which are intended only as column headings.

When a character or letter is typed into a cell, most spreadsheets assume that it is a text entry. Likewise, when a number is typed into a cell, most spreadsheets assume that it is a value or number entry on which calculations can be performed.

The procedure for entering text into a cell is simple. Move the cell pointer to the cell where the text should be placed, then begin typing the text. As the text is being typed, the characters are displayed in the formula bar and in the cell. After you have typed the characters, press the [ENTER] key to enter the text into the cell. Most spreadsheets also allow you to enter data into a cell by pressing either the [ENTER] key or any of the four arrow or direction keys.

Text can be edited later by using the Edit command. The Edit command varies among different spreadsheet programs, but it generally allows a user to correct or change the contents of the cell. The Edit command in Microsoft Excel is [F2]. You can also double-click on a cell to edit it.

Another way to change the contents of an existing cell is to point to the cell to be changed, type new content, and enter the new text into the cell. This deletes the existing content and inserts the new content in the same cell. This procedure can be used for changing text, values, or formulas.

Values Numbers that are entered into a cell and that can be used in making calculations are **values**. In Exhibit 3–1, the amount listed for each expense item is a value. Values can be entered as either positive or negative numbers. Negative values are usually represented with parentheses around them or a negative sign before them. For example, if you wanted to enter negative 20,000, the spreadsheet would show either (20,000) or <–>20,000.

Entering a value in a spreadsheet is similar to entering text. First, point to the cell where the value should be placed, then type the value. As the value is being typed, the characters are usually displayed in the formula bar and in the cell. After you have typed the value, press the [ENTER] key or a cursor key on the keyboard to enter the label into the cell. In Exhibit 3–1, notice that no commas or dollar signs are shown. A separate command is used to enter formatting codes. This is covered later in this chapter.

Formulas Calculations using the values in other cells are performed with **formulas**. For example, in Exhibit 3–4, the entry in cell D14 is a formula (=D10+D11+D12+D13) that adds the values of cells D10, D11, D12, and D13. Because the formula is placed in cell D14, the total is also placed there. The real power of a spreadsheet program is that formulas automatically recalculate totals if a cell value is changed. Thus, if any of the values in D10, D11, D12, or D13 were later changed, the program would automatically recalculate the total in D14.

Formulas can be entered using arithmetic operators or function commands or both.

values
Numbers that are entered into a spreadsheet program for the purpose of making calculations.

formulas
Expressions used in spreadsheet programs to automatically perform calculations on other values.

EXHIBIT 3–4

Entering arithmetic operator formula

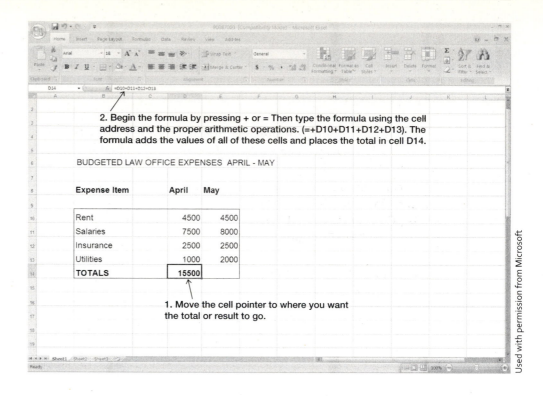

2. Begin the formula by pressing + or = Then type the formula using the cell address and the proper arithmetic operations. (=+D10+D11+D12+D13). The formula adds the values of all of these cells and places the total in cell D14.

BUDGETED LAW OFFICE EXPENSES APRIL - MAY

Expense Item	April	May
Rent	4500	4500
Salaries	7500	8000
Insurance	2500	2500
Utilities	1000	2000
TOTALS	15500	

1. Move the cell pointer to where you want the total or result to go.

EXHIBIT 3–5

Arithmetic operators

Arithmetic Operator	Name	Formula Example
+	Addition	= C10 + C11 or = 100 + 10
−	Subtraction	= C10 − C11 or = 10 − 10
*	Multiplication	= C10 * C11 or = 100 * 10
/	Division	= C10 / C11 or = 100 / 10

arithmetic operators

Symbols that tell a spreadsheet how to compute values. Examples include addition signs, subtraction signs, and multiplication signs.

Entering Formulas Using Arithmetic Operators One way to enter formulas is to use arithmetic operators and list each cell to be computed separately (see Exhibit 3–4). **Arithmetic operators** tell a spreadsheet how to compute values (see Exhibit 3–5). With this method, you point to the cell where the total should be placed. You then begin by typing an = (equal sign) or a + (plus sign). These tell the spreadsheet that a formula will be entered. When you have typed the formula, press the [ENTER] key or a cursor key to enter it.

In Exhibit 3–4, the formula in cell D14 uses the addition arithmetic operator (+) to tell the spreadsheet program to add the values in cells D10 through D13. This is an example of using an arithmetic operator. Spreadsheets also have arithmetic operators to subtract, multiply, and divide the contents of cells. For example, in Exhibit 3–4, if instead of adding cell D12 you wanted to subtract it, the formula would read =D10+D11−D12+D13, and the total would read 10500.

In most spreadsheets, you have the option of either typing the cell addresses of the cells to be included in the formula (e.g., typing =D10+D11+D12+D13 in Exhibit 3–4) or using the cursor keys to point to the cells to be included in the formula. The second option could be accomplished by simply pointing to the D10 cell, adding an arithmetic operator (+ in this case), and then pointing to the next cell reference to be included in the formula (D11 in this case) until the formula is complete. Spreadsheet novices usually find the pointing method of entering formulas easier.

Arithmetic operators can also be used to add, subtract, multiply, and divide numbers in addition to cells. For example, in addition to a formula using an arithmetic operator to add, subtract, multiply, and divide the values entered into cells (=D10+D11), arithmetic operators can also be used in a formula to add, subtract, multiply, and divide numbers themselves (=100+10). See Exhibit 3–5.

Entering Formulas Using Function Commands
Another way to enter formulas is by using function commands. A **function command** is a predefined or preprogrammed calculation that a spreadsheet can perform.

Function commands are designated by an = (equal sign) followed by the function name. For example, in Exhibit 3–6, the SUM function is used to add cells D10, D11, D12, and D13. Notice that the formula in Exhibit 3–6 reads =SUM(D10:D13). This means "add the contents of cells D10 through D13." This process of dealing with a group of cells is called entering a range (a range is a group of cells). One powerful feature that spreadsheets offer is the ability to work with a group or range of cells at one time.

Many different function commands are available in most spreadsheet programs. Some of the function commands represent long, complex formulas and make them easy to use. Both the arithmetic operators and the function commands yield the same results (compare the totals in Exhibits 3–4 and 3–6). However, for a long formula such as one that adds 100 cells together, to use the arithmetic operator method, you would have to type addition signs between all 100 cell addresses. The function commands make calculating large ranges of cells easy. For example, Exhibit 3–7 shows the Insert Function dialog box. Some of the more common functions are:

- MAX, which computes the largest value within a range of values
- AVERAGE, which computes the average of a range of values
- SUM, which adds numbers in a range and computes the total
- COUNT, which counts the number of cells that contain numbers within a range

function command
A predefined calculation used in a spreadsheet program to speed up the process of entering complex formulas.

EXHIBIT 3–6
Entering formulas with function command

Used with permission from Microsoft

EXHIBIT 3–7

Commonly used function commands in Excel

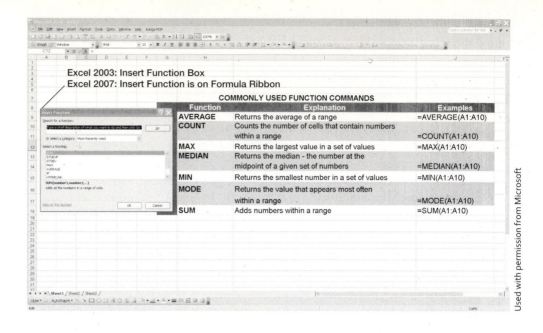

Function commands are entered in nearly the same way as arithmetic operator formulas. Point to the cell where the total should be placed. Next, enter the = sign, followed by the name of the function command and an opening parenthesis. Then, enter the beginning cell address of the range, followed by a colon (:) and the ending cell address of the range. Finally, close the parentheses and press the [ENTER] key to enter the formula into the cell.

A function formula may also be entered using the pointing method. The first step is to go to the cell where the total is to be placed. The next step is to enter the = sign, followed by an opening parenthesis: for example, =SUM(. The next step is to point to the beginning of the range that is to be included and type a colon (:). The colon anchors the range (i.e., it tells the spreadsheet program where the range is to start). The next step is to point to the end of the range. The final step is to type the closing parenthesis and hit the [ENTER] key to execute the command: for instance, =SUM(C10:C13). Using the pointing method is simpler than typing in the cell range for many people and is especially easy for beginning spreadsheet users. Entering formulas is covered in detail in the Excel 2007 and Excel 2003 Hands-On Exercises at Lessons 1, 2, 4, and 6.

Entering Formulas Using Both Arithmetic Operators and Function Commands Arithmetic operators and function commands can also be used together. For example, if you wanted to add cells C10, C11, C12, and C13 and then divide the total by 2, the formula would read =SUM(C10:C13)/2. This formula uses the SUM function to add the cells together and the division operator to divide the total by 2.

In any case, no matter how a formula is entered, whether by using arithmetic operators or using a function command, if the values change in the cells that are calculated, the spreadsheet will automatically recalculate the totals.

Other Spreadsheet Features

Spreadsheets can perform many functions, including changing cell widths, copying data and formulas, moving formulas, and sorting data.

Changing Cell Width Every cell has a cell width, sometimes called a column width. The **cell width** refers to the number of characters that can be placed in a cell. Cells in most spreadsheet programs have a starting value of nine; that is, a cell can hold nine characters or numbers.

Many times you will need to change a cell width to hold either large values (e.g., $200,000,000) or long labels. If a cell width is not large enough to hold the desired value, the cell will be filled with asterisks (*) until you enlarge it. Cell widths can also be shortened if needed. Making cells smaller allows more information to be seen on a page or computer screen at a time. The cell width is easily changed by pointing to the column to be changed and then executing the Column Width command, entering the number of characters the column should hold, and then pressing [ENTER] or clicking on OK.

Another way to change the column width is to use the pointing method. Point to the right border of the heading of the column to be changed. The pointer changes to a double arrow. Drag it to the right to expand the column or to the left to make the column smaller. When the mouse button is released, the column width is automatically changed. Lesson 1 in the Hands-On Exercises covers changing column width in detail.

Copying Data Spreadsheets have a Copy command that copies information from one part of a spreadsheet to another part or from one spreadsheet to another, while leaving the original intact (see Exhibit 3–8). Point to the cell to be copied and then click Edit > Copy. Then move the cell pointer to the location where the information is to be copied and press [ENTER]. Another way to do this is to place the mouse over the information to be copied, right-click, and click Copy. Then move the pointer to the new location and press [ENTER]. An even more convenient way to copy

> **cell width**
> The number of characters that can be placed in any given cell in a spreadsheet program.

Step 1
Put cell pointer on formula to copy command

The formula = D10+D11+D12+D13 uses relative cell references.

BUDGETED LAW OFFICE EXPENSES APRIL - MAY

Expense Item	April	May
Rent	4500	4500
Salaries	15000	15000
Insurance	2500	2500
Utilities	1000	2000
TOTALS	23000	

Autofill Command

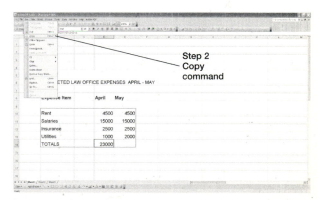

Step 2
Copy command

ETED LAW OFFICE EXPENSES APRIL - MAY

Expense Item	April	May
Rent	4500	4500
Salaries	15000	15000
Insurance	2500	2500
Utilities	1000	2000
TOTALS	23000	

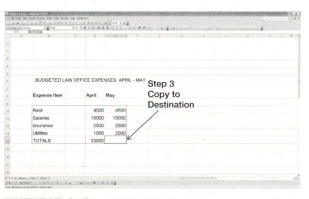

BUDGETED LAW OFFICE EXPENSES APRIL - MAY

Step 3
Copy to Destination

Expense Item	April	May
Rent	4500	4500
Salaries	15000	15000
Insurance	2500	2500
Utilities	1000	2000
TOTALS	23000	

BUDGETED LAW OFFICE EXPENSES APRIL - MAY

Expense Item	April	May
Rent	4500	4500
Salaries	15000	15000
Insurance	2500	2500
Utilities	1000	2000
TOTALS	23000	24000

The formula automatically changes when the Copy command is used, because it contains relative cell references

Step 4
Execute

EXHIBIT 3–8

Copying formulas-relative cell references

information (as long as the cells are adjacent to one another) is to use the AutoFill command. Notice in the fourth screen in Exhibit 3–8 that the pointer is on cell E14. Notice that there is a small box in the lower right corner of the pointer. To copy data, put the pointer on the cell you want to copy, position the pointer over the "AutoFill" box, drag it to the adjacent cells where the information is to be copied, and release the mouse button. The information is automatically copied. The AutoFill command also works with ranges of cells.

Copying Formulas   Copying formulas is a great time-saver. The process for copying formulas is exactly the same as for copying data generally, but it is important that you understand *how* formulas are copied.

Exhibit 3–8 shows an example of copying a formula from D14 to E14. Notice that the utilities expense has increased to 2,000 for the month of May (from 1,000 in April), thus making 24,000 the correct total for May expenses. Also note that even though the formula was copied from D14 to E14, the correct total of 24,000 is shown in E14.

Most new users assume that if the formula in D14, which is =D10+D11+D12+D13, is copied to E14, the formula in cell E14 will read "=D10+D11+D12+D13" and will put the wrong total of 23,000 in the cell. This would happen if a formula used absolute cell references. An **absolute cell reference** is a cell address that does not change when it is copied to a new location. Absolute references can be placed in a formula in most spreadsheets using the dollar sign (e.g., $D$9+$D$10+$D$11+$D$12). This would give the result most people expect.

However, most spreadsheets assume that users want relative cell references. A **relative cell reference** is a cell address that will automatically change to reflect its new location when it is copied. For example, look again at Exhibit 3–8. The formula in D14 is a relative cell reference. So, when it is copied to E14, the spreadsheet automatically changes it to read "=E10+E11+E12+E13." Thus, once a formula is entered, it can be copied time and time again instead of being entered from scratch each time. As with any electronic material, retyping increases the risk of entry errors, so take advantage of any tools that help you avoid retyping or reentering materials.

Suppose a relative cell reference/formula of "=C10+C11" was placed in cell C12. C12 is where the total formula will go. The relative cell reference in C12 actually tells the computer to "go to the cell two rows up from C12 [which is C10] and add the value in it to the value in the cell one row up from C12 [which is C11]." Thus, when a relative cell reference is copied, it just tells the computer how many cells to go up and over. The only thing that changes is where the formula is copied to. So, in our example, if the user copied the formula in C12 to D12, the computer would go to the cell two rows up from D12 (which is D10) and add the value in it to the value in the cell one row up from D12 (which is D11). The formula in Exhibit 3–8 is a relative cell reference.

There are times when you must use an absolute cell reference (see Exhibit 3–9). In Exhibit 3–9, the formulas in cells C7–C10 all use a combined relative cell reference and an absolute cell reference. To calculate cells C7–C10 (the 2012 salary) in Exhibit 3–9, you must take the salary in cells B7–B10 (the 2011 salary) times the salary increase figure in B4 (103.75 percent). Notice in Exhibit 3–9 that cell D7 shows the formula for cell C7. The formula in D7 is B7 (which is a relative cell reference— meaning go one cell over to the left) * (times) $B$4 (the dollar signs mean that this is an absolute cell reference; no matter where this formula is copied to, the application will go one cell over to the left and always multiply it times the value in the cell B4). If a relative cell reference were used for cell C7 it would read B7*B4. This would tell the application to take the cell one row over to the left times the cell three rows up and one column over. This would work fine for cell C7, but if cell C7 were copied to cell

---

absolute cell reference

A cell address in a spreadsheet program formula that does not change when it is copied to a new location.

relative cell reference

A cell address in a spreadsheet program formula that automatically changes to reflect its new location when it is copied.

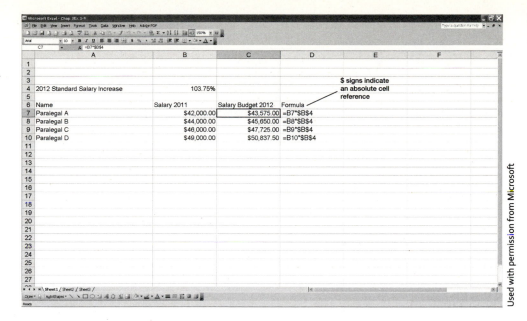

EXHIBIT 3–9

Absolute cell references

C8 (or C9 or C10), the formula would not work anymore. This is because in cell C8 the computer would take the cell one row over to the left (which is B8–that is correct) times the cell three rows up and one column over (which is cell B5). Notice that nothing is entered in cell B5; it is blank. The computer would enter $44,000 ($44,000 * 0 = $0). By the time the formula got to cell C10, the results would be very bad. The formula would take cell B10 (one cell over to the left), $49,000 (which is correct) times cell B7 (three rows up and one column over), $42,000. The result would be $2,058,000 instead of the correct answer of $50,837.50. Thus, the only way for the second part of the formula to work is to always (absolutely) reference cell B4.

Copying formulas with relative cell references is covered in detail in Lesson 1 of the Hands-On Exercises. Copying formulas with absolute cell references is covered in Lesson 4.

Moving Data   Moving data is similar to copying data. First, point to the cell to be moved, select Edit, then select Cut. Then point to the location where the information is to be moved and press [ENTER]. Another way to do this is to point to the cell to be moved, right-click, and then select Cut. You would then move the pointer to the new location and press [ENTER].

Inserting Rows and Columns   It is sometimes necessary to go back and insert additional rows and columns into a spreadsheet. If, for example, you want to insert an expense item (such as an equipment expense item) in Exhibit 3–6, you can do this easily. To insert a row or a column, move the cell pointer to where the new row or column should be inserted. Then execute the Insert Row or Insert Column command. One new row or column is inserted. To insert more than one row or column, drag the pointer down or over the number of rows or columns you want to add, right-click, and select Insert. Use extreme caution when inserting rows and columns after formulas have been created, because it is possible that the existing formulas will not include the new row or column.

Sorting Data   Sorting is the process of placing things in a particular order. Spreadsheets, like databases, can sort information. They can sort either values or text in ascending or descending order. In Exhibit 3–10, before sorting, the expense items are

EXHIBIT 3–10

Sorting data

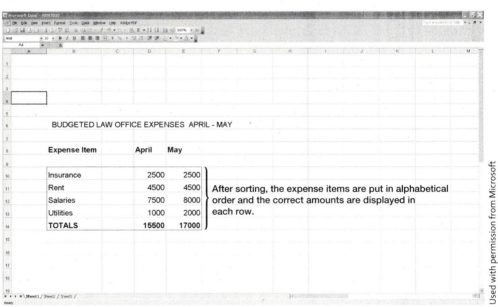

not in alphabetical order. To sort data, mark the data range of the information to be sorted, execute the Sort command (in Excel you would point to Data and click Sort), and then indicate which column to sort the data on and whether the information is to be sorted in ascending or descending order. In Exhibit 3–10, the data range must include not only the Expense Item column, but also the May and June columns. If the May and June columns were not included in the data range, the spreadsheet would put the expense items in alphabetical order, but would not move the corresponding dollar amounts. In Exhibit 3–10, with the data range properly selected, you would execute the Sort command, instruct the computer to sort the data by Column B, which is the Expense Item, in ascending order, and then select OK. The spreadsheet responds by placing the expense items and corresponding dollar amounts in alphabetical order.

Formatting Cells   Most spreadsheet programs allow users to indicate which format or type of values has been entered. For example, in Exhibit 3–10, the values in the spreadsheet should be represented in dollars.

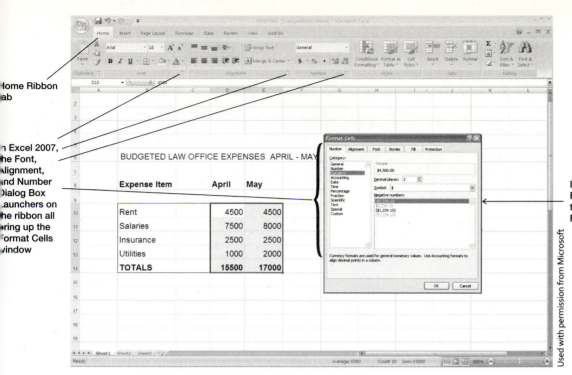

EXHIBIT 3–11
Formatting cells

Home Ribbon tab

In Excel 2007, the Font, Alignment, and Number Dialog Box Launchers on the ribbon all bring up the Format Cells window

In Excel 2003, selecting Format from the menu bar, then Cells brings up the Format Cells window

Used with permission from Microsoft

To change the format of the content of the cells to dollars, drag the pointer over the cells to be changed and execute the Format Cells command (in Excel 2007 or 2003, the command is right-click and then select Format Cells). In Exhibit 3–11, notice that when the Format Cells command is initiated, you may select Currency and the desired number of decimal places. After you select OK, the cell values are automatically changed to dollar signs.

Also, notice in Exhibit 3–11 that numbers can be formatted as percentages and other expressions. Most spreadsheets can change the format of cells in many ways, such as alignment, fonts and type sizes, borders, and patterns or backgrounds. Formatting cells is covered in detail in the Hands-On Exercises.

Saving and Retrieving Files Spreadsheets can be saved and retrieved for later use, just as word processing files and database files can. When working with any program, users should save their work often!

Printing Reports All spreadsheet programs allow for the spreadsheets to be printed. Printing large spreadsheets with many columns used to be difficult, because only a limited number of columns could be printed on a page. It often meant taping pages together. Now, however, most spreadsheets and printers allow pages to print in a condensed or compressed mode as well. This means that the data are printed smaller than normal, and it allows more information to be printed on a page. In Exhibit 3–12, notice that one of the options is the Fit to: command. This option allows a print selection to be compressed into a certain number of pages, including into a single page.

Most spreadsheets allow users to change margins, add headers or footers, indicate whether the page should be printed in portrait or landscape mode, and so on. **Portrait** refers to printing down the length of the page, whereas **landscape** refers to printing across the width of the page (see Exhibit 3–12).

Using Macros As we learned in Chapter 2, a macro is a previously saved group of commands or keystrokes that allows you to save commands or procedures so that

portrait
A method of printing that arranges data down the length of a page.

landscape
A method of printing that arranges data across the width of a page.

EXHIBIT 3–12

Page setup print options in Excel

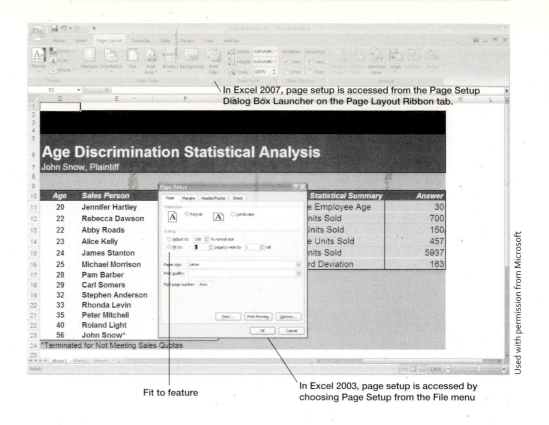

In Excel 2007, page setup is accessed from the Page Setup Dialog Box Launcher on the Page Layout Ribbon tab.

Fit to feature

In Excel 2003, page setup is accessed by choosing Page Setup from the File menu

Used with permission from Microsoft

they can be used again and again. For example, if you routinely print a spreadsheet each month a certain way, you could write a macro that would automatically save the keystrokes and commands you used to produce that result. This way, you could print the spreadsheet properly by running the macro, instead of reentering all the commands every time you wanted to print it out.

Charting and Graphing   The ability to visualize numerical information in a spreadsheet is beneficial. Most spreadsheet programs have graphing and charting capabilities built into them. After a graph (or chart—we will use the terms graph and chart interchangeably) has been set up, a link is created between the numerical information in the spreadsheet and the graph (see Exhibit 3–13). When the values in the spreadsheet are changed, the graph automatically reflects those changes.

Most spreadsheet programs have a chart wizard feature that takes the user through a step-by-step process and gives the user many options on how to set up a chart. Creating a chart in an Excel spreadsheet is easy. First, drag the pointer over the data that you want charted (see Exhibit 3–13) and then click on the Chart Wizard.

Many types of graphs and charts are available. The major types of graphs and charts are bar graphs, line graphs, pie charts, and stacked bar graphs. Most spreadsheets support these types of graphs. Graphs are often used in trials to convey complicated numerical data in an easy-to-understand manner. Lesson 2 in the Hands-On Exercises covers creation of a chart.

bar/column graph

A graph consisting of a sequence of bars that illustrate numerical values.

Bar/Column Graph   A **bar/column graph** consists of a sequence of bars that illustrate numerical values. Bar or column graphs are common and can be either horizontal or vertical. Vertical column graphs have columns that go straight up the page (see Exhibit 3–13), and horizontal bar graphs have bars that go across the page. These graphs are best used for comparing values at a specific point in time. For example, the bar graph in Exhibit 3–13 compares the office expenses for the months of April and May.

EXHIBIT 3–13

Linking the values in a
spreadsheet with a graph

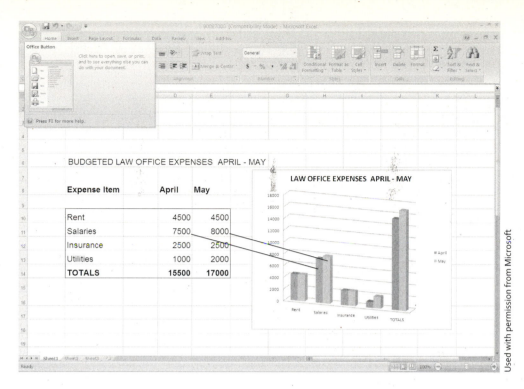

Bar/column graphs have many uses in legal organizations. A bar graph
might be used in a personal injury case to illustrate the large earning potential of a person before an accident and her reduced earning potential after the
accident. A bar graph might also be used in a breach of contract case to show
the profits a business was making before the breach of contract compared
with the reduced profits it made after the breach.

Line Graph A **line graph** plots the course of a value over time. In the line
graph in Exhibit 3–14, each line represents a month's worth of expenses.

line graph
A graph that plots numerical
values as a time line.

EXHIBIT 3–14

Line graph

Because line graphs plot changes over time, they are useful for plotting trends. For example, in Exhibit 3–14, notice that the expense for utilities rose in the month of May.

Pie Chart A **pie chart** represents each value as a piece or percentage of a total pie. In Exhibit 3–15, each expense item represents a slice of the pie, with the whole pie representing the total amount of expenses for the month of April. This chart shows that salaries are the biggest piece (or expense) of the pie (that is, of the firm's total expenses). Pie charts are best used for showing the relative contributions of the various pieces that make up a whole.

Stacked Column Graph A **stacked column graph** compares data by placing columns on top of one another. Like a pie chart, a stacked column graph shows the relative contributions of various elements to a whole. The difference is that rather than showing only a single entity or a single pie, a stacked column can show several. In Exhibit 3–16, each column segment represents a month, and each stack of columns represents an expense item. The stacked column allows users to see the allocation of an expense item over two months.

SPREADSHEET PLANNING

Planning is critical to developing a spreadsheet that accomplishes its intended purpose. Most spreadsheets are more complex than the law-office expense spreadsheet used as an example in this chapter. Most people find it helpful to draft a model of a spreadsheet on paper before actually beginning to enter it in the computer. Some of the most complex aspects of creating a spreadsheet concern the use of formulas. Entering formulas can get complicated quickly, especially when a spreadsheet requires a lot of formulas. Take your time and plan the formulas out carefully.

This section discusses a few rules to keep in mind when planning and using a spreadsheet.

pie chart
A chart that represents each value as a piece or percentage of a whole (a total "pie").

stacked column graph
A graph that depicts values as separate sections in a single or stacked column.

EXHIBIT 3–15
Pie chart graph

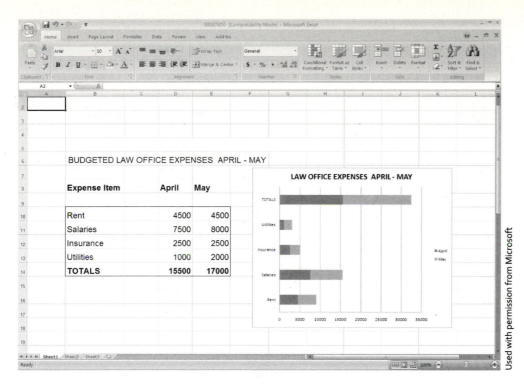

EXHIBIT 3–16
Stacked bar graph

Keep Your Spreadsheet Simple

Keep your spreadsheet as simple as possible. Complex spreadsheets are more likely to have errors. In addition, other people may have to use the spreadsheet, and a simple design will keep you from having to spend hours training them to do so. It is also common for even the person who designed a spreadsheet to forget certain aspects of the spreadsheet if she has not worked with it for some time. Finally, use easy-to-understand headings and titles. Say what you mean, and mean what you say. It is confusing to read titles that do not make sense to everyone involved.

Always Document Your Spreadsheet

Always document your spreadsheet well, making notes and narrative statements right in the spreadsheet itself. Always include a section called "Notes" in your spreadsheet. It is common to make assumptions when designing a spreadsheet (such as when entering formulas) and then later forget why or how you made them. Another technique is to add a comment directly to a cell. In Excel and other spreadsheets, you can add explanatory text to a cell itself. The Comment tool is a great way to add specific information about a cell, including any assumptions or justifications you have made regarding the value or formula entered. Users can show or hide comments as they wish, depending on their needs at the time (see Exhibit 3–17). Creating a comment is covered in Lesson 7 of the Hands-On Exercises.

Make a Template of Your Spreadsheet

A template is a blank spreadsheet that has had labels and formulas entered, but has no values filled in. Once a template is made and saved, copies of it can be made and given to other users; then the only thing they will have to do is enter the values. Some

EXHIBIT 3–17

Adding a comment to a cell in Excel

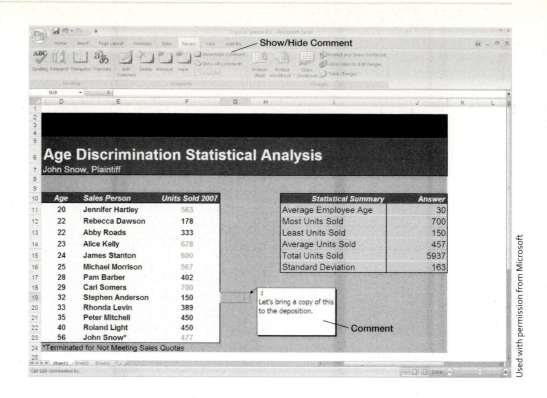

software companies also sell a variety of predefined templates. A template saves a user from having to rebuild the same spreadsheet over and over. Users can also access free templates online from software providers and other sources.

Leave Room in the Upper Left Corner

Do not start your spreadsheet in the far corner of the spreadsheet (for example, at cell A1); always leave yourself some room to include additional labels and notes. Start your spreadsheet no closer to the upper left corner than cell C4. This gives you room to add notes, dates, and so forth later on.

Use Cell Widths Wisely

Cell widths should be used wisely. Some people make all their columns 20 characters wide; the problem with this is that they can then see and print only four columns at a time, which makes a spreadsheet difficult to work with. It is better to use narrow columns, which maximize the amount of information you can see and allow the spreadsheet to be printed on one page. For long labels, keep the column width the same size, but wrap the text down to the next line, using the wrap text feature found in most spreadsheets.

Be Careful Inserting Rows and Columns

If you must insert additional rows and columns after a spreadsheet has been designed and entered into the computer, be sure that the formulas you have already entered are adjusted to take the new additions into account. A celebrated lawsuit was filed against Lotus Development Corporation over this problem. A construction firm designed a spreadsheet to allow it to bid on jobs. Staff would enter job costs into the spreadsheet, and the spreadsheet would calculate what the bid on a job should be. Unfortunately, at some point, the spreadsheet user inserted additional rows, and the old formulas did not pick up, or add, the job costs in the new rows. Subsequently, the construction firm bid several hundred thousand dollars too low on a job. The firm sued Lotus, but Lotus won the suit because the user had used the program improperly. Be sure to go back and double-check your formulas!

Rigorously Test Your Spreadsheet

Rigorously test your spreadsheet to make sure it is functioning as intended. It is easy to make a mistake entering a formula, but it is often difficult to recognize and find mistakes. Always enter test data in the spreadsheet, and use a calculator to spot-check that the formulas have been entered properly and are making the calculations correctly. Most spreadsheets have an option that allows you to see the formulas entered instead of the calculations. This is a nice feature when you are checking the logic and formulas of your spreadsheet.

Audit Formulas

To access this feature in Excel 2003, on the Tools menu, point to Formula Auditing, then click on Formula Auditing Mode. To access this feature in Excel 2007, point to the Formulas ribbon tab, then click on Show Formulas in the Formula Auditing group.

Occasionally Read the Spreadsheet Documentation

Most spreadsheet users employ only a fraction of the commands, operators, and function commands that are available in most spreadsheets. Although the commands covered in this book will get you started with spreadsheets, you will find that as you grow more proficient, many sophisticated features will help you solve tough problems. Take the time occasionally to read the Help features and other documentation for your spreadsheet program to learn more about its capacities and functionalities.

SPREADSHEETS IN THE LEGAL ENVIRONMENT

Numerical data are important in the outcome of many types of cases. Remember, if it involves money, it involves numbers. In some lawsuits, parties hire statisticians to research a matter in hopes that the final statistics or numerical data will support their case. Spreadsheets can be used to analyze statistical findings, look for trends, and so forth. Spreadsheet programs, like word processors and database management systems, are extremely flexible, so it is easy to use them to accomplish all types of tasks. Some common applications of spreadsheets in law offices include:

- Tax planning and tax returns
- Estate planning
- Calculations for bankruptcy actions
- Child support calculations
- Alimony payments
- Divorce asset distributions
- Truth-in-Lending statements for real estate transactions
- Amortization schedules
- Loan/payment calculations
- Calculations for collection actions regarding principal and interest due
- Present value and future value calculations regarding damages
- Lost wages and benefits calculations for worker's compensation claims

- Back wages and benefits regarding employment/discrimination actions
- Budgeting
- Accounting-related calculations

Damages Calculations

In many cases, the plaintiff (the person bringing the lawsuit) alleges that he is entitled to money damages—that is, that he should be compensated for whatever injury was sustained. The amount of damages a person should receive is always in dispute. A spreadsheet allows the law office personnel to test different options or assumptions.

A Simple Damages Calculation Exhibit 3–18 is an example of an easy damages projection. Assume that you represent the plaintiff, John Jones, in an automobile accident case and you must prepare an exhibit for the jury to show the amount of damages the plaintiff is seeking. This spreadsheet simply lists the damage items, the amounts asked for, and a total (i.e., a formula using the SUM function).

A More Complex Damages Calculation (Net Present Value) Spreadsheets can handle complex damages calculations as well, as shown in Exhibit 3–19.

Assume that your firm represents Wendy Jones, who suffered a severe injury on the job and is bringing a worker's compensation claim. Jones is 59 years old and was going to retire at age 65. Assume that because she is now totally disabled, she is entitled to six years of income from her employer. She was making $35,000 a year before she was injured, and on average, she has received increases of about 2 percent every year. Therefore, in the first year following the accident, assume that Jones would have received $35,000, and in every year after that, she would have received a 2 percent increase. Exhibit 3–19 automatically calculates what her gross earnings would have been until retirement, for a total loss of wages of $220,784.23.

Unfortunately, Jones is not entitled to a lump-sum payment of $220,784.23. This is because Jones could take the lump-sum payment, invest it at 6 or 7 or 8 percent, and by the end of the six years have considerably more than she would have earned at her job. Thus, the future payments must be reduced to their present, or current, value. Nearly all spreadsheets have a present value function that accomplishes this

EXHIBIT 3–18

Sample damages calculation

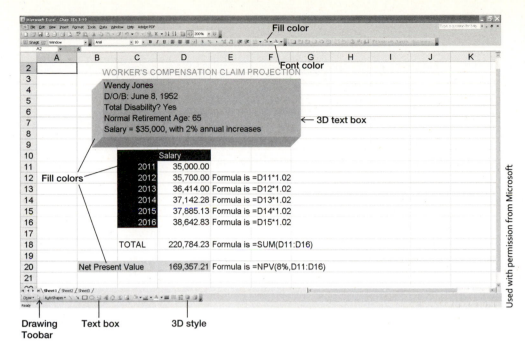

EXHIBIT 3–19
Complex damages
calculation

task easily. The spreadsheet in Exhibit 3–19 calculates that Jones should be awarded a lump-sum payment of $169,357.21 for future payments worth $220,784.23.

This type of calculation (reducing a payment schedule to a present value) is also useful when considering different settlement offers or options. Notice in Exhibit 3–19 that a number of graphic elements have been added to the spreadsheet. The spreadsheet includes a number of different fill (background) colors and textures, font sizes, styles, and colors. The spreadsheet also includes a text box that has been formatted in three dimensions (3-D). These are all standard features in Excel and other spreadsheets. In Excel 2003, these tools can be found on the Standard and Drawing toolbars (see Exhibit 3–19). In Excel 2007, these features can be found on the Insert ribbon tab. Notice in Exhibit 3–18 that an oval has been added to the spreadsheet around the total and that the word "Expenses" appears vertically in the spreadsheet. All of these graphical features are extremely easy to use and can give spreadsheets added visual impact.

Legal Organization Budgeting

Many legal organizations prepare a yearly budget to track expenses and income. The budget is used as a planning tool and as a means of spotting potential problems.

Real Estate Law

Spreadsheets are particularly helpful for legal organizations that practice in the real estate field. An example of spreadsheet use in this field is to create an amortization schedule.

Monthly Payment and Amortization Schedules   Spreadsheets can automatically calculate the monthly payment on a loan and produce an amortization schedule. The loan amortization schedule in Exhibit 3–20 is a template that comes free with Excel. Simply fill in the data in the Loan Information section and the spreadsheet does the rest. To access the template in Excel 2003, on the File menu click New, then click Templates on my computer . . ., then Spreadsheet Solutions, then Loan Amortization. In Excel 2007, click on the Office Button, click New, then click under Templates.

EXHIBIT 3–20

Loan amortization schedule

Ready to use
Excel template

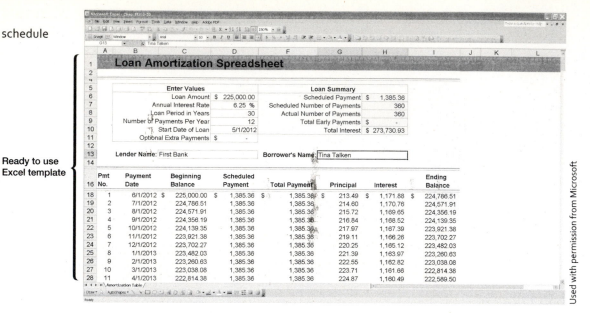

Family Law Cases

Spreadsheets are commonly used to help divide assets in a divorce. When a marriage is dissolved, it is the duty of the court to try to fairly distribute or divide the assets the parties have amassed during the marriage so that neither party gets more than her or his fair share. Spreadsheets are also used to calculate a party's child support obligations. A spreadsheet enables the user to lay out different division-of-asset scenarios or options for consideration. Spreadsheets can also produce lists of assets, family budgets, balance sheets, and income comparisons (such as between husband and wife). These documents are routinely prepared in many divorce cases.

Statistical Analysis

Spreadsheets can also be used to analyze statistics. Most spreadsheets have statistical functions that can help a user analyze a group of values. Suppose your firm represents the plaintiff John Snow, a salesman, in an age-discrimination suit against his former employer. The defendant company states that Snow was terminated because he did not sell enough units of its product. Snow must convince a judge that he was really terminated because the company wanted a younger workforce.

Exhibit 3–21 shows the names and ages of the company's salespersons and the units of product they sold. Looking at the statistical analysis part of the exhibit, notice that the average age of salespersons is 30 (far below Snow's age of 56—it appears that the company may be trying to hire young salespersons). This was arrived at by using the average function (AVG), which automatically totals the values in a range and divides by the number of values.

Now, look at the Most Units Sold cell. The spreadsheet automatically placed the highest value here, using the MAX function. Notice also that the minimum number of units was placed in the Least Units Sold cell, using the MIN function. Also, look at the Average Units Sold cell, which was calculated automatically using the AVG function. (Snow was 20 units above the average units sold—it certainly seems he can make a strong argument for his case.)

Finally, the standard deviation of the values (i.e., the standard deviation from the average of each value) is high, showing that the data vary widely. The formula

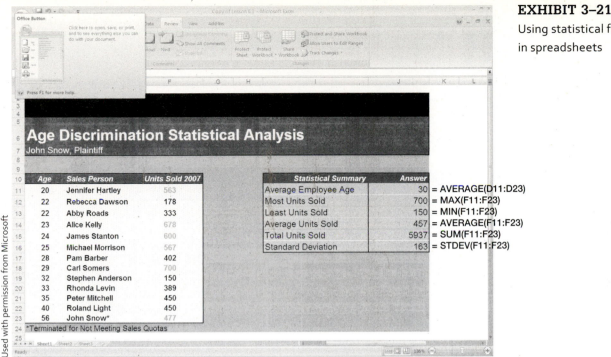

EXHIBIT 3–21

Using statistical functions in spreadsheets

for calculating standard deviations is not simple, but a spreadsheet user can find it by issuing a function command and marking the range. This is an example of how spreadsheets can turn hard tasks into easy ones.

Importing Spreadsheets into Other Programs

Sometimes it is necessary to include numerical information in a word-processing document. For example, you might want to incorporate part of a spreadsheet or a graph into a brief or pleading. In most cases, it is simple to paste a spreadsheet or graph into a word processing document.

Tracking Investments for Trusts and Estates

Sometimes attorneys or law firms act as trustees or fiduciaries for trusts and estates. Part of this responsibility often involves investing money on behalf of a trust or an estate. Such fiduciaries have a duty not to waste or neglect the trust or estate and to make reasonable investments.

Exhibit 3–22 is an example of a spreadsheet that tracks the progress of stock market investments. By tracking the current prices of the stocks, the firm can get an idea of how the investments are doing and whether it should sell them and buy something else. Notice the use of formulas in Exhibit 3–22. The market value formulas take the number of shares purchased times the current price of the stock. The dollar gain formulas subtract the total purchase price (the number of shares times the purchase price) from the market value. Finally, the percentage gain formulas arrive at results by dividing the dollar gain by the total purchase price.

ETHICAL CONSIDERATIONS

The primary ethical considerations regarding spreadsheets are accuracy and competence.

EXHIBIT 3–22

Using a spreadsheet to track investments for an estate

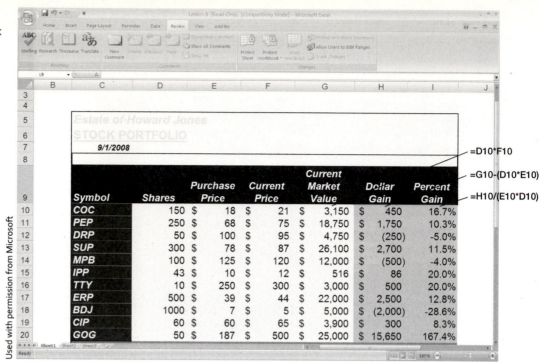

Used with permission from Microsoft

It is absolutely critical that the spreadsheets the paralegal produces be 100 percent accurate and well tested. If formulas do not correctly manipulate all the data they are supposed to, if formulas have wrong numbers in them, if data are not updated, or if there are any other errors in the spreadsheet, disaster will occur. Unfortunately, often when paralegals work with spreadsheets they are not just working with raw numbers, mathematics, and research—they are working with spreadsheets that relate to actual money and financial projections that have a dollar impact. Thus, errors in a spreadsheet typically have a negative financial impact as well.

These issues are not as much ethical matters (although this is a problem) as they are a malpractice risk. Most spreadsheet users fail to understand the likelihood of spreadsheet errors or the absolute importance of careful quality control of every spreadsheet, no matter how small.

How prevalent are errors in spreadsheets? A number of studies have shown that spreadsheet errors are relatively high. Cell error rates are typically around 5 percent. Thus, for every 20 cells you create, on average, you will have one error. As the total number of cells in a spreadsheet rises, so does the propensity for errors. One auditing firm found that 90 percent of all spreadsheets they reviewed that had 150 or more cells had one or more errors. In many cases the errors were serious. Every study that has been conducted on spreadsheet errors has found them at rates that would be unacceptable in most organizations.

So, what can paralegals do to minimize the potential for errors? They can:

- Double-check all numbers that are entered into a spreadsheet for accuracy.
- Triple-check every single formula in a spreadsheet, including using the Formula Auditing mode to print out all formulas.
- Make comments in specific cells regarding assumptions.
- Create a notes section at the bottom or top of the spreadsheet containing assumptions or other data the reader should be aware of.

- Be extremely careful when adding rows or columns to a spreadsheet in which formulas already exist. Double-check each inserted row or column to make sure it appears in the applicable formulas.
- Have someone else carefully review each spreadsheets, including formulas.
- Before using a new function, completely understand exactly what it does and ensure that it is working 100 percent correctly.
- Use a calculator to spot-check spreadsheets to make sure the formulas are accurate.
- Use the Protect feature to protect cells, particularly formulas, from being changed accidentally (see the following subsections).

If working with a spreadsheet is outside of your knowledge base or comfort zone, ask your supervising attorney to get an expert, such as an accountant or financial analyst, to prepare and/or review the calculations. In the end, it is far cheaper to do this than to discover an error later.

Password Protection

Passwords are an easy way to increase the security of your documents. Password-protecting spreadsheets is easy to do and should always be done if the spreadsheet is going outside of the firm. In Excel 2003, the command sequence is File > Save > Tools > General Options > Password to Open. In Excel 2007, the command sequence is Office Button > Save > Tools > General Options > Password to Open.

Protecting Cells and Spreadsheets

Protection is a useful security tool for spreadsheet use. When multiple people work with a spreadsheet, it is common for formulas and other data to be accidentally deleted or changed by users. If a formula, for example, is deleted and the recipient tries to correct the problem by writing a new formula, but makes an error, a large problem has been created that could go a long time without being noticed. One way to solve this problem is to use the Protect Cells feature found in most spreadsheets.

In Excel, for example, to protect all or part of a spreadsheet, you must turn on the protection feature. In Excel 2003, protection can be turned on by pointing to the File menu, then clicking Tools > Protection > Protect Sheet. In Excel 2007, protection can be turned on from the Review ribbon tab by checking Protect Sheet in the Changes group. *Note*: Cells can be protected against accidental deletion simply by turning on the Protect command (which a user can turn off at a later time) or can be password-protected, in which case protection cannot be turned off unless the user has the password. For example, suppose the creator of a spreadsheet wants to protect certain formulas in an Excel spreadsheet from being accidentally typed over. The spreadsheet creator does not want users to have to type a password if they want to edit the spreadsheet; the creator just wants to protect the formulas from accidental deletion. The spreadsheet creator would use Protect Sheet and leave the password blank. The creator would mark all of the cells that were not locked and in Excel 2003, point to the Format menu, then click Cells > Protection, and uncheck the Locked feature. In Excel 2007, the command is right-click, Format Cells > Protection. If a user then wanted to change a formula, he or she could not; instead, the user would get an error message stating that the cell is protected. However, all that user would have to do would be to click Tools > Protection > Unprotect Sheet to turn off the protection feature. The user would then be able to edit the formula. If the spreadsheet creator did not want the user to be able to do this, the creator could use the password feature to lock the spreadsheet cells he or she wanted to keep from being edited.

SUMMARY

Spreadsheet software calculates and manipulates data using labels and formulas. Spreadsheets use rows and columns, which look similar to those on an accountant's paper worksheet. A row is an area that extends across a page horizontally; a column is an area that extends down a page vertically. A cell is an intersection between a row and a column. The cursor, or cell pointer, in a spreadsheet indicates what cell is currently selected.

Three types of data can be entered into a spreadsheet: text, values, and formulas. Text is descriptive data, such as headings and titles, that are entered into a cell; text cannot be used in making calculations. Values are numbers that are entered into a cell and can be used in making calculations. Formulas perform calculations using the values in other cells. Arithmetic operations and function commands are used in constructing formulas; they instruct a spreadsheet how to make the desired calculations.

Copying data places information from one part of a spreadsheet into another part while leaving the original intact. When copying formulas, an absolute cell reference does not change to reflect the new location of the cell pointer. A relative cell reference will automatically change to reflect the new location of the cell pointer.

Most spreadsheets provide a variety of graphing capabilities. A bar graph consists of a sequence of bars that illustrate numerical values. A line graph plots the course of a value over time. A pie chart represents each value as a piece or percentage of a total "pie." A stacked bar graph compares data by placing bars on top of one another.

Paralegals can use spreadsheets to perform and track a huge variety of information, including damages calculations, budget plans and problems, and tax plans and tax return calculations.

KEY TERMS

absolute cell reference
arithmetic operators
bar/column graph
cell
cell address
cell pointer
cell width
column

formulas
function command
landscape
line graph
pie chart
portrait
relative cell reference
row

spreadsheet
spreadsheet software
stacked column graph
text
values
"what if" analysis

INTERNET SITES

Internet sites for this chapter include:

ORGANIZATION	PRODUCT/SERVICE	INTERNET ADDRESS
Microsoft	Microsoft Excel spreadsheet program	www.microsoft.com
Microsoft	Home page for Microsoft, containing a wealth of information, tips, and tricks	www.microsoft.com/excel
Corel Corporation	Quattro Pro spreadsheet	www.corel.com
About.com	General site about spreadsheets, with information and tips	www.spreadsheets.about.com

TEST YOUR KNOWLEDGE

1. An area on a spreadsheet that extends vertically up and down the page is called a _____.

2. An area on a spreadsheet that extends horizontally across a page is called a _____.

3. True or False: An intersection between a row and a column in a spreadsheet is called a *location*.

4. Descriptive data entered in a spreadsheet, such as titles and headings, are called _____.

5. Numbers entered in a spreadsheet are called _____.

6. Expressions used in a spreadsheet program to automatically perform calculations are called _____.

7. True or False: The plus sign, minus sign, multiplication sign, and division sign are examples of function commands.

8. Write two formulas for adding the following cells: A1, A2, and A3.

9. "=SUM," "AVERAGE," and "MAX" are examples of what kind of formulas?

10. Name two kinds of cell references.

11. Name three things that should be kept in mind when planning a spreadsheet.

12. True or False: It is difficult to make errors in spreadsheets because the built-in templates, formulas, and function commands are automatic.

13. One way to keep formulas and cells from being accidentally deleted is to use which command?

ON THE WEB EXERCISES

1. Using the "Internet Sites" listed in this chapter and a general Internet search engine (such as www.google.com or www.yahoo.com), research the issue of errors in spreadsheets. Write a two-page paper on your findings.

2. Go to www.microsoft.com/excel and, under the "Templates" section, view 10 of the many ready-to-use templates for Excel.

3. Research legal-related Excel templates, including tax, real estate, child support, financial planning, estate planning, and related subjects. Write a two-page paper summarizing the types of free and fee-based sites and templates you found.

QUESTIONS AND EXERCISES

1. Using a spreadsheet, track the daily price of any four stocks in which you have an interest for one week. Show the daily beginning stock price, ending stock price, and difference. Calculate the stock's total per-share movement for the week and calculate the stock's average price per share for the week.

2. Using a spreadsheet program, prepare an expense budget for a mythical start-up law firm for one year. Assume that the law firm will have four attorneys (two of whom are partners and two of whom are associates), two paralegals, and two secretaries. Be sure to include leased space, office equipment (computers, copiers, printers, phones, etc.), office supplies, utilities, and miscellaneous expenses.

3. Using a spreadsheet program, summarize the amount of time you spend attending class and studying for your classes for a week. Assume that you will be paid for the time spent studying or attending classes, but that you must present a detailed bill of your activities. The bill must be professional in appearance and be accurately calculated. Assume that you will be paid $60 an hour.

4. Using a spreadsheet program, enter the names, complete addresses, and telephone numbers of 20 relatives and/or friends. The list must be professional in appearance and sorted alphabetically by last name.

5. You have requested a new computer from your law firm in next year's budget. Your managing attorney has asked you to provide a detailed, itemized list of the equipment and the price for each component of the system. Your managing attorney is very frugal, so include a one-page memorandum (with the itemized listing) summarizing why the system you have selected is appropriate.

ETHICS QUESTION

You work in a state that requires use of a spreadsheet in the calculation of child support payments. The attorney you work for does not know how to use a spreadsheet. If the attorney is to take on the representation of a parent in a contested divorce case, what ethical issue(s) may arise?

Go to the Workbook to complete the Hands-On Exercises. There are exercises for Excel 2007 and Excel 2003.

Access an interactive eBook, chapter-specific interactive learning tools, including flash cards, quizzes, and more in your Paralegal CourseMate, accessed through CengageBrain.com.

CHAPTER 4

Legal Timekeeping and Billing Software

CHAPTER OBJECTIVES

After completing this chapter, you should be able to do the following:

1. Explain what timekeeping and billing are.
2. Explain the computerized timekeeping and billing process.
3. Describe the different types of legal fee agreements.
4. Identify why accurate billings are important to law firms.
5. List the basic features and functions of timekeeping and billing programs.
6. Describe how timeslips are entered into a timekeeping and billing system.
7. Explain how management reports generated from a timekeeping and billing system can help a firm.
8. Explain what electronic billing is.
9. Describe the factors for determining whether a fee is reasonable.

INTRODUCTION

A lawyer's time is the only thing he or she has to sell. Therefore, it is important to keep accurate records of how that time is spent. In the legal environment, the process of tracking time for the purpose of billing clients is called **timekeeping**. In addition to being paid for their time, attorneys must also be reimbursed for the expenses that they incur on each case (such as for postage, copies, court filing fees, expert witness costs, and so forth).

In the legal environment, the process of issuing bills to collect monies for legal services performed and for expenses incurred is called **billing**. This chapter introduces the principles of legal timekeeping and billing, compares manual and computerized billing systems, describes the computerized timekeeping and billing process, introduces the kinds of fee agreements attorneys and clients enter into, describes what a good billing system is intended to accomplish, shows how computerized timekeeping and billing software can improve efficiency and accuracy in this process, and discusses ethical issues related to timekeeping and billing.

timekeeping
Tracking time for the purpose of billing clients.

billing
The process of issuing invoices (bills) to collect monies for legal services performed and for expenses incurred.

89

INTRODUCTION TO TIMEKEEPING AND BILLING

Law firms, like all businesses, must generate income. As with other businesses, the running of law firms has a management side. One important management duty that law offices perform is to track the time and expenses of their staff and then generate accurate billings for clients so that law office staff can be paid. Attorneys spend their time advising clients, talking to witnesses, drafting documents, taking depositions, appearing in court, and undertaking other activities on behalf of their clients. All these activities must be tracked so that clients can be accurately billed for the work the attorneys do. In addition, the expenses attorneys incur on behalf of their clients must be tracked so that the attorneys can be reimbursed. Expenses incurred on behalf of clients include the cost of making photocopies of documents for a client's file, the cost of mailing letters and other documents, travel expenses incurred while working on a client's case, court filing fees, deposition transcription costs, and much more.

If time and expenses were not tracked, law firms could not generate bills, get paid, or adequately run the business. Although timekeeping and billing are not glamorous, they are necessary to the survival of nearly all law firms. Firms that do not put a priority on billing clients, on a regular and accurate basis, will most likely not be around long. It is simply bad business practice to work 70 hours a week, bill for 50 hours, and be paid for 30 hours.

The timekeeping and billing problem becomes even worse when large law firms have to track the time and expenses of hundreds of attorneys and hundreds of paralegals. A good timekeeping and billing system is an absolute necessity.

Why Do Paralegals Need to Know Timekeeping and Billing?

Paralegals need to know about timekeeping and billing for several reasons. In many private law practices, paralegals are required to track their time so it can be charged to the case(s) they are working on. Many law practices that use this system require paralegals to bill a minimum number of hours each year. It is important to remember that private law firms are fundamentally businesses—and like any other business, they need to make money, operate at a profit, and earn money for their owners. Therefore, the billing of time to a firm's clients is crucial to its operations and success as a business. It is not uncommon for a firm to require each paralegal to bill between 26 and 35 hours a week (1,352 and 1,820 hours annually). Paralegals may be terminated from their jobs if they fail to bill the required number of hours. Thus, it is necessary for paralegals to understand how timekeeping and billing work.

In addition, paralegals are sometimes put in charge of the timekeeping and billing system, including managing the timekeeping process and generating bills. This usually occurs in smaller law offices. In those situations, it is important for the paralegals not only to know the process, but also to know how to actually run and operate the system.

MANUAL VERSUS COMPUTERIZED BILLING SYSTEMS

Before legal billing software came along, bills were generated manually, using typewriters or word processors. The manual method was cumbersome and slow, commonly issued bills that contained mathematical errors, and often produced billings that were outdated or inaccurate. This was especially true of large firms with hundreds of clients.

Long ago, it was common for law firms to send out bills only when they needed to pay their own bills (rent, staff salaries, etc.). Attorneys often sat down with a client's file months after work had been performed and tried to remember what they did on the case and how much time it took to do it. Of course, these billings were very inaccurate; it is extremely hard to remember this type of information after the fact, even by the end of a day, let alone after weeks or months. In addition, with manual methods, the billing process took hours or days to complete, especially if a large number of bills were being done.

The more traditional way of handling manual billing is to send out bills based on timeslips that each attorney or paralegal fills out every day. A **timeslip** is a piece of paper or a computer entry that legal professionals use to record information about the legal services they provide to each client. Most timeslips contain information such as the name of the case worked on, the date a service was provided, a description of the service, and so on (see Exhibit 4–1). In addition to tracking time, all law firms must

timeslip
A slip of paper or computer record that records information about the legal services legal professionals provide to each client.

PC—Phone Conference	R—Review	Time Conversion	
LR—Legal Research	OC—Office Conference	6 Minutes 0.1 Hour	36 Minutes 0.6 Hour
L—Letter	T—Travel	12 Minutes 0.2 Hour	42 Minutes 0.7 Hour
D—Dictation	CT—Court Hearing	15 Minutes 0.25 Hour	45 Minutes 0.75 Hour
		18 Minutes 0.3 Hour	48 Minutes 0.8 Hour
		24 Minutes 0.4 Hour	54 Minutes 0.9 Hour
		30 Minutes 0.5 Hour	60 Minutes 1.0 Hour

Date	Client/Case	File No.	Services Performed	Attorney	Time Hours & Tenths	
5-7	Smith v. United Sales	118294	Summarized 6 depositions; Client; Δ (Defendant) Helen; Δ Barney, Δ Rose; Witness Forrest & Johnson	BJP	6.	5
5-8	Marcel v. True Oil	118003	PC w/Client Re: Settlement offer; Discussions w/Attorney; Memo to file Re: offer	BJP		3
5-8	Johnson v. State	118118	PC w/Client's Mother, PC w/Client; LR Re: Bail; Memo to file; R correspondence	BJP		75
5-8	Potential claim of Watkins v. Leslie Grocery	Not Assigned Yet	OC w/Client; (New client); Reviewed facts; Received medical records Re; accident; Conf. w/atty	BJP	1.	50
5-8	Smith v. United Sales	118294	Computerized searches on depositions for attorney	BJP		75
5-8	Jay Tiller Bankruptcy	118319	PC w/Creditor, Bank One; Memo to file; Client; LJ to Client	BJP		3
5-8	Potential Claim of Watkins v. Leslie Grocery	—	LR Slip & Fall cases generally; Standard of care	BJP	1.	00
5-8	Marcel v. True Oil	118003	Conf. w/atty. & Client Re: Settlement; Drafted & prepared LJ to Δs Re: Settlement offer	BJP	1.	10
5-8	Jay Tiller Bankruptcy	118319	Drafted Bankruptcy petition; OC w/Client; List of Debts; Fin. Stmt; Conf. w/atty	BJP	1.	00
5-8	Smith v. United Sales	118294	Drafted and prepared depo notice to Witness Spring	BJP		25
5-9	Seeley Real Estate Matter	118300	Ran amortization schedule to attach to 'Contract for Deed'	BJP		25

EXHIBIT 4–1

Typical manual timeslip/Time record form

EXHIBIT 4–2
Expense slip

Johnson, Beck & Taylor
Expense Slip

Expense Type & Code
1 Photocopies	4 Filing Fees	7 Facsimile	10 Travel
2 Postage	5 Witness Fees	8 Lodging	11 Overnight Delivery
3 Long Distance	6 Westlaw/Lexis	9 Meals	12 Other _____

Date   4-5-08   Case Name: Smith v. United   File No.   118294
Expense Code: 1   Quantity 20 pages   Amount File rate   ⟨Billable⟩ Non-Billable
Expense Code: 2   Quantity 4 packages Amount $4.66   ⟨Billable⟩ Non-Billable
Expense Code: Quantity sent   Amount   Billable Non-Billable
Name of Person Making Expense Slip: JBP

Description of Expense(s) Incurred:
Copies and postage re: Motion to compel 4/5
_____
_____
_____
_____

© Cengage Learning 2012

expense slip
A record of each expense item a firm incurs on behalf of the client.

also track expenses. An **expense slip** is a record of each expense item a firm incurs on behalf of a client (see Exhibit 4–2). Some common expenses include:

- copying costs
- court reporter fees
- electronic legal research (Westlaw/Lexis)
- expert witness fees
- filing fees
- overnight delivery charges
- postage
- travel expenses
- witness/subpoena fees

When a member of a firm incurs an expense for a client, such as by making copies of documents, using postage to send out material, or making a long distance telephone call, an expense slip is filled out. Then, usually on a monthly basis, manual billings are sent out, based on the timeslips and expense slips that have been collected. Although billings based on timeslips are more accurate than those based on memory, the billing process itself is still quite tedious and slow when done manually.

Computerized billing systems solve many of these problems. Exactly how much time a computerized time and billing program saves over a manual system is somewhat debatable, but a study by one attorney found that manual billing systems can take up to three times longer than computerized methods to produce bills every billing cycle (i.e., every time billings are sent, whether it be biweekly, monthly, or according to some other schedule).

timekeeper
Anyone who bills for time, including partners, associates, and paralegals.

Generally, timekeepers still must record what they do with their time on a timeslip, whether the billing system is manual or computerized. A **timekeeper** is anyone who bills out his or her time; this includes partners, associates, and paralegals. Usually, the information from paper timeslips is entered into the legal billing software on a daily basis. However, there is a growing trend for attorneys and paralegals to enter their time directly into the computerized timekeeping and billing system without using a separate timeslip at all. This is particularly true in law offices where all timekeepers are connected to a local area network. It is common for firms using computerized billing systems to produce monthly or even weekly bills, according to the wishes of the client.

In addition to alleviating cash flow problems, most legal billing software produces reports that management can use to help operate the law firm business (this is covered in more detail later in the chapter). Computerized timekeeping and billing systems also produce billings that are more accurate than those produced by manual methods, because all mathematical computations are performed automatically by the computer.

THE COMPUTERIZED TIMEKEEPING AND BILLING PROCESS

Timekeeping and billing software packages differ greatly from one another. However, the computerized timekeeping and billing process for most billing packages is as shown in Exhibit 4–3.

1. The Client and the Attorney Reach Agreement on Legal Fees

An attorney can bill for services in many different ways. At the outset of most cases, the client and the attorney reach an agreement regarding how much the attorney will charge for her or his services. Preferably, the agreement is in writing in the form of a

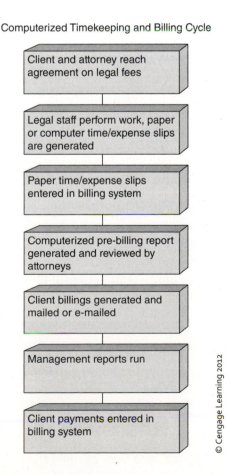

Computerized Timekeeping and Billing Cycle

Client and attorney reach agreement on legal fees

Legal staff perform work, paper or computer time/expense slips are generated

Paper time/expense slips entered in billing system

Computerized pre-billing report generated and reviewed by attorneys

Client billings generated and mailed or e-mailed

Management reports run

Client payments entered in billing system

© Cengage Learning 2012

EXHIBIT 4–3

Computerized timekeeping and billing cycle

contract. After the legal fee has been agreed on, the new matter is set up in the computerized billing package by entering the client's name and address, the type of case it is, the type of legal fee that has been agreed on, and any other relevant information the law office has identified for inclusion.

2. Legal Staff Perform Services and Prepare Timeslips

When attorneys or paralegals perform work on a legal matter for a client, they fill out a timeslip to track the exact services (either using a manual timeslip form or entering the information directly into the computer). Many timekeeping and billing programs also support data entry from a handheld computer or personal digital assistant (PDA). Expense slips are also generated this way.

3. Timeslips and Expense Slips Are Entered into the Billing System

If manual timeslips are used, the information they contain must be entered into the billing system. Usually the information is typed into the computer in roughly the same format as it appears on the timeslip. It is essential that the information be accurately entered into the computer. In addition, expense slips are entered into the computer to track the expenses the firm has incurred on behalf of a client.

4. A Pre-Billing Report Is Generated and Reviewed

pre-billing report
A rough draft compilation of billings.

After legal services have been performed and recorded in the time and billing software, the next step is for a **pre-billing report** to be generated. This is done before the final client bills are produced. A pre-billing report is a rough draft of the billings that eventually will be sent to clients (see Exhibit 4–4). The pre-billing report is given to the attorney in charge of the case for review or to a billing committee to make sure the billings are accurate.

Attorneys may choose to discount bills for a variety of reasons, including thinking the task should have taken less time than it actually did. Discounts are also given for good customers, because of the client's hardship, for professional courtesy or for friends, or because the billing looks unreasonable. This can, however, be very frustrating to a paralegal who has his or her time cut back. Typically, only the amount that is actually billed is counted against the target or minimum number of billable hours a paralegal is expected to work.

5. Client Billings Are Generated and Mailed or Emailed

Formal client billings (invoices) are generated by the billing system (see Exhibit 4–5). Most timekeeping and billing programs can produce many different billing formats. The computer automatically prints the bills, and they are subsequently mailed or emailed to the clients. Also, most computerized billing systems can now produce some form of electronic billing (see discussion later in this chapter) or can produce PDF files to be emailed.

6. Management Reports Are Generated

In most computerized timekeeping and billing programs, a wide variety of management reports may be generated. Management reports are not used for billing clients; rather, they are used to evaluate the effectiveness of a firm. For example, most programs generate a report that shows how much time is nonbillable (i.e., not chargeable to clients). If a firm has a lot of nonbillable time, it might indicate that the firm is not productive and is losing valuable time from its timekeepers.

EXHIBIT 4–4

Pre-billing report

```
                    JOHNSON, BECK & TAYLOR
8/01              Pre-billing Report              Page 1

Refrigeration, Inc.                          Corporate Matters
Miscellaneous Corporate Matters              Monthly
Case Number: Refrig-002                      Trust Balance: $2,825
P.O. Box 10083                               Case Rate: $125
500 East Fifth Street                        Case Attorney: MJB

Los Angeles, CA 90014
Phone: (213) 555-9342


                                        Previous Bill Owed $470.20


                        —Legal Fees—

7/6     MJB    Telephone conference with
               Stevenson re: June minutes        .50 hr         $62.50

7/7     MJB    Preparation of June minutes;
               prepared for review at next       1.00        $125.00 MJB
               meeting of the board of directors 1.50 hr     $187.50

7/9     MJB    Conference with Stevenson at home  .25 hr        none

                                                 1.75        $187.50 MJB
               Total Legal Fees ............     2.25 hr     $250.00

                     —Costs Advanced—

7/7     MJB    Photocopy documents; June 2005
               minutes (for board meeting)       $.25 ea
                                                 100 items      $25.00

               Total Costs Advanced .........                  $25.00



                    Continued on Page Two
```

Management reports can also be used to make management decisions, such as that particular types of cases are no longer profitable, the firm needs to raise hourly rates, or other such financial related decisions.

7. Client Payments Are Entered into the Billing System

Finally, payments made as a result of billings must be recorded or entered into the billing system, giving clients proper credit for the payments they have made.

The Billing Cycle

The timekeeping and billing process is a recurring cycle. Once bills are produced and payments are made for a period, the process starts over if more work is performed on a case. The timeslips for the new period are entered, bills are generated, and so forth. Once a year or so, old timeslips should be purged or deleted from the computer. Without the outdated information, the computer can operate faster.

In essence, manual systems go through the same process or cycle as do computerized systems, except that the pre-billing reports, final billings, and payments are all generated and recorded by hand. However, most manual systems do not have the capability to produce management reports.

EXHIBIT 4–5

Final client billing

JOHNSON, BECK & TAYLOR
555 Flowers Street, Suite 200
Los Angeles, California 90038
(213) 555-2342

Mary Smith   Billing Date: 8/02
Refrigeration, Inc.
P.O. Box 10083   Acct. Number: 4345AS3234
500 East Fifth Street   Previous Bal. in Trust
                                              $2,825.00
Los Angeles, CA 90014

RE: Refrigeration Miscellaneous Corporate Matters

DATE	PROFESSIONAL SERVICES	INDIV.	TIME	
7/6	Telephone conference with Stevenson re: June minutes	MJB	.50	$62.50
7/7	Preparation of June minutes: prepared for review at next meeting of the board of directors	MJB	1.00	$125.00
7/9	Conference with Stevenson at home	MJB	.25	$-0-
TOTAL FOR THE ABOVE SERVICES			**1.75**	**$187.50**

DATE	EXPENSES	
7/7	Photocopy documents; June minutes (for board meeting)	$25.00
TOTAL FOR ABOVE EXPENSES		**$25.00**
TOTAL BILLING		**$212.50**
CURRENT BALANCE IN TRUST		**$2,612.50**

KINDS OF LEGAL FEE AGREEMENTS

All bills are, of course, based on the fees the law firm charges. Legal fees can be charged and structured in many different ways. The kind of legal fee depends on the type of case or client matter, the specific circumstances of each particular client, and the law practice's preference for certain types of fee arrangements. Fee agreements may specify hourly rates, contingency fees, flat fees, or retainer fees.

Regardless of the type of agreement, a fee agreement should also specify what legal procedures, if any, the attorney is *not* obligated to provide to the client. For example, in Exhibit 4–6, paragraph 3 specifically excludes representation on appeal from this fee agreement. Another example of legal services commonly excluded is collection activities to collect the money awarded by the court or in a settlement. Of course, these activities may always be the subject of another (separate) fee agreement. If there is ambiguity in a fee agreement, the client will generally get the benefit of the doubt: Courts will assume that the legal professional drafted the fee agreement and included all the rights and privileges desired.

Hourly Rate Fees

hourly rate fee

A fee for legal services that is billed to the client by the hour at an agreed upon rate.

Hourly rate agreements are the most common. An **hourly rate fee** is a fee for legal services that is billed to the client by the hour at an agreed upon rate. For example, suppose a client hires an attorney to draft a business contract. The client agrees to pay $250 for every hour the attorney spends drafting the contract and advising the client. If the attorney spent four hours working on the contract, the client would owe the attorney $1,000 ($250 times 4 hours equals $1,000).

Hourly Rate Contract for Legal Services

This contract for legal services is entered into by and between H. Thomas Weber (hereinafter "Client") and Johnson, Beck & Taylor (hereinafter "Attorneys") on this _____ day of December, 201__. The following terms and conditions constitute the entirety of the agreement between Attorneys and Client and said agreement supersedes and is wholly separate and apart from any previous written or oral agreements.

1. Client hereby agrees to employ Attorneys and Attorneys hereby agree to represent Client in connection with a contract dispute in Jefferson County District Court of Client's claim against Westbridge Manufacturing.

2. Client agrees to pay a retainer fee of $5,000.00, which will be held in Attorney's trust account until earned.

{ *Hourly rate language* }

3. Client agrees to pay associate attorneys at $250.00 per hour, partners at $350.00 per hour, paralegals at $100.00 per hour and senior paralegals at $115.00 per hour for legal services rendered regarding the matter in paragraph (1). Attorneys are not hereby obligated to take an appeal from any judgment at the trial court level; if an occasion for an appeal arises, Attorneys and Client hereby expressly agree that employment for such an appeal must be arranged by a separate contract between Attorneys and Client.

4. Client agrees to reimburse Attorneys for all expenses incurred in connection with said matter: and Client agrees to advance all expenses requested by Attorneys during the duration of this contract. Client understands that he is ultimately responsible for the payment of all expenses incurred in connection with this matter.

5. Client understands that Attorneys will bill Client periodically (usually on a monthly or quarterly basis, depending on how quickly the case moves through the system) for copying costs at the rate of $.25 per copy, postage and handling costs, long-distance telephone costs, travel costs, and other costs, and that Client is obligated to make payments upon said billing for said fees and expenses described at paragraphs (2), (3) and (4) above, or otherwise satisfy said fees and expenses. Attorneys will also bill Client for all deposition costs incurred and Client is solely responsible for said deposition costs and Client will be required to advance the sum of **$10,000.00** (or more as necessary) or trial costs (including subpoenas, travel costs, and preparation costs) once the case is set for trial.

6. Client understands and agrees that this litigation may take two to five years or longer to complete and that he will make himself available for Attorneys to confer with and generally to assist Attorneys in said matter. Client agrees he will not discuss the matter of his litigation with any unauthorized person at any time or in any way. Client understands and agrees that Attorneys may withdraw from representation of Client upon proper notice. Client further understands that he can apply for judicial review and approval of this fee agreement if he so desires.

7. Client agrees that associate counsel may be employed at the discretion of Attorneys and that any attorney so employed may be designated to appear on Client's behalf and undertake Client's representation in this matter and such representation shall be upon the same terms as set out herein. **Client understands that Attorneys cannot and do not guarantee any particular or certain relief and expressly state that they cannot promise or guarantee Client will receive any money damages or money settlement.**

The undersigned hereby voluntarily executes this agreement with a full understanding of same and without coercion or duress. All agreements contained herein are severable and in the event any of them shall be deemed to be invalid by any competent court, this contract shall be interpreted as if such invalid agreements or covenants were not contained herein. Client acknowledges receiving a fully executed copy of this contract.

Date _____   _____

Date _____   Johnson, Beck & Taylor_____

NOTE: THIS IS ONLY AN EXAMPLE AND IS NOT INTENDED TO BE A FORM. CHECK WITH YOUR STATE BAR FOR A PROPER FORM.

EXHIBIT 4–6

Attorney/paralegal hourly rate contract

Hourly rate agreements can be complicated. Law offices have several specific types of hourly rate contracts, including:

- attorney or paralegal hourly rate
- client hourly rate
- blended hourly rate fee
- activity hourly rate

Some law practices use a combination of these as the basis of client billings.

attorney or paralegal hourly rate

A fee based on the attorney's or paralegal's level of expertise and experience in a particular area.

Attorney or Paralegal Hourly Rate The attorney's or paralegal's level of expertise and experience in a particular area determine the **attorney or paralegal hourly rate**. Exhibit 4–6 is an example of this type of contract. If a partner worked on a case, his or her hourly rate charge might be considerably more than an associate's or paralegal's hourly rate charge. Partners typically can bill from $300 to $600 or more an hour, compared with associates, who might bill $200 to $350 an hour. Paralegals typically charge from $65 to $135 (or more) per hour. The difference in price is based on the expertise and experience of the individual working on the case, her or his job title, and locally acceptable rates. In this type of fee agreement, it is possible for a client to be billed at several different rates in a given period if several attorneys or paralegals work on a matter, as they may all charge different rates.

client hourly rate

A fee based on a single hourly charge for the client, regardless of which attorney works on the case and what she or he does on the case.

Client Hourly Rate The **client hourly rate** method is based on only one hourly charge for the client, regardless of which attorney works on the case and what is done on the case. For example, if an insurance company hired a law practice to represent it, the insurance company and the law practice might negotiate a client rate of $200 per hour for attorneys and $85 an hour for paralegals. This means that no matter which attorney or paralegal works on the case, whether the attorney or paralegal has one year's or 20 years' experience, and regardless of what the attorney or paralegal does (e.g., making routine phone calls or appearing in court), the insurance company will be charged $200 an hour for attorney time or $85 an hour for paralegal time.

blended hourly rate fee

A single hourly rate that is set by taking into account the mix of attorneys working on the matter.

Blended Hourly Rate Fee An hourly rate that is set taking into account the blend or mix of law office staff working on a matter is a **blended hourly rate fee**. The "mix" includes the associates, partners, and sometimes paralegals working on the matter. Some states allow the "blend" to include only associates and partners, whereas other states allow paralegals to be included. The advantage to this is that billing is simpler, because there is one rate for all paralegal and attorney time spent on the case. The bill is easier for the law office to produce and easier for the client to read. Some states allow paralegals to have their own "blend," which results in one rate for all paralegals (whether experienced or inexperienced, senior or junior, etc.) who work on the matter.

activity hourly rate

A fee based on hourly rates that vary depending on the type of service or activity performed and the degree of difficulty of the activity.

Activity Hourly Rate An **activity hourly rate** is based on the different hourly rates attaching to the type of service or activity actually performed. For example, offices using this approach might bill legal staff time to clients as follows:

Court appearances	$350 per hour
Legal research by attorneys	$225 per hour
Drafting by attorneys	$175 per hour
Telephone calls by attorneys	$150 per hour
Legal research by paralegals	$ 80 per hour
Drafting by paralegals	$ 70 per hour

This sliding scale hourly fee is based on the difficulty of an activity.

Contingency Fees

contingency fee

A fee collected if the attorney successfully represents the client; typically a percentage of the total recovery.

A **contingency fee** agreement entitles the attorney to a certain percentage of the total amount of money awarded to the client. If no money is recovered, the attorney collects no legal fees, but is still entitled to be reimbursed for all expenses incurred (see Exhibit 4–7). Contingency fees are typically used by law firms that represent plaintiffs in personal injury, worker's compensation, civil rights, medical malpractice, and other types of cases in which monetary damages may be awarded. The individual

---

Contingency Fee Contract for Legal Services

Date:
Name: D.O.B.
Address: Phone:

1. I hereby employ **Johnson, Beck & Taylor** (hereinafter "attorneys") to perform legal services in connection with the following matter as described below:
   Personal injury claims arising out of an automobile accident which occurred January 12, 2010, on Interstate I-70.

2. I agree to pay a nonrefundable retainer fee of $2,500; plus,

3. I agree attorneys will receive 20% of any recovery, if prior to filing suit;
   I agree attorneys will receive 25% of any recovery, if prior to pretrial conference;
   I agree attorneys will receive 33% of any recovery, if after first trial begins;
   I agree attorneys will receive 33% of any recovery, if after appeal or second trial begins.
   Attorneys are not hereby obligated to take an appeal from any judgment at the trial court level; if an occasion for an appeal arises, attorneys and client hereby expressly agree that employment for such an appeal will be arranged by a separate contract between these parties. Further, I agree that attorneys will be entitled to the applicable above-mentioned percentage of recovery minus whatever a court may award, if I am a prevailing party and the court awards fees following my request therefore.

4. As to the expenses of litigation: I agree to reimburse attorneys for all expenses incurred in connection with said matter, and any expenses not fully paid as incurred may be deducted from my portion of any recovery. I agree to advance any and all expenses requested by attorneys during the duration of this contract. I agree to make an advance of expenses upon execution of this contract in the amount of $1500.00. I understand that these litigation expenses do not pertain to the retainer fee or percentage of any recovery, and I am ultimately responsible for the payment of all litigation expenses.

5. I understand that attorneys will bill client periodically, and that client is obligated to make payments upon said billing for said fees and expenses described at paragraphs (2), and (4), or otherwise satisfy said fees and expenses.

6. I understand and agree that this litigation may take 2 to 5 years, or longer to complete, and that I will make myself available to attorneys to confer with, and generally to assist attorneys in said matter. I will not discuss the matter of my litigation with any unauthorized person at any time in any way. I understand and agree that attorneys may withdraw from representation of client at any time upon proper notice.

7. I agree that associate counsel may be employed at the discretion of Johnson, Beck & Taylor, and that any attorney so employed may be designated to appear on my behalf and undertake my representation in this matter and such representation shall be upon the same terms as set out herein. Attorneys have **not** guaranteed, nor can they guarantee, any particular or certain relief.

   The undersigned herewith executes this agreement with a full understanding of same, without coercion or duress, and understands the same to be the only agreement between the parties with regard to the above matter, and that if any other terms are to be added to this contract, the same will not be binding, unless and until they are reduced to writing and signed by all parties to this contract. I acknowledge receiving a fully executed copy of this contract. Further, the undersigned Client understands that said Client is entitled to apply for judicial review and approval of this fee agreement, if Client so desires.

Date

Date   Johnson, Beck & Taylor

NOTE: THIS IS ONLY AN EXAMPLE AND IS NOT INTENDED TO BE A FORM. CHECK WITH YOUR STATE BAR FOR A PROPER FORM.

Contingency fee language (bracket marking paragraph 3)

EXHIBIT 4–7

Contingency fee contract

who would like to bring the lawsuit usually has little or no money to pay legal fees up front. Contingency fees typically range from 20 percent to 50 percent.

Contingency fee agreements must be in writing. Exhibit 4–7 shows a sample contingency fee contract. Some states put a cap (a maximum percentage) on what an attorney can collect for claims in areas such as worker's compensation and medical malpractice. For example, some states prohibit attorneys from receiving more than a 25 percent contingency fee in a worker's compensation case.

By their nature, contingency fees are risky, because if no money is recovered, the attorney receives no fee. However, even if no money is recovered, the client must still pay legal expenses such as filing fees and photocopying. Contingency fees and hourly fees also may be used together. When clients agree to this arrangement, some offices reduce their hourly fee and/or lessen the percentage of the contingency portion of the fee.

Flat Fees

flat fee
A fee for specific legal services that is billed as a fixed amount.

A **flat fee** (sometimes called a fixed fee) is a fee for specific legal services that is billed as a specific dollar amount. Some offices have a set fee for handling certain types of matters, such as preparing a will or handling an uncontested divorce, a name change, or a bankruptcy. For example, suppose a client agreed to pay an attorney a flat fee of $500 to prepare a will. No matter how many hours the attorney spends preparing the will, the fee is still $500. Flat fee agreements are usually used when a legal matter is simple, straightforward, and involves few risks.

Retainer Fees

The word *retainer* has several meanings in the legal environment. Generally, retainer fees are monies paid by the client at the beginning of a case or matter. However, there are many types of retainers. When an attorney or paralegal uses the term *retainer*, it could mean a retainer for general representation, a case retainer, a pure retainer, or a cash advance. In addition, all retainer fees are either earned or unearned.

earned retainer
The money the law office or attorney has earned and is entitled to deposit in the office's or attorney's own bank account.

operating account
Bank account used by a law firm for the deposit of earned fees and payment of law firm expenses.

Earned versus Unearned Retainers   There is a *very* important difference between an earned retainer and an unearned retainer. An **earned retainer** means that the law office or attorney has done work to earn the money and is entitled to deposit the money in the office's or attorney's **operating account**. Firms use monies from the operating account to pay the attorney's or law office's operating expenses, such as salaries and rent.

An **unearned retainer** is money that is paid up front by the client as an advance against the attorney's future fees and expenses; it is a kind of down payment. Until the money is actually earned by the attorney or law office, it belongs to the client. According to ethical rules, unearned retainers may *not* be deposited in the attorney's or law office's normal operating (checking) account. Unearned retainers must be deposited into a separate trust account and can be transferred into the firm's operating account only as they are earned.

unearned retainer
Money that is paid up front by the client as an advance against the attorney's future fees and expenses. Until the money is actually earned by the attorney or law office, it actually belongs to the client.

A **trust or escrow account** is a separate bank account, apart from a law office's or attorney's operating account, where unearned client funds are deposited. As an attorney or law office begins to earn money by providing legal services to the client, the attorney can bill the client and move the earned portion from the trust account to his or her own law office operating account.

trust or escrow account
A bank account, separate and apart from a law office's or attorney's operating bank account, where unearned client funds are deposited.

The written contract should set out whether the retainer is earned or unearned. However, in some instances the contract may be vague on this point. Typically, when a contract refers to a non-refundable retainer, this means an earned retainer.

Additionally, in many contracts, flat fee rates, as discussed earlier, are said to be non-refundable and thus are treated as earned. However, some state ethical rules regulate this area heavily: Some hold that all flat fees are a retainer, so they are considered unearned and must be placed in trust until they are "earned out." Hence, whether a retainer is earned or unearned will depend on your state's ethical rules and on the written contract.

Where Does the Interest Go? All bank accounts earn interest, even if the interest is not paid to the account holder. The money in a trust account belongs to the client, but the account is in the name of the law firm. So, who gets the interest? The law firm cannot keep interest earned on client funds. It might seem that the easy answer is to pay the interest to the client, especially if the amount held in trust is large enough or is held in the trust account long enough. However, that is not usually either possible or feasible.

The problem is twofold: First, the amount of interest that any individual client might earn is typically very small. (Remember that, in most instances, a single trust account contains funds belonging to many clients.) Second, it costs money to calculate and remit the exact amount of interest that might be owed to each client. For example, it might cost a firm $20 to send a client a check for less than $1.00. So, who gets the interest?

The answer is IOLTA, which stands for "Interest on Law Office Trust Accounts." Banks participating in the IOLTA program take the interest earned by trust accounts and pay that money to the state IOLTA program. The money is then used to fund or support legal aid or indigent defense programs in the state.

Cash Advance Retainer One type of retainer is a **cash advance**: this money is unearned and is an advance against the attorney's future fees and expenses. Until the attorney does the work to earn the money, it actually belongs to the client. The cash advance is a typical type of unearned retainer.

For example, suppose a client wishes to hire an attorney to litigate a contract dispute. The attorney agrees to represent the client only if the client agrees to pay $200 per hour with a $10,000 cash advance against fees and expenses. The attorney must deposit the $10,000 in a trust account. If the attorney deposits the cash advance in her own account (whether it is the firm's account or the attorney's own personal account), the attorney has violated several ethical rules. As the attorney works on the case and bills the client for fees and expenses, the attorney will write checks out of the trust account for the amounts of those billings. The attorney must tell the client that money is being withdrawn and keep an accurate balance of how much the client has left in trust. So, if after a month the attorney has billed the client for $500, the attorney would write a check for $500 from the trust account, deposit the $500 in the attorney's or the firm's own bank account, and inform the client that the remaining retainer (trust balance) is $9,500. If the case ended at this point, the client would be entitled to a refund of the $9,500 remaining in trust.

cash advance
Unearned monies that are paid before services are rendered, to cover the attorney's future fees and expenses.

Retainer for General Representation Another type of retainer is a **retainer for general representation**. This type of retainer is typically used when a client such as a corporation requires continuing legal services throughout the year. The client pays a specific amount, typically up front or on a prearranged schedule, to receive these ongoing services. For example, suppose a small school board would like to be able to contact an attorney at any time with general legal questions. The attorney and the school board could enter into this type of agreement for a fee of $7,500 every 6 months. The school board could contact the attorney at any time and ask general questions, but the attorney would never receive more (or less) than $7,500 for the six-month period regardless of how often they did so.

Retainers for general representation allow the client to negotiate and anticipate what the fee will be for the year. This type of agreement usually covers only general legal advice, and does not include matters such as litigation. Depending on the specific arrangements between the client and the attorney, and on the specific state's rules of ethics, many retainers for general representation are viewed as being earned, since the

retainer for general representation
A retainer typically used when a client such as a corporation or school board requires continuing legal services throughout the year.

client can call at any time and get legal advice. Retainers for general representation resemble a flat fee agreement. The difference is that in a flat fee agreement, the attorney or law office is contracting to do a specific thing for a client, such as prepare a will or file a bankruptcy. In the case of a retainer for general representation, the attorney is agreeing to make himself available to the client for all nonlitigation needs.

case retainer
A fee that is billed at the beginning of a matter, is not refundable to the client, and is usually paid at the beginning of the case as an incentive for the office to take the case.

Case Retainer   Another type of retainer is a **case retainer**, which is a fee that is billed at the beginning of a matter, is not refundable to the client, and is usually paid to the office at the beginning of the case as an incentive for the office to take the case. For example, a client comes to an attorney with a criminal matter. The attorney agrees to take the case only if the client agrees to pay a case retainer of $1,000 up front plus $200 an hour for every hour worked on the case. The $1,000 is paid to the attorney as an incentive to take the case and thus is earned. The $200 per hour is a client hourly rate charge. Because the case retainer is earned, the attorney can immediately deposit it in the office's own bank account.

Another example of use of a case retainer is a case involving a contingency fee. Suppose a client comes to an attorney asking her to file an employment discrimination case. The attorney agrees to accept the case only if the client agrees to a 30 percent contingency fee and a non-refundable or case retainer of $1,000. Again, the earned retainer is an incentive for the attorney to take the case and can be deposited in the attorney's or the office's own bank account.

pure retainer
A fee that obligates the office to be available to represent the client throughout the agreed upon time period.

Pure Retainer   A rather rare type of retainer is a **pure retainer**. A pure retainer obligates the law office to be available to represent the client throughout the time period agreed upon. The part that distinguishes a pure retainer from a retainer for general representation is that the office typically must agree not to represent any of the client's competitors and not to undertake any type of representation adverse to the client. Some clients, typically major corporations, think that listing the name of a prestigious law firm as counsel has a business value that they are willing to pay for.

Retainers for general representation, case retainers, and pure retainers are usually earned retainers, and a cash advance is an unearned retainer. However, *the language of the contract determines whether amounts paid to attorneys up front are earned or unearned.* The earned/unearned distinction is extremely important and is yet another reason all fee agreements should be in writing.

Value Billing

Recently, much has been written in the legal press about why private law practices should stop billing by the hour and use a different billing method. The reasons for the change from hourly billing include:

- The client never knows during any stage of the work how much the total legal fee will be.
- Clients sometimes avoid calling (or otherwise communicating with) paralegals and attorneys because they know they will be charged for the time, even if it is a simple phone call.
- Clients have trouble seeing the relationship between what is performed by the paralegal or attorney and the enormous fees that can be incurred.
- Hourly billing encourages lawyers and paralegals to be inefficient (i.e., the longer it takes to perform a job, the more revenue they earn).
- Many law offices force attorneys and paralegals to bill a quota number of hours a year, which puts a tremendous amount of pressure on the individual paralegal and attorney.

Value billing has been proposed as an alternative to the traditional system. The **value billing** concept uses a type of fee agreement that is based not on the time required to perform the work, but on the basis of the perceived value of the services to the client. Value billing typically requires that the attorney and client reach a consensus on the amount of fees to be charged. Because of increased competition in the legal environment and because of the power of the client as a buyer of legal services, clients are demanding that they have a say in how much they are going to pay for legal services, what type(s) of service will be provided, and what quality of legal services they will get for that price.

LEGAL EXPENSES

Under most ethical canons, attorneys must charge for the expenses they incur on behalf of a client. Expenses include the costs of photocopies, postage for mailing letters and documents regarding a case, long distance telephone calls regarding the case, and so forth. Legal expenses for cases that are litigated or filed in court can sometimes be very high. They include court reporter fees (fees charged by a court reporter to transcribe hearings, oral statements, trial testimony, etc.) and expert witness fees (fees charged, usually by the hour, by subject matter experts to give testimony), just to name two.

TIMEKEEPING AND BILLING FOR PARALEGALS

Many law offices are still firmly wedded to the billable hour concept, and thus set billable hour quotas that paralegals must meet. As indicated previously, an average number of billable hours for paralegals ranges from 1,400 to 1,800 hours annually. Historically, this was not the case. In the late 1950s, 1,300 billable hours was thought to be realistic. The minimum number of billable hours varies greatly depending on the location and size of the law office and on the types of cases it handles.

Recording Time

A **billable hour** consists of 60 minutes of legal services. Clients expect to receive a full 60 minutes of legal services when they are billed for one hour. Interruptions, calls home, and checking personal email are not billable. It is imperative that legal professionals take great care when billing clients for their time.

There are several different ways to actually record and/or track your time. One method is to bill time in tenths of an hour, with 0.5 being a half-hour and 1.0 being an hour. Every six minutes is a tenth of the hour, so you would be billing for six-minute intervals. Billing in tenths works out as follows:

0–6 minutes	=	0.1 hour
7–12 minutes	=	0.2 hour
13–18 minutes	=	0.3 hour
19–24 minutes	=	0.4 hour
25–30 minutes	=	0.5 hour
31–36 minutes	=	0.6 hour
37–42 minutes	=	0.7 hour
43–48 minutes	=	0.8 hour
49–54 minutes	=	0.9 hour
55–60 minutes	=	1.0 hour

As an alternative, some offices bill using a quarter of an hour as the smallest increment of time, as follows:

$$0\text{–}15 \text{ minutes } = 0.25 \text{ hour}$$
$$16\text{–}30 \text{ minutes } = 0.50 \text{ hour}$$
$$31\text{–}45 \text{ minutes } = 0.75 \text{ hour}$$
$$46\text{–}60 \text{ minutes } = 1.0 \text{ hour}$$

Although the quarterly basis is easier to use, it is not as accurate as the tenth-of-an-hour system. Suppose you took a five minute phone call from a client and your average billing rate was $70 an hour. Using the tenth-of-an-hour system, the fee for the phone call would be $7.00 (0.1 hour times $70 equals $7.00). However, using the quarterly system, the fee for the phone call would be $17.50, since 0.25 is the least possible billable interval (0.25 times $70 equals $17.50), or more than twice as much.

It is important that you include as much detail as possible when completing your time records, that the language be clear and easily understandable, and that the time record itself be legible. Clients are usually more willing to pay a bill when they know exactly what service was performed for them. For example, compare these bill excerpts:

1. Telephone conference—0.50 hr., $35.00.
2. Telephone conference with client on Plaintiff's Request for Production of Documents regarding whether client has copies of the draft contracts at issue—0.50 hr., $35.00.

Most clients prefer the latter, as they are able to see, and hopefully remember, exactly what specific services they received. Which of these bills would *you* rather receive?

Timekeeping Practices

If the average paralegal is required to bill between 1,400 and 1,800 hours a year, it is very important that he or she take the timekeeping function extremely seriously. The following are some suggestions regarding time tracking.

- *Find out how many hours you must bill annually, monthly, and weekly up front, and track where you are in relationship to the quota.* One of the first things you should do when you start a new paralegal job is find out how many billable hours you must submit. If the office requires that you bill 1,400 hours a year, budget this on a monthly and weekly basis, and keep track of where you are so that you will not have to try to make it all up at the end of the year.
- *Find out when timesheets are due.* Find out exactly what day of the week timesheets are due, so that you can submit yours on time.
- *Keep copies of your timesheets.* Always keep a copy of your timesheet for your own file in case the original is lost or misplaced. Having a copy also allows you to go back and calculate the number of billable hours you have put in to date.
- *Record your time contemporaneously on a daily basis.* One of the biggest mistakes you can make is to not record your time as you go along during the day. If you wait until the end of the day and then try to remember all the things you did, there is absolutely no way you will be able to accurately reconstruct everything. In the end, you will be the one who suffers, doing work you did not get credit for. Keep a timesheet handy and fill it out as you go along.
- *Record your actual time spent; do not discount your time.* Do not discount your time because you think you should have been able to perform a job faster.

If it took you four hours to finish an assignment and you worked the whole four hours, there is no reason to discount the time. If the supervising attorneys think a discount is warranted, they can decide to do so, but it is not up to you to do that. However, if you made a mistake or had a problem that you do not think the client should be billed for, tell your supervising attorney, and let him or her help you make the decision.

- *Be aware if billable hours are related to bonuses or merit pay increases.* Be aware of how billable hours are used. In some law offices, billable hours are used in allocating bonuses and merit increases, and may be considered in performance evaluations, so know up front how your office uses the tally.

- *Be ethical.* Always be honest and ethical in the way you fill out your timesheets. Padding your timesheets is unethical and simply wrong. Eventually, wrongdoing regarding timekeeping, billing, or handling client funds will become apparent.

- *Be aware of things that keep you from billing time.* Be aware of distractions and things that decrease your productivity, such as:

  - People who lay their troubles at your feet or who are constantly taking your attention away from your work. An appropriate approach is to say, "I would really like to hear about it at lunch, but right now I am very busy."

  - Time wasted trying to track down other people or trying to find information you need.

  - Constant interruptions, including phone calls. If you really need to get something done, go someplace where you can get the work done and tell others to hold your calls. However, check in every once in a while to return client phone calls. Client calls should be returned as soon as possible (note also that calls with clients probably constitute billable time!).

Billing for Paralegal Time—Paralegal Profitability

Many law offices bill for paralegal time as well as for attorney time. Many clients prefer this, because the paralegal hourly rates are much lower than the attorney hourly rates. The average actual billing rate for paralegals ranges from $65 to $135 per hour.

For example, assume that an associate attorney and a paralegal can both prepare discovery documents in a case and that the task will take seven hours. If the paralegal bills at $75 an hour and the associate bills at $150 an hour, the cost to the client if the paralegal does the job is $525, whereas the cost if the associate drafts the discovery is $1,050. Thus, the client will have saved $525 simply by allowing the paralegal to do the job. The client would still have to pay for the attorney's time to review the paralegal's work, but that cost would be minimal. This strategy represents substantial savings to clients.

The question of whether law offices can bill for paralegal time was considered by the U.S. Supreme Court in *Missouri v. Jenkins,* 491 U.S. 274 (1989). In that case, the plaintiff was successful on several counts in a civil rights lawsuit and was attempting to recover attorney's fees from the defendant under a federal statute. The statutory language provided that the prevailing party could recover "reasonable attorney's fees" from the other party. The plaintiff argued for recovery for the time that paralegals spent working on the case as well as for the time that attorneys spent. The defendant argued that paralegal time was not "attorney's fees." Alternatively, the defendants argued that if they did have to pay something for paralegal time, they should have to pay only about $15 an hour, which represented the overhead costs to the office for a paralegal.

The Court noted that paralegals carry out many useful tasks under the direction of attorneys and found that "reasonable attorney's fees" refers to the reasonable fee for work produced, whether it be by attorneys or paralegals. The Court also found that under the federal statute, paralegal time should not be compensated for at the overhead cost to the office, but should be paid at the prevailing market rates in the area for paralegal time. The Court noted that the prevailing rate for paralegals in that part of the country at that time was about $40 an hour and held that the office was entitled to receive that amount for paralegal hours worked on the case. Thus, it is clear that offices can bill for paralegal time if they choose to do so. The case also reminds us that purely clerical tasks or secretarial tasks cannot be billed at the paralegal rate—or any other rate.

Although the *Missouri v. Jenkins* case was a landmark decision for paralegals, the opinion involved the interpretation of a specific statute, the Civil Rights Act. Fee questions arise in many different situations, and if another court is deciding a fee question other than in the context of the Civil Rights Act, it may reach a different decision. Since *Missouri v. Jenkins* was decided, many courts in many different jurisdictions have allowed the recovery of paralegal time at the prevailing local rate. In addition, courts have also found that billing for an attorney's time spent on a matter is not reasonable (for purposes of court awarded fees) if the tasks performed "are normally performed by paralegals." Thus, many courts have recognized the unique niche that paralegals fill in the legal field.

FUNCTIONS OF A SUCCESSFUL BILLING SYSTEM

An often forgotten requirement for any billing system is that it must please the firm's customers or clients: The quality of the billing system is determined in large part by whether the firm's clients are satisfied with the billings and whether they pay the bills that are sent to them. One of the quickest ways for a firm to lose a good client is by mishandling the client's money in some way, by overbilling the client, or by giving the client the impression that its money is being used unjustly or unfairly. In addition, mishandling a client's money is a top reason that attorneys are disciplined. A good billing system, whether or not it is computerized, must do several things, including accurately track each client's account, provide regular billings, and itemize the services performed. In short, a billing system should satisfy the law office customers so that they are willing to make timely payments.

Accurately Track How Much a Client Has Paid the Firm

A successful billing system must be able to accurately track how much clients have paid the firm, and whether the payments were made in cash, through a trust account, or otherwise. Although this may seem easy, it often is not. Consider how you feel when a creditor either loses one of your payments or misapplies it in some manner. This is especially important for a law firm because in many instances large sums of money are involved. Payments can be lost, not entered into the billing system, or applied to the wrong client's account. It is important that the firm take great care with what goes into and comes out of the billing system, and that the information be accurate.

Send Regular Billings

We all expect to receive regular billings for routine things, such as credit card balances, utility use, and so forth. This makes budgeting and financial planning much easier. Likewise, most clients like to receive timely billings, at least monthly.

Imagine the frustration of a client who receives a quarterly billing that is four or five times more expensive than expected. Regular billings will alert clients to how they are being billed and how much they need to budget for legal services. In addition, if a client sees timely bills that are higher than were planned for, he can tell the firm how to proceed so as to limit future bills before costs are incurred. This at least gives the client the option of cutting back on legal services instead of having to overspend and get angry at the firm for not communicating the charges on a timely basis.

Provide Client Billings That Are Fair and Respectful

Billings that are fair and courteous are essential to a good billing system. If a client believes that the firm is overcharging for services or that the billings are curt and unprofessional, the client may simply not pay a bill, or may delay payment. If you ever speak to a client regarding a bill, always be courteous and respectful, and try to understand the situation from the client's point of view. If a dispute arises, simply make notes on the client's side of the story, relay the information to the attorney in charge of the matter, and let the attorney resolve the situation.

Provide Client Billings That Identify What Services Have Been Provided

It is important for the client to know exactly what services she received and what the bill covers. Bills that just say "For Services Rendered" are for the most part a thing of the past. Although the format of the bill will depend on the client, it is recommended that invoices indicate exactly what service was performed, by whom, on what date, for how long, and for what charge. With an itemized record, the client can see exactly what the firm is doing and how hard the staff is working, and may thus be more willing to pay the bill.

Provide Client Billings That Are Clear

Finally, billings should be clear and free of legalese. They should be easy to read and contain the information a client wants to see. Payments on billings that are complicated and hard to understand are often held up while the client tries to decipher the bill.

COMPUTERIZED TIMEKEEPING AND BILLING: SOFTWARE

Many different billing and timekeeping programs are available. As with most software applications, competing programs offer a wide range of diverse features, structures, and prices. Some programs just do timekeeping and billing; others offer functionalities in a variety of related areas such as general ledger, accounts payable, accounts receivable, payroll, trust accounting, docket control and calendaring, and case management. Programs are available for all sizes and types of law firms. Some timekeeping and billing software packages are designed for particular sizes of law firms, usually designated as large (100 to a thousand attorneys), medium (25 to 100 attorneys), and small (1 to 25 attorneys).

This text only covers the basics of timekeeping and billing software; the manner in which any particular package handles these functions will depend on the package. In this section you will learn to understand the fundamentals of computerized timekeeping and billing: the main menu and the primary tasks that most timekeeping and billing programs perform; the client information screen and how client records are set up in timekeeping and billing programs; how time and expense slips are entered into the billing system; how client bills are produced; and what management reports most systems can run (such as case/client lists, aged accounts receivable reports, and timekeeper productivity reports). This text also touches on the nature of and systems involved in electronic billing.

Main Menu/Fundamental Tasks of Timekeeping and Billing Programs

Exhibit 4–8 shows the main menu of Tabs3, a popular timekeeping and billing program. Exhibit 4–8 is a good example of the functions found in most timekeeping and billing programs. These include entering and maintaining client accounts and preferences, entering time records, tracking attorneys' fees, entering and tracking expenses, recording client payments, managing client trust funds (some programs do this and others do not), managing and tracking client accounts, generating and managing pre-bills and final bills/statements, tracking accounts receivable, and producing management reports. Some of these tasks and activities are discussed in more detail in this chapter, but these are the general functions that most timekeeping and billing programs provide.

Entering Client-Related Information

Before timekeeping data can be entered into the computer or a bill can be generated for a client, certain information regarding the client must be entered into the

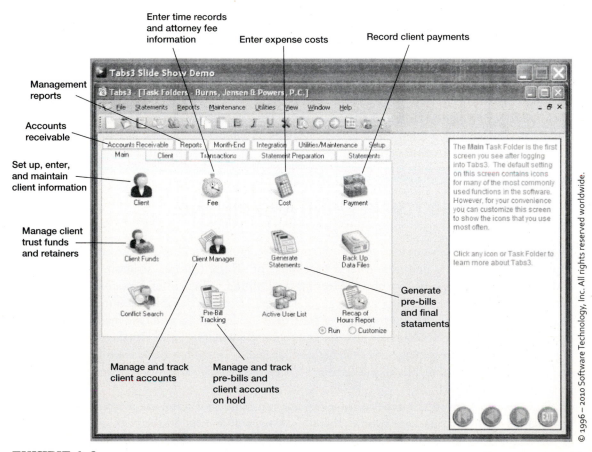

EXHIBIT 4–8

Timekeeping and billing program main menu

EXHIBIT 4–9
Client information screens

timekeeping and billing software. Exhibit 4–9 shows two client information screens in a timekeeping and billing system. Information such as a client's name and address and client identification number must be entered. Fee related information must also be entered, such as how the case will be billed and whether the fee is an hourly rate, a flat fee, or another type of fee, and who is the primary timekeeper for the file (see Exhibit 4–9). Most legal billing programs are very flexible regarding how cases are to be billed. Notice in the second screen of Exhibit 4–9 that the billing frequency for this particular client is monthly. This can be changed depending on how often the client wants to be billed. The Billing Preferences option allows a firm to set up different billing formats for each client. Some clients may want complete details and a description of every action that was performed on their behalf—who performed it, how long it took, and so forth. Other clients may want only a very brief description of what services were performed. Bill preference options allow you to control this type of information.

Exhibit 4–10 shows the accounts receivable and fund balances screen for a client. This client information screen gives an overall view of the client's account and billing status, as well as information related to any funds the client may have in trust.

Time Record Data Entry

Once the basic information about a firm's clients has been entered into the timekeeping and billing software, specific timekeeping information can be entered into the computer. Many timekeepers now enter their own timeslips directly into the computer. Time records can also be entered remotely, using a laptop, handheld computer, or PDA. The timekeeper enters the information into the PDA offsite, such as at a courthouse or deposition; then, when she gets back to the office, she synchronizes the PDA with the main computer and billing program. Alternatively, a timekeeper may complete a manual timeslip and have a clerk enter it into the computer.

Exhibit 4–11 shows a typical time record entry screen. In the Timekeeper field, the timekeeper's initials (or name) are entered. (Remember, a timekeeper is anyone who bills for his or her time.) In Exhibit 4–11, the timekeeper's name is Michael

EXHIBIT 4–10
Client information—Accounts receivable and fund balances screen

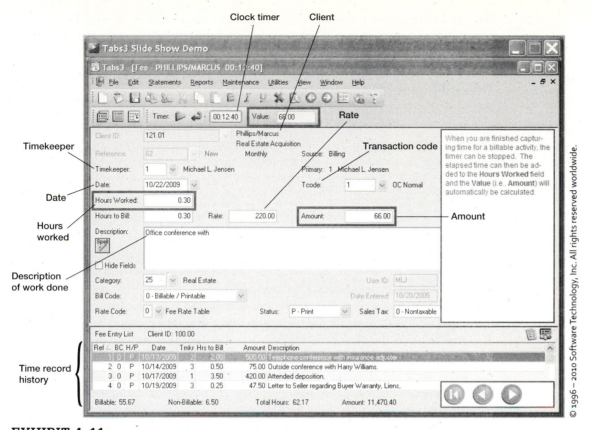

EXHIBIT 4–11

Entering a time record

Jensen. Many programs allow the user to "pop up" a list of all the possible time-keepers in a firm. Notice the clock/timer feature in Exhibit 4–11. It shows that the timekeeper has been performing a task for the client for 12 minutes and 40 seconds. Many timekeeping and billing programs allow users to interactively turn on a clock or meter as they are providing legal services to clients so that they know exactly how much time they have spent on a matter. Exhibit 4–11 also shows the current hours worked on the project (three-tenths of an hour), the rate at which the client is being billed ($220 an hour), and the current amount being charged to the client for the task. The Tcode field in Exhibit 4–11 accepts transaction codes; in this example, the code is 1, which in this system represents an office conference. Other standard transaction codes represent legal research, court appearances, depositions, drafting, and so forth.

The Client ID field indicates which client is to be billed for this time record. In Exhibit 4–11, the client is Marcus Phillips and the matter is a real estate acquisition. Most programs allow the user to select a client's account from a list of active clients. The Description field contains a listing of what services were performed. This can be detailed or brief, depending on the particular client's needs. The Date field, obviously, shows when the services were provided. The bill code in Exhibit 4–11 shows that the service is billable, as opposed to nonbillable. The time record screen in Exhibit 4–11 even shows a history of past time records that have been entered for this client.

Expense/Cost Record Data Entry

The data entry screen for entering expense or cost records is nearly the same as the time record data entry screen in most programs. It will include areas for entering a client ID, date, transaction code (for example, fax costs), and units (such as the number of pages faxed). Many programs also display an expense history, similar to the history of past time records shown at the bottom of Exhibit 4–11.

Pre-Billing and Final Statements

Generating bills is the most important aspect of any timekeeping and billing program. In general, the timekeeping and billing program takes all the time and expense slips for a period, assembles them by client, and calculates the amount due for each slip for each client. It then includes any past due balances and client payments, and calculates a total amount due for that period for each client.

Once all the timeslips and expense slips for a period have been entered into the timekeeping and billing system, usually the next step in preparing client bills is to generate a pre-billing report. Most programs give you the option to produce either drafts (pre-bills) or final bills. The pre-billing tracking screen shows when pre-bills for the selected clients were run and gives you the option of putting a "hold" on the account or going ahead and issuing final statements.

One of the first steps in generating pre-bills or bills is to select which time records and expense slips to include. Users can also select time and expense records by client ID, timekeeper, billing frequency, location, or status of files, among other things (see first screen of Exhibit 4–12).

Once the pre-billing report has been generated, it is up to the individual timekeepers or decision makers to decide if changes should be made to the bills. It is usually fairly simple to make changes in bills and to correct any mistakes. Once the information is accurate, the final step is to generate the actual client billings.

In many programs, the format of a bill is set up in the client information screen (see second screen of Exhibit 4–12). Law firms use many different formats to bill clients. For example, some bill formats contain only general information about the services provided, whereas other formats show greater detail. The look and format of billings depend on the law firm, its clients, the type of law practiced, and so forth. Thus, it is important that any timekeeping and billing package be flexible as to client billing formats and have a variety of formats easily available.

Producing detailed bills takes work. It requires timekeepers to prepare accurate, current timeslips of what work they have done. This seems easy enough, but it is not. It is sometimes difficult to convince timekeepers to write down each service they perform for each client. However, most clients strongly prefer detailed billings. So, although itemized billings are sometimes inconvenient for the timekeepers and take longer to produce, if the bill is paid in the end, the extra work has "paid off."

Management Reports

management reports
Reports used to help managers analyze whether the office is operating in an efficient, effective, and profitable manner.

Almost all timekeeping and billing software packages can produce a wide variety of management reports (see Exhibit 4–13). **Management reports** are used to help law office managers analyze whether the office is operating efficiently and effectively. Management reports can be used to track problems an office may be experiencing and to help devise ways to correct any problems. The following subsections explain some common management reports and how law office staff use them.

Case/Client List   Most billing packages allow the user to produce a case or client list. An accurate list of all active cases is very important when a firm is trying to effectively manage a large caseload. Most reports list clients not only by name, but also by the appropriate account number (called the client identification number by some programs). This cross-listing is useful when trying to locate a client's identification number.

EXHIBIT 4–12
Generating final bills

Aged Accounts Receivable Report

The **aged accounts receivable report** shows all clients that have outstanding balances owed to the office and how long these balances are past due. This report allows management to clearly see which clients are not paying and how old the balances are. This report also is helpful for identifying and following up with clients who are slow to pay their bills.

aged accounts receivable report
A report showing all cases that have outstanding balances due and how much these balances are past due.

EXHIBIT 4–13

Management reports

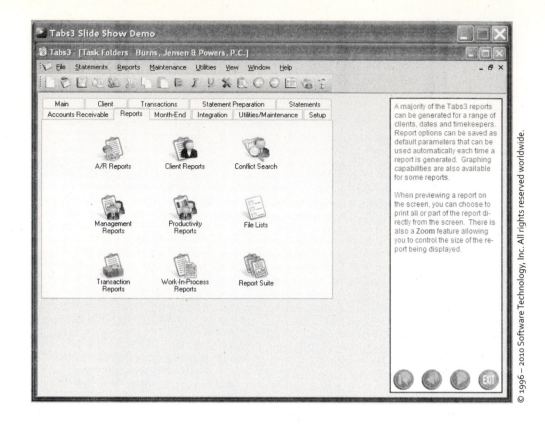

Most programs allow such a report to be run according to the type of case. Thus, management can see what types of cases (criminal, divorce, tax, etc.) have the most aged accounts. If one particular type of case has more than its share of aged accounts, it might be more profitable to stop taking such cases. So, from a management perspective, this can be a very important and useful report.

Note that aged account information should not appear on bills sent to clients. Bills with balances that are more than 30 days old should simply say "past due."

Timekeeper Productivity Report   The amount of billable and nonbillable time being spent by each timekeeper is shown in the **timekeeper productivity report**. This report can be used to identify which timekeepers are the most diligent or productive. Most packages allow a productivity report to be run for a quarter or a whole year.

Case Type Productivity Report   The **case type productivity report** shows which types of cases (criminal, personal injury, bankruptcies, etc.) are bringing in the most revenue. Obviously, this report shows which types of cases are the most profitable and which are the least profitable. Management can use this report to decide which areas of law to concentrate on to become more profitable.

Electronic Billing

When using **electronic billing**, law firms bill clients in a fashion that conforms to standard billing codes and uses a standard electronic format, using such means as the Internet. Many large clients, such as Fortune 1000 corporations and other businesses, demand that law firms bill them using electronic means. For large clients, electronic billing is a big improvement over traditional paper billing, although it introduces a certain amount of rigidity and places some administrative burden on the law firm.

---

timekeeper productivity report

A report showing how much billable and nonbillable time is being spent by each timekeeper.

case type productivity report

A report showing which types of cases (e.g., criminal, personal injury, bankruptcy, etc.) are the most profitable.

electronic billing

Client billing that uses a standard electronic format, using such means as the Internet, and conforms to standard billing codes.

Electronic billing is actually a term of art; it does not mean, for example, just sending a bill as a PDF or Microsoft Word email attachment to the client. Rather, electronic billing means sending bills that conform to the Uniform Task-Based Management System (UTBMS, a standard way of referring to timekeeper tasks) and comply with the Legal Electronic Data Exchange Standard (LEDES). LEDES is a standardized, uniform billing format in which to output billing data to clients regardless of the timekeeping and billing system that produced the bill.

Some timekeepers do not like e-billing because it mandates that they keep track of their time according to rigid, inflexible UTBMS codes. Many e-billing vendors are application service providers (ASPs), third-party vendors that set up the e-billing part of the system, receive data from law firms, and operate the software over the Internet. Clients are able to see bills (from any law firm they use) in a standard format and then customize the reports they output to meet their particular needs.

Some clients are even taking e-billing to the next level by contracting with their own ASP clearinghouses to audit bills, to ensure that the bills they receive are in strict compliance with the client's internal requirements. If the law firm's bill does not meet the client's requirements, the ASP rejects the bill and the client does not even get the electronic data. For example, if a client requires that each task be billed for separately (itemized), the client's clearinghouse would reject bills that include block entries covering three or four separate activities (e.g., "drafting letter to client; legal research for discovery motion, drafting discovery motion; telephone call with witness: 5 hours").

INTEGRATING TIMEKEEPING AND BILLING, ACCOUNTING, AND CASE MANAGEMENT

In a fully automated legal organization, the "back office" computer system will have at least three main components: (1) timekeeping and billing software, (2) accounting software, and (3) case management software. Timekeeping and billing have already been discussed in this chapter. Accounting software handles the financial side of the legal organization: receiving and applying money, making deposits, issuing checks, paying taxes, tracking aged accounts receivable, writing payroll checks, and the like. Case management software helps a legal organization provide services to clients by tracking client cases; tracking schedules, appointments, deadlines, and things to be done in cases; and tracking case-related information such as opposing parties and opposing counsel. For example, when a new client comes to a legal organization with a matter to be handled, case management software would be used to set up the new case, including client name, client address, client matter/case name, type of case, things to be done, and so forth. The same client will have to be set up in the time and billing system (to receive bills, have monies applied correctly, etc.), by entry of such data as client name, client matter, and when payments are made and recorded in the time and billing system. The legal organization's accounting software will need to know this so that deposits can be made, accounts receivable balances adjusted, and so on. The point is that all of these back-office systems have to be able to communicate with each other and share information; otherwise there will be much duplication of effort, and the possibility of error will increase greatly because of repetitive data entry.

Software manufacturers typically handle integration in one of three ways. (1) Separate software programs (from different manufacturers) exchange information among themselves (this is becoming much more common, but does not always work as promised). (2) One manufacturer makes a product that handles all of the back office needs of the legal organization (this is also fairly common). (3) Integration is ignored and the legal organization must duplicate its efforts. It should be fairly clear that it is most efficient to design legal organization computer systems that are integrated and share information seamlessly across functions.

WHAT TO LOOK FOR IN TIMEKEEPING AND BILLING SOFTWARE

As with most software, no single timekeeping and billing program is best for all attorneys and all firms. Attorneys bill clients in very different formats and ways. The size of the firm also plays a role in choosing the right package. A timekeeping and billing package that works for a five-member law firm may not work well for a fifty-member firm.

Although paralegals do not always play a part in deciding which timekeeping and billing package to purchase, often they are consulted. (They may even be charged with the task of researching the software available and making recommendations!) When considering purchasing timekeeping and billing software, keep in mind that the billing program should do the following:

1. Be flexible, allowing the firm to charge different hourly rates, mix different fee arrangements, and so on.
2. Provide a wide variety of billing formats for different types of clients. An inflexible program that allows only one or two billing formats is usually not a good idea.
3. Be easy to use. Programs that allow users to look up information instead of memorizing keystrokes are almost always easier and more convenient to use.
4. Give the user the flexibility to bill each client whenever the user wishes, instead of having to bill all clients at one time.
5. Allow users to define a list of timekeepers and activities. Such programs are almost always easier and faster to use than programs that have predefined lists.
6. Include plenty of room for a description of the legal service provided. Some programs allow only one or two lines, which is often inadequate for recording a complicated entry.
7. Permit users to edit timeslips or expense slips instead of reentering slips that have mistakes in them.
8. Offer plenty of management reports and formats to help management operate the firm.
9. Utilize a robust security system, such as passwords, to keep unauthorized or unwanted users from accessing the system. Some programs have different levels of security; for example, a secretary might have access to the password that allows him to enter data, but not to the password to run bills or management reports. Security is an important aspect of any system.
10. Have the ability to integrate with accounting and case management software.
11. Include the ability to comply with the UTBMS and LEDES protocols.

THE ETHICS OF TIMEKEEPING AND BILLING

More ethical complaints related to timekeeping and billing are filed against attorneys and law offices than all other types of complaints combined. It is important that paralegals completely understand the ethics of timekeeping and billing. In years past, timekeeping and billing complaints were viewed simply as "misunderstandings" between the client and the law office. More recently, state bars have come to see timekeeping and billing disputes as having major ethical implications for attorneys. In fact, such disputes were often not simply misunderstandings; law offices were sometimes flagrantly violating ethical rules regarding money and financial issues.

Timekeeping and billing complaints by clients do not just lead to ethical complaints against attorneys. They may also turn into the basis for criminal fraud charges filed against attorneys and paralegals.

Ethical Considerations Regarding Legal Fee Agreements

We should stress several important ethical considerations regarding fee agreements. The first is that *all fee agreements should be in writing*, especially when a contingency fee is involved. Second, contingency fees should not be used in criminal or domestic relations matters. Third, only a reasonable fee can be collected. Disputes regarding attorney handling of fees are taken seriously and can lead to adverse ethical findings or worse.

Fee Agreements Should Be in Writing

It is highly recommended that, as a matter of course, all fee arrangements be in writing. The days of a handshake cementing an agreement between an attorney and a client are long gone. There is no substitute for reducing all fee agreements to writing. If the firm and the client have a dispute over fees, the document will clarify the understanding between the parties.

Why is it so important for legal fee agreements to be in writing?

1. Clients file more ethical complaints against attorneys and law offices for fee disputes than for any other type of dispute or problem.
2. The client and the attorney may (will) forget what the exact fee agreement was unless it is reduced to writing.
3. In a factual dispute regarding a fee between a client and an attorney, the evidence is typically construed in the light most favorable to the client.

Contingency Fee Agreements Must Be in Writing

When a contingency fee is involved, most jurisdictions state that the agreement *must* be in writing for the office to collect the fees. The primary reason that a contingency fee agreement must be in writing is that in many cases, large sums of money are recovered; the difference between 20 percent and 30 percent may be tens of thousands of dollars. Contingency agreements are risky for the attorney, and they simply must be reduced to writing so that the client and the attorney both know what the proper percentage of fees should be. It also is important that the contingency agreement state—and the client understand—that even if there is no recovery in the case, the client must still pay for expenses.

Contingency Fees Are Not Allowed in Criminal and Domestic Relations Proceedings in Some Jurisdictions

Many jurisdictions prohibit contingency fees in criminal and domestic relations proceedings as a matter of public policy. For example, assume that an attorney agrees to represent a client in a criminal matter. The client agrees to pay the attorney $10,000 if the client is found not guilty, but the attorney will receive nothing if the client is found guilty. This is an unethical contingency fee agreement. It rewards the attorney not for efforts, but for results that are not entirely within the attorney's control; thus, the attorney may be tempted or pressured to engage in unethical or even criminal pursuits to ensure the desired verdict.

To avoid such possibilities and protect the public interest, contingency fees in these types of cases are prohibited.

Only a "Reasonable" Fee Can Be Collected

It is important to keep in mind that no matter what the contract or legal fee agreement is with a client, attorneys and paralegals can receive only a "reasonable" fee. Unfortunately, there is no absolute standard for determining reasonableness, except that reasonableness will be determined on a case-by-case basis. However, most states have set out a number of factors to be considered in determining reasonableness:

1. The time and labor required, including the novelty and difficulty of the questions involved, and the skill required to perform the legal services.
2. The likelihood that acceptance of the legal matter will preclude the lawyer from accepting other cases.
3. The customary fee in the area for such legal services.
4. The outcome of the matter, including the amount involved.
5. Any time limitations imposed by the client or by the circumstances.
6. The type, nature, and length of the professional relationship with the client.
7. The ability of the lawyer involved, including experience, reputation, and ability.
8. Whether the type of fee was fixed or contingent.

Rules of Many State Bars Provide for Oversight/Arbitration on Fee Issues

One of the ways in which state bar associations and courts have dealt with the plethora of fee disputes is by providing for immediate and informal review and/or arbitration of fee disputes. Many state ethical rules and court rules provide that clients have the right, at any time, to request that the judge in the case or an attorney representing the state bar review the reasonableness of the attorney's fees. In many states, the attorney is required to inform the client of this right. In those states, the judge or attorney hearing the matter has the right to set the fee and determine what is reasonable under the particular facts and circumstances of the case.

Fraud and Criminal Charges

Charging an unreasonable fee is no longer simply a matter of ethics. Attorneys and paralegals have been criminally charged with fraud for intentionally recording time and sending bills for legal services that were never provided. Criminal fraud is a false representation of a present or past fact made by the defendant, upon which the victim relies, and which results in the victim suffering damages.

Criminal charges for fraud are not filed against attorneys and paralegals when there is simply a disagreement over what constitutes a reasonable fee. Criminal charges are filed when an attorney or paralegal acts intentionally to defraud clients. This usually happens when the attorney or paralegal bills for time when he or she did not really work on the case, or in instances in which the office intentionally billed a grossly overstated hourly rate far above the market rate.

Interestingly, many of the most recent criminal cases are being brought against well-respected law offices (both large and small) specializing in insurance defense and corporate work. Some insurance companies and corporations, as a matter of course when a case has been concluded, hire an audit firm or independent attorney to go back and audit the legal billings and files to be sure they were billed accurately. In some instances, these audits have concluded that intentional criminal fraud was perpetrated, and the cases were referred to prosecutors who filed criminal charges. No matter what type of firm is involved, intentionally overstating bills can lead to very big problems.

Ethical Problems

The general subject of timekeeping and billing brings up a wide variety of ethical issues and considerations, only a few of which are mentioned here. No matter what kind of timekeeping and billing system your office uses, whether it be manual or computerized, it is critically important that the underlying agreement between the law office and the client be in writing. Second, ethical rules state that only a "reasonable" fee can be collected from clients. It is very important that bills be accurately produced the first time and that no errors occur, so that only a "reasonable" fee is collected. Data entry is absolutely crucial to timekeeping and billing. If a timeslip is entered twice so that a client is billed twice for the same service, if a payment is not recorded to a client's account, or if a client is overcharged for legal services, the firm could lose that client or be faced with an ethical complaint. Thousands of ethical complaints are filed every year against attorneys regarding timekeeping and billing practices, so it is of utmost importance that this function be handled properly.

Several difficult ethical problems regarding timekeeping and billing are explored in this section, although they have no definite answers or solutions. The rule in deciding ethical questions such as these is to use your common sense and notions of fairness and honesty.

Can You Bill More than One Client for the Same Time? From time to time a paralegal or attorney has the opportunity to bill more than one client for the same time period. This is known as double billing. For instance, while you are monitoring the opposing side's inspection of your client's documents in case A, you are drafting discovery for case B. Another example: while travelling to attend an interview with a witness in case A, you work on case B.

If you were the client, would you think it is fair for the attorney to charge full price for travel time related to your case while also billing another case? Reasonable approaches are to bill only the case you are actively working on, to split the time between the cases, or to bill the case you are actively working on at the regular hourly rate and bill the case you are inactively working on at a greatly reduced rate. Be fair and honest; your clients as well as judges and others looking at your time records will respect you for it.

When Billing by the Hour, Is There an Ethical Obligation to Be Efficient? Does the firm have to have a form file, rather than researching each document anew each time? Must an office use a computer to save time? These types of ethical questions are decided on a case-by-case basis. The point is that billing by the hour rewards people for working slowly: the more slowly they work, the more they are paid.

Common sense tells you that if you were the client, you would want your legal staff to be efficient and not to "milk" you for money. The real issue is whether the attorney or paralegal acted so inefficiently and charged so much, when compared with what a similar attorney or paralegal with similar qualifications would charge in the same community, that the fee is clearly unreasonable. When judges rule on the reasonableness of fees, there is no doubt that they will consider what a reasonably efficient attorney or paralegal in the same circumstances would have charged. Use your common sense and be honest and efficient, because someone in your office might have to justify your time and charges someday.

Should You Bill for Clerical or Secretarial Duties?   Law offices cannot bill clients for clerical or secretarial time or tasks. These tasks are viewed as overhead costs, a normal part of doing business. An easy, but unethical, way to bill more hours is for a paralegal to bill time to clients for clerical functions such as copying documents or filing materials. Paralegals clearly should not bill for time spent performing these types of clerical tasks. Paralegals bill time for professional services, not for clerical functions. If you are unsure about whether a task is clerical, ask your supervising attorney, or record the time initially and point it out to the supervising attorney and let him or her decide.

Should You Bill for the Mistakes of the Law Office?   This is another tough problem. People make mistakes all the time. Clients generally feel that they should not have to pay for mistakes; after all, the reason they went to an attorney in the first place was to get an expert to handle their situation. This decision should be left for each law office to decide, but generally the practice of billing for mistakes is discouraged.

Must a Task Be Assigned to Less Expensive Support Staff When Possible?   Common sense and efficiency will tell you that tasks should be delegated as low as possible. Clients should not have to pay for attorney time when the task could be completed by an experienced paralegal. In addition, this arrangement is more profitable for the law office, because higher-paid persons are freed to do tasks for which they can bill clients at their normal rates.

SUMMARY

In the legal environment, the process of tracking time for the purpose of billing clients is called timekeeping. The process of issuing bills for the purpose of collecting monies for legal services performed and for expenses is called billing. Timekeeping and billing software is the second most popular kind of software for law offices, right after word processing.

The computerized timekeeping and billing process or cycle includes the following steps: the client and the attorney reach an agreement with regard to how fees will be calculated; the attorney performs legal services and prepares manual or computer timeslips; paper timeslips and expense slips are entered into the timekeeping and billing software; a pre-billing report is generated; client billings are generated; management reports are generated; and client payments are entered into the computer.

Many types of fee arrangements are available, including hourly rate fees, contingency fees, flat fees, and retainers.

Every timekeeping and billing program has a screen where relevant information about each client is entered. The client information screen usually shows and receives client information such as name, address, identification number, fee arrangements, bill formatting options, and the like.

The data entry screen is where timeslips and expense slips are entered into the computer. Computerized timeslip entry screens look much like manual timeslips.

Generating accurate and timely client bills is an important function of any timekeeping and billing system. Many timekeeping and billing programs allow users to choose from among several different billing formats.

Management reports are used to help management analyze whether a law firm is operating efficiently and effectively. Many programs allow you to generate a case or client list, aged accounts receivable report, timekeeping productivity report, case type productivity report, and more.

Many ethical complaints are filed against attorneys due to timekeeping and billing issues. It is important to have written fee agreements, bill honestly and accurately, and bill only reasonable fees.

KEY TERMS

activity hourly rate
aged accounts receivable report
attorney or paralegal hourly rate
billable hour
billing
blended hourly rate fee
case retainer
case type productivity report
cash advance
client hourly rate

contingency fee
earned retainer
electronic billing
expense slip
flat fee
hourly rate fee
management reports
operating account
pre-billing report
pure retainer

retainer for general representation
timekeeper
timekeeper productivity report
timekeeping
timeslip
trust or escrow account
unearned retainer
value billing

INTERNET SITES

ORGANIZATION	PRODUCT/SERVICE	INTERNET ADDRESS
Abacus Data Systems, Inc.	Abacus Silver, timekeeping, billing, accounting and case management software	www.abacuslaw.com
Aderant	CMS Open Billing	www.cmsopen.com
IOLTA	Information about IOLTA and IOLTA programs	www.iolta.org
Juris	Juris legal timekeeping and billing software	www.juris.com
LEDES	Legal Electronic Data Exchange Standard (LEDES)	www.ledes.org
LexisNexis	PC LAW legal timekeeping and billing software	www.pclaw.com
Micro Craft, Inc.	Verdict Time & Billing	www.micro-craft.net
Omega Legal Systems	Omega Billing & Accounting	www.omegalegal.com
Orion Law Management Systems	Timekeeping and billing software	www.Orionlaw.com
Perfect Law Software	Timekeeping and billing software and comprehensive back office systems	www.perfectlaw.com
ProVantage Software, Inc.	Timekeeping and billing software and comprehensive back office systems	www.provantagesoftware.com
Rainmaker Software, Inc.	Rainmaker Gold timekeeping and billing software	www.rainmakerlegal.com
Sage Software	Timeslips legal timekeeping and billing software	www.timeslips.com
Software Technology, Inc.	Tabs3 legal timekeeping and billing software	www.Tabs3.com
Thomson	Elite Enterprise and Prolaw timekeeping and billing software systems	www.elite.com

TEST YOUR KNOWLEDGE

1. What is the difference between timekeeping and billing?

2. Name four types of hourly rates.

3. When a lawyer takes a percentage of the recovery in the case, it is called a _____ fee.

4. True or False: It is strongly recommended that all fee arrangements be in writing.

5. True or False: A flat fee agreement must be in writing.

6. A retainer that can be deposited in the firm's or attorney's operating checking account is called a(n) _____ retainer.

7. True or False: An account where unearned client monies are deposited is called a trust fund.

8. A retainer for general representation is a(n) _____ retainer.

9. A case retainer is a(n) _____ retainer.

10. A cash advance retainer is a(n) _____ retainer.

11. For what activity do clients file the most ethical complaints against lawyers?

12. True or False: A contingency agreement can be used in all kinds of cases.

13. True or False: If a client signs a contract with an attorney and the fee turns out to be clearly excessive, it doesn't matter, because a contract was signed and the contract prevails.

14. Name four of the eight factors that courts use to determine if a fee is unreasonable.

15. True or False: Paralegals can bill for time spent doing photocopying and other clerical tasks.

16. Define electronic billing.

17. True or False: Integrated programs that include timekeeping and billing, accounting, and other features do not really offer the modern law office much advantage.

ON THE WEB EXERCISES

1. Using the "Internet Sites" listed in this chapter or a general Internet search engine (such as www.google.com or www.yahoo.com), research three timekeeping and billing programs. Compare the features, price, training options, and other information about the products and write a three-page paper on your findings, including which program you liked the best and why.

2. Using the "Internet Sites" listed in this chapter or a general Internet search engine (such as www.google.com or www.yahoo.com), research legal electronic billing. Write a three-page paper on the results of your research. Include what it is; how it works; what, if any, problems there are regarding implementation of electronic billing; and what benefits clients and legal organizations derive from electronic billing.

3. Using the "Internet Sites" listed in this chapter or a general Internet search engine (such as www.google.com or www.yahoo.com), find a minimum of three articles on legal timekeeping and billing. Write a one-page summary of each article.

4. Visit five state bar association websites and find three articles on either legal timekeeping, billing, or legal fees.

5. Go to the Georgia Bar Association's website at www.gabar.org and use the Search tool to find a sample contingency fee agreement. Go to several other state bar association websites and try to find another sample contingency fee or hourly rate contract agreements.

6. Visit the National Association of Legal Assistants website at www.nala.org and review the latest NALA National Utilization and Compensation Survey Report. Read and print out the section related to paralegal billing rates. If you have difficulty finding it, try using the "Search" feature on the website. If you still have trouble finding it, use www.google.com and search on the full title.

7. Go to the ABA Law Practice Management Section home page at www.abanet.org and find two articles on timekeeping, billing, fees, and financially related matters. Summarize the articles in a two-page paper.

QUESTIONS AND EXERCISES

1. You are a new paralegal and have worked for a medium sized law office for three months. It has been a tremendous experience for you, as you learned how the office does business; its policies and procedures; what type of service you are expected to give to clients; where resources are; and how to use resources, such as the office's computer systems, law library, copy machines, and form files. Although it has taken time for you to learn these things, you have also been productive and have received several compliments on the quality of your work.

   One day, you read in the office's staff manual that all paralegals are required to bill 1,500 hours annually or face possible discipline. You immediately contact your supervisor and ask whether, as a new paralegal, you will be expected to bill this amount. Your supervisor responds, "Of course. You were told that when you were hired." You immediately begin gathering copies of your timesheets to compile your total. You also request that the billing department send you the total numbers of hours you have billed to date. When you get the report from billing, you panic; you have billed only 300 hours. What do you do now, and how could you have avoided this unfortunate situation?

2. On June 30, a billing goes out to Susan Simon, one of the clients whose cases you have been working on. Ms. Simon calls you a few days later and complains about the amount of time shown on the bill. She is extremely rude and discourteous. Ms. Simon flatly states that she thinks she is being overbilled. How do you handle the phone call?

3. You are interviewing a new client. The client wants to hire your office to help negotiate the purchase of a small business. The seller has proposed $20,000. The new client would be willing to pay this amount, although she thinks it is a bit high, but she does not feel comfortable negotiating with the seller and would rather have an attorney involved in the deal for her protection. However, she is suspicious of paralegals and attorneys and is especially concerned about how much it will cost to get the representation she needs. You inform the client that the attorney will be the one who actually talks to her about the fee issue, but that typically this type of case is taken on an hourly basis and that the attorney will be able to give her only a very broad estimate of what the total matter will cost. The client states that this would be unacceptable to her because she "does not have a lot of money to pay overpriced attorneys." The client also states that she would like this matter settled as soon as possible. You must prepare a memorandum to the attorney outlining the issue and possible solutions. What type of fee arrangement would you suggest to the attorney? Please keep in mind the client's anxieties and her particular needs.

4. Recently, your office has found a niche in representing spouses collecting on past due child support. In most cases, your clients have little money to pay you with and are financially strapped, because they no longer have the income of their former spouses to support their children and have not been receiving the child support. In some cases, large amounts of money are owed, but finding the former spouses has proven difficult. Your supervising attorney decides that the best way to handle these types of cases is on a one-third contingency basis. Your supervising attorney asks for your comments. How do you respond?

5. Yesterday was a hectic day. Although you wanted to record your time earlier, you just could not get to it. Record your time now, using a spreadsheet. Build the spreadsheet so it has columns for the date, client/case name, timekeeper, services rendered, billable time, and nonbillable time. For each activity listed, decide whether it is billable or not billable. Record your time, first using tenths of hours.
   You should also fill out expense slips for items that should be charged back to clients. Build the spreadsheet to include date, client/case name, type of expense, and cost. The firm charges 25 cents each for copies and 50 cents per page to send a fax. Assume that long-distance phone calls cost 25 cents a minute. Total the cost of each expense slip. As best you can recall, this is how your day went:

   8:00 a.m.–8:12 a.m.: Got a cup of coffee, talked to other law office staff members, reviewed your schedule/things-to-do sheet for the day, and reviewed the email in your inbox.

   8:13 a.m.–8:25 a.m.: Talked to your supervising attorney (Lisa Mitchell) about some research she needs done on the grounds to support a motion to dismiss *Johnson v. Cuttingham Steel*. Ms. Mitchell also asked you to find a bankruptcy statute she needs for *Halvert v. Shawnee Savings & Loan*.

   8:26 a.m.–8:37 a.m.: A paralegal from another office calls to remind you that the paralegal association you belong to is having a meeting at noon and that you are running the meeting.

8:38 a.m.–8:40 a.m.: One of your least favorite clients, John Hamilton, calls to ask you when he is supposed to be at your office to prepare for his deposition tomorrow. You access the weekly schedule electronically and read him the information he needs.

8:40 a.m.–8:50 a.m.: You find the information you need for the motion to dismiss in *Johnson v. Cuttingham Steel* in a motion in another case you helped to prepare last month. The research is still current, and Ms. Mitchell is pleased that you found it so fast. You note that it took you two hours to research this issue when you did it the first time. You copy the material Ms. Mitchell needs (five pages) and put it on her desk, and also send it to her electronically.

8:55 a.m.–9:30 a.m.: You speak with a witness you have been trying to contact in *Menly v. Menly*. The call is long-distance. The call lasts 15 minutes and writing the memo to the file documenting the call takes 15 minutes.

9:30 a.m.–9:54 a.m.: Ms. Mitchell asks you to contact the attorney in *Glass v. Huron* regarding a discovery question. You spend 10 minutes on hold. The call is long-distance but you get an answer to Ms. Mitchell's question.

10:00 a.m.–10:15 a.m.: Coffee break and talk with attorney about the ballgame.

10:15 a.m.–10:45 a.m.: One of the secretaries informs you that you must interview a new client, Richard Sherman. The person who was supposed to see Mr. Sherman got delayed. Mr. Sherman comes to your office regarding a simple adoption. However, in talking to Mr. Sherman you find out that he also needs someone to incorporate a small business that he is getting ready to open. You gladly tell him that your office has a department that handles this type of matter. You take down the basic information regarding both matters. You tell the client that you will prepare a memo regarding these matters to the appropriate attorney and that one of the office's attorneys will contact him within two days to further discuss the matter. You also copy 10 pages of information that Mr. Sherman brought.

10:45 a.m.–10:54 a.m.: One of the secretaries asks you to cover her phone for her while she takes a quick break. Because the secretary always helps you when you ask for it, you gladly cover the phone for a few minutes. Ms. Mitchell asks you to send a fax regarding *Stewart v. Layhorn Glass*, so you use this time to send the six-page fax.

10:55 a.m.–12:00 noon: Yesterday Ms. Mitchell asked you to organize some exhibits in *Ranking v. Siefkin*. The deadline was noon today. You finally have some free time to organize the exhibits.

12:00 noon–1:00 p.m.: Lunch.

1:00 p.m.–2:00 p.m.: You work on a pro bono criminal case for a client whom Ms. Mitchell is representing on appeal. In an effort to become familiar with the case, you read some of the transcripts from the trial.

2:00 p.m.–3:30 p.m.: Ms. Mitchell hands you a new case and says that your firm will be representing the defendant, Maude Pinchum. She asks you to read the petition and client file, analyze the case, and draft interrogatories to send the plaintiff. You spend the rest of the day working on this case.

3:30 p.m.–3:45 p.m.: Make personal phone calls.

3:45 p.m.–5:00 p.m.: Continue working on Pinchum case.

ETHICS QUESTION

It is the first day of your new job as a paralegal. As you perform your first job assignment, you discover that it is taking longer than you think it should. You do not want your boss to think that you are incompetent or lazy, so when you submit the bill for your time, you report only half the time you actually spent on the assignment. What ethical issues, if any, are raised by this scenario?

Go to the Workbook to complete the Hands-On Exercises.

CourseMate   Access an interactive eBook, chapter-specific interactive learning tools, including flash cards, quizzes, and more in your Paralegal CourseMate, accessed through CengageBrain.com.

CHAPTER 5

Databases, Case Management, and Docket Control Software

CHAPTER OBJECTIVES

After completing this chapter, you should be able to do the following:

1. Define relevant terms, including database, field, record, table, and query.
2. Explain what a docket control system is.
3. Explain what case management is.
4. Describe the computerized docket cycle.
5. Describe how a computerized case management system can prevent cases from being forgotten or overlooked.
6. Discuss why docket control and case management are important to a legal organization from an ethics perspective.

INTRODUCTION

Why are case management and docket control important? This is why.

A client sued his former attorney (and the attorney's partners) for legal malpractice for failing to file a medical malpractice claim in a timely manner. Nearly two years earlier, the client had met with the Michigan attorney regarding a claim against a hospital for medical malpractice. After the initial meeting, the client made repeated telephone calls and sent letters to the attorney. However, the attorney never responded to the client's communications. Twenty months later, the attorney finally responded with the following letter.

> My sincere apologies for the delay in responding to your earlier communications; however, we have been making a thorough inquiry into the facts of your alleged complaints. We have not been able to find an expert to make the appropriate causal relationship to support our theories of possible malpractice. Accordingly, we are not going to be proceeding on your claim and will close our file.

Within two weeks, the client sought the advice of another attorney and filed a legal malpractice claim against the first attorney. A jury awarded the client $150,000 in damages against the attorney for allowing the statute of limitations on the medical malpractice claim to lapse. *Gore v. Rains & Block*, 189 Mich. App. 729, 473 N.W.2d 813 (1991).

WHAT IS A DATABASE?

database management system (DBMS)
Application software that manages a database by storing, searching, sorting, and organizing data.

All businesses, including legal organizations, must maintain and track information. Businesses routinely use database management systems to collect and analyze information. A **database management system (DBMS)** is application software that stores, searches, sorts, and organizes data. A **database** is a collection of pieces of related data. For example, a database can be anything from a list of appointments, to a card catalog in a library, to an address book. These databases, whether or not they are on a computer, contain related information: appointments, listing of books, and addresses, respectively. They are organized by the date of the appointment; by the subject, title, and/or author of the book; and by the name of the person. A DBMS allows users to track and organize this kind of information using a computer.

database
A collection of related data items. Databases are created because the information contained in them must be accessed, organized, and used.

DBMSs are used in millions of businesses to manage and track vital information. They are powerful and flexible and can be used for thousands of different purposes. For example, a law firm might use a DBMS to track its clients' names and addresses; a manufacturer might use a DBMS to track its inventory of parts and finished products. A DBMS not only stores or holds information, but can also organize that information in a relevant manner. For example, the law firm might need an alphabetical list of its clients' names and addresses to be used for reference purposes. The manufacturer might use a DBMS to generate an inventory list of products by completion date. It is sometimes easy to think of databases simply as organized lists, catalogs, or compilations of information.

In the legal environment, organizations use databases to track many kinds of information. Legal organizations use DBMSs to track specific information about a particular case, such as the many thousands of documents in large cases. This process is called litigation support. Each document is entered into a litigation support system, which is another kind of DBMS.

A DBMS allows users to manipulate data as they wish. For example, if a legal organization wanted a list displaying only its clients' names and home phone numbers on a report (and no other information), a query report could be developed to display this information while still leaving the underlying data unchanged. Even though a vast amount of information is entered into a database, that information need not be displayed or printed out in every report. Information in a database is selected and used as needed.

Database software is flexible, powerful, and convenient to use and operate because it allows users to:

- Store and retrieve information easily
- Arrange and rearrange data over and over without affecting the data itself
- Update and change information
- Add or delete information
- Search for information
- Sort and organize information
- Print information in many different formats

Legal organizations and paralegals use databases for a wide variety of purposes in addition to litigation support. They may maintain an opposing attorney database, forms database, class action database, judges database, legal research database, conflict of interest database, factual database (for a specific case), expert witness database, library catalog database, active file database, inactive file database, licensed software database, marketing database, trial database, and many others.

Microsoft Access is a common and widely available database program, typically used for "small" databases that may contain several hundred or even several thousand records. However, for large databases that contain millions of records, Access would not be appropriate.

EXHIBIT 5–1

Client database structure

Fields

Table

A data value (8 records x 8 fields = 64 data values).

One record
(8 records
total)

© Cengage Learning 2012

DATABASE STRUCTURE

Databases are organized into tables, fields, records, and data values.

Table

A **table** is a collection of related information stored in rows and columns. A database is made up of tables that contain related information and the tools necessary to manipulate the data. The entirety of the data in Exhibit 5–1 is a table.

A table stores information about a particular topic. The table in Exhibit 5–1 stores contact information about a law office's clients. Many databases have more than one table. Having additional tables simplifies and speeds up searching or querying the database and in some ways makes the database easier to manipulate. Instead of having one file with everything dumped in it, the database creator has broken up the information into smaller subunits while still keeping the various information elements connected or related to each other.

Field

A **field** is a column in a table that contains a category of information. (It is common for DBMSs to refer to fields as columns.) For example, Exhibit 5–1 shows eight fields in the table:

1. Last Name
2. First Name
3. Address
4. City
5. State
6. Zip
7. Home Phone
8. Case Number

Fields will differ from database to database. For example, in a docket control database used to track and control a legal organization's deadlines and appointments, the fields might include date of event, event description, case name, and place of event. The client information database in Exhibit 5–1 uses other fields relevant to its purpose.

All databases must have fields where data are input and collected. Large databases commonly have hundreds of fields in which to enter information.

Record

A **record** is a collection of fields treated as a unit. It is essentially one row in a table. In Exhibit 5–1, each record has all the information for one client entry—that is,

table
A collection of related information stored in rows and columns.

field
A column in a table that contains a category of information.

record
A collection of fields that is treated as a unit; essentially, one row in a table.

the complete set of field data for one entry. A total of eight records, or clients, are entered in Exhibit 5–1. Large databases may have millions of records. For example, litigation support databases in large class action cases involving thousands of plaintiffs can easily have millions of records.

Data Value

A **data value** is one item of information and is the smallest piece of information in a table. For example, in Exhibit 5–1, each individual piece of information is a data value (e.g., "Winslow," "Harriett," "Allen," "San Diego," etc.). There are 64 data values in Exhibit 5–1. Multiply the number of records times the number of fields for each table to compute the total number of data values (e.g., 8 records x 8 fields = 64 data values).

COMMON DATABASE TERMS

Most database programs use tools, sometimes called objects, that allow users to manipulate the data therein. Some common tools include forms, queries, and reports.

A **form** allows a user to view, enter, and edit data in a special (custom) format designed by the user.

A **query** extracts data from a table based on criteria specified by the user. A query allows you to search for and sort only the information you are looking for at that time. Queries create a specific view of data and allow you to answer specific questions. Once you create a query, you can save it and then use it whenever you need to. After a query has been created, you must run or execute the query to see the results.

A **report** prints data from a table or query in a format designed and specified by the user. Whereas forms are designed to be used on the screen, reports are designed to be printed. A report consists of information that is pulled from tables or queries, as well as information that is stored with the report design, such as labels, headings, and graphics.

CALENDARING, DOCKET CONTROL, AND CASE MANAGEMENT

The practice of law is filled with an array of appointments, deadlines, hearings, and many other commitments for every case that is handled. Considering that a single legal professional can have a caseload of between 20 and 100 cases at any one time, just staying organized and on top of all of the things that must be done is a big job. It is extremely important that these dates, deadlines, and commitments be accurately tracked and that the legal work get done accurately and on time—for ethical reasons, customer service reasons, general business/profitability reasons, and malpractice avoidance reasons. All legal organizations must track deadlines, whether they use manual systems or computers or both. Most legal organizations now use some type of computerized method to track deadlines.

This chapter discusses specific law-office database programs that assist legal professionals with computerized calendaring, docket control, and case management. Though these terms each have a fairly specific meaning, they are often (somewhat confusingly) used interchangeably.

Calendaring is a generic term used to describe the recording of appointments and other schedule items. Many personal information managers (PIMs), such as Microsoft Outlook, fall into this category. These programs can be used by any business to manage appointments and scheduling. In addition, most include a host of other general productivity tools as well.

Docket control is a legal-specific term that refers to entering, organizing, and controlling the appointments and deadlines for a legal organization. Docket control is sometimes referred to as a tickler or a tickler system because it "tickles" the memory for upcoming events.

Case management (sometimes called practice management) is also a legal-specific term, but it always means more than just tracking appointments and schedules. The breadth of features in current case management programs seem to grow every day. Some of the features found in case management programs include docket control (scheduling/appointments), things to do, a contact information database (name, address, email, phone, etc.) organized by case (parties, co-counsel, opposing counsel, judges, etc.), case notes, document assembly, integrated billing, email, and more. In case management programs, all data are tied to cases. This is very helpful for legal organizations that view and organize most of their data according to what case a piece of information is tied to. This is a different approach than general calendaring/PIM applications.

As the legal software market has matured, more legal software manufacturers have entered it. In addition, nearly all of the current legal products available in this market are significantly more sophisticated and targeted at meeting the needs of attorneys, paralegals, and legal organizations. The products today do far more than just docket control. The end result is that currently, legal organizations really only use two kinds of products to handle calendaring and docket control functions:

1. Generic calendaring/personal information management programs such as Microsoft Outlook. These are found in many legal organizations because they come as a part of the Microsoft Office suite program (bundled together with word-processing, spreadsheet, and database programs) and because they typically have an email component.

2. Full case management programs that have a wide array of features for handling client cases in addition to calendaring and docket control. The advantage of case management programs to legal organizations is that information is organized by case/matter.

Most PIMs and case management programs can now synchronize with handheld computers (PDAs); this enhances the ability of attorneys and paralegals to access and control their appointments, scheduling, and things-to-do lists. Also, nearly all legal organizations operate in a computer network environment. Most PIMs and case management programs now have network-based group scheduling capabilities so that users can share information related to scheduling/case management. Throughout the rest of this chapter, we use the terms docket control or case management to describe the process of tracking appointments, deadlines, and schedules in legal organizations. This chapter presents general information about docket control in legal organizations and gives an overview of the features found in many legal case management programs.

INTRODUCTION TO DOCKET CONTROL/CASE MANAGEMENT

Docket control/case management works differently depending on the specific legal organization, the type(s) of cases handled, and the organization's or users' philosophies on how the function should be managed. In many legal organizations, each attorney and paralegal enters docket control information in a central office-wide system, but they still manage their own dockets. In others, secretaries enter and manage all dockets. Some of the events that are regularly tracked include appointments, deadlines and reminders, and hearing and court dates.

---

docket control
A legal-specific term that refers to entering, organizing, tracking, and controlling all the appointments, deadlines, and due dates for a legal organization.

case management
A legal term that usually encompasses functions such as docket control, deadlines, things to do, contact information by case, case notes, document assembly, document tracking by case, integrated billing, and email.

Appointments

During the course of a case or legal matter, a legal professional will have many appointments: meetings with clients and co-counsel, witness interviews, interoffice meetings, and so forth. Keeping appointments is very important. Law offices that constantly reschedule appointments with clients may find their clients going to other attorneys who provide better service.

Deadlines and Reminders

statute of limitations
A law that sets a limit on the length of time a party has to file a suit. If a case is filed after the statute of limitations has run (expired), the claim is barred and is dismissed as a matter of law.

The practice of law encounters deadlines at practically every stage of a legal matter. One of the most important types of deadlines is a statute of limitations. A **statute of limitations** is a law that sets a limit on the length of time a party has to file a suit. For instance, some states impose a five-year statute of limitations on lawsuits alleging a breach of a written contract. That is, if a lawsuit is brought or filed more than five years after a contract is breached or broken, the lawsuit is barred by the statute, and the court will dismiss the action. The purpose of a statute of limitations is to force parties to bring lawsuits in a timely fashion. Otherwise a defendant might be prejudiced by loss of evidence, the inability to find witnesses, or the inability of witnesses to recall relevant information. If an attorney allows a statute of limitations to expire without filing a case, he or she will likely be liable for legal malpractice.

Many other deadlines are set after a case has been filed. In some courts, the judge and the attorneys on both sides meet and schedule the deadlines for the case. These deadlines may look something like those in Exhibit 5–2. These deadlines must be tracked and adhered to. An attorney who does not adhere to the deadlines may cause the case to be dismissed or may be sanctioned. Courts are usually reluctant to extend deadlines once they have been set.

Because attorneys and paralegals are usually busy working on more than one case at a time, a legal organization must have a system for tracking upcoming deadlines. This is done not only by calendaring the deadline itself, but also by creating reminder notices, or ticklers, in the calendar so that a deadline does not catch a person by surprise. For example, Exhibit 5–2 shows a January 30 deadline to file a motion to dismiss; the attorney or paralegal may want to be reminded 30, 15, and 5 days before this deadline. Therefore, reminder notices would be issued on January 1, January 15, and January 25, in addition to the deadline itself being recorded on January 30. It is common for an attorney or paralegal to request more than one reminder for each deadline.

EXHIBIT 5–2
A typical case schedule

Deadline Item	Deadline Date
Motion to Dismiss must be filed by	Jan. 30
Response to Motion to Dismiss must be filed by	Mar. 1
Discovery (interrogatories, requests for production, and depositions) must be completed by	July 1
Summary Judgment motion must be filed by	July 15
Response to Summary Judgment motion must be filed by	Aug. 1
Pretrial Order must be filed by	Sept. 1
Settlement conferences must be completed by	Sept. 15
Pretrial motions must be completed and decided by	Oct. 15
Trial to start no later than	Dec. 1

Some deadlines are automatically set by the prevailing rules of procedure. Rules of procedure are court rules that specify the procedures that must be followed when litigating cases. For instance, in some courts the rules of procedure hold that when a final decision in a case is rendered, all parties have 30 days after that to file an appeal.

April 15, the date on which federal income tax returns are due, is an example of an automatic or procedural deadline that must be tracked by a law office that practice tax law. Thus, tracking of this automatic or procedural deadline should be built into the office's docket system, so that appropriate reminders are issued, returns are not filed late, and penalties are avoided.

Hearings and Court Dates

Hearings and court dates are formal proceedings before a court. It is extremely important that these dates be carefully tracked; courts have little tolerance for attorneys who fail to show up for court. In some instances, the attorney can be fined or disciplined for missing a court date.

A large case that is being litigated in court may require hundreds of entries into the docket system. Exhibit 5–3 lists some common docket entries, including both substantive items and entries related to law-office management.

EXHIBIT 5–3

Common docket control entries

Accounts receivable review due dates

Answer and other pleading due dates

Appeal filing dates

Appellate briefs and arguments

Billing due dates

Board of directors meeting dates

Commercial law action dates

Copyright, trademark, and patent renewal dates

Corporate securities filing due dates

Corporation filing due dates

Discovery due dates

Employee benefit annual filing deadlines

Expiration dates for statutes of limitations

Insurance coverage renewal dates

Judgment renewal dates

Lease renewal dates

License renewal dates

Notary certificate expiration date

Performance evaluations of staff

Probate and estate tax due dates

Probate inventory and appraisal completion dates

Property tax return due dates

Stockholder meeting dates

Tax return due dates

Trial court appearance dates

Trial court brief due dates

Unemployment tax report due dates

Will and trust review dates

Withholding tax report due dates

© Cengage Learning 2012

MANUAL DOCKET CONTROL

Attorneys have used manual docket control methods for centuries. The most popular manual docket systems use a simple calendar.

Calendar

Small law offices sometimes use a simple, one-page-a-day calendaring system. Many calendars provide space or a section dedicated to recording "things to do" or reminders, in addition to providing space to write in or schedule appointments.

Before the advent of computerized systems, deadlines and reminders (i.e., ticklers) would be entered into the calendar as cases were opened. Notices from courts, attorneys, and so forth that were received in the mail would also be entered on the calendar. In addition to the due date or appointment date, any reminders also had to be manually entered into the calendar. This process could be time-consuming. For instance, for a deadline with two reminders, the information would have to be manually entered a total of three times.

Although manual calendaring systems may work for small offices that make few entries, they do not work well for large offices that have many attorneys and many appointments and deadlines. They simply do not have enough room to enter all the appointments, unless each attorney has his or her own calendar—and this is dangerous because it does not reveal conflicts.

Many calendaring systems are decentralized. In a decentralized system, each attorney or timekeeper has her or his own calendar and staff to record appointments, things to do, reminders, and so forth. This can be problematic for the administrators of the firm; because they do not have a centralized system at their disposal, they never know where an attorney or other person should be without tracking down that person's secretary. This problem is compounded when a staff meeting for the entire office must be scheduled. Instead of going to a centralized calendar, checking what dates are available, and scheduling the meeting, the organizer must contact each attorney, compile a list of available dates for each attorney, find dates and times that are acceptable to all parties, and then notify each party of the date and time of the meeting.

Manual calendaring systems also lack the ability to track information by case. For example, if a client asked to see all the upcoming events for her case, a staff person would have to go through the calendar and manually put together a list. Depending on the case, there could be many entries. Again, this is a time-consuming and inefficient process.

Yet another problem with a manual calendaring system is that successive calendars must be purchased every year (one for 2011, one for 2012, one for 2013, etc.). It is also difficult to schedule dates far in the future—five years down the road for a statute of limitations entry, for instance—because you need the appropriate calendar.

TYPES OF COMPUTERIZED DOCKET CONTROL SYSTEMS

A legal organization can use a variety of computer programs to schedule and track events. The organization can choose a generic calendaring/personal information manager program or a case management program. Most of these programs can be purchased for stand-alone computers or for local area networks. Networked systems, whether they are generic or legal-specific, have the principal advantage of allowing individual users throughout an organization to see and have access to the calendars of other users in the office.

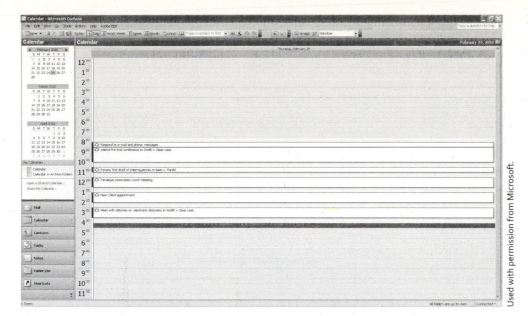

EXHIBIT 5–4

Calendaring/PIM program:
Microsoft Outlook

Generic Calendaring and Personal Information Manager Programs

Generic calendaring programs computerize the functions of a paper desk calendar. Because they are generic and can be used by any type of business, they lack many features that are particularly helpful to a legal organization. These types of programs are usually very inexpensive and typically manage only calendaring, things to do, contacts, and email functions.

A generic **personal information manager (PIM)** program consolidates a number of different tasks into one computer program. Most PIMs include calendaring, things to do, a contact database that tracks names and addresses of people, note-taking, email, and other tasks. Exhibit 5–4 shows Microsoft Outlook, which is a PIM that often comes bundled with Microsoft's Office suite of programs.

The generic calendaring and scheduling software market has matured, and most new programs now are PIMs. PIMs are very popular and convenient to use, as they allow you to organize a number of related tasks into one easy-to-use interface. Generic PIMs, such as the one shown in Exhibit 5–4, are not specifically suited to the needs of legal professionals, but still have useful features; some legal organizations use these programs. For example, for consistency purposes a corporate law department might use a product like Microsoft Outlook, which can be implemented throughout the corporation, instead of a legal-specific program that only the legal department can use. However, as good as some PIMs are, they fundamentally lack the crucial ability to track information by case, and also lack the power, functionalities, and resources of true case management programs.

personal information manager (PIM)
System that consolidates a number of different tasks into one computer program. Most PIMs handle or provide functions for calendaring, things to do, a contact database that tracks names and addresses of people, note-taking, email, and other tasks.

OVERVIEW OF COMPUTERIZED LEGAL CASE MANAGEMENT AND DOCKET CONTROL

The case management (sometimes called practice management) niche of the legal software market is mature and competitive, and the available programs are rich with features. Some case/practice management programs are designed for specific legal specialties, such as real estate, tax, collections, criminal defense, and so forth. Most case management programs, however, are designed for a broad spectrum of

EXHIBIT 5–5

Daily calendar and menu bar/toolbar in a case management program

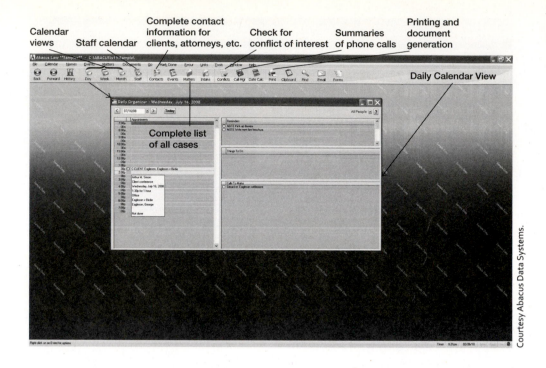

Calendar views · Staff calendar · Complete contact information for clients, attorneys, etc. · Check for conflict of interest · Summaries of phone calls · Printing and document generation · Daily Calendar View · Complete list of all cases

Courtesy Abacus Data Systems.

legal organizations, no matter what type of law they practice. Currently, the case management market is so competitive that no one product enjoys clear dominance. Further, many practicing paralegals do not use a case management program. In lieu of a case management program, many law offices use a PIM, such as Microsoft Outlook. Although this section covers the basics of case management software, the manner in which any particular package handles these tasks and functions will depend on the package.

Main Menu: Fundamental Tasks of Case Management Programs

Exhibit 5–5 shows the daily calendar and menu for AbacusLaw, a popular case management program. Exhibit 5–5 is a good example of the functions found in most case management programs, which include providing calendars in a variety of different views; capturing complete contact information for clients and others; tracking and managing events (e.g., appointments, reminders, things to do, and calls to make); recording information about matters and case files, including links to documents and case notes; checking conflicts; managing phone calls; and calculating dates, among others. Some of these tasks and activities are discussed in more detail here, but these are the general functions that most case management programs provide.

Contacts/Name Tracking

Before events such as appointments and reminders can be calendared for a case or matter in a case management system, you must first input or create basic contact information for the client. This is a good example of how a generic database function (client list) has been modified for the specific needs of legal professionals. Exhibit 5–6 shows a contact/name entry for a new client, Sherry Richards. You can enter contact information including address, phone, and email, among other items. In addition, the type or class of name entry is entered from a list; in this instance the contact is a client. Judges, vendors, colleagues, attorneys, and anyone the legal professional comes in contact with can be entered as contacts/names. Notice in Exhibit 5–6 that the client can be assigned to "linked matters," such as cases or legal matters; "linked

Assigned attorney

EXHIBIT 5–6

Entering a new client

Courtesy Abacus Data Systems.

events," such as calendar entries; "linked documents," such as legal documents; and "linked names," such as opposing counsel or other people associated with the client or the client's case. The ability to link contacts/names with cases and other case-related information is what separates case management systems from PIMs. Also, notice in Exhibit 5–6 that there is a space for initials to indicate which attorney has been assigned to the client. This allows the case management system to track and produce reports regarding which attorneys are assigned to which cases.

Matters/Cases

Exhibit 5–7 shows that a new matter has been created, *Richards v. EZ Pest Control*, and that the matter has been linked to Sherry Richards's contact/name record.

Matters associated with Sherry Richards

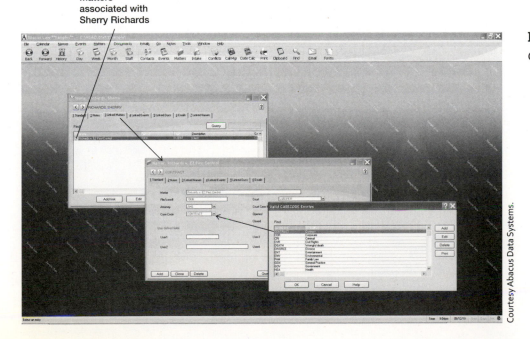

EXHIBIT 5–7

Creating a case/matter

Courtesy Abacus Data Systems.

In addition, the new matter shows the attorney assigned to the case (here AMS), the case code (here a contract case), and the court, among other things. If Sherry Richards brought additional legal matters to your firm, you would simply create the new matters in the "Adding a new Matter" window and link that case to her contact/name record. You can also find the linked names for the case, all events associated with the case, and all linked documents that are related to the case. These capabilities allow you to have a tremendous amount of information at your fingertips.

Events

Once client contact and case matter information has been entered in the case management system, events can be entered and associated with the client or case. In Exhibit 5–8, an appointment has been entered and associated with Sherry Richards and with the matter *Richards v. EZ Pest Control.* The event window in Exhibit 5–8 allows the user to select who the event is for (Arthur M. Simon) and what kind of event it is (an appointment). Notice also in Exhibit 5–8 that valid "what" entries include appointments, client conferences, and many other standard event types. Events can also include reminders, things to be done, calls to be made, trials, hearings, and many other legal-related items.

In Exhibit 5–8, there are two numerals next to "Reminders": a "**1**" and a "**3**." This means that one and three days before the actual event, a notice will appear in the Reminders section of the daily calendar that this event is coming up. In Exhibit 5–8 there is also a priority field, which allows you to assign various priorities, such as "high" or "low," to events. There is also a field for Status; in this instance, an "**N**" in Exhibit 5–8 stands for "not done." This allows you to track events that did not get completed.

Users can also create recurring entries in most case management systems. A **recurring entry** is a calendar entry that happens repeatedly, typically daily, weekly, monthly, or annually. For instance, if an office has a staff meeting every Monday morning, the entry could be entered once as a weekly recurring appointment. Notice the <u>R</u>ecur menu item on the menu bar in Exhibit 5–8. This is where a recurring entry would be designated in the case management program shown in Exhibit 5–8.

recurring entry
A calendar entry that must be done regularly or often.

EXHIBIT 5–8

Creating a new event

Recurring
Entry

Reminders   Status

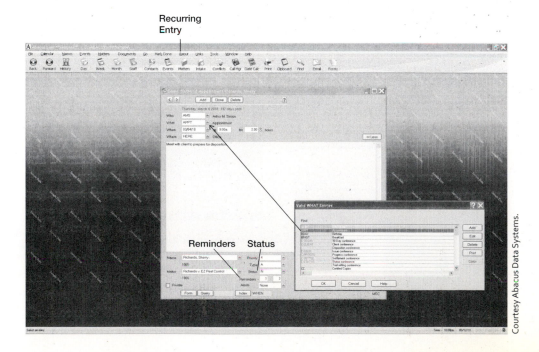

Courtesy Abacus Data Systems.

Linked Events tab

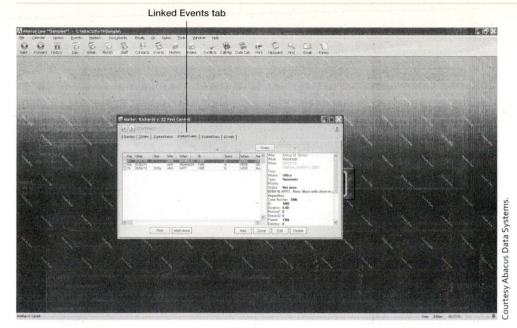

EXHIBIT 5–9

List of linked events by matter/case

Exhibit 5–9 shows the Matter screen for *Richards v. EZ Pest Control*, except that now the Linked Events tab is selected. Notice that you get a quick snapshot of exactly what deadlines are coming up in the case. They include the two reminders and the appointment mentioned earlier. By linking events to the matter and the name/contact, you have a powerful tool with which to manage a case.

Most case management programs allow a user to create rule-based entries. In a **rule-based entry**, one event automatically triggers the addition of a list of subsequent calendaring events based on a rule that was programmed into the application. For example, in Exhibit 5–10, a rule entitled "New case" has been created. This rule says that on the day it is executed, staff will meet with the client; that one day after the initial meeting, a conflict check entry/event will automatically be generated; and that an entry/event will be entered for a client file to be opened. Seven days after the initial meeting, the case management program will automatically create an event for a confirmation letter to the client,

rule-based entry
A method of entering events in a case management system so that entering one event automatically triggers creation of a list of subsequent calendaring events, based on a rule that was programmed into the application.

EXHIBIT 5–10

Entering rule-based events

EXHIBIT 5–11

Calendar views

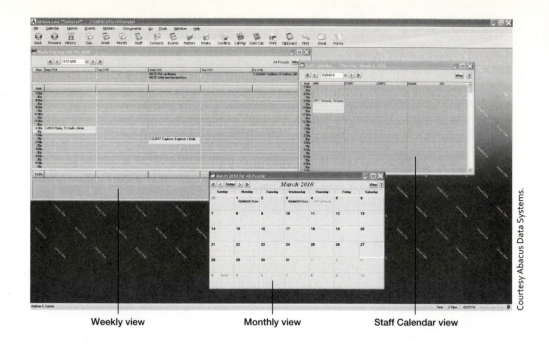

Weekly view   Monthly view   Staff Calendar view

and fourteen days after the initial conference an entry/event will be created to draft a fee contract. All of this will take place automatically after the New case rule is executed.

Most case management programs allow you to program your own rules (as shown in Exhibit 5–10). Additionally, most case management programs have court-based rules that users can purchase. Using court-based rules that automatically generate many events is a large timesaver when a legal organization has many cases to handle.

Calendar Views

All case management programs come with a number of calendar views with which users can see their calendars. A daily calendar view is shown in Exhibit 5–4, but there are several additional views as well. Exhibit 5–11 shows a weekly view, a monthly view, and a Staff Calendar view. The Staff Calendar view shows the calendars for one day for different staff side by side.

Date Calculator

Some case management systems have a date calculator that automatically calculates the number of days between dates. For instance, suppose you receive a set of interrogatories that must be answered within 30 days. If you receive the interrogatories on January 2, 2012, when are the responses due? The "Date Calculator" window in Exhibit 5–12 shows that the responses are due on February 1, 2012. Date calculators are handy features, particularly when you need to calculate precise deadlines.

Notes/Case Diary

Most case management systems provide a place in which to maintain a case diary or notes for the file. This gives legal professionals a centralized area to place their notes, record summaries of phone calls, and share other information. The notes section allows you to create a running diary of what is happening in a case as it progresses. This is particularly helpful when multiple people are working on a case. If anyone wants an update of the case, all that person has to do is read the notes.

EXHIBIT 5–12

Date calculator

Document Assembly and Generation

Case management programs can store extensive information about a case, including items such as parties, attorneys, case-related information, and case numbers. Most case management programs can assemble this information into a merged document (see Exhibits 5–13A and 5–13B). A legal professional can therefore automatically generate standard letters, forms, pleadings, and reports either from the case management program itself or in combination with a word processor such as Word or WordPerfect. Also, in some programs, when you create a document using document generation, the case management system automatically notes this, including the date, in the case diary/notes. The ability to automatically generate standard letters and forms from a case management program is a tremendous time saver.

Synchronizing with PIMs/PDAs

Most case management systems will synchronize calendars with PIMs such as Outlook and devices such as PDAs. Thus, if a corporate law department wanted to use a

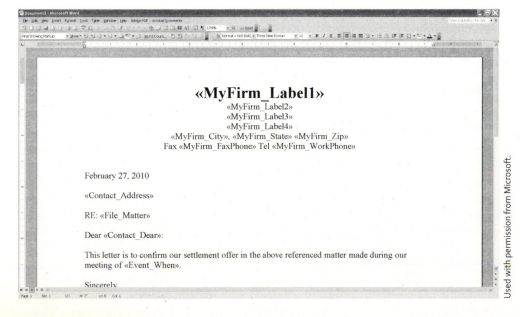

EXHIBIT 5–13A

Information setup for document generation in a case management program

EXHIBIT 5–13B

Case management program document assembly/ generation

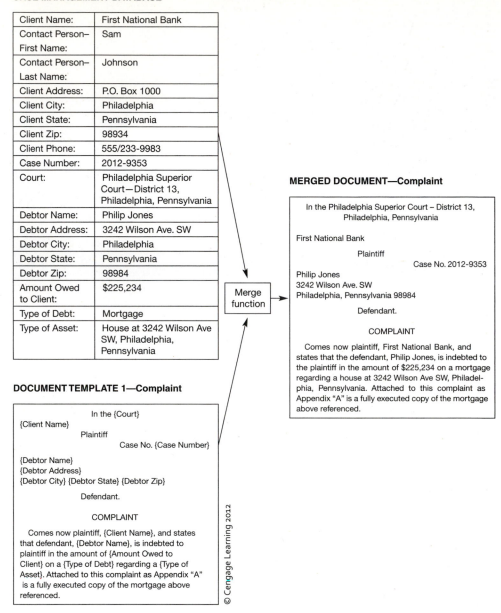

CASE MANAGEMENT DATABASE

Client Name:	First National Bank
Contact Person– First Name:	Sam
Contact Person– Last Name:	Johnson
Client Address:	P.O. Box 1000
Client City:	Philadelphia
Client State:	Pennsylvania
Client Zip:	98934
Client Phone:	555/233-9983
Case Number:	2012-9353
Court:	Philadelphia Superior Court—District 13, Philadelphia, Pennsylvania
Debtor Name:	Philip Jones
Debtor Address:	3242 Wilson Ave. SW
Debtor City:	Philadelphia
Debtor State:	Pennsylvania
Debtor Zip:	98984
Amount Owed to Client:	$225,234
Type of Debt:	Mortgage
Type of Asset:	House at 3242 Wilson Ave SW, Philadelphia, Pennsylvania

Merge function

MERGED DOCUMENT—Complaint

In the Philadelphia Superior Court – District 13, Philadelphia, Pennsylvania

First National Bank

Plaintiff

Case No. 2012-9353

Philip Jones
3242 Wilson Ave. SW
Philadelphia, Pennsylvania 98984

Defendant.

COMPLAINT

Comes now plaintiff, First National Bank, and states that the defendant, Philip Jones, is indebted to the plaintiff in the amount of $225,234 on a mortgage regarding a house at 3242 Wilson Ave SW, Philadelphia, Pennsylvania. Attached to this complaint as Appendix "A" is a fully executed copy of the mortgage above referenced.

DOCUMENT TEMPLATE 1—Complaint

In the {Court}
{Client Name}
Plaintiff
Case No. {Case Number}

{Debtor Name}
{Debtor Address}
{Debtor City} {Debtor State} {Debtor Zip}

Defendant.

COMPLAINT

Comes now plaintiff, {Client Name}, and states that defendant, {Debtor Name}, is indebted to plaintiff in the amount of {Amount Owed to Client} on a {Type of Debt} regarding a {Type of Asset}. Attached to this complaint as Appendix "A" is a fully executed copy of the mortgage above referenced.

case management system, but the rest of the corporation was using Outlook, the two could be set up to share and/or synchronize information so that the entries in the case management program would not have to be entered manually in Outlook.

Conflict of Interest Searches

Most case management programs allow users to do conflict of interest searches. Because the database tracks clients, parties, counsel, and an enormous amount of other case-related information, the conflict search can be very comprehensive. In Exhibit 5–14, the user executed a conflict of interest search on "Richards." The case management program returned with two possible hits, a matter/case (*Richards v. EZ Pest Control*), and a contact name-client (*Sherry Richards*).

Email Interface

Most case management programs include an email interface that allows users to send emails in conjunction with the program and to link emails with cases. This is

Conflicts of interest
search for "Richards"

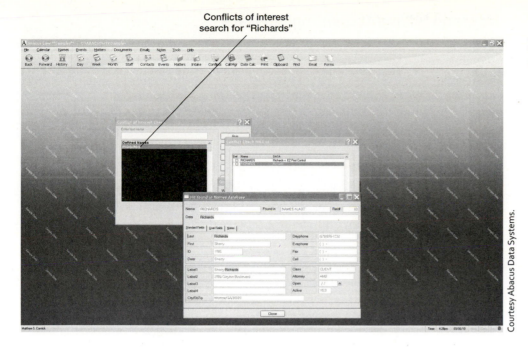

EXHIBIT 5–14

Conflict of interest check

Courtesy Abacus Data Systems.

extremely important given the heavy use of emails in communicating with clients and in handling client matters.

Document Tracking

Most case management programs can now associate documents with cases. A link can be made between a document or file and a matter or contact in a case management program. This allows legal professionals to index and manage case documents directly from the case management program. Exhibit 5–15 shows that a user has linked the electronic "COMPLAINT" word-processing file with the matter and name of the client. Thus, when you pull up the matter window, you can click the Linked Documents tab and see a list of all of the electronic documents in that case.

Linked documents   Path

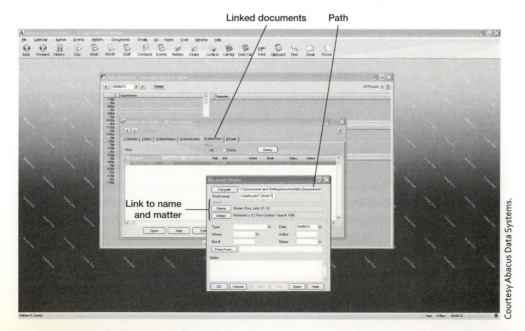

Link to name
and matter

EXHIBIT 5–15

Linking documents to matters, cases, and/or contracts

Courtesy Abacus Data Systems.

Time and Billing/Accounting Interface

Many case management programs share information with timekeeping and billing programs, and in some instances with accounting programs as well. Thus, when you create a case event (such as an appointment), you can automatically generate a time record for the event without having to retype all the information. Some case management programs have separate time and billing modules available for purchase, whereas others can interface with many popular legal time and billing programs.

Reporting

Most computerized systems allow users to generate a vast number of standard reports covering every aspect of case management. Most systems also come with a report writer feature that enables users to write customized reports and queries.

IMPLEMENTING CASE MANAGEMENT SYSTEMS—WHY THEY FAIL

Much has been written in the legal press regarding the fact that while case management programs have never been better, many legal organizations have been slow to implement them. Even when they have been purchased and implemented, it appears that many legal professionals are not using them. A commonly mentioned reason why legal professionals fail to use case management systems is a simple lack of training. This problem has two facets. First, because a case management system can be expensive, a firm may stop short of purchasing the training tools needed to train staff to use the new system. Second, overly busy legal professionals may not attend the training that is offered.

THE DOCKET CYCLE

The docket cycle refers to how information is entered into a case management program. There are three primary ways in which information can flow into and out of such a program: centralized, decentralized, and combined cycles.

Centralized Docket Control Cycle

In a centralized docket control cycle, one person typically is responsible for inputting all docket entries into the case management program. This is usually a secretary, but in some cases may be a paralegal. In this type of system, step one is for a user to manually complete a docket slip. The second step is for the secretary/keyer to enter the event into the docket control program. The third step is for reports to be generated, and the last step is for entries to be marked "done."

Decentralized Docket Control Cycle

In a decentralized docket control cycle, each user enters docket information directly into the computer, controlling his or her own docket. In this type of system, the first step is for the user to make a docket entry in the case management program. Next, the user views or prints reports as necessary; third, the user marks entries "done." The advantage of this system is that users have ultimate control over their own dockets. The disadvantage is that each user, instead of a clerk or secretary, is doing data entry.

Combined Docket Control Cycle

In a combined docket control cycle, a user can decide whether to enter information into the program or have a clerk/secretary do it. Some docket control programs allow multiple people to enter data into a user's schedule. For example, some networked docket programs allow both an attorney and her secretary to enter information into the attorney's schedule. Both have full access to the attorney's calendar.

In this type of system, the first step is for either the user or a third party to make a docket entry in the case management program. Second, either the user or the third party views or prints reports as necessary; third, either the user or the third party marks entries "done." In some ways, this is the best of both worlds: The user still has control over his calendar, but can delegate the data entry to someone else.

ETHICAL AND MALPRACTICE CONSIDERATIONS

The ramifications of missing deadlines and otherwise failing to track the progress of cases can be severe. In fact, two types of negative outcomes can result from case neglect: an ethics board proceeding against the attorney and/or a legal malpractice claim filed against the attorney or firm. An attorney who neglects a case can be disciplined by a state ethics board. Discipline in an ethics case may include reprimand, suspension, or even disbarment. In a legal malpractice case, the attorney involved is sued for damages for providing substandard legal work. These types of cases are not remote or obscure. Thousands of legal ethics and malpractice proceedings are filed throughout the country every year alleging case neglect.

Ethical Considerations

A nationwide statistical study of attorney disciplinary opinions found that the two primary reasons that clients file disciplinary proceedings against attorneys, and that courts discipline attorneys, are (1) attorneys failing to communicate with the clients and (2) attorneys neglecting or not diligently pursuing client cases. This confirms what studies have shown since the early 1980s. Both of these problems are easily preventable when attorneys and paralegals use good docket control systems and effective time management.

It is common for state rules of professional conduct to provide guidance on these issues. They typically state that attorneys should be competent in the area in which they practice and that they should be reasonably prepared to represent the client. These state rules also state that the attorney must act with reasonable diligence and promptness when representing a client. Finally, an attorney must keep the client reasonably informed about what is going on with representation of the client.

Competence and Adequate Preparation An attorney must be competent to represent the client. That is, the attorney must have a reasonable knowledge of the area of law in which the client needs representation, or, if the attorney does not know the area of law well, must put in the preparation time to become familiar enough with the case area to represent the client adequately.

The amount of preparation considered "adequate" depends on the type of legal matter the client presents. Major litigation, for example, will require far more preparation time than drafting a simple will. The point is that attorneys should not undertake to represent a client if for some reason they cannot do it with the required skill and/or cannot dedicate an appropriate amount of preparation time.

Diligence Attorneys must act with a reasonable degree of diligence in pursuing the client's case. Attorneys should carry through to conclusion all legal matters undertaken for a client unless the relationship is properly and clearly terminated. If doubt exists about whether an attorney-client relationship exists, the attorney should clarify the situation in writing.

Communication with Clients An attorney also must communicate regularly with a client. Legal professionals need to keep in reasonable contact with the client, both to explain general strategy and to keep the client reasonably informed regarding the status of the client's legal matter. "Reasonableness" always depends on the facts and circumstances of the particular case.

Clients become extremely frustrated when they pay for legal services and then the attorney refuses to take their calls, answer their letters, or otherwise communicate with them. Often, paralegals are more accessible to clients than attorneys are, so they can play an important role in communicating with clients.

Legal Malpractice Considerations

In addition to the ethical breaches involved in neglect of a client's legal matter, the client may have a legal malpractice claim against the attorney for negligence. The general theory in a **legal malpractice** claim is that the attorney breached an ordinary standard of care applicable to a reasonable attorney under those circumstances. In a legal malpractice case, both the plaintiff and the defendant must rely on attorneys who are expert witnesses to testify that the defendant either did or did not act as a reasonable attorney would have in the same situation.

A computerized case management system that is used correctly and effectively will greatly decrease an attorney's or law office's chances of being the subject of ethical complaints or malpractice suits. In fact, some malpractice insurers will refuse to write malpractice insurance for a law office that does not have an effective docket control system. However, ultimately the responsibility lies with the individuals working at the law office. Even the most technologically advanced software cannot prevent an attorney or paralegal from forgetting to enter a deadline in the case management system or putting in a wrong date when entering a docketing deadline.

---

legal malpractice
An attorney's breach of an ordinary standard of care that a reasonable attorney would have adhered to under the same circumstances.

SUMMARY

The practice of law involves many appointments, deadlines, hearings, and other commitments that must be carefully tracked. Docketing means entering, organizing, and controlling appointments and deadlines for a legal organization. Database programs, including case or practice management computer systems, offer legal organizations a wide variety of features for doing these tasks, including docket control, contact information, case notes, document assembly, document tracking, integrated billing, email, and conflict checking. Personal information managers such as Outlook are contact- and calendar-based programs, as opposed to case management systems, which are matter- or case-based systems.

Case management programs can link and create relationships among contact information, matters/cases, events, and documents and combine them into one integrated system. Other features include various calendar views, date calculators, notes/case diaries, synchronization with PIMs and PDAs, time and billing interfaces, and reporting capabilities.

The docket control cycle of tracking legal/case events differs depending on whether a legal organization has a centralized, decentralized, or combined procedure for entering docket entries into its docket system.

Manual docket systems are prone to mistakes, are slow and cumbersome to administer, are generally inflexible, and cannot provide the amount or quality of information that a computerized case management system can.

A legal organization can use either generic calendaring programs or true case management software for docket control. Computerized case management systems can perform functions such as maintaining perpetual calendars, making recurring entries, alerting the user to possible scheduling conflicts, providing for centralized or decentralized case management, generating past due reports, performing document assembly, and tracking case information. Most case management programs can also generate many types of reports, such as daily calendar reports for an individual or a firm, per-case docket reports, and free time reports.

Attorneys and law firms that fail to maintain an accurate docketing system may be subject to malpractice lawsuits and sanctions such as disbarment or suspension from the practice of law.

KEY TERMS

calendaring	docket control	record
case management	field	recurring entry
data value	form	report
database	legal malpractice	rule-based entry
database management system (DBMS)	personal information manager (PIM)	statute of limitations
	query	table

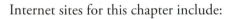

INTERNET SITES

Internet sites for this chapter include:

ORGANIZATION	PRODUCT/SERVICE	WORLD WIDE WEB ADDRESS
Abacus Data Systems	AbacusLaw (legal PIM/case management)	www.abacuslaw.com
ADC Legal Systems	Practice management system	www.perfectpractice.com
Amicus Attorney	Amicus Attorney legal case management	www.amicusattorney.com
Bridgeway Software	Law Quest (case management for corporate law departments)	www.bridge-way.com
Chesapeake Interlink, Ltd.	Practice management system specializing in personal injury practices	www.needleslaw.com
Client Profiles	Practice management system	www.clientprofiles.com
Compulaw	Compulaw (case management)	www.compulaw.com
Corporate Legal Solutions, Inc.	Practice management system for corporate legal departments	www.caseandpoint.com
Corprasoft, Inc.	Practice management system for corporate legal departments	www.corprasoft.com
Lawex Corp.	Legal case management	www.trialworks.com
Legal Files Software	Legal Files (legal PIM/case management)	www.legalfiles.com
LegalEdge Software	Case management for criminal defense law offices, attorneys, prosecutors, and general practitioners	www.legaledge.com
LexisNexis	Time Matters (legal PIM/case management)	www.timematters.com
Orion Law Management Systems	Practice management system	www.orionlaw.com
Perfect Law Software	Practice management system	www.perfectlaw.com
RainMaker Software	Practice management system	www.rainmakerlegal.com
Software Technology	Tabs3 and PracticeMaster (legal PIM/case management)	www.tabs3.com
Solutions in Software, Inc.	Practice management system	www.casemanagerpro.com
Thomson Elite	Elite practice management system and Pro Law practice management system	www.elite.com

TEST YOUR KNOWLEDGE

1. True or False: An application program that stores and searches data is called a database.

2. A _____ is a collection of related information stored in rows and columns.

3. True or False: Calendaring and docket control are purely secretarial functions with little relationship to the practice of law.

4. _____ is a legal-specific term that always means more than just tracking appointments and schedules.

5. What is the difference between PIMs and case management programs?

6. Case management systems allow users to link or create relationships among which types of information? (name three)

7. What is a rule-based case management event entry?

8. What benefits do document assembly features offer to case management users?

9. True or False: Case management systems are universally accepted in most law offices and have a high success rate when they are implemented.

10. True or False: There is virtually no connection or relationship among ethical claims, legal malpractice, case management, and docket control.

ON THE WEB EXERCISES

1. Research and write a paper on computerized case management and docket control systems. Use one of the websites in the "Internet Sites" section of this chapter. Obtain demonstration copies of the programs if you can. Compare and contrast at least two of the different products that are available. Which one were you most impressed with, and why?

2. Visit several bar association websites (including that of the Georgia Bar Association, at www.gabar.org) and find three articles on case management, docket control, or a related subject. Write a short paper summarizing the articles you found.

3. Visit the American Bar Association Technology Resource Center at www.abanet.org, and review any materials it provides on case management software. Write a short paper summarizing the article(s) you found.

4. Using a law library, state bar journal, legal research database, or the Internet, write a paper that summarizes a minimum of three attorney discipline cases regarding failure to complete work on time. Be sure to include an analysis of the case, the court's or tribunal's findings, the ethical rules that were at issue, the rules that were violated, and what discipline was imposed.

QUESTIONS AND EXERCISES

1. A legal organization is considering moving to a computerized case management system even though its manual system has worked adequately. Give some reasons why a computerized case management system is a good idea for this organization.

2. A medium-sized law firm handles most of its cases by appointing an attorney and a paralegal for every case. How can a computerized case management system help in this situation?

3. Several of your firm's clients have complained because they never get notice of what is going on with their cases, what deadlines have been set, or even when to call after a major event has taken place in their cases. How could a case management system help?

4. Research your state bar's disciplinary proceedings regarding attorneys who have been disciplined for client neglect. Write a short paper on one of the cases.

5. Contact three legal organizations in your area, find out how they control or manage their dockets (manual or computer method), explain their procedures in detail, and then compare and contrast the three.

6. Set up and maintain a docket of class assignments for a semester using a PIM such as Outlook or a word processor. For quizzes and assignments, give yourself one three-day reminder before the assignment or quiz is due, in addition to recording the quiz or assignment itself. For exams or lengthy papers, give yourself three reminders: a ten-day reminder, a five-day reminder, and a three-day reminder, in addition to docketing the exam date or paper deadline itself.

ETHICS QUESTION

A law firm has just installed the latest and greatest case management program. The attorneys and paralegals diligently attended all of the training classes required to master the new software program. All client and case matter information was uploaded into the new program. However, when inputting data, one of the paralegals entered the wrong date for a court hearing on an opposing party's motion for summary judgment. The opposing party won its motion by default because the law firm failed to appear on behalf of its client. What ethical issues, if any, are raised by this scenario?

Go to the Workbook to complete the Hands-On Exercises.

Access an interactive eBook, chapter-specific interactive learning tools, including flash cards, quizzes, and more in your Paralegal CourseMate, accessed through CengageBrain.com.

CHAPTER 6

Electronic Discovery

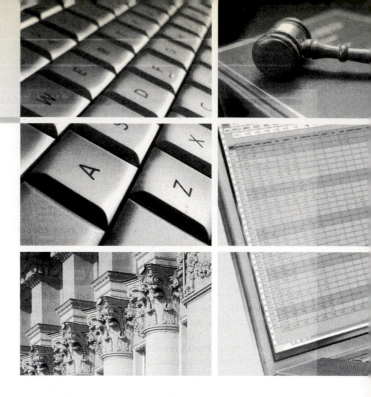

CHAPTER OBJECTIVES

After completing this chapter, you should be able to do the following:

1. Explain why electronic discovery is an important aspect of litigation.
2. Identify the term that the Federal Rules of Civil Procedure use for all electronic data, and understand its scope.
3. Explain the purpose of the "meet and confer" pretrial conference that parties must have pursuant to the Federal Rules of Civil Procedure.
4. Discuss the duty of parties to preserve electronic information.
5. Understand the different steps of an electronic discovery procedure.
6. Explain what native and image formats are.

ELECTRONIC DISCOVERY OVERVIEW

electronic discovery (e-discovery)

The process of producing and receiving litigation documents in electronic format.

discovery

The pretrial stage of litigation where parties disclose to each other information about their case.

Electronic discovery or **e-discovery** refers to the process of producing and receiving litigation documents in electronic format. The **discovery** stage of litigation, which takes place before trial, is when parties disclose information about the case to each other. For decades, discovery has revolved around (1) taking pretrial oral testimony from parties and witnesses in the form of depositions; (2) the exchange of written requests for information and interrogatories, and the responses to these requests; (3) the exchange of statements of fact, called requests for admissions, which each party must admit or deny; and (4) the production of hard-copy documents in response to either a *subpoena duces tecum* (a command for a witness to appear at a certain time and place and bring documents or records) or a request for the production of documents. Document production is a crucial aspect of discovery because documents sometimes tell a story different from that of witnesses. Documents can establish facts and timelines, support conclusions, reveal complex ideas, and support inferences that are vital to any litigation.

For decades, documents have been produced in hard-copy format. In complex litigation, each party would send a request for the production of documents; in response, the other party would copy the documents (sometimes hundreds or even thousands of boxes) and give the copies to the requesting party. The requesting party would then have to sort through the boxes by hand, gleaning information slowly to learn what it could about each document and the relevance of that document to the case issues.

The use of computers in all sizes of businesses and in every aspect of life has fundamentally altered how information is exchanged. Today, most "documents" are created in an electronic format (on a computer). Recent studies have shown that more than 95 percent of all documents are now electronic. Web pages, databases, emails, word-processing files, spreadsheets, accounting information, billings, payroll, corporate records, personal digital assistant (PDA) files, and other documents are all stored electronically. North Americans alone send approximately 4 trillion emails each day. Practically every document produced in most organizations, large or small, is created or transmitted in an electronic format.

Many courts have held that the production of hard-copy documents when electronic versions are available is unacceptable. These courts have been on the forefront of mandating the production of electronic documents. The federal courts, for example, have adopted rules regarding the discovery of electronic documents. However, electronic documents are not tangible, unlike hard-copy documents, which can be read by anyone, which have physical dimensions, and which can be observed and examined. Electronic documents thus present many more complexities and problems than hard-copy materials when it comes to producing them in litigation.

Electronic information is said to be distributed, meaning that it is not held in just one place. Electronic information in large organizations can be dispersed among hundreds of servers, thousands of desktop computers, thousands of laptops, and hundreds or thousands of PDAs, thumb drives, CD-ROMs, DVDs, and even home computers when employees have taken documents home to work on them. Controlling, discovering, and copying information in a distributed electronic environment is not easy. Also, many companies outsource goods, services, information, administration, operations, production, technology, and other functions. Controlling and discovering information in an outsourced environment is not easy, either.

Electronic documents exist in countless formats, a fact that increases the complexity of producing and reading those documents. Some documents are in standard formats, but many others come from completely proprietary systems owned, licensed, and controlled by vendors. Computer systems themselves come from a large variety of manufacturers, and many of these systems are not necessarily standard. Just accessing data from all of these computer systems and file formats is a daunting task. Computers run a variety of operating systems; come in different sizes; and have various memory, components, and other hardware and software that further increase the complexity of producing electronic documents in litigation.

It is easy to destroy a paper document; it is difficult to destroy an electronic document. As we will see, a single document can exist in many different electronic files—and "delete" does not really mean delete. It is difficult to alter a paper document; it is easy to alter an electronic document. Furthermore, every time you look at an electronic file (even if you do not make any changes to it), you may well change the document's metadata (which is considered an integral part of the document itself). People understand what a paper document is. Very few people (and even fewer lawyers) have any understanding of what an electronic document really is. That is the essence of the problem presented by electronically stored information (ESI).

All of these issues, and many more, make the exchange of electronic data inherently complex. Why is this an important issue for paralegals? Because paralegals have historically been the legal professionals with "boots on the ground" handling, tracking, and managing document production. In many legal organizations, paralegals are the ones working with clients and vendors regarding electronic document requests.

More than ever before, paralegals must have outstanding technological skills to be effective.

Chapter 7 discusses litigation support software, which is closely associated with electronic discovery. However, although electronic discovery and litigation support are pieces of the same puzzle and are closely aligned, they are different. Electronic discovery is the process of receiving or providing electronic information during the discovery process. In contrast, litigation support software organizes, stores, retrieves, and summarizes the information acquired through discovery for use in litigation.

THE FEDERAL RULES OF CIVIL PROCEDURE AND ELECTRONICALLY STORED INFORMATION

The Federal Rules of Civil Procedure (FRCP) were amended in December 2006 specifically to address the issue of electronic discovery. Some state courts have followed the lead of the federal courts and adopted similar rules. It is certain that additional states will do so in the next few years. The FRCP now refer to any electronic data as **electronically stored information (ESI)**. FRCP 34(a) states that ESI includes "writings, drawings, graphs, charts, photographs, sound recordings, images, and other data compilations stored in any medium from which information can be obtained or translated." ESI is a term of art, and it is used broadly by the FRCP so that any new form of electronic information will be covered by the rules.

> The wide variety of computer systems currently in use, and the rapidity of technological change, counsel against a limiting or precise definition of electronically stored information. Rule 34(a)(1) is expansive and includes any type of information that is stored electronically. A common example often sought in discovery is electronic communications, such as email. The rule covers—either as documents or as electronically stored information—information "stored in any medium," to encompass future developments in computer technology. Rule 34(a)(1) is intended to be broad enough to cover all current types of computer-based information, and flexible enough to encompass future changes and developments. References elsewhere in the rules to "electronically stored information" should be understood to invoke this expansive approach. (FRCP, Rule 34, Comment from 2006 Amendment.)

Mandatory Meet and Confer Sessions

FRCP 26(f) clearly states that as soon as practicable, attorneys for the parties must meet and confer to discuss issues related to ESI, including the preservation of discoverable information and any issues relating to disclosure or discovery of ESI, such as the format(s) in which ESI should be produced.

The rules create an expectation that the attorneys involved will work collaboratively regarding the exchange of ESI, that games of "hide the ball" should not take place, and that any matters related to the production of ESI will be openly discussed early in the case. The Judicial Conference Rules Advisory Committee noted that "the parties' discussion should pay particular attention to the balance between the competing needs to preserve relevant evidence and to continue routine operations critical to ongoing activities." Another goal of the meet and confer session is for the parties to understand the volume of the materials to be reviewed, sampled, and possibly produced. Businesses, particularly large ones, have an enormous volume of data (terabytes of information representing tens of millions of pages of hard-copy data), and the parties need to come to terms with what is discoverable (that is, what is and is not subject to the rules of formal discovery).

---

electronically stored information (ESI)
The term used by the Federal Rules of Civil Procedure to refer to all electronic data, including writings, drawings, graphs, charts, photographs, sound recordings, images, and other data compilations stored in any medium from which information can be obtained or translated.

The Challenges of Electronically Stored Information

An electronic document differs from a paper document in many ways. The existence (or nonexistence) and replication of ESI are two of the most important.

There's So Much of It   The staggering amount of ESI is compounded by the fact that ESI can replicate itself without the user realizing it. For example, if I hand you a printed document, only one copy of the document exists unless you or I consciously create one or more copies. ESI seems to have a mind of its own. For example, when I send you an email, there is a copy on your computer. And a copy on my computer. And one on your server. And one on my server. And whenever one of our systems makes a backup copy of the electronic data, there's another copy. If you forwarded the email to someone, or if I had sent the email to five people, then even more copies of the email would have been created. And what if my original email evokes a response? The response email may contain the original email within it. That creates even more copies.

In addition, whenever you create a Word document or Excel spreadsheet, as you are working on the document, your computer is making "temporary" backup copies of the data. These copies are deleted when you save the document, but (as we shall see) delete does not always mean delete. Along the same lines, whenever you print a document or a screen off the Internet or a photo from a flash drive, the computer creates a copy of the image (called a spool file) and prints the spool file. The spool file is then deleted . . . or is it? A computer may retain copies of images it has printed even if those images were never saved on the computer.

Where does ESI come from? Nowadays, it can come from almost anywhere. It can be gleaned from:

- Computers (home and office; desktop and laptop)
- Network drives and servers
- Electronic storage devices (CDs, DVDs, flash drives, backup tapes, external hard drives)
- PDAs, BlackBerries, iPods, iPads, MP3 players
- Cell phones
- Instant messages (IMs)
- Voice mail
- Web history

Also consider that relevant information may be available from sources such as:

- Records from a credit card company, providing details of a consumer's purchase
- A hotel or office building, providing information regarding the use of a hotel room key or pass card
- An automobile computer, providing information regarding details of use of the car at a particular time (speed, brake usage)
- Global Positioning System (GPS) devices in automobiles and cell phones, which may be able to pinpoint a person's location at a particular time

A printed document has no secrets: What you see is what there is. In contrast, an electronic document has so much more than just its apparent content; it has metadata. Metadata is information about the document, such as the precise time the document was created, accessed, modified, and copied. However, every time you open a document—just open it—you may permanently change the metadata. That's because by opening the document (or, in some programs, just copying a file without opening the file), you change the date the file was last accessed. If opposing counsel requests the production of ESI and you copy the electronic files in an attempt to comply with the request, you may thereby permanently change the metadata. That can lead to sanctions; this is an example of spoliation.

You Can't Get Rid of ESI when You Want To As most folks now know, just hitting "delete" does not mean that a file is actually gone. When you delete a file, all you have done is made the disk space occupied by that file available to be written over. Depending on the computer's storage capacity, the size of the deleted file, and the amount of new data being put on the hard drive, it can be a long time before a "deleted" file is actually written over. Even then, computer forensic professionals may be able to recover the deleted information. In addition, sometimes only part of a deleted file is written over; the remaining disk space is called slack. So, even when a deleted file is partially written over, some of it may be relatively accessible. In addition, because there may be so many copies of an electronic file, unless you destroy all of the copies, the ESI will still exist.

Notwithstanding the foregoing, ESI is often destroyed at the most inconvenient times. Sometimes this spoliation is not intentional. Most businesses have a regular schedule, whereby old computer backup tapes are written over after a specific amount of time. Big problems can arise even when a party in litigation institutes a **litigation hold**: instructions designed to prevent the destruction of evidence, including ESI and its metadata, pending litigation. Numerous court decisions have held that litigants may be subject to sanctions if evidence is subsequently destroyed, even if steps were taken to prevent the destruction. According to the premiere e-discovery case, *Zubulake v. UBS Warburg*, once a party is aware that litigation is likely, that party has an affirmative obligation to prevent the destruction of all relevant evidence, including metadata.

Duty to Exchange and Preserve Electronically Stored Information

The FRCP, in no uncertain terms, specifically require that the parties preserve and exchange ESI. No longer can there be any argument that electronic data are not discoverable under the FRCP because they are somehow not "documents." FRCP Rule 26(a)(1)(B) provides that "without awaiting a discovery request," a party *must* provide to the other party "a copy of, or a description by category and location of, all documents, electronically stored information, and tangible things" that are in that party's possession or control. The FRCP therefore make it mandatory for the parties to disclose the existence and location of ESI even before they receive discovery requests. In addition, FRCP Rule 34(a) specifically requires that the producing party allow the requesting party to copy, test, and sample discoverable information, including ESI. This is particularly important when large amounts of data might have to be produced. This allows the requesting party to look at and inspect data, including the format of the data, before it is actually produced. **Sampling data** also refers to the process of testing a database to see if it contains information relevant to the subject matter of the case. The FRCP contemplate a very open environment regarding the preservation and exchange of ESI. An important thing to note, in FRCP Rule 34(b)(iii), is that a producing party only has to produce information in one form; hence, if a producing party produces ESI, it need not also produce hard copies.

In addition, as soon as a potential party reasonably anticipates litigation, it becomes obligated to preserve electronic data. Most businesses routinely discard, erase, or write over their electronic records. Upon the reasonable anticipation of litigation, parties must stop their normal practice of document destruction and put a litigation

litigation hold
An order suspending destruction or disposal of all relevant hard-copy and electronically stored information, instituted when a party reasonably anticipates litigation.

sampling data
The process of testing data to determine if it is appropriate for production.

hold in place. A litigation hold for ESI would include stopping all destruction of data possibly relevant to the subject matter of the litigation, no matter what its form; the hold extends to emails, voicemails, calendars, information in handheld devices, word-processing files, spreadsheets, databases, hard disk drives, and all other forms of ESI. Failure to institute or comply with a litigation hold may lead to claims that the ESI was subjected to spoliation. **Spoliation** refers to the destruction or alteration of relevant documents or other evidence in litigation.

In one case, an organization terminated an employee for viewing sexually explicit material on the Internet. The employee sued, alleging racial discrimination and claiming that someone had either stolen his password and used his computer to view the material, or that a previous user of the hard drive had viewed the material. The employee argued that the hard drive would prove his innocence. Unfortunately, the organization's IT staff wiped the drive clean, reformatted it, and reissued it to another employee. The court stopped short of actually fining the organization, but in its ruling it strongly reprimanded the organization for destroying the central piece of evidence in the case.

The seminal case in this area is *Zubulake v. UBS Warburg* (actually, a series of cases decided in the U.S. District Court for the Southern District of New York). The genesis of these cases is a claim of employment discrimination. In the ensuing litigation, the female employee requested that the corporation produce hundreds of emails, which she argued would bolster her claim of discrimination. The corporation reported that the emails were no longer available, having been deleted from the corporation's computers. The Court ruled that the defendant had a duty to maintain the emails and a duty not to delete the emails. Further, that duty was triggered by the corporation's knowledge that an employee was complaining about sexual harassment and that it was likely litigation would result.

The Electronic Format of ESI

The electronic format in which ESI is produced is extremely important. FRCP 34(b) allows the requesting party, at least initially, to specify the form in which the ESI is to be produced. The producing party can object to the form requested, but must specifically state the reason for the objection and what format it proposes to use for the ESI. FRCP Rule 34(b)(i) requires that a party producing ESI shall produce it as it is kept in the usual course of business, and goes on to say, in 34(b)(ii), that if the requesting party does not specify a format, the responding party is required to produce the ESI in the format in which it is ordinarily maintained or in reasonably usable format (see FRCP Rule 34(b)). For example, suppose a Microsoft Word 2003 file is subject to production in discovery. In Microsoft Word 2003, the native format of a Word file is ".doc." That is, Microsoft Word 2003 files all have the file extension ".doc" (e.g., "letter.doc"). Would it be acceptable for the producer to produce the ".doc" file in a PDF format instead of its native ".doc" format? If the request for production did not state a format, then the production in PDF—a reasonably usable format—would most likely be allowed. Native format (discussed later in this chapter) generally refers to the file structure/program in which a piece of information was originally created. If the requesting party had wanted a Microsoft Word 2003 file to be produced as a ".doc" file, the request should have specifically so stated.

No Duty to Produce Inaccessible Data if There Is Undue Burden or Undue Cost

The FRCP create two classes of ESI: **accessible data** and **inaccessible data**. FRCP Rule 26(b)(2)(B) says that ESI need not be produced if the source is not reasonably

spoliation
The destruction of relevant documents (or other materials) in litigation.

accessible data
Data that have not been deleted and can be accessed without the use of special tools and/or software.

inaccessible data
Data that can be accessed only with the use of special tools and/or software.

accessible because of undue burden or undue cost. If the producing party uses this rule to avoid discovery, it must be ready to give specific factual reasons to back up its claims of inaccessibility. In addition, some courts have allowed the requesting party's expert to examine the system in question to determine whether the ESI is in fact inaccessible. ESI that might fall into this category includes electronic data that have been erased, fragmented, or stored on out-of-date storage systems that are no longer supported by the organization. In any case, the producing party may still be required to produce the ESI if the requesting party can show that the information is important, relevant, and unavailable from any other source.

Claims of Privilege Can Be Asserted after Inadvertent Production

Information obtained within the context of a privileged communication (such as between attorney and client, doctor and patient or between spouses) is generally outside the scope of discovery. Federal Rule of Civil Procedure 26(b)(5)(B) provides a process for a producing party to recover information that was inadvertently produced when it was in fact privileged. This is sometimes referred to as the **clawback** provision. When producing parties are requested to produce millions of pages of ESI, it is probable (perhaps highly likely) that from time to time privileged information will be inadvertently produced. If this happens, the rule states that the party receiving the information "must promptly return, sequester or destroy the specified information and any copies it has and may not use or disclose the information until the claim is resolved." The receiving party may also bring the matter to the court to decide if the ESI is in fact privileged.

clawback
The ability to have privileged material that has been produced inadvertently returned with no waiver of privilege.

Safe Harbor Regarding Electronic Information Lost through Routine, Good-Faith Operation of an Electronic Information System

According to the FRCP, parties that act in good faith but inadvertently destroy ESI during routine operation of their information systems are not subject to sanctions. This **safe harbor** provision covers inadvertent routine deletion of information such as emails to create additional space, or the regularly scheduled recycling of backup tapes. Rule 37(f) of the FRCP states that "a court may not impose sanctions under these rules on a party for failing to provide electronically stored information lost as a result of the routine, good-faith operation of an electronic information system." This rule assumes, however, that the party in question has acted in good faith, including discussing the issue of preservation of ESI with the other party, putting a litigation hold in place, and making some effort to not intentionally destroy ESI.

safe harbor
A provision of the FRCP providing that parties who act in good faith but inadvertently destroy ESI as a routine part of their information systems handling are not subject to sanctions for that destruction.

PRODUCING AND RECEIVING ESI

When it comes to ESI, legal professionals must be prepared both to request ESI from other parties and to assist the client in producing the client's own ESI for other parties. Reduced to its essence, e-discovery is not significantly different from traditional discovery. Parties must be sure to preserve and assemble the requested material; the material must be reviewed and culled to remove privileged, irrelevant, or redundant material; and it must be produced to the requesting party. Still, the devil is in the details, and there are details aplenty in e-discovery. Let's look at how e-discovery differs from traditional discovery.

EXHIBIT 6–1

Electronic discovery
reference model

Electronic Discovery Reference Model

Electronic Discovery Reference Model / © 2009 / v2.0 / edrm.net

Courtesy of EDRM [edrm.net].

Exhibit 6–1 shows the Electronic Discovery Reference Model (courtesy of edrm. net), which describes the following stages of e-discovery:

Information management—Getting your electronic house in order to mitigate risk and expenses should e-discovery become an issue, from initial creation of electronically stored information through its final disposition.

Identification—Locating potential sources of ESI and determining its scope, breadth, and depth.

Preservation—Ensuring that ESI is protected against inappropriate alteration or destruction.

Collection—Gathering ESI for further use in the e-discovery process (processing, review, etc.).

Processing—Reducing the volume of ESI and converting it, if necessary, to forms more suitable for review and analysis.

Review—Evaluating ESI for relevance and privilege.

Analysis—Evaluating ESI for content and context, including key patterns, topics, people, and discussion.

Production—Delivering ESI to others in appropriate forms and using appropriate delivery mechanisms.

Presentation—Displaying ESI before audiences (at depositions, hearings, trials, etc.), especially in native and near-native forms, to elicit further information, validate existing facts or positions, or persuade an audience.

Clients Must Preserve ESI: Preservation Letter to Client

Early in the process (even before an actual case is filed), attorneys and paralegals must inform clients that they must not destroy ESI. This includes not deleting emails, reformatting hard drives, destroying backup tapes, or otherwise erasing data that might be discoverable in litigation. Legal staff should also document the instructions and process in a preservation letter to the client, so it can be proven at a later time, should the issue arise, that there was no intentional destruction of ESI.

Sending a Preservation Letter to the Opposing Party

If the opposing party has ESI, it is recommended that a preservation letter be sent as soon as possible, even before litigation is commenced, to the party or its counsel

EXHIBIT 6–2

Sample preservation letter (requesting institution of litigation hold)

Dear Sir or Madam:

As critical evidence in this matter exists in the form of Electronically Stored Information ("ESI") contained in the computer systems of ABC Company, this is a notice and demand that such evidence identified below in paragraphs 2 through 5 be immediately preserved and retained by ABC Company until further written notice from the undersigned. This request is essential, as the printed contents of text and images contained in a computer file do not completely reflect all information contained within the electronic file. Additionally, the continued operation of the computer systems identified herein will likely result in the destruction or spoliation of relevant ESI due to the fact that electronic evidence can be easily altered, deleted, or otherwise modified. Failure to preserve and retain the ESI outlined in this notice will subject ABC Company to legal claims for damages and/or evidentiary and monetary sanctions.

1. For purposes of this notice, "Electronically Stored Information" shall include, but not be limited to, all text files, spreadsheets, email files and information concerning email (including logs of email history and usage, header information and any "deleted" files), Internet history files and preferences, graphical image files (including .JPG, .GIF, .BMP, and TIFF files), databases, calendar and scheduling information, computer system activity logs, and all file fragments and backup files containing ESI.

2. Please preserve and retain all ESI generated or received by [insert appropriate date].

3. Please preserve and retain all ESI containing any information about [insert appropriate date].

4. Unless and until all potentially relevant ESI has been preserved, ABC Company must refrain from operating (or removing or altering fixed or external drives and media attached thereto) stand-alone personal computers, network workstations, notebook and/or laptop computers used by [insert names of appropriate persons].

5. ABC Company must retain and preserve all backup tapes or other storage media, whether on-line or off-line, and refrain from overwriting or deleting information contained thereon, which may contain ESI identified in paragraphs 2 through 4.

stating that ESI should not be destroyed (see Exhibit 6–2). It is recommended that this letter be as specific as possible, because normal business operations must still continue and an overly broad letter will make compliance difficult and burdensome. A specific preservation letter puts the other parties on notice regarding what type of information they should be preserving. A specific request issued early in the matter makes it difficult for the other side to argue that ESI was accidentally deleted. If specific hard drives are at issue in a case, the preservation letter should also state that new software, encryption, defragmenting, data compression, and other processes that change the file structure of the hard disk should not be implemented until a copy of the hard drive is secured.

Items to Be Negotiated between the Attorneys/Parties at the Meet and Confer Session

During the meet and confer session, the parties should negotiate agreements concerning the following items:

- Exchange of basic system data
- Exchange of listing of electronic collections of data
- Exchange of information related to backup and archival data and its preservation, including standard dates, times, and reuse of storage devices
- Discussion of how the principal actors store data (laptop, PDA, voicemail, email, calendar, word-processing, etc.)

- Agreement to a common document production format, including methods of dealing with native-format documents
- Whether metadata is being produced in whatever file formats are agreed to
- Any privilege related to ESI
- Disclosure of databases
- Any inaccessible data

Catalog All Client ESI

Before the meet and confer session takes place, the attorney and/or paralegal should meet with the client to specifically catalog and understand all sources of the client's ESI. The catalog is crucial in preparing for the meet and confer session, because the legal representatives must document exactly what the client has. In addition, it is important to document this process, because if opposing counsel later makes spoliation accusations, the attorneys will have documentation to support the claim that reasonable measures were taken to prevent loss of or damage to ESI. Exhibit 6–3 contains a sample checklist that can be used with clients to catalog their systems and ESI issues. Exhibit 6–3 can also be used as a tool when requesting ESI from the opposing party.

Assisting Clients in Producing ESI

Attorneys and paralegals should begin thinking about helping a client to produce ESI as soon as the client walks in the door. There are three primary ways for clients to produce ESI. The first is to hire a professional third-party vendor to go on site and assist the client's information technology (IT) staff in collecting the ESI. This has the advantage of involving a third party; if the opposing party claims that not all of the data was produced, the vendor can speak to the authenticity and completeness of the review. This is the easiest method for the law firm, but the most expensive one for the client. The second way is for the client to gather all the data and send it to the law firm. The success of this option depends on the expertise of the client's information technology staff. Also, it still leaves the client open to claims from the opposing side that not all of the information was produced. A third option is for the ESI to be remotely collected by a third-party vendor.

Each of these options has advantages and disadvantages. The decision should be made on a case-by-case basis depending on the unique circumstances in each instance.

Document Formats

Electronic documents can be saved in thousands of formats and structures. **Native format** refers to an associated file structure as defined by the original creating application. As noted earlier in this chapter, the native format for a Microsoft Word 2003 document is ".doc." Native formats cause problems because often the native format requires use of the original application to view or search a document. (For example, a copy of Microsoft Word 2003 may be needed to read and access a ".doc" file.) However, some large third-party vendors have developed proprietary software solutions that allow users to see ESI in native format without using or even having the original program.

Many electronic documents can be converted to vendor-neutral file structures such as PDF (Portable Document Format) or **TIFF (Tagged Image File Format)**. These are sometimes called **image format** or static-format file structures because the image of the document is displayed as it would have been in the original application, although the viewer need not have or use the original application to do so.

native format
A file structure as defined by the original application in which the file was created.

image format
A file structure that shows an image of a document as if it were being viewed in the original application, without the need to use or even have the original application.

TIFF (Tagged Image File Format)
A vendor-neutral file structure that produces image format documents.

Item	Date Range (x/xx/xx to xx/xx/xx)	Program Created In	Format of Data	Physical Location of Data	Estimated File Size/Volume
Email files and attachments					
Calendar files					
Contact/task list files					
Word-processing files					
Spreadsheet files					
Database files					
Graphic/sound files					
Accounting/billing/budgeting files					
Sales files					
Marketing files					
Internal/operations report files					
Payroll files					
PDF files					
Presentation files					
Files stored in file management systems					
Voicemail (and voicemail files in email)					
Network logs, audit trails, and monitoring software					
Data that is hosted by application service providers					
Internet-related files					
Intranet/Extranet					
Backup/archive data					
Personal digital assistants (PDAs) and smart phones					
Telephone logs					
Laptops					
Servers					
Portable storage devices (thumb drives, CD-ROMS, DVDs, zip disks, memory sticks, etc.)					
Disaster recovery storage and storage in other sites					
Home computers					

Listing of basic information system data, including

- Network type/configuration/structure
- Operating system
- Class/type of computers used
- All application programs (custom and off-the-shelf)
- Backup/archival systems and backup protocols
- Name of the system administrator
- Encryption systems (ask for keys)
- Email client/server
- Janitorial (email deletion) programs

EXHIBIT 6–3

Checklist of items to review for ESI

A downside of some image formats, such as TIFF, is that the metadata associated with the file are no longer present. In addition, some litigants have purposefully converted documents from a native format that the requesting party could process (such as Microsoft Word) to an image format, to remove the metadata and make it more expensive and difficult for the requesting party to work with the document. The PDF image format can associate metadata, so it offers an advantage over TIFF.

The term **legacy data** refers to information on obsolete computer media (anyone remember floppy disks?) or created using obsolete programs. Imagine finding some old disks that may or may not contain relevant information. What if reading the disks requires a computer program that is no longer on the market? These are problems we did not have when information existed only on paper. Law firms have to depend on the expertise of computer professionals to obtain and work with legacy data.

Metadata

Metadata is information stored electronically in files that may identify the origin, date, author, usage, comments, or other information about that file. Parties are generally entitled to the production of the metadata accompanying ESI. Parties often use metadata to prove their theory of a case. In one case, for example, a woman brought a class action against an employer, arguing that age was a determining factor in the employer's decision to lay off workers. The employee requested that the spreadsheets that had been used to analyze layoff options be produced in the native format, so the hidden formulas could be analyzed. The employer provided the spreadsheets with the cells locked so that the formulas and other metadata could not be viewed. The court ruled that the employer had to produce the documents in their native format, which included being able to access the metadata.

There are two different types of metadata: system metadata and application metadata. System metadata is information the computer operating system creates and uses to track the location of the data on the hard drive. Some examples include the file name; dates of creation, modification, printing, and so forth; and size of the file. To see this yourself, open a Microsoft Word file and then click on "Properties." You will see something similar to Exhibit 6–4; the first screen is an example of system metadata.

legacy data
Data created with obsolete computer media and programs.

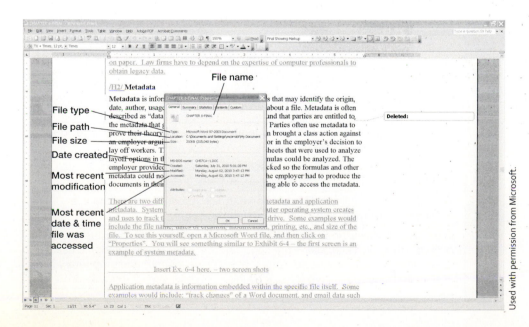

EXHIBIT 6–4A
System metadata

Used with permission from Microsoft.

EXHIBIT 6–4B

Application metadata

Application metadata is information embedded within the specific file itself. Some examples include Track Changes information in a Word document, and email data such as "From:," "To:," "Cc:," and the like. This metadata moves with a document when it is copied. The specific examples of application metadata will change depending on the specific computer application. The second screen in Exhibit 6–4 shows a typical email; some of the application metadata have been called out.

Using In-House Staff or Hiring Third-Party Vendors

When a party is producing documents pursuant to a production request, it is necessary to decide whether the party wants its own information technology department to prepare the ESI or whether a third-party vendor will be hired to coordinate the production. A number of factors must be weighed in this decision. Three key factors include the amount of data to be produced, the amount of time the party has to produce it, and the complexity of transferring the data itself. Exhibit 6–5 shows a process that a client and legal team might follow to produce documents in a case.

EXHIBIT 6–5

Steps in e-discovery production process

No.	E-Discovery Production Steps
1.	Legal team issues letter to client advising them to preserve data related to litigation.
2.	Legal team meets with client to discuss strategies and problems related to ESI early on in case, including cataloging the ESI and discussing any special problems (unique or uncommon file formats, location of files/access, dates of files that may be requested, and any problems such as backup issues, etc.)
3.	If litigation is imminent, client and legal team decide whether production will be handled by a third-party vendor or the client's internal information technology (IT) team.
4.	If a third party will be used, a request for proposal may be issued, bids received, and a vendor selected.
5.	Parties to the lawsuit have a meet and confer conference to disclose ESI information and try to reach an understanding/resolution on ESI issues, including format of requested ESI.
6.	Document request is received. Legal team analyzes the request and decides if a protective order should be sought.
7.	Legal team meets with client and third-party vendor/client's IT team regarding production strategy, timelines, and any problems.
8.	Third-party vendor/client's IT team harvests ESI, processes the data into a common file format, and creates a database.
9.	Legal team reviews the ESI gathered. Sufficient time is allowed so that relevance and privilege issues are considered. If a third-party vendor is used it is usually done at their site or remotely using the Internet and proprietary custom software. Such review includes the ability to search the database.
10.	ESI is produced and delivered to the opposing party.

In a Fortune 500 business merger, the U.S. Department of Justice requested a large amount of documents in a number of categories in conjunction with the merger. The organizations and their attorneys decided that the document production was too large for the organizations' own IT departments to handle. Instead, they issued a request for proposals and hired a third-party vendor. The vendor assisted the businesses in producing more than 30 million pages of documents in less than 60 days. To make matters worse, the Department of Justice required some files to be in their native format, whereas other files were to be produced as TIFF files. The vendor had special proprietary software that allowed the attorneys to review the ESI in a single database/platform while still being able to deliver the documents to the Department of Justice in multiple formats and meet its deadlines and requirements.

In another large case regarding potential fraud and conspiracy allegations arising out of a complex multiparty transaction, a law firm representing the plaintiff reviewed more than 30 gigabytes of restored email from the defendants. The attorneys hired a consulting firm to assist them in reviewing the production. Using specialized software, the attorneys and consultants narrowed the millions of documents to a little more than 10,000 documents and created a database to store, search, and retrieve them. In the end, the review was a success and led to a stronger case. The strategy allowed them to focus on 10,000-plus documents rather than millions. They were able to find what they needed without wading through every single document, which would have taken more than a year. Because of the third-party's capabilities, they accomplished the review of the records in a few months.

It is thus obvious that third-party vendors specializing in e-discovery can help in both producing and receiving documents. The downside of third-party vendors is the cost. Large third-party vendors can charge between $300 and $500 an hour and this is just the cost of the professionals who consult and work with the data. There may also be conversion costs and other expenses related to working with the data, and these charges can run into the tens of thousands of dollars, depending on the needs of the attorneys and clients. Nevertheless, the cost is well worth it if the ESI is usable, meets the needs of the attorneys and users, and prevents the client from being sanctioned by a court for failure to comply with ESI rules.

What Services Do Third-Party Vendors Provide and How Do They Work?

Whether a client must produce or receive ESI, third-party vendors can be helpful. Exhibit 6–6 shows a list of services that most high-quality e-discovery vendors can provide.

This is a developing market; as legal organizations become more involved in ESI, the use of e-discovery vendors will rise. The following is a more detailed explanation of the services that third-party vendors may provide.

Harvesting Data As mentioned previously, third-party vendors can assist clients in **harvesting data**, that is, collecting from the client's information systems the data that must be produced. Depending on the size of the production, the age of the data (for example, if the required ESI includes legacy data), its location, the amount of data, and its native format, data harvesting can be either routine or extremely complex. Because most production requests are time sensitive, it is important to have a plan for how the data will be harvested in advance of the actual production request and to know in what format the data will have to be processed.

De-duplication **De-duplication** or **de-duping** is the process of marking or deleting records that are duplicates. For example, think of the number of duplicate records

harvesting data
The process of collecting ESI from the client's information systems.

de-duplication (de-duping)
The process of marking or deleting records that are duplicates.

EXHIBIT 6–6

High-quality third-party
e-discovery vendor services

- Analyze IT infrastructure and make recommendations on producing/
  receiving ESI
- Authenticate and provide testimony regarding ESI, including providing
  workflow certification affidavits regarding software processes, accuracy
  test results, and anything that shows the validity of the processing,
  searching, and filtering methods
- Ability to harvest, restore, and read a large variety of standard and unique
  file formats, databases, and structures, including ability to restore backups
  and harvest restored data
- Harvest, de-dupe, and filter dataset as needed
- Process and produce data set in an electronically searchable format
- Present data in an easy-to-use viewable interface, no matter the format of
  the original data, and include options such as Bates numbering, redaction,
  document tagging, and notes
- Preserve metadata
- Integrate paper documents and ESI into one database
- Provide data recovery and forensic services
- Deliver native format and image files to opposing party

© Cengage Learning 2012

that are generated when a group of people exchange a series of emails. De-duping reduces the dataset, which makes searching the data more efficient. It is also less expensive to produce and process the data, because de-duping can significantly cut down
on the amount of data to produce.

data filtering

The process of searching
and culling the data to find
relevant information and
reduce the overall size
of the dataset.

Data Filtering **Data filtering** is the process of searching and culling the data to find
relevant information and reduce the overall size of the dataset. Many third-party vendors
claim that by using advanced filtering software, they can reduce the size of a dataset by
75 percent. When millions of documents are at issue, the ability to reduce the dataset
by 75 percent—to even several hundred thousand relevant documents—can represent
an enormous savings in both time and money. Producers of documents can use filtering to help narrow the universe of potentially relevant and responsive documents so
that document production requests can be met in a timely, cost-effective, and efficient
manner. Requesting parties can also use filtering when they receive a large amount of
data and need to reduce that dataset to a more manageable size.

Processing Data If third-party vendors are producing the ESI, they can harvest it
and then produce it on CDs, DVDs, hard disks, or whatever media and in whatever
formats have been agreed to. If they have been hired to receive data that have been
produced, some vendors can convert the data to a common file format and create a
unified database, which can then be filtered and viewed.

Viewing Data Whether a vendor is producing documents for the client to review before the documents are sent to the requesting party, or is filtering data that have been
produced by the other party, the vendor may provide the client with proprietary viewing
software. This allows the attorney, paralegal, or client to view documents in one central
window no matter what format the files are in. The viewing software provided by many
vendors allows the user to see, magnify, print, add Bates numbers, redact information, add
bookmarks/tags/notes, and in some cases view the metadata associated with the ESI.

Computer Forensics

Computer forensics is used to recover, authenticate, or analyze electronic data. Computer forensics can be used in a number of ways, including instances in which it is

suspected that electronic data have been deleted or modified, or when advanced computer expertise is necessary concerning extremely complex computer issues. Using advanced computer forensic techniques, experts can in some cases reconstruct or recover previously deleted or destroyed information. Computer forensics is sometimes used in lawsuits to recover data that has been destroyed or to prove that electronic data was intentionally deleted or destroyed.

Deleted data is data that at one time was active on a computer, but has since been deleted. "Deleted" data may stay on storage media, either completely or partially, until they are overwritten. As an analogy, consider a traditional blackboard. Imagine that a teacher has written some information on the blackboard and also wrote "Do Not Erase" on it. Now imagine that the teacher has erased the "Do Not Erase" note. The information will continue to remain on the blackboard until someone actually erases it. Computers work in a similar fashion. When you "delete" something, you have essentially removed the "Do Not Erase" sign from that portion of the computer's memory, but the data will remain fully intact and available (to IT professionals who know how to find it) until new data are written over it.

Even after data have been overwritten, some information may still remain, such as directory entries. **Soft deletions** refers to information that has been deleted and is not available to the user, but which nonetheless has not been overwritten. Soft deletions can often be fully restored with complete integrity.

> **deleted data**
> Data that at one time were active on a computer, but which have since been deleted.

> **soft deletions**
> Information that has been deleted and is not available to the user, but which nonetheless has not been overwritten; can often be fully restored, with complete integrity, by forensic experts.

Chain of Custody

When dealing with ESI, as with any evidence, it is important that the chain of custody be preserved. One must be able to systematically trace ESI back to anyone who has had access to it. Only through an intact chain of custody can one prove that such access was never improper and that the ESI was never contaminated from the time it left the hands of the opposing party to its introduction in court. It is imperative to be able to prove that no information was added, deleted, or altered. Experts can make a forensic copy of the data with matching marks to prove that the copy is complete. Exhibit 6–7 shows a sample chain of custody log. Unless a proper chain of custody and authentication is established, ESI data will never be admitted as evidence in a case.

Overreliance on Third-Party Vendors

Legal professionals must be careful when delegating work, including ESI-related work, to third-party vendors. They must ensure that they closely watch and scrutinize the vendors and the vendors' work. In several high-profile cases, attorneys who delegated too much of the responsibility for ESI-related matters to vendors were reprimanded by judges and sued by clients for malpractice when the third-party vendor's or expert's advice was wrong.

ETHICAL CONSIDERATIONS

Perhaps we will not all become experts in the area of ESI or e-discovery, but we all need to know the basics so we can properly inform and protect our clients. Regardless of the precise language of a state's rules of professional responsibility, legal professionals have an ongoing responsibility to act in the best interests of their clients, to act zealously for their clients, and to act competently for their clients. In light of those duties, legal professionals may have an affirmative obligation to ensure that clients are aware of the dangers and opportunities that ESI presents. For example:

- Clients should be advised to prepare a document retention plan and to implement the plan immediately once the reasonable threat of litigation appears.

CHAIN OF CUSTODY LOG

Specific Description of Item	Lomax 40 Gb. Hard Drive
Evidence ID #	1001
Evidence Serial Number	2934809234
Evidence Custodian	Steven Keys, IT Director, Chase Limited Co.
Case/Matter	Chase Limited v. Wax, Layman Mortgage Bankers
Case No.	2011-23434

Name of Person Receiving Evidence	Date	Time	Place of Collection or Receipt	Purpose of Transfer	Signature of Person Receiving Item
Lisa Jenkins, Alpha Data Collection & Forensic Scientists, Inc.	1/3/12	9:50 a.m.	Chase Limited Co, Exec. Headquarters, 64 Wall St. NY, NY	Copy and Review of Hard Drive to Determine if Confidential Trademark Secrets Were Released	*Lisa Jenkins*
Steven Keys, IT Director, Chase Limited Co.	1/17/12	4:00 p.m.	Chase Limited Co, Exec. Headquarters, 64 Wall St. NY, NY	Return of Hard Drive - Hard Drive Appears in Same Condition as it Left	*Steven Keys*

EXHIBIT 6–7

Chain of custody log

- Clients should be advised not to destroy (or attempt to destroy) ESI when there is a reasonable potential for litigation.
- Clients should be advised to create and enforce a policy regarding the use of email, computers, and other sources of ESI, to limit the creation of information that may be discovered and used in later litigation.
- Clients should be told that they need to learn about their own computer systems, so that they can discuss these issues with the "techies."

Law offices will also need to be able to handle and discuss issues relating to computers and ESI competently. This means that either attorneys are going to have learn all this stuff, or they will have to hire someone who understands the legal process and ESI. Sounds like a job for a paralegal!

SUMMARY

Electronic discovery refers to the process of producing and receiving litigation documents in electronic format. The Federal Rules of Civil Procedure refer to any electronic data as electronically stored information. In the FRCP, ESI includes "writings, drawings, graphs, charts, photographs, sound recordings, images and other data compilations stored in any medium from which information can be obtained or translated."

The FRCP have many provisions regarding ESI, including the duty of the parties to meet and confer early in the case to discuss ESI. Each side also has a duty to preserve evidence in a case, which may mean having the client put a litigation hold in place, and to willingly and cooperatively exchange ESI. The FRCP provide that data that are inaccessible may or may not have to be produced, depending on the circumstances. Even after a document has been produced, if it is privileged the receiving party may be required to return or otherwise destroy the document, and may not disclose or use it. The FRCP also have a safe harbor provision stating that

if a party acts in good faith but inadvertently destroys ESI as part of routine operation of its information system, a court may not sanction the party.

Documents may be produced in native format, the file structure defined by and associated with the original creating application. Some ESI may be produced in image or static formats, which yield an image of the document as it would appear in the original application without any need for the original application. Metadata is information that is stored electronically in files that may identify the origin, date, author, usage, comments, or other information about a file. Parties are generally entitled to the metadata that accompanies ESI.

Third-party vendors may be used when producing or receiving litigation documents. Third-party vendors may provide a number of services, including harvesting data, which is the process of collecting ESI from the client's information system; and filtering data, which is the process of searching and culling data to find relevant information and reduce the overall size of the dataset.

KEY TERMS

accessible data
clawback
data filtering
de-duplication (de-duping)
deleted data
discovery
electronic discovery (e-discovery)

electronically stored
   information (ESI)
harvesting data
image format
inaccessible data
legacy data
litigation hold

native format
safe harbor
sampling data
soft deletions
spoliation
TIFF (Tagged Image
   File Format)

INTERNET SITES

ORGANIZATION	PRODUCT/SERVICE	WORLD WIDE WEB ADDRESS
Alpha Systems	Electronic discovery services	www.alpha-sys.com
Altep, Inc.	Electronic discovery services	www.altep.com
Attenex Corp.	Electronic discovery services	www.attenex.com
Capital Legal Solutions	Electronic discovery services	www.capitallegals.com
CaseCentral	Electronic discovery services	www.casecentral.com
Cricket Technologies	Electronic discovery services	www.crickettechnologies.com
Daticon, Inc.	Electronic discovery services	www.daticon.com
Discover-e Legal	Electronic discovery services	www.discover-e-legal.com
DocuLex, Inc.	Electronic discovery services	www.doculex.com
Electronic Discovery Reference Model	Resource for e-discovery	www.edrm.net
Electronic Evidence Discovery Inc.	Electronic discovery services	www.eedinc.com
Fios Inc.	Electronic discovery services	www.fiosinc.com
Forensics Consulting Solutions	Electronic discovery services	www.forensicsconsulting.com
Guidance Software, Inc.	Electronic discovery services	www.guidancesoftware.com
IE Discovery Inc.	Electronic discovery services	www.iediscovery.com
Kroll OnTrack	Electronic discovery services	www.krollontrack.com
LexisNexis	Electronic discovery services	www.applieddiscovery.com
Planet Data Solutions	Electronic discovery services	www.planetds.com
Sedona Conference	Resource for e-discovery	www.sedonaconference.com
Xact	Electronic discovery services	www.xactids.com

TEST YOUR KNOWLEDGE

1. Define the term electronic discovery.
2. By what name do the Federal Rules of Civil Procedure refer to electronic data?
3. True or False: Under the FRCP, parties are required to disclose information about ESI even before they receive a discovery request.
4. What is a litigation hold?
5. True or False: Under the FRCP, if a party produces a document in ESI format, it still may have to produce a hard copy of the document.
6. What does the "clawback" provision in the FRCP entail?
7. According to the FRCP, when might a party be required to produce inaccessible data?
8. What is the safe harbor provision of the FRCP?
9. Destruction of relevant documents in litigation is called _____.
10. True or False: Data harvesting is searching and culling data.

ON THE WEB EXERCISES

1. Go to three of the e-discovery websites in the "Internet Sites" section of this chapter and compare and contrast the services of the vendors. Which one were you most impressed with, and why? Write a one-page summary regarding your research.

2. Using a general search engine such as www. google.com or www.yahoo.com, find the Federal Rules of Civil Procedure as amended in 2006 and read Rules 26 and 34. Summarize what you find regarding ESI in a two-page paper.

3. Using a general search engine such as www. google.com or www.yahoo.com, find three articles on e-discovery. Write a short paper summarizing the articles you found.

4. Using a general search engine such as www. google.com or www.yahoo.com, or a legal search engine such as www.findlaw.com, find one case related to e-discovery, either cited in an article or reproduced in full. Write a one-page summary of the case.

5. Using a general search engine such as www. google.com or www.yahoo.com, find a sample of a request for proposals that a law firm might send to e-discovery vendors for document production services related to a large case.

6. Using a general search engine such as www. google.com or www.yahoo.com, find a draft preservation letter for a client and an opposing party.

7. Using either a general search engine or a law-specific site such as Westlaw or LexisNexis, research whether your state has adopted rules related to electronic discovery. If so, how are those rules similar to or different from the federal rules described in this chapter?

QUESTIONS AND EXERCISES

1. A legal organization is trying to decide whether to recommend to a client the use of a third-party e-discovery vendor for document production in a case. What factors should the firm consider in making this recommendation?

2. You are a new paralegal in a law firm and a client you are working with cannot understand why it should preserve unfavorable evidence. Write a one-page memo explaining how you would try to convince the client to preserve this (and similar) evidence.

3. You are a new paralegal in a law firm and you are trying to convince a client to spend $300 an hour for data-filtering services from a third-party vendor in a case in which 20,000 documents will be produced. Write a one-page summary of how you would handle the matter.

ETHICS QUESTION

A client in a divorce case comes into his attorney's office clutching a handful of papers. Excitedly, the client says, "See, I told you my wife was having an affair. And here are the emails to prove it!" The client then places the papers on the attorney's desk. What, if any, ethical issues are raised by this scenario?

Access an interactive eBook, chapter-specific interactive learning tools, including flash cards, quizzes, and more in your Paralegal CourseMate, accessed through CengageBrain.com.

CHAPTER 7

Litigation Support Software

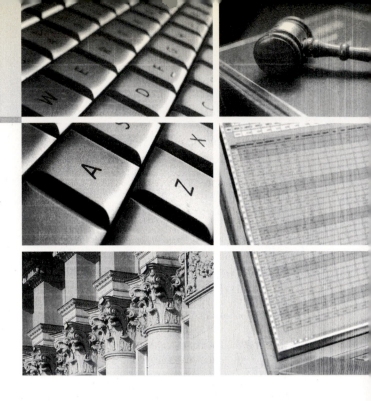

CHAPTER OBJECTIVES

After completing this chapter, you should be able to do the following:

1. Explain what litigation support is.
2. Explain why computerized litigation support methods are more successful than manual methods.
3. Explain why a legal organization might use a litigation support service provider.
4. Identify the three major types of litigation support systems.
5. Describe the litigation support process.
6. Identify and use various search methods to retrieve litigation support data.

INTRODUCTION

litigation support software
Program that assists attorneys and paralegals in organizing, storing, retrieving, and summarizing the information that is gathered during the litigation of a lawsuit.

Litigation support software assists attorneys and paralegals in organizing, storing, retrieving, and summarizing information that is gathered for the litigation of a lawsuit. During the course of a lawsuit, large quantities of information are generated and acquired. Litigation support software helps to manage and control this information so that it is presented in a usable form to the attorney(s) working on the case. This chapter introduces the fundamentals of computerized litigation support and describes how it can be used effectively in the practice of law. This chapter covers tracking of the information and documents used in litigation, manual litigation support methods, types of computerized litigation support systems, the litigation support process, the purchase of litigation support systems, and questions and fears about using computerized litigation support.

TRACKING INFORMATION AND DOCUMENTS USED IN LITIGATION

During litigation, the legal team (including attorneys, paralegals, and others) must organize, summarize, control, and understand a great deal of information so that it can be presented to a factfinder (such as a judge, jury, or administrative hearing officer) in a way that defeats the opposition's case and best promotes the client's interests. This is not an easy task, as legal issues, factual issues, and legal theories constantly change both during the course of the litigation and at trial. The more parties there are, the more complex the issues are, the more documents there are, the more attorneys/ paralegals there are, and the higher the stakes, the harder it is to succeed at organizing and controlling the information.

The information and documents that must be tracked in litigation vary according to the type of case. However, the following are some of the documents most commonly tracked:

- *Litigation documents*—Documents prepared during the course of the lawsuit; they include pleadings, motions, briefs, correspondence and email between the attorneys and the court, discovery documents, deposition transcripts (including summaries), expert witness reports, and other documents filed in the case.

- *Factual documents*—Documents that arise out of the subject matter of the litigation; they might include contracts, correspondence, emails, business/ financial records, photographs, diagrams, and other information concerning the parties or relevant to the lawsuit. Factual documents also include anything that might be presented as evidence in the case to prove or disprove the claim.

- *Knowledge management documents*—Documents and information that are used to help strategize, analyze, and administratively prepare the case. The focus of knowledge management is on information rather than documents. Knowledge management materials might include chronologies and timelines of the case, analyses of the issues, legal precedent, case law, management/tracking of the case docket, lists of witnesses and exhibits, internal reports or analyses of the facts of the case, and other information. In litigation, these documents, which are prepared by or for the legal professionals, are known as work product.

The following subsections explore each of these areas in more detail.

Litigation Documents

Litigation documents are prepared during the course of the lawsuit. They are extremely important, both because they are filed with a court, typically under deadlines, and because they contain the basic theories and strategies for winning the case. It is important that the legal team involved have control over these documents. Types of litigation documents include pleadings, motions, briefs, discovery documents, and miscellaneous documents.

Pleadings Formal documents filed with a court, usually stating a party's contentions regarding specific issues, are called pleadings. The complaint, answer, counterclaim, crossclaim, and third-party claim are types of pleadings.

Motions and Briefs During the litigation, motions and briefs are filed to argue the position a party is taking on how the case should proceed in court. These can be voluminous, especially if the issues are complex. Motions and briefs are critical to a case because they set forth the legal and factual theories of each party to the case. Some of the more important motions typically filed include motions to dismiss and motions for summary judgment; both of these motions seek to dismiss the lawsuit before it ever reaches the factfinder or the trial stage.

Discovery Documents Discovery documents include interrogatories, requests for admissions, requests for production of documents, depositions, and expert witness reports, among others.

Interrogatories Interrogatories direct a series of questions or written requests for information to an opposing party in a lawsuit. Interrogatories must be answered under oath and returned to the issuing party.

Requests for Admissions A request for admissions is a series of statements of fact directed to an opposing party in a lawsuit. The receiving party must either admit or deny each of the statements in the request for admissions.

Requests for Production of Documents A request for production of documents is a series of requests or instructions directing an opposing party in a lawsuit to produce documents and electronically stored information (ESI) that are in its possession or control so that the requesting party can examine those items. In some cases, especially those that are complex or span a number of years, anywhere from a thousand to a million documents or more may be produced. The documents that are actually produced in response to such a request are discussed in the section on factual documents.

Depositions A deposition is oral testimony that is taken before a court reporter who transcribes the testimony word for word. Depositions can be taken of parties or nonparty witnesses.

Expert Witness Reports An expert witness report is produced by an expert witness, and states the factual basis for the expert's opinion on a matter.

Miscellaneous Documents Miscellaneous documents in litigation include notes, internal memorandums, and external correspondence (both on paper and email).

Notes Written records of conversations and events are made from the first time a client steps in the door until the conclusion of a lawsuit.

Internal Memorandums Internal memorandums and emails are documents that are more formal than handwritten notes and are usually circulated only within a legal organization. They may be notes to a client's file, requests to other members of the firm to do things, or an exchange of information between individuals on a legal team.

External Correspondence Letters, email, and written communications that are exchanged between attorneys and their clients, between opposing attorneys, between attorneys and potential witnesses, and between attorneys and the court all fall into the category of external correspondence.

Factual Documents and Electronically Stored Information

Factual documents pertain to the subject matter of the litigation. Depending on the case, these can range from a couple of sheets of paper to a million or more documents. For example, suppose a jet airliner crash is being litigated. Factual documents that might be produced in the case include years of maintenance records, Federal Aviation Administration (FAA) registration and other documents, passenger lists, technical design schematics (possibly on many areas of the plane), computer models, and memorandums and email from aeronautical engineers regarding the actual manufacturing of the aircraft, among many others. Again, the kinds of documents that will be important in the case depend on the specific facts and the complexity of the case. Any information that might be presented to the factfinder as evidence to prove or disprove a claim falls into the category of factual documents.

Although many factual documents are discoverable, some are not. Some such documents might be classified as attorney work product, and as such are privileged and not discoverable.

Knowledge Management

In addition to tracking litigation documents and factual documents in a case, legal professionals must also track and organize internal organizational knowledge about a case. Knowledge management usually deals with a class of information prepared internally by legal professionals, and may cover a wide variety of miscellaneous information that can be helpful when litigating a case. Here are some examples of internal organizational knowledge:

- Chronologies or timelines of the facts of a case, which are often critical in presenting theories as to what, when, how, and why things happened in a case (for example, the timelines produced using TimeMap).

- Analyses and strategies regarding factual issues, legal issues, evidentiary issues, and other matters to be addressed at trial or at other stages of the litigation.

- Analysis of current case law and how it will affect the present case at various stages of the litigation.

- Scheduling and docket control reports, which can be important in litigation because they constitute a factual summary of the litigation process, including how and when things were accomplished in the case. This can be particularly important in large cases that are litigated over many years. In many cases, attorneys and clients strategize the timing of the litigation; this may include use of stalling/delaying techniques or attempts to "push" a case through to trial.

- Case diaries and notes made during litigation.

- Other internal reports, such as queries and searches that reveal cause and effect in evidence; reports about witnesses (such as a report listing every time a witness's name was brought up in the lawsuit); and anything else that provides information or knowledge regarding a case that is not a litigation or factual document but may nonetheless be important to the case.

WHY LITIGATION SUPPORT?

A typical case often involves hundreds of documents and extensive electronically stored information (ESI). When complex litigation is undertaken, the mountains of documents and ESI that are generated can be astounding: Some complex cases may involve a million factual documents and ESI files and several years' worth of litigation documents. Can you imagine trying to hold all of that information in your head?

The purpose of litigation support, whether through manual or computerized methods, is to organize the litigation documents, factual documents, and knowledge management in a case so that all of the information is useful to the attorney. For example, suppose that an attorney is questioning a witness in court and realizes that the witness is changing his testimony from what he said at a prior deposition. If the attorney can show this, she can prove a point and impeach the witness (create doubt as to the witness's credibility). However, if the attorney is unable to find the exact place in the volumes of deposition transcripts where the witness's prior—and different—answer was given to the same question, the opportunity to impeach the witness is lost. This is how litigation support wins or loses cases.

The goal of litigation support is to make sure the second outcome of this scenario does not happen. At trial, and throughout litigation, attorneys are engaged in cross-examining hostile witnesses, preparing their own witnesses, and making objections and other legal arguments. To effectively handle a case, attorneys must be backed up by a support system that can help them quickly find the information they need.

MANUAL LITIGATION SUPPORT METHODS

One type of manual litigation support system is a simple index, produced on a word processor, that lists key issues, facts, and/or other items to remember. A printout of this index is usually kept in a notebook for use at trial. The major limitation of this manual system is that it is impossible to cover all the topics that might be brought up during the course of a trial. Also, the index must be continually updated as new issues arise.

Another type of manual litigation support system used for case organization is an index-card system, usually based on key issues. For every essential document in the case, one or more index cards are prepared. If a document is related to two different key issues, then two index cards must be prepared, summarizing the document's contents relevant to those issues. Each card is then filed behind the appropriate issue divider.

Although the index-card system is more sophisticated than the simple index listing, it also has several disadvantages:

1. This type of manual system is time-consuming and tedious to set up, as the cards must usually be prepared by hand or typed. In addition, the process is slow, because a single document might pertain to many issues, all of which must be indexed.
2. Because this type of system is tedious, it encourages entry of the fewest possible documents, instead of thoroughness and entry of all relevant (or possibly relevant) documents.
3. This type of system is useful only for simple searches.
4. Other types of indexes, such as document author and chronological indexes, usually cannot be created from an index-card system—at least not without a substantial investment of time.
5. The system is vulnerable to human error, such as misfiling of cards.
6. If cards are not put back properly, are lost, or if the system should be knocked off a desk and the cards scattered, it could be a major disaster.

Manual litigation support systems, whether they use an index-card system or other manual methods, do not suit the modern legal environment well, because they are inherently inflexible and unable to meet changing needs and circumstances. A lawsuit is a dynamic environment, where key issues can change in an instant. What was important one minute may become unimportant the next. Especially at trial, the litigation support system must be flexible and adaptable to reflect progression of the case.

OVERVIEW OF COMPUTERIZED LITIGATION SUPPORT

Computerized litigation support solves many of the problems associated with manual methods, and has many benefits in addition. Many different kinds of computerized litigation support software are available, and litigation support can be provided either in-house, by existing staff, or outsourced to a litigation support service provider.

Manual vs. Computerized Litigation Support

A comparison of the time- and cost-saving features of computerized methods over manual methods shows why computerized litigation support is popular. The productivity and cost-saving features of computerized litigation support are substantial. Computerized litigation support can also be viewed as a service to clients: simply put, legal organizations with computerized litigation support can provide better-quality representation and take less time to do it.

General Benefits of Computerized Litigation Support

General benefits of computerized litigation support include data storage, retrieval, and search capabilities; flexible organization and use of information; and the ability to analyze and share information.

Electronic Storage and Immediate Retrieval Using electronic technologies, computers can store a vast amount of data in a fraction of the space required for hard-copy documents. External hard drives and other storage media can hold millions of document images and pages of text. In addition, document images can be retrieved almost immediately and repeatedly, without the hard copy (original) of the document being lost or affected in any way.

Searches/Queries Using database technology, thousands of electronic documents can be searched in seconds, allowing immediate retrieval of the document you are looking for.

Organization/Control Electronic documents can be numbered, incorporate links to other electronic documents, be annotated with electronic notes or comments attached to them, and be organized or sorted in many different ways without affecting the documents themselves.

Analytical Reports Analytical reports can be assembled from queries and searches on documents. Information can be gathered or revealed that would never come to light using manual methods.

Flexibility Computerized litigation support is inherently flexible, in that it can be changed and adapted according to the requirements of different cases. Information can be presented in a number of different "looks" and formats, and can also be exported to many different computer programs, including word-processing, spreadsheet, presentation graphics, or trial presentation software.

Sharing of Information A huge benefit of computerized litigation support is that information can be shared with others over a local area network or the Internet, giving a variety of users access to the information 24 hours a day, 7 days a week.

Mobility Litigation support databases that include electronic images and transcripts can be downloaded to a flash drive and thus made completely transportable, unlike heavy, bulky boxes of hard-copy records.

Preservation of Information and Theories Because litigation support creates a record of factual documents, litigation documents, and case knowledge, the information can be preserved and quickly passed along to others if the attorneys or paralegals working on a case change.

Types of Computerized Litigation Support

Many computerized litigation support programs and options are currently available. The legal market for computerized litigation support programs is continually growing, offering new and exciting ways to organize, control, and present information. All of these products have their own strengths and weaknesses. A brief summary follows (in-depth coverage is included later in this chapter).

Document Abstracts Using a litigation support program or database management program, abstracts of documents can be entered into the computer. An "abstract" is basically a short summary of a single document. The fields in the database usually include document number, document type, author, date, subject, summary, and others. The abstracts can then be used to organize, track, sort, and summarize the documents in the case. In addition, the abstracts can be searched and queried.

Full-Text Retrieval In a full-text retrieval system, the entire text of a document is available for user searches and queries. Unlike a document abstract, which contains only summary information, a full-text system includes all of the text of the document; hence, searches and queries have more data to pull from. Two types of documents that full-text systems can search on include real-time transcription files and electronic discovery (ESI).

> ***Real-Time Transcription*** With real-time transcription, an attorney or paralegal connects a computer to a court reporter's transcription machine and, using specialized transcription software, gets an electronic, rough-draft version of the transcript within seconds of the testimony being spoken. The transcription, which is full text, can be searched or queried using a full-text retrieval system.
>
> ***Electronic Discovery*** Most litigation support programs now support the ability to store electronic documents such as emails, word-processing files, spreadsheets, and other ESI that is produced during discovery. With a full-text retrieval system, the entire electronic discovery database may be searched and queried.

Imaging Documents can be imaged so that an electronic "photograph" of the document is maintained in the computer. The image cannot be searched (like full text), and there is no summary (as found in an abstract system), but the document can be viewed in its entirety electronically. Among other benefits, this preserves the original document and obviates the need to make numerous paper copies.

Case Management Software Case management software can be used in a litigation support capacity to electronically track and manage the scheduling and docket control of a case. In addition, you can use this software to create case diaries and notes, track legal research for the case, generate documents, and much more.

Analytical Software Analytical litigation support software can be used to create case outlines, chronologies, timelines, analyses of the issues and witnesses in a case (including reports that link documents and facts to issues or witnesses), and much more.

Trial Presentation Software Once litigation support information is in an electronic format, it can be exported to trial presentation software and presented to factfinders in a visually compelling manner. (This topic is covered in Chapter 9.)

External or Internal Litigation Support

Legal organizations have two main options when deciding how to go about providing litigation support for a case. They can either use an external litigation support service provider, or they can handle the project in-house. Alternatively, they can use a combination of both. All of these options have strengths and weaknesses.

Litigation Support Service Providers A **litigation support service provider** is a company that, for a fee, sets up a litigation support system and enters all the documents necessary to handle a case. The advantage of using a litigation support service provider is that the work is essentially done by someone else. The service provider consults with the law firm or attorney on how the system is to be set up. Once the structure of the system has been decided, the law firm delivers the documents and/or ESI to be entered to the service provider. The service provider then enters the documents into its computer or downloads/converts the ESI so that it can be used by the provider's system. When an attorney wants to search for or retrieve information, he connects to the service provider's computer, via the Internet, to access the data. Alternatively, the service provider can save the information to a DVD or flash drive. Even if the content is constantly being changed, or multiple people need access to the information, users can easily access the data using the Internet, because the data are centrally located on the service provider's computer. Some vendors offer electronic discovery services as well as litigation support services.

The main advantage of a service provider is that the labor-intensive task of data entry is performed by the service provider, not the law firm's staff. In addition, the law office does not have to hire, train, pay, manage, and then lay off extra employees. Also, because they specialize in this area, litigation support service providers can bring a great deal of experience, technological power, and knowledge to bear on the project.

The main disadvantage of using a litigation support service provider is cost: these services can be very expensive. Most service providers charge a consulting fee, a fee for entering information into the computer, a fee for each time an attorney or a firm connects to the computer, a fee for each search of information in the computer, and a storage fee. Nevertheless, using a service provider becomes economical when a case involves tens of thousands of documents.

In-House Computerized Litigation Support Systems An **in-house computerized litigation support system** uses a firm's or an attorney's own staff and computer to perform litigation support. Many litigation support programs are available for in-house use.

The advantage of in-house litigation support systems is that they are significantly less expensive than hiring a service provider. They also give a legal organization or attorney more control over a project. This is important, because the attorney is ultimately responsible for the litigation process and the success or failure of a suit. In-house systems also enable a legal organization or attorney to use litigation support even for small cases for which it would not be cost-effective to hire a service provider.

The disadvantage of an in-house computerized litigation support system is that a significant amount of front-end work is associated with setting up and entering information into the system. The setting-up and document-entry tasks take staff away from other duties and can eat up a lot of time. However, this problem can be somewhat alleviated by hiring temporary employees to enter, or *code*, documents into the system. The problem with temporary employees is that they often have no experience in litigation support. The choice of whether to use a service provider or an in-house system will depend on the circumstances of a case.

litigation support service provider
A company that, for a fee, sets up a litigation support system and enters all documents necessary for a case.

in-house computerized litigation support system
A litigation support system set up by the firm's or attorney's own staff on their own computer(s).

Combination of Providers An alternative to using either in-house or third-party litigation support is to use a combination of the two. For example, a service provider might be hired to consult with a law firm regarding ESI and to assist with converting the ESI to a format compatible with the firm's own litigation support program. Given the complexity of ESI and all of the technical issues involved, this alternative sometimes serves a firm well and saves staff from having to do all the work themselves.

Litigation Support in Legal Organizations

The use of litigation support has grown in recent years as software has become easier to use and the variety of litigation support programs has risen. In many firms, paralegals use this software more than anyone else. Two of the most popular litigation support programs are Summation and CaseMap.

TYPES OF COMPUTERIZED LITIGATION SUPPORT SYSTEMS

As indicated earlier, there are five major types or functions of litigation support software: document abstracting, full-text retrieval, imaging, case management, and analytical. Many litigation support programs can perform one or more of these functions. The lines between these different programs/functions are somewhat blurred. Exhibit 7–1 shows an overview of the programs. The following subsections describe each of the different types of litigation support programs.

Document Abstract Litigation Support Systems

document abstract litigation support system
Software that allows users to enter document abstracts or summaries into a computer and then search and retrieve the information contained in those abstracts or summaries.

A **document abstract litigation support system**, also called an indexing system, allows users to enter document abstracts or document summaries into a computer and subsequently to search and retrieve information contained in the abstract or summary. Exhibit 7–2 is an example of a document abstract. Notice in Exhibit 7–2 that abstracts of several documents are shown. The fields shown include document ID (Docid), document type, date, summary, author, and privilege. A short description of each document appears in each of these fields (according to how the user entered the information). For example, in Exhibit 7–2, document ID number EDC000001 is a spreadsheet dated 3/22/1999.

This is exactly how a document abstract database/litigation support program is designed. The system is, in essence, a database, and many legal organizations use generic database programs to create their document abstract litigation support systems. However, many prepackaged litigation support systems include an abstracting module. One main difference between a generic database program and a litigation support program with an abstract function is that the program designed specifically for litigation support will already have appropriate fields designed and set up for abstracting. For example, Exhibit 7–3 shows the standard fields for the document abstracting feature in Summation iBlaze, a popular litigation support program. Users can customize the fields or the form, but it is convenient to have a predesigned form to start with.

objective/bibliographical coding
System in which only basic information about documents (document number, document name, date, author, recipient, and so forth) is recorded in a document abstract database. The coder makes no subjective characterizations about the document.

There are two ways to construct a document abstract database: objective/ bibliographical coding or subjective coding. **Objective/bibliographical coding** records only basic information about a document, including document number, document name, date, author, recipient, and so forth. Whoever is coding the document need not know anything about the case because he or she is only entering information that comes from the face of the document. The coder makes no subjective judgments about or characterizations of the document. Objective coding is fairly fast and straightforward. It might be used in very large cases in which there are hundreds of thousands of documents. Objective coding is often outsourced to a litigation support service provider, because the coders do not have to know anything about the case to input the data.

Type of Program/Function	Description	Strengths	Weaknesses/Limitations
Document Abstract	A database where abstracts or summaries of documents are entered. Each document is a record and each record contains fields such as doc. number, name, date, type, author, subject, etc. The database can either be setup to be objective/biographical data or can be subjective and include why the document is significant to the case	• Provides a short summary of each document that can usually be read quickly • Excellent for drafting exhibit lists • Can produce a chronology of documents • Can produce reports based on any of the field names, documents sorted by author, subject, type, etc. • Can be linked to file with full text, images or photos • Document reports can be sorted as needed • Documents can be searched on • Can be used to identify relationships between documents, people, etc.	• The full text of a document cannot be searched • The document must be coded and the abstract entered into the database
Full-Text Retrieval	The full text of documents is available for searches. Hard-copy documents are scanned and run through optical character recognition software or electronic files are used (such as elec-tronic deposition transcripts or electronic discovery)	• The entire text of a document can be searched for individual words and phrases • Can be used for searching for words in depositions, trial transcripts, documents obtained from electronic discovery, and word processing documents • Can be used to impeach witnesses when testimony does not match • Annotations and notes can be attached to an electronic document without it affecting the underlying document itself • Electronic documents can have electronic Bates numbers added	• Uniform words are not always used (Jim, James, Jimmy, Mr. Smith) • Cannot produce indexes and reports like an abstract system
Imaging	Produces a "photograph" of the document	• Produces an exact electronic duplicate of the hard copy that can be instantly viewed • Can be included in electronic presentation graphic programs • Thousands of documents can be stored on flash drives and easily transported almost anywhere	• Cannot be searched on • Cannot produce indexes and reports like an abstract system
Case Management	Organizes docket control, scheduling, case diaries, document assembly/generation, legal research, and some document tracking capabilities and makes date available over a network to the whole legal team	• Captures information such as case diaries/notes, docket control, legal research, timekeeping, phone log, etc. that is not typically maintained by other litigation support programs/functions	• Is not a substitute for abstract, full-text retrieval, or imaging
Analytical Software	Creates chronologies, timelines, and tools for analyzing, issues, facts, witnesses, and other aspects of a case	• Creates documents for analyzing important aspects of a case	• Is typically not a substitute for abstract, full-text retrieval, or imaging

EXHIBIT 7–1
Different types/functions of litigation support programs

EXHIBIT 7–2

Document abstract litigation support

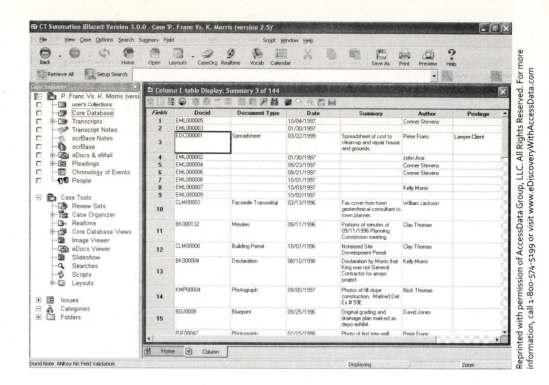

EXHIBIT 7–3

Blank document abstract form in Summation iBlaze

subjective coding

Entering information in a document abstract program about what the document means, including what case issues the document is relevant to or notes about the document.

Subjective coding allows the coder to enter into the document abstract program information about what the document means, including to which case issues the document is relevant or notes about the document itself. Subjective coding takes longer than objective coding because much more thought must go into the abstracting. Exhibit 7–3 is an example of a subjective document abstract; note that "Summary," "Attorney Notes," "Issues," and other such fields are included in the design. To subjectively code documents, the coder needs to have a good understanding of the facts and legal issues involved in the case. There are pros and cons involved with both objective and subjective coding, so the particular circumstances of the case should determine which is used.

At the bottom of Exhibit 7–3, notice the field that says "Linked Document." The litigation support program in Exhibit 7–3 is able to link another file, such as an image file, an electronic discovery file, or the full text of a file, to the document abstract. Exhibit 7–4 shows an example of a linked file.

Exhibit 7–5 shows a completed record in a document abstract system. Compare Exhibits 7–5 and 7–3. Notice that although the forms are somewhat different, many of the field names are similar. The following explains the fields in Exhibit 7–5.

EXHIBIT 7–4

Linking an email or full-text document to a document abstract

Document Reference No.:	2342
Document Title:	Employment Contract
Type of Document:	Contract
Date of Document:	February 22, 2002
Author of Document:	Jim Hill
Recipient of Document:	Mary Rhodes
Subject of Document:	Employment
Physical Location of Doc.:	Box 211
Importance (1-10):	8
Names Mentioned:	Jim Hill; Mary Rhodes; RXY Corp.
Issues:	Liquidated damages; material breach; noncompete
Description 1:	This employment contract sets out the terms and conditions of Mary Rhodes's employment.
Description 2:	There is a provision in the contract requiring each party to act in good faith to the other.
Keywords:	Employment, contract, damages, noncompete
Notes:	
Source of Document:	Plaintiff
Production History:	Plaintiff's Deposition Exhib. 1
Plaintiff's Exhibit No.:	62
Defendant's Exhibit No.:	27
Beginning Bates No.:	734
Ending Bates No.:	744
Attorney Comments:	Was signed without attorney's advice
Authenticated:	Y/N
Stipulated:	Y/N
Offered during what witness:	Jim Hill
Admitted:	Y/N
Privileged/Confidential:	NO

EXHIBIT 7–5

Completed record in a document abstract system

Document Reference Number Before document abstracts or summaries are entered into a computer, each physical document must be given a reference number or bar code. Unless each document is given a reference number and stored in order, there is an excellent chance that documents will get lost. Throughout the course of litigation, documents are moved, handled, and used so frequently that a reference number is the only way to keep a document from being misfiled (unless the legal organization uses electronic document imaging). In addition, the only link between the information contained in the litigation support system and the hard copy of a document is this number.

Document Title If the document being entered has a title, that name can be entered in the Document Title field. Coding rules (discussed later) provide guidelines so that documents are given uniform, informative titles. Also, your coding rules should include directions for how to assign titles to untitled documents like memos and letters, so that you can quickly and accurately retrieve such documents when necessary.

Type of Document The Type of Document field indicates whether a document is a letter, contract, memorandum, pleading, or other type. Again, coding rules are set so that similar documents are given the same name (sometimes referred to as vocabulary control). For instance, you would not want one letter entered into this field as a "letter" and another similar type of letter entered as "correspondence." It is important that there be strict uniformity. Many litigation support programs use drop-down menus with set options for fields like this, as limiting the available choices ensures uniformity.

Date of Document The date of a document is entered in the Date of Document field. Undated documents are also captured in this field. The date of a document is a critical feature in a litigation support system. Throughout the litigation of a case, the law office will frequently use the software's functions to provide chronologies of events and compare documents by date.

Author of Document and Recipient of Document These fields record the personal and organizational author and the recipient(s) of each document.

Subject of Document This field records what the subject or topic of a document is.

Physical Location of Document Physical location refers to the place where the actual original document is stored, whether it is in a numbered box, a file drawer, a flash drive, or some other place.

Importance This field records the relative importance of each document entered. This is usually accomplished using a numbering system or scale, such as a range between 1 and 10, with relatively unimportant documents being assigned a 1 and critical documents getting a 10. This allows users to sort documents based on their relative importance. This function is useful at trial, as it is possible to forget or overlook important documents that have not been admitted into evidence. Because the rating input into this field is subjective, it is usually decided by an attorney or a paralegal.

Names Mentioned In this field, a user enters the names of people and organizations mentioned in a document. This allows users to search for people's names and obtain a list of all documents that concern them. It is useful at trial or in preparing for the deposition of a particular witness or party. It is sometimes useful to separate these names into two fields: a Persons Mentioned field and an Organizations Mentioned field.

Issues The Issues field allows a user to note when a document concerns a key issue in a case. The user can then search the database for all documents that pertain to a specific issue. This is helpful throughout the litigation of a case, as it allows an attorney to get a handle on specific issues and determine which (and how many) documents pertain to those issues.

Description, Keywords, and Notes These fields are where a user enters notes or a summary of the documents.

Source of Document The source field allows a user to track where a document came from: whether it was produced in discovery by the opposing side, whether it was given to the attorney by her own client, and so forth. It is always important to keep the history of a document straight. This can be as simple as indicating whether the document came from plaintiff or defendant or as specific as giving a person's name as the document creator/provider.

Production History This field allows a user to track how a document has been used in litigation. For instance, if a document was used as an exhibit in a particular deposition, this fact could be tracked in the production history field.

Plaintiff's and Defendant's Exhibit Number Each party to the lawsuit prepares its own list of potential documentary exhibits and gives each document an exhibit number. The resulting lists are exchanged during discovery, allowing each party to know how the other party numbered a particular document for tracking purposes.

Beginning and Ending Bates Number Every page of every document is usually given a reference number, using either a Bates stamp or a computer-generated label or number. A **Bates stamp** is a machine that marks a page with a sequential number and then automatically advances to the next number. When all the pages have been numbered, they are maintained in numerical-order files. This makes documents easier to locate. The Bates numbers (beginning and ending for each document) are then entered into the computer. Depending on the case and how the document must be tracked, a document may have either a document reference number, Bates numbers, or both.

Bates stamp
Marks a page with a sequential number and then automatically advances to the next number.

Attorney Comments Comments are simply personal notes about the document that an attorney wants to remember. They can function merely as reminders, or they can become important work product if a different attorney takes over litigation of the case or an aspect of the case.

Authenticated A check in this field means that the document has been "authenticated" for evidence purposes. Some documents are self-authenticating, which means that by statute they are admissible into evidence without further proof (such as of origin or creator).

Stipulated Notes in this field relate to whether the parties have stipulated or agreed to the admissibility of the document.

Offered during What Witness At trial, documents are offered into evidence during witness testimony. This field records which witness was on the stand testifying when the document was offered.

Admitted This field tracks whether the judge admitted the document into evidence.

Privileged/Confidential This important field relates to whether the document is privileged or confidential and thus should not be produced in discovery. Proper notations here can save a great deal of time and trouble, as all users can immediately see whether a given document is privileged rather than relying on memory or reasoning.

Use of Document Abstract Systems Document abstracts can be helpful when attorneys are litigating cases. For example, suppose an attorney is representing Mary Rhodes in a case for breach of employment contract against her former employer. The attorney's task is to cross-examine Jim Hill, Rhodes's former supervisor, at trial. To prepare for the cross-examination, the attorney would like to see every time Hill's name was mentioned in any of the documents that the plaintiff has been able to obtain in discovery. This is a simple task using a computerized document abstract litigation support system. You simply instruct the system to search for every document abstract that mentions Hill's name. You then instruct the system to print a list of all the documents where the search term was found (see Exhibit 7–6). With this list, you can then use the document reference number to pull the original of a document for the attorney's inspection.

Document abstracts can also be used to give the attorney a chronological list of all (or a subset) of the documents by sorting on the dates of the documents. This type of list is important when the attorney is trying to put together time frames and sequences of events in cases. Document abstract systems are sometimes called document indexing systems, because the printouts they produce are nothing more than indexes (see Exhibit 7–6).

A legal professional can use document abstracts as a quick reference to refresh his or her memory about the documents involved in a case (see Exhibit 7–2). Notice in Exhibit 7–2 that a document abstract system can be used to prepare a list of exhibits for trial. Document abstract systems can also be used to search for and sort reports based on any of the field names in the database. Thus, a report could be run for all documents that were authored by "Jim Hill," or every document that concerned the issue of "liquidated damages," or every document that was produced by the plaintiff. Document abstract databases can produce an infinite number of reports, searches, and queries, depending on the user's particular needs at the time.

Disadvantages of Document Abstracts There are several disadvantages of using document abstracts. The first is that if subjective abstracting is to be used, the persons preparing the document abstracts must be trained in *exactly* what the issues of the case are. That is, nonlawyers have to make decisions about evidence and relevance, so the lawyer is in essence delegating legal judgments to nonlawyers. There is a fairly high potential for errors: for instance, irrelevant information that has no real bearing on the case may be entered in the abstracts, whereas relevant and important

EXHIBIT 7–6

Document abstract search report on the name "Jim Hill"

SEARCH REQUEST:	"Jim Hill"		
Document Ref. No.	Type of Document	Recipient of Document	Date of Document
2342	Contract	Mary Rhodes	2/22/08
2346	Letter	Mary Rhodes	2/27/08
2359	Letter	John Hays	3/30/08
2365	Memo	John Hays	4/10/08
2377	Memo	John Hays	5/06/08
2390	Letter	Mary Rhodes	6/01/08
2400	Letter	Bill Green	6/30/08

information might be left out. As long as experienced, highly skilled paralegals do the abstracting, there is little reason to worry, but if data entry clerks or untrained temporary staff are used, this could present a real problem.

Also, abstractors must be careful to use a controlled vocabulary so that information is entered uniformly into the abstracts. If information is not entered uniformly, searches of the document abstracts will be inconclusive. For example, if one abstractor referred to an important incident as a "collision," another abstractor referred to the same thing as an "accident," and another referred to the incident as a "wreck," anyone searching the document abstract database would encounter a significant problem, because he or she would have to do three different word searches to get all the information about the same incident.

Another disadvantage of using document abstracts is that the issues in a lawsuit change constantly. This is particularly true in complicated cases (for which full litigation support can be invaluable). When issues are added or modified, documents must be reviewed again and the abstracts updated.

Finally, the facts that the document abstract database itself does not contain the full text of documents, and that the documents have to be coded and entered into the system, may also be viewed as disadvantages.

Full-Text Retrieval Litigation Support Systems

A **full-text retrieval litigation support system** enables users to search and retrieve information contained in the full text of any documents stored in the system. Unlike document abstract systems, they are not set up like a database. They do not have fields or a file structure. In full-text retrieval systems, a whole document, not just an abstract or a summary, is entered and stored.

The full text of a document can be entered into a computer in several ways: by scanning, keyboard entry, and/or word processing; computer-aided transcription; real-time transcription; service providers; or electronic discovery.

Scanners Optical character recognition (OCR) scanners translate hard-copy documents into a computer-readable format almost instantly. Once a document is scanned into a computer, the document file is saved to a disk for later retrieval by the full-text retrieval litigation support system. OCR is not 100 percent accurate. Most OCR systems have accuracy rates of around 99 percent, so documents must be thoroughly reviewed for accuracy. (This need for checking and proofreading is a primary disadvantage of OCR systems, as these tasks take a great deal of time.)

Keyboards and Word Processing A word processor can be used to type the content of a document into a computer. Once the complete document is input into the computer, the file is then saved to a disk for later retrieval by the full-text retrieval litigation support system. Accuracy and the need for proofreading are concerns with this method as well. Also, the format and "look" of the original document are lost, as are handwritten and nontext markings.

Computer-Aided and Real-Time Transcription According to most court rules, a court reporter must record deposition testimony, court hearings, trials, and other types of formal proceedings. **Computer-aided transcription (CAT)** is a process that automatically converts a court reporter's notes into a computer-readable format. Before CAT, a court reporter, using a shorthand reporting machine to abbreviate common words and phrases by certain keystrokes, recorded the testimony as it was given. The court reporter then deciphered the notes and prepared a full transcript of the testimony, using either a typewriter or a word processor.

full-text retrieval litigation support system
Software that enables a user to search (and retrieve information from) the full text of documents stored in the system.

computer-aided transcription (CAT)
A process that automatically deciphers a court reporter's notes and converts them into a computer-readable format.

Most CAT systems automatically prepare a transcript in computer-readable format. The court reporter then makes any necessary corrections and saves the file. Because the file is saved in a machine-readable format, the court reporter can, in addition to selling attorneys hard copies of transcripts, provide transcripts in electronic format. Most full-text retrieval systems can use the electronic file of a transcript automatically. Thus, using CAT, it is easy and fairly inexpensive to get the full text of depositions and other formal documents into a full-text retrieval system.

In addition, many court reporters now have **real-time transcription** available. With this system, a cable attaches the court reporter's equipment to the attorney's computer (which has the appropriate software preloaded). As the court reporter types, the testimony appears on the attorney's computer screen within seconds. Most court reporters go back and edit the transcript documents, but it is possible for an attorney to get a rough draft of the transcript almost immediately, which can be extremely valuable at trial or deposition.

real-time transcription
System through which an attorney or paralegal connects a computer with the appropriate software to the court reporter's transcription machine, so that within seconds of the testimony being spoken, a rough-draft version of the transcript appears on the computer screen.

Service Providers   Some service providers allow users to rent their trained personnel to scan data and design a full-text retrieval system.

Electronic Discovery   Electronic discovery is a process during which discovery "documents" (emails, word-processing documents, spreadsheets, databases, etc.; see Chapter 6) are produced electronically. Many times attorneys want documents produced electronically because it is more difficult to destroy electronic documents. Backup tapes can be requested before documents are destroyed or possibly altered, and additional information can sometimes be learned from the metadata in electronic documents that hard-copy documents do not supply. Electronic documents can contain other documents, such as attachments, that may or may not show up on hard copies or automatically print out. Having documents produced electronically allows users to do full-text retrieval on the items produced without having to take the separate step of putting the documents through an OCR system.

Use of Full-Text Retrieval Systems   Full-text retrieval systems allow users to conduct searches on the full text of a document. In the breach of employment contract example used earlier, the attorney representing Mary Rhodes has a listing of all the documents that have Jim Hill's name in them. However, the attorney would also like to see a listing of every time Hill's name is mentioned in the 15 depositions that were taken in this case. This will save the attorney from having to reread all 15 depositions and will take the attorney right to the parts relating to Hill. This cannot be done using a document abstract system, but it is quite easy using a full-text retrieval system. The user simply tells the system to search the 15 deposition files for the name *Jim Hill* or to search each file separately for the name *Jim Hill* (depending on the litigation support system). Most systems respond either by producing a list of the found occurrences (see Exhibit 7–7) that includes the deposition name and page

EXHIBIT 7–7
Full-text retrieval search on the name "Jim Hill"

SEARCH REQUEST:	"Jim Hill"
Found Occurrences:	19

Deposition Name	Deposition Page
Depo of Mary Rhodes	Page 24, 34, 56, 67, 89, 94
Depo of Bill Green	Page 11, 23, 44
Depo of John Hays	Page 10, 15, 16, 19, 20
Depo of Alice Hall	Page 15, 16, 17, 45, 46

© Cengage Learning 2012

number of each occurrence; or by displaying each found occurrence on the computer screen. Some full-text systems have the capability to search across many different files at the same time.

Notice in Exhibit 7–8, just to the left of the word "Search" (just underneath the toolbar), that the user has entered the search term "drainage." Also notice, to the left of the screen under "Case Explorer," that check marks have been placed next to all of the transcripts for the case. The check marks mean that when the search on "drainage" is done, all of the transcripts will be included in the search at one time. Also notice in Exhibit 7–8 that the full text of the Conner Stevens deposition is displayed and the search term "drainage" has been highlighted.

A powerful feature found in many full-text retrieval systems allows users to add annotations (electronic sticky notes) to the file without affecting the transcript itself. Notice in Exhibit 7–8 that a line near the "drainage" hit has been highlighted and that a note has been created reminding the user to ask Stevens about other properties with drainage problems.

In addition to being able to conduct searches on the full text of a document, some full-text systems can produce a summary or digested version of a transcript or document. Full-text systems are also convenient if a document or transcript is lost, because the full text can be retrieved and printed. In addition, full-text retrieval avoids the potential of important issues or aspects of a case being missed. Finally, most full-text retrieval systems can even be used to search a firm's own word-processing documents, such as correspondence, memorandums, and other documents prepared in-house.

Disadvantages of Full-Text Retrieval Several disadvantages are associated with full-text retrieval systems. One disadvantage is that they tend to take up a large amount of hard disk space. This may strain the physical limits of storage space on a computer system, although the availability of optical storage devices and large internal and external storage devices now make this less of a problem.

Another disadvantage is the substantial amount of time and money that can be expended in entering the full text of documents. In some instances, only the most important documents are entered in full-text format, whereas in others all of the depositions, pleadings, and transcripts are in full text. This often depends on how much

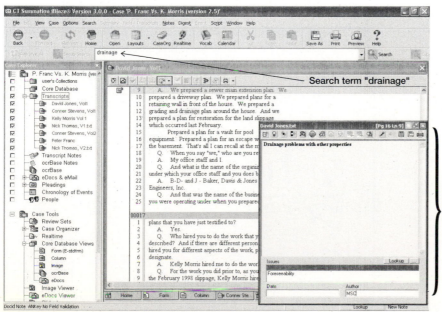

EXHIBIT 7–8

Full transcript search and electronic annotation of full-text documents of the information can be obtained in a computer-recognized format or how much of the data can be scanned into the computer.

Yet another disadvantage is that because the vocabulary entered into the system is not controlled, it may be impossible to find all occurrences of a subject. In some cases, subjects are referred to as concepts, and it is difficult to search on concepts. For example, the person Jim Hill in the preceding example may be referred to in documents as "Mr. Jim Hill," "Mr. Hill," "Jim," "the boss," "supervisor," and so on.

A final disadvantage is that a user cannot manipulate data and report formats as with an abstract system, because a full-text system has no fields to work with. It is quite difficult even to create chronologies using such a system.

Document Imaging Litigation Support Systems

Document imaging is a litigation support method in which documents are scanned into a computer and the documents' actual images (similar to photographs) are retained in the computer, either on a hard disk, flash drive, or another device (see Exhibit 7–9). Document images offer several advantages over paper. With document imaging, paper is handled only once, when it enters the legal organization and is scanned into the computer. Thereafter, reviewing, copying, and filing can be done electronically. Unlike paper documents, imaging allows multiple people on a network to access and view the same document at the same time without moving from their computers and without requiring staff to pull the actual document. Document imaging also reduces the need for physical storage space; many file cabinets' worth of documents can be stored on one DVD. Anyone who has worked with paper documents in a legal office can testify that there is always a risk of losing files or documents, especially during pretrial preparation and at trial, because documents are constantly being used and moved by many different people. Document images solve this problem, because the document is always available for review.

A disadvantage of document imaging is that the images take up a lot of electronic storage space. Also, each document must be scanned into the computer, which requires obtaining a certain amount of computer hardware or hiring a firm to scan the

EXHIBIT 7–9

Document imaging: Sample document image

documents. There is also a risk of inaccuracy with scanned images; if the initial scan is not properly done, the image may be blurred or unreadable in part.

Document images themselves typically cannot be sorted or searched, unlike the information in a document abstract or full-text retrieval system. However, scanned images can be turned into searchable text using OCR software. Also, some systems allow scanned images to be linked to an electronic abstract of the document. Scanners, including those with OCR, are readily available and inexpensive. This is becoming a popular option in litigation support. In addition, software is available that will electronically enter Bates numbers and allow legal team members to manipulate the images.

Another useful aspect of document imaging is that electronic discovery service providers can now take just about any kind of ESI and convert it to TIFF or PDF image files and then electronically convert the information to text as well. In this way, the service provider can provide both an exact image of a document and the full text of it. Document imaging, whether it is hard copy or electronic, can be a very powerful and important tool in providing support to litigators.

Case Management

Many current case management systems now include features that are helpful to litigators, such as comprehensive docket control (including a historical representation of what has transpired in the case in the way of deadlines, appointments, hearings, etc.). In addition, case management software may allow for creation of comprehensive case diaries/notes about the case, lists of documents that have been generated in the case, records of legal research prepared for the case, timekeeping records, document tracking, and other such features. Case management systems are discussed in depth in Chapter 5.

Analytical Software

Analytical litigation support programs help legal professionals analyze a case from a number of different perspectives and draw conclusions about cause-and-effect relationships between facts and evidence in a case. Analytical litigation support programs help legal professionals conceptualize and think about facts, documents, people, and related matters and the relationships among them. For example, the first screen in Exhibit 7–10 is a chronology of facts in a case. Notice in Exhibit 7–10 that not only are the dates and facts listed, but a source for each fact is also listed, with a note of whether it is key to the case, whether the "fact" is disputed or undisputed, and what factual or legal issue it is linked to. Notice in the second screen of Exhibit 7–10 that an analysis of the legal issues has been conducted. Each factual/legal issue in the case has been broken down and facts, documents, and people have been linked to each issue. Notice further in this screen that the issue of "Age Discrimination" has been highlighted and a list of the facts that support the claim has been opened. This allows litigators to literally see, very specifically, what evidence is required and available to prove (or disprove) each issue.

Exhibit 7–11 is an example of an analytical tool that builds a timeline of the facts in a case. In Exhibit 7–11, the top of the timeline represents one account of the facts of the case and the bottom of the timeline represents another. This can be an invaluable tool in court when trying to present evidence to a jury. If there are many discrete pieces of evidence in a case, a visual timeline may make it easier for the trier of fact to better understand the facts.

Another kind of analytical litigation support program is called an outliner. An outliner helps the legal professional create outlines for opening and closing arguments,

analytical litigation support programs
A type of software that helps legal professionals analyze a case from a number of different perspectives and draw conclusions about cause-and-effect relationships between facts and evidence in a case.

EXHIBIT 7–10

CaseMap litigation support analytical software

EXHIBIT 7–11

TimeMap litigation support analytical software

questioning witnesses, and other uses. Although an outline can be created in a word processor, outlining programs offer special features that can assist in and speed up the process of drafting an outline.

In summary, analytical litigation support programs are powerful tools that help legal professionals understand their own case, identify the strengths and weaknesses of the case, and persuade the factfinder about the meaning and pertinence of evidence in a case. In the Hands-On Exercises for this chapter, you will have the opportunity to gain hands-on experience with the analytical litigation support programs CaseMap and TimeMap.

Integrated Litigation Support Systems

Document abstract systems are beneficial when a user needs an index of documents, such as a chronological listing. Indexes cannot be made effectively using a full-text retrieval system. However, full-text retrieval systems are useful for searching the full text of depositions, transcripts, and so forth when completeness and exhaustivity are required. Imaging is useful when a user needs immediate access to the documents themselves. Analytical software is helpful in analysis of a case.

Integrated litigation support systems offer the best of all worlds, essentially providing a database program for entering document abstracts, a full-text retrieval system for searching the full text of documents, imaging management software, real-time transcription, and even analytical tools.

As mentioned earlier, many litigation support programs are currently on the market. Several of them offer all of these capabilities in a single program. The main downside to a fully integrated litigation support package that includes all of these features is that such programs, which are so powerful and do so many things, are fairly complex. They are not necessarily easy to learn to use, and may require significant technical support in addition to good initial training.

THE LITIGATION SUPPORT PROCESS

Many questions and problems must be resolved when setting up a litigation support system for a particular case. Every case has different facts and issues. Therefore, different needs and requirements must be taken into account for each case. Five steps should be taken when setting up a litigation support system for a particular case (see Exhibit 7–12).

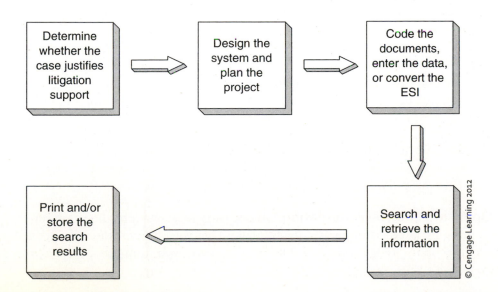

EXHIBIT 7–12

Litigation support software

© Cengage Learning 2012

1. Determine Whether the Case Justifies Litigation Support

The first step in the litigation support process is to determine whether the case is worth the time and expense required to design and set up the system and enter the data. Before litigation support was available on personal computers, the thinking was that only large or complex cases justified the expense of litigation support. Now, however, even attorneys with routine cases are using litigation support to organize documents and evidence.

Several issues and factors must be considered when determining whether a case should be entered into a litigation support system.

How Many Parties and Witnesses Are Involved? If only a few parties and witnesses are involved, a case might not justify the expense of litigation support. If, however, numerous parties and witnesses are involved, it might be wise to use a litigation support system for optimum organization of the parties, witnesses, and documents.

How Many Issues Are Involved? If only a few issues are involved, it might not be worth the expense of litigation support. However, if a large number of issues are involved in a case, it might be prudent to use a litigation support program to keep the issues clear and separate.

How Complex or Difficult to Grasp Are the Issues? If the issues in a case are easy to understand, a litigation support system might not be required. Obviously, the converse is also true.

How Long Is the Litigation Expected to Last? Litigation that is expected to last a long time has its own inherent problems. A turnover in the attorneys and paralegals working the case is very possible. If the information they need was never entered into a database for later retrieval, or is lost, they may have to start over—this is an expensive and time-consuming proposition and may raise ethical issues in addition to the practical problems the firm faces.

How Large Are the Damages? If a case involves the possibility of large damages, it is probably worth the time and expense to use a litigation support system.

How Many Documents Have Been Produced and Must Be Tracked? If thousands of documents are to be tracked, computerized litigation support may be the only way to effectively manage the case documents. In the past, some books on litigation support suggested that a case must have 1,000 to 10,000 documents before computerized litigation support pays off. This is probably not true anymore. Whether a case can benefit from litigation support depends on many issues other than just how many documents are involved. Computerized litigation support can be used effectively in small cases as well as large ones.

Does the Client Request Automation? In some instances, a client may ask that computerized litigation support be used. Nowadays, legal organizations may have to have this capability to accommodate client needs and desires.

Is Opposing Counsel Automating? If one party to a lawsuit has litigation support, this puts all other parties at a disadvantage. Therefore, in some cases, if opposing counsel begins using computerized litigation support, your firm may be forced to do so as well.

2. Design the System and Plan the Project

Once the decision has been made to put case information into a litigation support system, the next question is how the system should be set up; that is, what type of system will be used? System design includes planning what level of detail the fields of the database will have (when using abstracts), what information will be tracked, how many fields the database will have (when using abstracts), what documents will or will not be included, what will be done with duplicates, what information will be needed during the litigation, and how the database will be used at trial.

Users must also decide whether a brief summary of a document's characteristics will be sufficient or whether the full text of each document will be needed. If the system design is poorly thought out, the litigation system will surely fail. It is important that users think the system through clearly and take all options into account when approaching system design. The responsible attorney and paralegal should help design the system, as they will most likely have the clearest understanding of the facts and issues in the case.

In some cases, a budget must be drawn up so that the firm can decide what resources can be devoted to a project. The budget will also affect the decision on whether a service provider will be used or whether the system will be developed in-house.

When developing a system design, users should consider two questions.

Which Type of System Will Be Used? In designing a litigation support system for a case, it is first necessary to decide which type of system will be used: document abstract, full-text retrieval, document imaging, or a combination. Each case is different, but many firms use a combination. For example, it might be beneficial to use a full-text system to track depositions and testimony and to use an abstract system and document imaging to track documents. It is important to determine, at the beginning of the project, what you want to get out of the litigation support system, so that the system can be designed to accomplish those goals accurately, effectively, and swiftly.

What Kinds of Information Should Be Entered? The next question concerns what kinds of information should be entered into the system. For example, when using a full-text retrieval system, the designer must determine what documents should be scanned in: do you scan all documents, or just those that are relatively important?

One way to go about answering this question is to identify all the relevant issues of fact and law in the case, the relevant parties, and the documents that will affect the factfinding. All the information concerning these questions should be tracked.

3. Code the Documents and Enter the Data, or Convert the ESI

Once the design is complete, the user should enter test data into the system to see if the design really can accomplish what it is intended to. If the design holds up, the information must then be entered into the litigation support system. *Coding* of documents refers to the process of deciding what information will be entered into the system and what form it will take.

In many instances, clerical staff enter objective data into the litigation support database (in an objective/biographical document abstract design). Because all the information must be entered into the database in the same format (so that searches retrieve all the information relevant to the request), coding rules must be developed. Coding rules limit the vocabulary that can go into a litigation support system; hence the name controlled vocabulary. It is important to understand that what you put into the system is what you get out of it. For instance, if you were entering a piece of correspondence into a document abstract litigation support database, you could enter many different abbreviations and synonyms into the Document Type field, such as *letter, lt, ltr,* and *correspondence.* The coding rules tell data entry operators exactly what vocabulary choices they have to select from (e.g., the rules might say, "The following types of documents should be entered into the Document Type field: letters, pleadings, memos, notes."). A description of exactly what is meant by each title should also be provided. The format for entering a date might be "MM, DD, YY"; the formula for entering a name in a name field might be "LAST, FIRST"; and so on. Some programs permit designers to set up fields that do not accept variants in data entry; if a term or spelling is not on the "approved" list, it cannot be input.

It is important that all information entered into the database be uniform and as objective as possible. The use of coding rules will keep clerical staff from guessing when entering information. Coding rules should be drafted for all fields in the litigation support database. Note that some firms use codes or abbreviations instead of words. For example, a firm could code a statute of limitations issue in the Subject of Document field as the number 1 instead of using the words *statute of limitations.* In addition to enhancing uniformity, this strategy helps reduce the number of data entry errors, because far less typing is involved in entering a single number.

Fields that require subjective determinations (such as the Importance field) must be entered by trained paralegals or attorneys, not clerical staff. Remember the ethical issues and possibilities for unauthorized practice of law inherent in these judgments.

Some litigation support programs allow users to set up exactly what information can and cannot be entered into the system. For example, in the Date field, the user can instruct the system to accept only dates between January 2012 and January 2013. If a clerical staff person tries to enter a date before January 2012, the program will not allow the document to be entered. In this way, data can be verified right on the spot, as it is entered.

It is sometimes hard to determine how long it will take to enter case information into a litigation support system. This will depend on what level of detail is being entered into the system, how many people are entering data, how many documents are being entered, and so on. However, once a staff member has coded documents or entered information into a computer, the next time will be considerably easier for that person. Experienced coders make a big difference in how fast data are entered into the system.

It is also important to take into account the use of ESI in the case. Using service providers or other tools, a user may be able to quickly convert ESI into formats compatible with a litigation support program. These formats will often include images and the full text of documents.

4. Search and Retrieve the Information

Using the proper search and retrieval techniques helps users obtain the information needed. An in-depth discussion of different search/retrieval techniques and strategies is presented later in this chapter.

5. Print and/or Store the Search Results

It is sometimes necessary to produce a hard copy of search results or to save the search results. The design of the litigation support system must allow this, as well as electronic transmission and access.

SEARCHING AND RETRIEVING LITIGATION SUPPORT DATA

Accurate searching and retrieval of documents are very important and take some practice at first. In some instances, you may have to make four or five changes to a search request to get a litigation support system to retrieve the information you want. Litigation support programs, whether they are document abstract or full-text retrieval systems, generally provide the same type of search features. Nevertheless, the syntax for entering the search requests varies from one program to another.

When a search request (sometimes called search criteria) is entered, a litigation support program searches through every word in the documents or abstracts associated with that case, looking for matches. If a match is found, the program will show a list of the occurrences and where they were found. In most programs, a user has the option of pulling up and viewing on the screen the text surrounding a match.

Most programs allow a user to enter several different kinds of searches, including single-word searches, wildcard searches, Boolean logic searches, and proximity searches (see Exhibit 7–13).

Single-Word Searches

A **single-word search** searches a database for matches to a single word. For example, in Exhibit 7–13, the user requested that the program find any match to the single word *approve*. The system responded by retrieving a list of only the occurrences where the word *approve* was found. The potential problem with single-word searches is that derivatives or synonyms of words will not be found. For example, the single-word search for *approve* would not find derivatives or forms of the word, such as *approval,* nor will it find synonyms such as *accept, affirm,* and *ratify.*

single-word search
A computer search that scans a database for matches to a single word.

Search Type	Search Request	Words Found
Single word	approve	*approve*
Wildcard	approv*	*approve, approved, approval, approving*
Super wildcard	*approv*	*disapprove, disapproved, disapproval, disapproving, approve, approved, approval, approving*
Boolean OR	approval OR consent	*approval, consent*
Boolean AND	approval AND rate	*approval rate*
Boolean NOT	approval NOT rate	*approval but not approval rate*
Proximity—word	approval w/4 w rate	*approval* and *rate* where they are within four words of one another (the four words are retrieved each time)
Proximity—line	approval w/4 l rate	*approval* and *rate* where they are within four lines of one another (the four lines are retrieved each time)
Proximity—paragraph	approval w/4 p rate	*approval* and *rate* where they are within four paragraphs of one another (the four paragraphs are retrieved each time)
Proximity—page	approval w/4 pp rate	*approval* and *rate* where they are within four pages of one another (the four pages are retrieved each time)

EXHIBIT 7–13
Search types and examples

© Cengage Learning 2012

Single-word searches are useful when you know exactly what you are looking for, or when the document coders used a controlled vocabulary for entering the information.

Wildcard Searches

wildcard search

A computer search that scans a database for derivatives of a word.

Searching a database for derivatives of a word is called a **wildcard search**. Most litigation support programs, as well as most database programs, use an asterisk (*) to enable wildcard searches. For example, if you wanted to retrieve all the derivatives of the word *international,* you user would enter the search request as follows: "internation*". The system would respond by showing all matches to the words *international, internationally,* and so forth.

super wildcard search

A computer search that scans a database for derivatives of a word, using variations both in front of and in back of the root word.

Some litigation support systems can also perform what one program calls a super wildcard search. A **super wildcard search** searches a database for derivatives of a word that vary both before and after the root word. For example, the search request "*approv*" would find all occurrences of the words *disapprove, disapproved, disapproval, disapproving, approve, approved, approval,* and *approving.*

Wildcard searches are beneficial when you are not sure what derivatives of the word or words being searched for might appear in the documents.

Boolean Logic Searches

Boolean logic search

A computer search that allows a search request to include or exclude words, or use other search criteria, so that the search is either refined or broadened.

A **Boolean logic search** allows a search request to include or exclude words or other search criteria so that the search is either refined or broadened. Boolean searches are sometimes called logic searches or *OR, AND, NOT* searches.

OR The Boolean search operator OR is used to include synonyms of words in a search request. For example, if you wanted to search for the word *approval* and also wanted to include all synonyms of the word, so that you would not miss any occurrences of words such as *consent* and *permission,* you would enter the search request as follows: "approval OR consent OR permission." This request would find all occurrences of *any* of these three words throughout the database.

AND The Boolean search operator AND is used to include two or more words in a search request. For example, you might want to find any occurrences of the phrase *approval rate.* Using a Boolean search, the request would be as follows: "approval AND rate." This request would find all occurrences where the words *approval* and *rate* were located.

NOT The Boolean search operator NOT excludes words from a search request. For example, if you wanted to find the word *approval* but did not want to find the term *approval rate,* you would enter the search request as follows: "approval NOT rate." This search would find all the occurrences of the word *approval* in the database, but would not treat occurrences of *approval rate* as "hits."

Proximity Searches

proximity search

A computer search that scans a database for words that are in a given proximity to one another.

Searching a database for words that are within a given distance from one another is called a **proximity search**. For example, you could employ a proximity search if you wanted to find the name "Cindy" within two words of the name "John." The syntax of a proximity search will depend on the program, but a typical proximity search might look like this: "Cindy w/2 John".

Proximity searches can usually be performed based on the number of words, lines, paragraphs, or pages between two or more words. They are usually available only on full-text retrieval systems.

LITIGATION SUPPORT TIPS

There are advantages and disadvantages to using abstracts, full-text retrieval, imaging, case management, and analytical litigation support systems. To obtain the advantages of each, you really need to use all of them.

A mistake beginners sometimes make is to throw every possible document into the database. Generally, "big is bad," whether it is a big document abstract database, full-text database, or image database. The database should be only as big as you absolutely have to have to get the information you need. As much as possible, include only relevant documents. (Basically, this follows the "garbage in–garbage out" rule.) Bigger databases slow down performance.

Bigger databases also will yield more "hits" or documents than smaller ones. For example, if you search 1,500 documents and you get 40 documents back, this is manageable. You can just work your way through the 40 documents until you find what you need. However, if your database has 150,000 documents and you get 4,000 documents back, the database is basically useless. If you have a really big document collection, try to break it up into smaller document collections whenever possible. Finally, follow the rules in Exhibit 7–14.

QUESTIONS AND FEARS ABOUT COMPUTERIZED LITIGATION SUPPORT

People often share several common fears and questions about converting their manual litigation support systems to a computerized version: How long will it take to enter data? Is training hard? Can you convert a case to a computerized system in the middle of the case, or must you make that decision at the very beginning? What are the most popular programs? Can computerized litigation support be used in the courtroom?

How Long Will It Take to Enter Data?

The question of how long it takes to enter data into a litigation support system is hard to answer, because so many variables are involved. Three major variables must be considered:

1. How big is the litigation? (In other words, how many documents will have to be entered? How many witnesses are involved?) Small- to medium-sized cases with a few hundred documents and 20 to 30 witnesses can be entered in a week or two using a document abstract program, depending on some of the other variables listed here. Large cases with thousands of documents may take several months or more to complete. A lot depends on what information is to be contained in the support system and the complexity of the issues.

2. Are you using a full-text retrieval or a document abstract system? If you are using a full-text retrieval system, how will the full text be entered? If documents can be scanned into the computer or are available on disk through electronic discovery, as opposed to being typed into the computer, the process will be much faster.

3. How many people experienced with litigation support will be entering the data? Experienced people can input data much faster than people with little or no experience. In addition, many firms believe that it is smarter to have their experienced people do only the coding of the forms and to hire typists to actually enter the data into the computer. Another thing to consider is that if you begin the process of inputting data and find that you are running short of time or are shorthanded, many good litigation support service bureaus can come in and finish the inputting job for you.

How Long Will It Take to Learn a Litigation Support Program?

Generally speaking, most litigation support programs are not difficult to learn. The real trick is not learning the program itself, but learning how to set up and design the system so that you are able to retrieve the information you need when you need it. You want to be able to get at information quickly and accurately, especially when the

EXHIBIT 7–14

Litigation support tips

1. **Efficient and clean databases work best.** When you design and populate a litigation support database, keep it simple and straightforward, and enter only *relevant* information. Do not clutter your database with irrelevant information that will slow down the speed of the system or may retrieve unnecessary information during searches.
2. **Be an expert on the facts and legal issues in the case.** Before you can truly design a litigation support database that will meet your needs, you must fully understand the facts and legal issues of the case and understand the significance of the documents or information that you will be tracking.
3. **Legal documents are easier to search on than discovery documents.** You can search legal documents (depositions, pleadings, hearings, transcripts) more easily than discovery documents produced by parties.
4. **It is easier to search on documents that you produce rather than on documents the other party produces.** You can search your own documents more easily than documents you have never seen before.
5. **Searching on concepts is more difficult than searching on proper names or dates.** You can search for names and dates more easily than concepts. Concepts can be ambiguous and require you to be creative regarding what words might be used to describe them, whereas dates and names are usually straightforward and standard.
6. **Complex Boolean searches can be difficult to master.** It is sometimes difficult to construct complex Boolean searches that retrieve everything you need. It is sometimes easier to break down complex searches into smaller chunks.
7. **A quality team of legal staff who are educated on the specifics of the case and are using a well-thought-out database are more valuable than armies of untrained temporaries.** Computers cannot take the place of a good legal team. Armies of untrained office staff notwithstanding, often only an attorney or a paralegal is going to recognize the implications of a piece of evidence. Quality is more important than quantity.
8. **One piece of the pie is not enough.** Litigation support users truly need document abstract, full-text, and imaging capability for documents. The best approach is usually to standardize with one software package that can handle it all and search all of the modules at one time. And don't forget case mangement and analytical applications, they also add great value to litigation support.
9. **Don't build an inflexible litigation support database.** Design your database from the beginning for multiple purposes and multiple users. This way, if the players or the issues change you will be prepared.
10. **Carefully number every page of every document.** Assign every document/page a Bates number, or use alternative technologies such as bar coding. To admit a document into evidence, you typically need a hard copy of the document. Thus, you must be able to lay your hands on the document. The only way this is possible is for your documents to be carefully numbered so that the needle can be found in the haystack under pressure and when it counts. If you will use imaging, you will need electronic Bates numbering as well.
11. **Make standardized rules.** Establish rules to govern the inputting of information and stick to them. Create and distribute a list of standardized rules for inputting data, and train all staff that are entering data on them. Data in the database must be consistent or problems will arise.
12. **Use the fewest amount of people possible to enter data.** The more people that are involved in entering information into the database, the more you have to train, the more you have to audit, and the harder it is to manage.
13. **Do quality audits and test as you go along.** Again, quality is more important than quantity. Don't wait until the end of the project to find out half the data was entered wrong. Do periodic quality audit checks as you go along, and test the data regularly to make sure the database is working properly. "Garbage in—garbage out" applies to databases.
14. **Input trial exhibit numbers for your opponents.** Input the opposing party's trial exhibit numbers into the database so that you will be able to quickly find your copy in the corresponding database folder when the opposing party offers the exhibit into evidence.

EXHIBIT 7–14
(*Continued*)

15. **Don't wait until trial to enter your documents.** Enter all documents in the database as they come into the case if possible. Preparing for trial is hard enough without trying to do a big project like creating a litigation support database at the last minute.
16. **Update the database every day at trial.** Update the database after each day of trial with all exhibits, so at the end of trial you will have an up-to-date list of what was offered and admitted.
17. **Print hard copies of documents and make backups.** Print a paper copy of anything you could not live without at trial and make *regular* backup copies of your databases. Computer systems sometimes fail and usually at the worst possible moment.

pressure is on and time is of the essence, such as at trial. This is something that you will quickly pick up, because you will gain experience with each new case you work on. As you become more experienced, the process will get much smoother.

Do You Have to Computerize a Case from the Beginning?

Cases can be switched over to a litigation support program even after they have started. In fact, it might be a good idea to wait a few weeks to begin designing a system until after the adversary answers some of your more important arguments. This will allow you to see where the crux of the litigation will lie. If you design a litigation support system without knowing even the basics of how an adversary will argue the case, you may not end up with a very good system; you need one that can adapt to changes required to meet the adversary's arguments.

However, it is best not to wait until a case is almost ready to go to trial, because in many instances you will not be able to get all the information you need into the system in time. Further, a litigation support system can be quite helpful in the middle of a litigation process, for tasks such as preparing to take depositions of key witnesses and framing your arguments for motions and memorandums.

Can Computerized Litigation Support Be Used in the Courtroom?

Computerized litigation support systems are welcome in most courtrooms. Laptop computers are commonplace, not only for the litigators but also for the judges, court reporters, and other judicial staff. It is not uncommon to see separate tables for computers and litigation support staff in the courtroom. This is a real benefit for litigators, because searches in the litigation support system can be performed right in the courtroom whenever information is needed.

ETHICAL CONSIDERATIONS

In many cases, litigation support means the difference between winning and losing. This is particularly true in large cases where the litigants have much at stake; in some high-stakes cases, hundreds of millions of dollars may be at issue. Whether the case is large or small, though, the law office has the ethical duty to present its client's case as well as it possibly can. This includes being competent and acting diligently. If a litigation support system is set up poorly, if the litigation support system is not used competently, or if the litigation support system fails entirely, then the client's case suffers. In addition, in most situations the client is actually paying for staff time and expenses to set up and use the litigation support system. If the litigation support system fails, then not only does the client's case suffer, but the client is also billed and pays for a service from which it did not get any benefit. Litigation support definitely carries ethical responsibilities, in that it is an extremely important aspect of any client's case and often determines whether the client wins or loses.

SUMMARY

Litigation support software is designed to assist attorneys in organizing information that has been gathered during litigation. The purpose of these programs is to help attorneys find the information they need to adequately work on and try a case.

Manual litigation support methods do not work well in the legal environment, because they are not flexible enough for the ever-changing pace of modern lawsuits. Computerized litigation support methods can adapt to this changing environment, because they allow users to search an unlimited amount of data in many ways.

Computerized litigation support can either be performed by a litigation support service provider or done in-house. Service providers offer a number of advantages, including being able to draw on their knowledge and experience, having someone other than the legal team be fully responsible for the litigation support system, being able to tie electronic discovery duties and litigation support together, and being able to handle and work with tens or even hundreds of thousands of documents, among others. However, the law office (and ultimately the client) may pay a lot for these services.

Whether litigation support is performed by a service provider or in-house, a legal organization must decide whether a document abstract or document summary system will be used and whether full-text, imaging, case management, or analytical programs, or a combination of all of them, will be used.

A document abstract litigation support system allows users to enter document abstracts summaries into a computer and subsequently to search and retrieve information contained in the abstracts or summaries. Full-text retrieval systems enable users to search and retrieve information contained in the full text of documents entered into the system. In some instances, a document abstract system will be used to track documents, and a full-text retrieval system will be used to track depositions and other types of testimony in the same case.

Document imaging allows a legal professional to see the actual image of a document, as opposed to seeing its full text or an abstract of the document. Document imaging can be accomplished by scanning hard-copy images into a computer or by converting electronic documents into an image file format such as TIFF or PDF.

Analytical litigation support software helps legal professionals view a case from a number of perspectives and helps them conceptualize and think about facts, documents, people, and the relationships among them. This type of software includes programs that create timelines or outlines of cases, as well as itemize facts, documents, issues, and people.

Some litigation support systems now offer document abstract, full-text retrieval, imaging, and analytical tools in one program. These powerful packages offer the advantages of all these types of systems, but are typically complex. No matter what type of litigation support system is used, it is necessary that users carefully plan the design of the system, taking into account what type of information is most relevant to the case and how it will be used during litigation and at trial. A litigation support system that is poorly planned will surely fail and perhaps cause the case to be lost.

KEY TERMS

analytical litigation support programs
Bates stamp
Boolean logic search
computer-aided transcription (CAT)
document abstract litigation support
   system
document imaging

full-text retrieval litigation support
   system
in-house computerized litigation
   support system
litigation support service provider
litigation support software
objective/bibliographical coding

proximity search
real-time transcription
single-word search
subjective coding
super wildcard search
wildcard search

INTERNET SITES

Internet sites for this chapter include:

ORGANIZATION	DESCRIPTION	WORLD WIDE WEB ADDRESS
1360 Studios, Inc.	Transcript Manager Pro transcript management	www.transcriptmanagerpro.com
Access Data Group, LLC	Summation litigation support products	www.summation.com
Anacomp	Case Logistix litigation support program	www.caselogistix.com
C2 Legal	E-discovery and litigation support services	www.c2legal.com
CaseCentral	E-discovery and litigation support services	www.casecentral.com
Cricket Technologies	E-discovery and litigation support services	www.crickettechnologies.com
DT Software Inc.	Data searching and litigation support	www.dtsearch.com
Gigatron Software	Transcription software	www.gsclion.com
I Conect Development	E-discovery and litigation support services	www.iconect.com
Kroll Ontrack	E-discovery and litigation support services	www.krollontrack.com
LexisNexis	CaseMap and TimeMap litigation support	www.casesoft.com
LexisNexis	Concordance litigation support	www.lexisnexis.com/concordance
Real Legal	Litigation support and transcript management products	www.reallegal.com
Rosen Technology Resources	E-discovery and litigation support services	www.rosentech.net
Zylab	E-discovery and litigation support products	www.zylab.com

TEST YOUR KNOWLEDGE

1. True or False: Litigation support software primarily assists legal professionals in responding to electronic discovery requests.

2. True or False: Litigation support is an easy task because, for the most part, legal issues, factual issues, and legal theories are static during the litigation of a case.

3. Distinguish between litigation documents and factual documents.

4. What is knowledge management?

5. Name three benefits of computerized litigation support.

6. Distinguish document abstracting, full-text retrieval, and imaging.

7. What advantages does use of a litigation support service provider offer?

8. Differentiate between objective and subjective coding in relation to creating document abstracts.

9. What is a controlled vocabulary, and in what litigation support system is this important?

10. What type of search uses "AND," "OR," and "NOT"?

ON THE WEB EXERCISES

1. Using the addresses listed in the "Internet Sites" section of this chapter, visit the websites of the following three vendors: Case Logistix, CT Summation (iBlaze), and LexisNexis (Concordance litigation support software). Write a two-page paper that summarizes the features of each product.

2. Visit the American Bar Association's website and search for articles on litigation support. Find three articles on the topic. Write a one-page summary of each article.

3. Using a general search engine such as www.google.com or www.yahoo.com, research computer-aided transcription and write a two-page article on what it is, how it works, and why it is helpful to practicing legal professionals like attorneys and paralegals.

QUESTIONS AND EXERCISES

1. As the chief litigation paralegal, you are preparing to have clerical staff enter approximately 1,000 documents into a computerized litigation support system. You are concerned that the information may not be entered uniformly, because 10 different people will be doing this data entry work. What should you do to solve the problem? Give a detailed answer.

2. An attorney in your firm is having trouble deciding whether she should switch her staff from their manual litigation support system to a computerized system. Tell the attorney what you think about the situation.

3. You have been asked to give your opinion as to whether a litigation support database should be created for a particular case. The case involves approximately 200 documents, which average

150 pages each. The issues are complex, and four attorneys will need five months to try the case. Damages requested are minimal, but the public relations damage to your client could be devastating should your client lose. The opposing counsel may or may not use a litigation support database; your firm does not know. Should the case be entered into a litigation support database? Why or why not?

4. Using this chapter as a guide, and specifically the tips in Exhibit 7–14, design a litigation support system for one of the following types of lawsuits:

   • High-speed auto accident involving multiple cars, multiple witnesses, and no evidence of design defects

   • Wrongful termination claim based on age discrimination and involving multiple witnesses

- Securities fraud case in which investors claim they invested in a company that withheld information about its true financial situation
- Medical malpractice claim involving the wrongful death of a patient undergoing a medical procedure
- Product liability class action against a manufacturer alleging design defects in a tractor

Your design should consider what type of litigation support method you will use, who will enter the data and how, what type of information will be entered, when it will be entered, what issues will be disputed at trial, and other such information. Prepare a (minimum) three-page summary of your design, including specifics of how you arrived at your design.

ETHICS QUESTION

You work as a paralegal for a small law firm. Your firm does not use any of the litigation support tools discussed in this chapter. When your firm gets a new client with a very complex case, the new client agrees to pay a portion of the costs of acquiring a new litigation support software package. In return, the firm will be able to work more efficiently and produce more work per hour billed to that client. One of the attorneys suggests that the firm use the litigation support program for other clients' cases too. What, if any, ethical issues are raised by this scenario?

Go to the Workbook to complete the Hands-On Exercises.

CourseMate   Access an interactive eBook, chapter-specific interactive learning tools, including flash cards, quizzes, and more in your Paralegal CourseMate, accessed through CengageBrain.com.

CHAPTER 8

The Internet, Computer-Assisted Legal Research, and Electronic Mail

CHAPTER OBJECTIVES

After completing this chapter, you should be able to do the following:

1. Explain the different types of services the Internet offers.
2. Discuss problems with using the Internet for research.
3. Explain what a listserv is.
4. Describe the difference between a subject-oriented search engine and a metasearch engine.
5. List resources for finding precise legal information on the Internet.
6. List resources for finding factual information on the Internet.
7. Explain why manual research and computerized research complement one another.
8. Explain what is involved in planning a search query.
9. Formulate simple search queries for Westlaw or LexisNexis.

INTRODUCTION TO THE INTERNET

The Internet is one of the world's largest computer networks; it is variously described as a "network of networks," "the information superhighway," or "cyberspace." It connects hundreds of millions of computers and thousands of networks around the world. Unlike Westlaw, LexisNexis, or other online services, no one owns the Internet as a whole or runs it. The Internet simply connects thousands of computers that use the same network protocol or language. Each network on the Internet is independently owned and operated. To access the Internet, all a user needs is a computer, communication software, communication technology such as a cable modem, and an account with an Internet access provider.

When you do **computer-assisted legal research (CALR)**, you use a computer to search for and retrieve legal information. The two best-known and most-used CALR service providers are Westlaw and LexisNexis.

computer-assisted legal research (CALR)
Research method in which computers are used to find and retrieve legal information.

Connecting to the Internet

To connect to the Internet, you need a computer, a modem or cable modem, a means of connecting to the Internet, Internet software, and an **Internet service provider (ISP)**. An ISP provides its users with Internet services such as the World Wide Web, email, listservs, newsgroups, and many others. Some of the largest ISPs include Comcast and AT&T. Users now have many options for connecting to the "information superhighway," such as DSL, cable modem, T1 line, and others. These options, though more expensive than a traditional telephone line, have much larger bandwidths and thus are much faster at carrying and displaying video, sounds, and graphics. Most legal organizations now use one or more of these faster options.

Internet service provider (ISP)
Supplies users with Internet services such as the World Wide Web, email, listservs, newsgroups, and others.

World Wide Web

The **World Wide Web** is an Internet system, navigation tool, and interface that retrieves information using Internet addresses and links to web pages. To access the Web, you need a web browser program such as Microsoft Internet Explorer, Google Chrome, Bing, or Firefox.

The Web is a graphical and multimedia interface. Web pages can contain text, graphical images, moving pictures, animation, and sound, and often use hypermedia or hypertext links. If you are at a web page that references another website and supplies a hypermedia or hypertext link, all you have to do is click the link to be taken immediately to the new website. The millions of websites available on the Web include many law-related websites.

To find information on the Web, you often need to use a search engine. Whether you are looking for legal materials or nonlegal materials, there are tricks for how to find the desired information quickly and accurately.

Many legal organizations have their own web pages, as well as intranet and/or extranet sites. All of these are covered in detail in this chapter.

World Wide Web
An Internet system, navigation tool, and graphical/multimedia interface that retrieves information using links to other web pages. To access the Web, a user needs a web browser program.

Web Browser Software

To access the World Wide Web, you must have web browser software installed on your computer. A **web browser** is the interface or program that allows you to see web pages. Two popular web browsers are Microsoft's Internet Explorer and Firefox. After a web browser has been properly installed, you simply load the browser software, which then connects to your ISP. Once connected to the ISP, the browser software loads your home web page.

Everything on the Web has a unique address, known as a **uniform resource locator (URL)**. When a web browser loads, it automatically defaults to the user's home URL. You can change your home URL at any time by entering the new URL in the browser, or by changing the setting in the software's "Preferences" section.

web browser
The interface or program that allows the user to see web pages.

uniform resource locator (URL)
The address of a web page.

Electronic Mail

Electronic mail (email) enables users to send and receive messages almost instantly. Because the Internet is one of the largest networks of computers in the world, it allows hundreds of millions of users to send messages to each other, whether it is across a city or across the world. When a user obtains an Internet account, she or he is given an email address, which is what other people will use to send email to that user. Sending and receiving email is very straightforward: users send messages, receive messages, and manage their mailboxes with a mail program. Email is discussed in more detail later in this chapter.

electronic mail (email)
Computerized communication function that enables users to send and receive messages almost instantly.

File Transfer Protocol (FTP)

File Transfer Protocol (FTP)
A tool or standard for transferring electronic files over the Internet.

File Transfer Protocol (FTP) is a tool or standard for transferring files over the Internet. In many cases, administrators copy certain files to public directories on their FTP servers. Users can then download the files from the FTP server. There are publicly available FTP sites, allowing access to millions of files. FTP software lets you choose a computer to connect to and then enables you to upload or download files, including text, pictures, sounds, cases, and statutes. You can download files using an Internet browser or a special FTP program.

Listservs

listserv
An electronic mailing list that allows people on the list to send messages to and receive messages from everyone on the list via email.

A **listserv** (a short name that stands for "list server") is an electronic mailing list that allows people on the list to send email messages to and receive messages from everyone on the list. To join a listserv, you send an email indicating that you want to subscribe. After you have been added to the listserv, you receive copies of any emails sent to that listserv. Also, when you send an email to the listserv, everyone on the listserv gets a copy of your message.

A listserv is an easy way for people to communicate through email. There are thousands of listservs on the Internet, each dedicated to a particular topic or area of interest. You can find listserv mailing lists by searching "listserv" using a search engine (described later in this chapter).

Instant Messaging

instant messaging (IM)
Communication function that allows users to converse in real time with other users who are using the same IM program. As soon as a user connects to the Internet, the user will know which of his or her colleagues are signed on and be able to send them messages.

Instant messaging (IM) allows users to "converse" electronically, in real time, with other users. As soon as a user of an instant messaging program connects to the Internet, he or she will know exactly which colleagues are signed on to the Internet. IM software allows you to send any or all of them a message, even if they all use different ISPs.

Blogs

blog
A website with information contained in posts (writings resembling diary or journal entries) that are arranged in reverse chronological order.

A **blog** (short for weblog) is a website with information contained in "posts" that are arranged in reverse chronological order. Blog postings resemble diary or journal entries, and may contain links to other websites or articles.

There are many law-related blogs on the Internet, including specialized blogs on certain types of law and even paralegal-related blogs (see paralegalgateway.typepad.com and estrinlegaled.typepad.com). Law-related blogs are sometimes called "blawgs." A good way of finding blogs on the Internet is to use Google's blog search tool, blogsearch.google.com.

RSS

RSS
A group of formats that are used to publish and distribute news feeds, blogs, and podcasts.

RSS is a group of formats that are used to publish and distribute news feeds, blogs, and podcasts. RSS allows users to "push" news, blog updates, and other information to RSS readers and web pages. Users can subscribe to RSS feeds and access the updated information as soon as it comes in. Free RSS reader programs are widely available on the Internet.

There are many legal-related RSS feeds, including one for recent U.S. Supreme Court opinions (www.law.cornell.edu/supct/rss/supct_recent.rss) and one for recent copyright information from the U.S. Copyright Office (see www.copyright.gov).

Podcasts

podcast
An audio or video recording that is posted on the Internet and made available for users to download so they can listen or watch it on a computer or mobile computing device.

A **podcast** is an audio or video recording that is posted on the Internet and is typically made available for users to download so they can listen to it on a computer or mobile computing device. Music, lectures, blogs, and other recordings can be made available as podcasts and can also be pushed to users using an RSS format. You can search for podcasts by subject matter (including legal-related podcasts) at www.allpodcasts.com and www.itunes.com.

USE OF THE INTERNET IN LEGAL ORGANIZATIONS

Most, if not all, legal organizations are connected to the Internet and are using it in a variety of ways. Some of the most common uses include performing legal research, performing factual and business research, using email to communicate with clients and colleagues, accessing court records, filing documents electronically, marketing, taking online depositions, and conducting online learning.

Performing Legal Research on the Internet

A great deal of legal material is available on the Internet. Unfortunately, unlike Westlaw and LexisNexis, it is not all available in one place: it is scattered all over the Internet. The positive side of legal research on the Internet is that most of the information is free. The resources available include federal case law, federal legislative materials, government regulations, and state case law. Later in this chapter, we explore in detail the process of finding legal materials and conducting legal research on the Internet.

Performing Factual and Business Research on the Internet

You may undertake factual research to find people and information about people, find expert witnesses, find evidence useful for impeaching experts and other witnesses, gather information regarding businesses, and look for facts in newspaper articles and other sources about cases or witnesses. Later in this chapter, we discuss in more detail how to perform factual research on the Internet.

Using Email to Communicate with Clients and Colleagues

Email is a very convenient form of communication for legal professionals. It is nearly instantaneous, creates a record for both tracking and saving information, is inexpensive, is easy to use, and is convenient (unlike the telephone, you don't have to play telephone tag with busy callers). Its use is widespread, so many clients, colleagues, vendors, and others can be reached via email. Email programs even allow you to send or attach documents, such as word-processing documents, to an email message.

Email has been wholeheartedly accepted by the legal community, and is now used as much as (if not more than) the telephone for both internal communication with colleagues and external communication with clients, courts, and other legal organizations. Email is covered in depth later in this chapter.

Accessing Court Records and Filing Documents Electronically

Most courts allow legal professionals to access court records electronically, which is often more convenient (and almost always faster) than calling clerks or other staff for information or hard copies of documents. Many courts also allow documents to be filed electronically. Electronic filing offers time savings, cost savings, and convenience over filing of paper documents.

Marketing a Law Firm on the Internet

Law firms have realized that having a web page means that the firm can be marketed 24 hours a day, 7 days a week, to a potential nationwide and even worldwide audience. Law firm web pages are covered in more detail later in this chapter.

Taking Online Depositions

Attorneys can take depositions using an online deposition service. Typically, an attorney would use this kind of service to participate in an out-of-town deposition from his or her own office. The online deposition service provides live video and two-way audio on a secure Internet feed. Many such services also provide real-time transcription. The attorney is able to see and hear the witness, court reporter, and opposing counsel on his or her computer monitor and ask questions, make objections, and do nearly everything the attorney would do if he or she were at the deposition site. Some services even provide private online messaging so that information can be shared (securely and confidentially) between co-counsel.

Online Learning

The Internet is used to deliver online learning seminars and materials in a variety of areas to participants in legal organizations. Legal organizations can save thousands of dollars in travel costs when employees do their learning online; the organizations also experience productivity increases, since staff members never have to leave their desks.

This capability is very useful for fulfilling continuing education requirements, among many other learning opportunities. Legal organizations may also be able to supply (as well as receive) online learning content, such as seminars or webinars on specialized legal topics; or act as sponsor or host for an online course or seminar created and presented by a third party.

SEARCHING AND FINDING INFORMATION ON THE WORLD WIDE WEB

Searching the Web for information is one of the most common uses of the Internet for paralegals. If you do not have a URL for a desired website, or if you do not know exactly which website you want to access, you must use a search engine to try to find it. Unfortunately, it often is not easy to find the exact information you are looking for, due to the breadth and depth of information available on the Web. There are millions of different websites and more than 1 billion web pages on the Internet; therefore, you must learn how to find what you need quickly and precisely.

Search Engines

Most search engines use computerized functions or algorithms called spiders to search or "crawl" the Web to compile their databases. Once the spiders find a website, they typically index many of the words on the public pages at the site. Web page owners may also submit their URLs to search engines for crawling and eventual inclusion in the search-engine databases.

When you enter a search in a search engine, you are asking the engine to search its database; it is not actually searching the Web at that moment. In addition, no search engine covers the entire Web. Some search engines are better at finding particular kinds of information than others. Which search engine you use should depend on the particular information you are looking for. There are a number of different types and ways of classifying search engines.

individual search engine
Search engine that compiles its own searchable database.

An **individual search engine** compiles its own searchable database. One popular general individual search engine is Google (www.google.com). In addition to individual search engines that are general in nature, such as Google, there are also **specialty search engines**. A specialty search engine searches only in specific topical areas. Examples are www.searchgov.com, which searches government-related websites; and www.findlaw.com, which searches only law-related websites.

specialty search engine
Search engine that searches only in specific topical areas or sites.

Another kind of search engine is a **metasearch engine**. A metasearch engine does not crawl the Web or compile its own database. Instead, it sends the user's search request to a number of different individual search engines, eliminates the duplicate hits, and sorts or ranks the sites retrieved. Metasearch engines provide a quick overview of a subject and can be used to quickly find which engines will probably yield the best results for your particular search. Popular metasearch engines include www.metacrawler.com and www.dogpile.com.

A **subject directory** is a site maintained by an organization's staff, who select sites to include in the directory database. A popular subject directory is Yahoo (www.yahoo.com). Yahoo editors organize directory hierarchies into subject categories; the "Web Site Directory" at www.yahoo.com is an example of this. It should be noted that the line between search engines and subject directories is becoming somewhat blurry, with each sometimes combining both types of search techniques.

Many search engines or subject directory sites, such as Yahoo, are also portals. A **portal** is a "jumping-off" point for many things on the Web, offering searching, hierarchical directories, news, sports, shopping, entertainment, and much more. The basic portal concept is that a user will go to one place on the Web to start and then fan out to a number of other sites from that one starting point. FindLaw.com is a popular legal portal.

Another way to find information on the Web is to use a gateway site such as a **library gateway**. A library gateway is a collection of databases and information sites arranged by subject. These gateways usually support research and reference needs by pointing users to recommended, academically oriented pages on the Web. Exhibit 8–1 is an example of a library gateway.

Another way to find information on the Web is to use a **subject-specific database** that collects materials on a single subject. For example, CareerBuilder.com is a subject-specific database that is totally devoted to finding jobs. The open-position database in CareerBuilder.com usually contains hundreds of thousands of listings. There are many such subject-specific databases on the Web.

The **invisible Web**, sometimes called the deep Web, refers to the fact that a large portion of the World Wide Web is not accessible to search-engine spiders. For one

metasearch engine
Search engine that does not crawl the Web or compile its own database, but instead sends the user's search request to a number of different individual search engines and then eliminates duplicates and sorts the sites retrieved.

subject directory
A site maintained by a staff of people who select sites to include in the directory.

portal
A "jumping-off" spot for many things on the Web, offering searching, hierarchical directories, news, sports, shopping, entertainment, and much more.

library gateway
A collection of databases and information sites arranged by subject.

subject-specific database
A database devoted to a single subject or area.

invisible web
Term for the large portion of the World Wide Web that is not accessible to search engine spiders. This includes PDF files, password-protected sites, some databases, documents behind firewalls, and other data/sites.

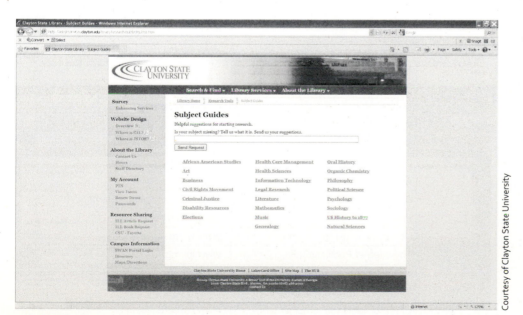

Courtesy of Clayton State University

EXHIBIT 8–1
Library gateway

reason or another, search engines cannot access these sites/pages; they may be password protected, in databases, behind firewalls, or otherwise invisible or inaccessible to the search engines. It is estimated that more than 50 percent of the Web falls into this category.

For example, a search engine will not find a job opening that is listed in Careerbuilder.com, because that site is a database and individual entries therein are protected. To access "invisible" websites, you must point your web browser directly to the desired site (which, of course, means that you must know its exact URL, and often that you must have permission to enter or access the site). Exhibit 8–2 shows a variety of websites for search engines, gateways, and databases on the Web.

Search Strategies

The following subsections describe a variety of general strategies for searching the Web.

EXHIBIT 8–2

Search engines, gateways, and databases of interest to paralegals

Name of Site	Web URL (Address)
General Individual/Subject Directory Search Engines	
All The Web	www.alltheweb.com
AltaVista	www.altavista.com
Excite	www.excite.com
Google	www.google.com
Lycos	www.lycos.com
MSN Search	http://search.msn.com
Northernlight	www.northernlight.com
WebCrawler	www.webcrawler.com
Yahoo	www.yahoo.com
Specialty Search Engines	
Google US Government	www.google.com
SearchGov (Government)	www.searchgov.com
SearchEdu (Education)	www.searchedu.com
SearchMil (Military)	www.searchmil.com
Pandia Newsfinder (News)	www.pandia.com/news
Metasearch Engines	
Dogpile	www.dogpile.com
Ixquick	www.ixquick.com
Kartoo	www.kartoo.com
Metacrawler	www.metacrawler.com
Library Gateways	
Academic Information	www.academicinfo.net
Digital Librarian	www.digital-librarian.com
Infomine	http://infomine.ucr.edu
Librarians' Index to the Internet	www.lii.org
The Internet Public Library	www.ipl.org
Virtual Library	www.vlib.org
Subject-Specific Databases	
Careerbuilder.com (employment)	www.careerbuilder.com
WebMD (health/medical information)	www.webmd.com

EXHIBIT 8–3

Advanced Search options in Google

Think about Your Search Different searches require different strategies. If you are looking for general information about a topic, a subject directory search engine such as Yahoo.com or a metasearch engine such as dogpile.com are good places to start. If you are looking for a very narrow topic or specific piece of information, consider what the subject matter is and use a specialty search engine or a database to find the information. For example, if you were looking for government-related information, it would be best to start with a government search engine such as SearchGov (www.searchgov.com); if you were looking for information on a detailed medical issue, it would be best to search WebMD (www.webmd.com). The more detailed or specific the information you are looking for, the more specialized your search engine or database will most likely have to be. See Exhibit 8–2 for a listing of search engines.

Use Advanced Search Options Most search engines have an area on the title page that directs you to advanced search. Advanced search options allow you to tailor your search so that it does not return thousands of documents. For example, in Exhibit 8–3 the user has entered the exact phrase she is looking for (freedom of speech). She has also directed Google to return files in Portable Document Format (PDF) only. Note that she could have limited it to other file formats as well, such as Word, Excel, or PowerPoint. Exhibit 8–3 also shows that she limited the search to web pages that have been updated in the past month, in the hopes of getting only current articles; and that she limited the search to the title of the page, in order to get articles directly on point. Using advanced options is a great way to increase efficiency and get better search results more quickly.

Read the Help or Search Guide Files for the Search Engines You Use Different search engines may require you to use different syntax for entering searches. Always read the help file for the search engine you are currently using to make sure you are entering search commands correctly. Users all too commonly assume that the commands are the same in various search engines, only to find out later that a search was not performed properly because the syntax was incorrect for the search engine used.

Make Your Search Query Specific To return only relevant documents, make your search query specific. For example, if you are searching for documents about the United States Supreme Court Rules, do not search on the overly broad topic of

"United States Supreme Court." Use modifiers, such as the following, to make your search as specific as possible.

- *Use + (plus) and − (minus) signs.* Use plus and minus signs to force inclusion or exclusion of a word in searches. For example, if the search was: *+Roosevelt −Theodore,* the search would find documents with "Roosevelt" but without the word "Theodore." If you wanted results that included Franklin Roosevelt but not Theodore Roosevelt, the query would be *+Roosevelt +Franklin −Theodore.* The plus and minus signs work in many but not all search engines; be sure to consult the help guide for each engine you want to use.

- *Search for phrases using quotation marks.* If you are looking for a specific phrase, put the phrase in quotation marks so that the search engine will retrieve only documents that have the words exactly as you typed them. For example, "*Joint tenants with rights of survivorship*" would retrieve sites and documents with exactly those words in exactly that order, but not ones where those words appear scattered throughout the document.

- *Combine plus and minus signs and phrases.* You can also combine the plus and minus signs and phrase searching in one query: for example, "*Franklin Delano Roosevelt*"−"*New Deal*"+"*World War II*". This query would yield results that had the exact phrase "Franklin Delano Roosevelt" and the phrase "World War II," but did not have the phrase "New Deal." (Again, be sure to consult the help guide for each engine you want to use to find the correct format and syntax for the search.)

Put Your Most Important Words First Usually, the best strategy is to put the most important or most specific word first in the search.

PERFORMING LEGAL RESEARCH ON THE INTERNET

You can perform legal research on the Internet, but it is not at all like researching on Westlaw or LexisNexis. In Westlaw and LexisNexis, you can look up, choose, and go to thousands of databases instantly; searches go through a uniform search engine using uniform Boolean language; and information is formatted neatly, succinctly, and uniformly. Even so, it still takes time, training, and experience to become proficient at using Westlaw or LexisNexis.

When performing legal research on the Internet in general (rather than through a proprietary service), you will find that little is uniform. You must search for and find information where you can, and you must learn the nuances of many different search techniques and languages. There is no one central depository of information. As with any kind of legal research, the more experience you have, the better, but it takes time, training, and experience to get good at it.

You can expect to find the following legal information on the Internet, by using the sites listed in Exhibit 8–4:

- Indexes by legal topic (tax law, intellectual property, family law, etc.)
- Government sites (extensive)
- United States Supreme Court cases (extensive)
- Federal appellate court cases (extensive)
- Federal district court cases (partial)
- Federal laws, regulations, and legislative bills (extensive—including *United States Code, Federal Register, Congressional Record, Code of Federal Regulations*)

Subject	Additional Information	Web URL (Address)
Legal Research Engine/Portal		
All Law	Legal search engine/portal	www.alllaw.com
FindLaw	Legal search engine/portal	www.findlaw.com
Internet Legal Research Group	Legal search engine	www.ilrg.com
Lawguru	Legal search engine/portal	www.lawguru.com
General Starting Points (Federal/State Case Law, Statutes, and Legal Subject Matter)		
Hieros Gamos	Large collection of links to legal resources	www.hg.org
Law Research	Large collection of links to legal resources	www.lawresearch.com
Legal Information Institute at Cornell	Large collection of links to legal resources	www.law.cornell.edu
Virtual Chase	Large collection of links to legal resources	www.virtualchase.com
WashLaw Web at Washburn University	Large collection of links to legal resources	www.washlaw.edu
Federal Government Information, Regulations, Laws, Bills, U.S. Code		
FedWorld	Government information	www.fedworld.gov
First Gov	Government search engine	www.firstgov.com
Google US Government	Government search engine	www.google.com/ig/usgov
SearchGov	Government search engine	www.searchgov.com
Code of Federal Regulations	Database for the Code of Federal Regulations	www.law.cornell.edu
GPO Access	Wide variety of federal government resources	www.gpoaccess.gov
Cornell Legal Information Institute	Wide variety of federal government resources	www.law.cornell.edu
Library of Congress	Bills, resolutions, Congressional Record	http://thomas.loc.gov
Legal Forms		
Internet Legal Resource Guide Forms	Free legal forms database	www.ilrg.com
Legal Encyclopedia and References		
Findlaw Legal Dictionary	Legal dictionary	dictionary.lp.findlaw.com
Law About (from Cornell Law School Legal Information Institute)	Legal encyclopedia	www.law.cornell.edu
Law Dictionary	Legal dictionary	http://dictionary.law.com
Legal Dictionary	Legal dictionary	www.legal-dictionary.org
Federal Courts		
Administrative Offices of the U.S. Courts	Links to all federal courts	www.uscourts.gov
Federal Courts Finder	Links to all federal courts	www.law.emory.edu
State Courts		
National Center for State Courts	Information on state (and federal) courts	www.ncsconline.org
Fee-Based Legal Research		
Casemaker.com	Online fee-based legal research	www.casemaker.us
Fastcase.com	Online fee-based legal research	www.fastcase.com
Lexis	Full online fee-based legal research	www.lexis.com
Lexisone.com	Fee-based legal research for small firms	www.lexisone.com
Loislaw.com	Online fee-based legal research	www.loislaw.com
Versuslaw.com	Online fee-based legal research	www.versuslaw.com
Westlaw	Full online fee-based legal research	www.westlaw.com

EXHIBIT 8–4

Legal research starting points

- Federal Rules of Civil Procedure, Federal Rules of Evidence, Federal Rules of Criminal Procedure, Federal Rules of Bankruptcy Procedure; Uniform Commercial Code
- Executive orders (extensive)
- State court cases (extensive)
- State statutes (extensive)
- Legal forms
- Legal references (extensive)

Legal Research on the Internet—An Example

If you wanted to read the U.S. Supreme Court opinion *New York Times Co. v. Sullivan,* 376 U.S. 254 (1964), on the Internet, you could take many avenues to get there. Because an historic case like this is readily available on the Internet, it would be a waste of money (unless you had a flat-rate agreement) to use Westlaw or LexisNexis. As indicated previously, you need to determine where your starting point will be. Although you could start at FindLaw, Lawguru, or another legal search engine, it is probable that an important case like this would be on Cornell's Legal Information Institute site (www .law.cornell.edu). Go to Cornell's site and click "Read the law," then "Supreme Court," and then "By party—historic." You will see an alphabetical list of historical decisions. Clicking "New York Times Co. v. Sullivan" will display the case on your screen.

In November 2009, the legal research landscape changed dramatically, as Google made it possible to search state and federal case law. The method of searching and the search results are strikingly similar to those you would see if you used Westlaw or LexisNexis. The first screen of Exhibit 8–5 shows the Google home page; from there,

EXHIBIT 8–5

Google Scholar

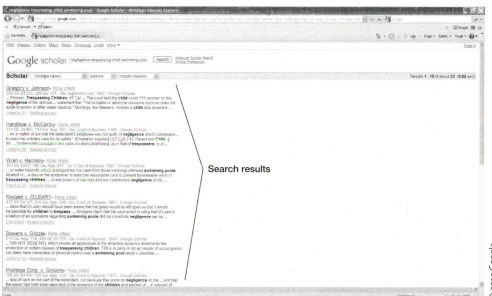

EXHIBIT 8–5

(*continued*)

choose Google Scholar. The second screen shows the Google Scholar page that gives you the choice of searching articles (including patents) or legal opinions and journals. Choosing the latter and clicking "Advanced Scholar Search" takes you to the third screen, where you can enter a search query (request) and specify the jurisdiction. In this example, we are looking for cases in Georgia that include the terms "negligence," "trespassing," "child," and "swimming pool." Finally, the fourth screen of Exhibit 8–5 shows the results of this search.

Performing Factual Research on the Internet

The Internet is best suited to factual research, because such a wide variety of information is available. The myriad of factual situations encountered in a law office means that you may need information, and thus have to do factual research, on a huge variety of topics. Here are some examples of common situations in which a paralegal might be asked to do factual research:

- You are performing collections work and you need to do a skip-trace on a debtor who has left the area.
- Your firm has a client who was adopted, and the client wants your firm to find his birth parents.
- A crucial witness for a case you are working on has disappeared, and you need to find the witness or her relatives or neighbors so you can get a message to her.
- The attorney you are working for has to cross-examine the other party's expert witness and has asked you to find out everything you can about the expert for impeachment purposes.
- Your corporate law department needs to find reputable local counsel to litigate a breach of contract case halfway across the country.
- One of your firm's best clients is considering a merger offer from another company. You have been asked to find out as much as possible about the other company, using materials that include SEC filings, annual reports, stock prices, and any news reports on the company for the past year.
- Your firm is considering getting involved in a medical malpractice case and you need to do some general background research regarding a specific type of surgery and medical condition.
- Your client is considering purchasing a piece of real estate and you have been asked to find out as much about the property as you can.
- During litigation, the opposing party has made numerous statements to the press; you have been asked to find every such occurrence and document exactly what the person said for impeachment purposes.
- Your client was involved in an automobile collision and you have been asked to get a photograph of the intersection where it happened.

In all these situations, the Internet would be useful for finding information. Exhibit 8–6 shows listings of fact-related websites by subject. Such sites can help you find everything from an email address, to who is an inmate in a federal prison, to financial data on a publicly traded company—and much, much more.

Unfortunately, there is no standard or uniform way of entering or finding information factual information on the Internet. The Internet is a virtual haystack of enormous proportions, and finding the right needle takes time and effort; the user may have to look in many, many sites to find it, or may never find it. Searching for information on the Internet is like anything else: becoming good at it takes time and experience. The more time you spend doing it, the better you will become, the more resources you will acquire, and the more tricks you will learn. The following section covers additional information regarding factual research on the Internet classified by subject.

General Information

A huge variety of general information is available on the Internet, although the quality and accuracy of this information varies enormously. General search engines are one excellent way to search for general information on the Internet. Exhibit 8–6 lists Internet sites for dictionaries, encyclopedias, maps, a Zip Code finder, thesauruses, resources for finding attorneys, and more. One extremely helpful Internet tool for

Name/Subject	Additional Information	URL Web (Address)
General Sites		
Dictionary	Dictionary	www.dictionary.com
Dictionary	Merriam-Webster	www.webster.com
Encyclopedia	Encyclopedia	www.reference.com
Encyclopedia	Encyclopedia Britannica	www.britannica.com
Encyclopedia	High Beam Encyclopedia	www.encyclopedia.com
General factual research site	Good starting point for any research project	www.virtualchase.com
Maps	MapQuest	www.mapquest.com
National lawyer directory	FindLaw	www.findlaw.com
National lawyer directory	Martindale-Hubbell	www.martindale.com
Google Maps	Satellite and street level images for major cities	http://maps.google.com/
Thesaurus	Thesaurus	http://thesaurus.reference.com
Zip Codes	U.S. Postal Service	www.usps.gov
Public Records (Free)		
Court cases/criminal cases (federal)	PACER (Public Access to Court Electronic Records)—Provides access to an index of filings in federal district, bankruptcy, and appellate courts	http://pacer.uspci.uscourts.gov
Criminal records	Virtual Chase.com—Excellent links to federal and state resources related to criminal records	www.virtualchase.com www.sexoffender.com
Criminal records—Sex offenders	Sex offender database	
Public record links and research strategies	Virtual Chase.com—Excellent links to public records	www.virtualchase.com
Public record portal	BRB Public Information Records—Large portal to many sites with public records	www.brbpub.com
Real estate records	NETR Online—Real estate public records	www.netronline.com
State public records	Public record information is available from individual state websites. Many, but not all, states have a standard Web address: www.state.XX.us (at XX enter the state's two-letter abbreviation). Examples: Florida = www.state.fl.us; New York = www.state.ny.us	
Vital records information	Births, marriages, deaths, divorces	www.vitalrec.com
Public Records (Fee Based)		
Public and court records	Court Records.Org—Various public information, including criminal histories, property ownership, and the like in one place	www.courtrecords.org
Public records	Accurint—Wide variety of online information	www.accurint.com
Public records	BRP—Wide variety of public information	www.brbpub.com
Public records	CLEAR—Wide variety of online information	https://clear.thomsonreuters.com/
Public records	Courthouse Direct—Various information, including criminal histories, property ownership, and the like in one place	www.courthousedirect.com
Public records	DCS Information Systems—Wide variety of online information	www.dnis.com
Public records	KnowX—Wide variety of online information	www.knowx.com
Public records	Search Systems—Wide variety of online information	www.searchsystems.net
Public records	USDatalink Information Services—Wide variety of online information	www.usdatalink.com

EXHIBIT 8–6

Factual research starting points

legal organizations is sites that provide free access to satellite images of a geographic area. These images are useful in a variety of contexts, including auto accidents, some criminal matters, and insurance and property casualty litigation.

Finding People, Addresses, Phone Numbers, and Email Addresses		
People, addresses, phone locator	List of links for finding people	www.pipl.com
Links and articles on finding people	Finding people	www.virtualchase.com
People, addresses, phone numbers	Database America	www.databaseamerica.com
People, addresses, phone numbers, email addresses, Yellow Pages	Bigfoot	http://search.bigfoot.net
People, addresses, phone numbers, email addresses, Yellow Pages	Infospace	www.infospace.com
People, addresses, phone numbers, email addresses, Yellow Pages	Yahoo	www.people.yahoo.com
Email addresses	Internet Address Finder	www.iaf.net
People	Classmates.com	www.classmates.com
People	Social networking site	www.facebook.com
People	Social networking site	www.myspace.com
Other Information about People		
General information about people (living and dead)	Family Finder Index—Includes information from U.S. Census, marriage, Social Security	www.familytreemaker.com
Government record search	Search of government records for finding people	www.global-locate.com
Death database	Ancestry	www.ancestry.com
Federal campaign donors	Federal Candidate Campaign Money Page	www.tray.com
Federal prison inmates	Federal Board of Prisons	www.bop.gov
Genealogy links	Genealogy-related website links	www.cyndislist.com
Military personnel	Listing of military personnel (small monthly cost)	www.militarycity.com
Physician list	American Medical Association	www.ama-assn.org
News and Directories		
News	Directory of News Links	www.newslink.org/menu.html
News	Chicago Tribune	www.chicagotribune.com
News	Los Angeles Times	www.latimes.com
News	New York Times	www.nytimes.com
News	USA Today	www.usatoday.com
News	Wall Street Journal	www.wsj.com
News	ABC News	www.abcnews.com
News	CBS News	www.cbsnews.com
News	CNN	www.cnn.com
News	Fox News	www.foxnews.com
News	NBC News	www.msnbc.com
Researching Businesses		
Business phone/address listings	Bigfoot	http://search.bigfoot.net
Yellow Page	Yellow Pages	www.bigyellow.com
Federal Securities and Exchange Commission	Electronic Data Gathering, Analysis and Retrieval (EDGAR) database	www.sec.gov/cgi-bin/srch-edgar
Federal Securities and Exchange Commission	Required public filings for public companies	www.sec.gov

EXHIBIT 8–6

(*continued*)

Public Records

Searching for public records on the Internet is an art form. In some instances, success requires more luck than science. Generally, public records do not contain personal information such as birth date, Social Security number, or medical or financial information. Nevertheless, much information is maintained in government records, which are public. Every state, every county, every city has different rules for what information is public and what is posted online, including what form it takes, what can or cannot be searched, and at what cost. There is little uniformity even in national

Annual reports for companies	Public Register's Annual Report Service	www.prars.com
Business information	Business-related information	www.hoovers.com
Business information	Business-related information	www.companiesonline.com
Complaint information	Better Business Bureau	www.bbb.org
Finding Expert Witnesses		
Expert witnesses	Expert witness directory	www.expertpages.com
Expert witnesses	Expert witness directory	www.expertwitnessnetwork.com
Expert witnesses	Expert witness directory	www.expertwitness.com
Expert witnesses	Expert witness directory	www.jurispro.com
Expert witnesses	Technical Advisory Service for Attorneys	www.tasanet.com
Expert witnesses	Washburn University School of Law	www.washlaw.edu/
Medical-Related Information		
Medical dictionary	Medical dictionary	www.medterms.com
Medical Dictionary Online	Medical dictionary	www.online-medical-dictionary.org
Medical Conditions Glossary	Medical conditions	www.medical-conditions.org
MedLinePlus Medical Dictionary	National Library of Medicine	www.nlm.nih.gov/medlineplus/ mplusdictionary.html
Stedman's Electronic Medical Dictionary	Medical dictionary	www.stedmans.com

© Cengage Learning 2012

EXHIBIT 8–6

(*continued*)

public record searches. It pays to know a lot about the jurisdiction in which you are seeking information. This takes time.

It is also important to realize that often information published on the Internet, even when you *can* find it, is not as complete as information maintained at the source (such as a courthouse or public recorder's office). By some estimates, less than half of public records are available on the Internet, and many of those that are available are incomplete. Therefore, once you have found a helpful public record, it is recommended that you check the actual source to see if other or further information is available.

The information available in public records is vast. Public record information for a specific jurisdiction might include:

- Vital statistics (births, deaths, marriages)
- Corporate records, such as secretary of state filings and Securities and Exchange Commission filings
- Corporation commission filings
- Court records
- Criminal records
- Licenses (law, medical, nursing, public accounting, insurance, etc.)
- Sex offenders
- Adoptions
- Bankruptcies
- Campaign contributions
- Copyrights, trademarks, and patents
- Property-related information
- Judgments/liens
- Building permits and zoning
- Foreclosures
- Environmental records
- Motor vehicle records
- Driver's license records

A good place to start is with the jurisdiction and entity that keeps the information. Is the information stored by a city, county, state, or federal government? You need to know this type of information before you can do a meaningful search. For example, suppose you wanted to know the value of a defendant's property holdings in Houston, Texas. You could start at a fee-based public records site, but a better and less expensive way would be to start with the jurisdiction in which you are interested, and determine where such information is held. This may sound easy or obvious, but it can take some time to track this down if you are not familiar with the area or entity. In Houston, and in much of the United States, property is tracked by county, not city. Trying to search for property records for the City of Houston would be futile. However, once you know that Houston is in Harris County, Texas, you could search for the county in an Internet search engine and be directed to its website. You could then find the Harris County Appraisal District website, and use their record search tool to search by the name of the defendant to find all of the defendant's property holdings (and their appraised value) in Harris County. Some U.S. counties even include pictures of the property.

The information is all right there. However, to find this kind of information, you may not be able to just "Google" it. This is how the "invisible Web" works. The more you know about what you are looking for, where it is stored, and what names or labels it goes by, the better you will be at finding the information you are looking for.

The Internet is full of websites that charge for retrieving public information. Some provide great value and access to information that would be very difficult to find on your own; others are not worth the time, money, and effort required. Again, it helps to know exactly what you are looking for. Before using a pay site, ask a lot of questions and ask for references.

Finding People and Information about Them

Obviously, there is a lot of information about people on the Internet. Sure, you can "Google" someone by putting the name in a search engine, but many times this does not work well. First of all, if you are conducting a nationwide search for a common name, you will get back thousands of hits. Even if the name is uncommon, you can still expect to get back dozens, if not hundreds, of hits. The more information you have about who you are looking for, the better. Nevertheless, when trying to locate someone, it is recommended that you start with the obvious, such as searching for the person's name in Google, Yahoo, and the other general search engines listed in Exhibit 8–2, even though doing so will most likely turn up many hits.

To reduce the number of irrelevant hits, it is recommended that you search for exact matches using quotation marks, such as "Steven Rich," or (even better) "Steven A. Rich" or "Steven A. Rich" + Buffalo. If you do not find who you are looking for, the next step is to use the resources in the "Finding People" section of Exhibit 8–6. Enter the query carefully, making sure that you have spelled the name correctly, and use many variations based on the information you have. Being creative sometimes works, particularly if you know any information about the person that can be used during the search process to narrow the results.

News

The Internet has vast numbers of news-related sites. Sometimes you may need to find background information related to business dealings or companies. News sites provide broad-based information that is sometimes invaluable (see Exhibit 8–6). Another good tool for this purpose is Google's News Alerts (www.google.com/alerts). Google News Alerts (see Exhibit 8–7) allow users to have Google automatically

EXHIBIT 8–7

Google Alerts

conduct searches and email the results to them. Notice in Exhibit 8–7 that the user has entered "interstate commerce clause" as the search term. The user can then indicate what she would like Google to search (e.g., news, blogs, the Web, newsgroups, listservs) and how often. This is a convenient way to stay on top of changing events. For example, if your client was in a crash in a Toyota Corolla, you might want to stay current on information related to the vehicle, such as recalls, other crashes, and so forth. RSS feeds, covered earlier in this chapter, can also be extremely helpful in staying up to date on news and blogs that are relevant to a case.

Researching Businesses

The Internet is the perfect tool for researching information about companies, businesses, and organizations. Not only can you find a wealth of information using general search engines and news-related sites, but you can also find out a great deal of other information from more specialized sites. For publicly traded companies, the U.S. Securities and Exchange Commission's (SEC) Electronic Data Gathering Analysis and Retrieval (EDGAR) database (www.sec.gov) is a good place to start. The SEC requires publicly traded companies to file extensive current information, almost all of which is publicly available. Corporate websites, press releases, litigation documents, judicial decisions, public records such as state attorney general filings, and much more are readily available on the Internet as well.

Expert Witnesses

Finding lists of expert witnesses is an easy task using the Internet. There are many sites devoted to this one topic, and many general legal sites also offer numerous databases for finding an expert witness in practically any area (see Exhibit 8–6).

Medical-Related Information

Exhibit 8–6 lists a few sites for general medical information. These are often a good starting point for research into medical issues or conditions; you can follow up with searches more narrowly tailored to the issue of interest. There is a huge amount of medical- and health-related information on the Internet, but in this area you must be particularly careful about site and information authorship, sponsorship, accuracy, substantiation, and currency.

Internet Browser Tools

Internet browsers such as Microsoft Internet Explorer and Firefox have several features that are invaluable when you are conducting Internet research. The Find feature in Microsoft Internet Explorer, **[CTRL]+[F],** allows you to search for words on an open web page. It is common, when using general search engines, to click a link and be taken to pages and pages of text without being able to see where your search terms were found. Using the Find feature, you can re-enter a search term and be taken directly to its location in the document.

bookmark

A tool that enables a user to quickly and easily go back to a website or web page.

Another helpful feature is **bookmarks** (sometimes called favorites). Bookmarks and favorites allow you to save shortcuts to particular web pages. Not only can you save shortcuts, but you can also arrange the shortcuts into groups by setting up folders such as "news websites," "legal research sites," or "public record sites." Because serious Internet users may have hundreds of bookmarks or favorites, the ability to manage them in folders is critical.

LEGAL ORGANIZATION INTRANETS AND EXTRANETS

An intranet is an internal network designed to provide and disseminate information to internal staff using the look and feel of the World Wide Web. Similar to how the Internet provides information to the public, an intranet provides information to a legal organization's internal users. Users access an organization's intranet by using a web browser.

Legal organizations use intranets for a variety of purposes, but their primary functions are to allow people to share internal information, improve knowledge and teamwork, and streamline internal processes. Information usually included on intranets includes human resource policies, procedural manuals, training information, forms, access to databases, articles, and links to external websites.

An extranet is a secure Web-based site that allows clients to access information about their cases and collaborate with the legal professionals who are providing services to them. An extranet employs a variety of security measures to ensure that the general public does not have access to the site, and that only clients or other authorized users can view it. Extranets can enable document exchanges; sharing of information, case strategies, calendars, and updates; forums for collaboration; and much more. Extranets are particularly helpful when a legal matter is complex, multiple parties or multiple co-counsel are involved, and sharing of information is critical to the success of the matter. An extranet allows a legal organization to distribute information to one central spot where everyone involved can access it, no matter what their geographic location, time zone, or computer platform.

ELECTRONIC MAIL

Electronic mail (email) allows users to send and receive messages via computer or PDA. When an Internet account is opened, the user is given an email address and can then send and receive messages. Hundreds of millions of people use email every day to communicate.

Email use has many advantages. First and foremost are its low cost and tremendous capabilities. With inexpensive email, messages can be sent almost instantaneously nearly anywhere in the world; word-processing, sound, and graphic files can be attached to email messages; messages can be sent, read, and replied to at the user's convenience;

"telephone tag" can be made a thing of the past; messages can be sent to groups of people at the same time; users can get their messages from anywhere; and messages can be saved, tracked, and managed electronically. A common client complaint is that legal professionals are often very busy and hard to reach. Email allows legal professionals and clients to communicate with one another quickly and conveniently.

Email in the Legal Environment

Email is now a major means of communicating with clients, other attorneys, and courts, and most paralegals use email every day in their jobs. Email is being used in legal organizations for everything from routine correspondence, to billing, to newsletters, to filing court papers. Most clients now demand email access to their lawyers and paralegals. The security of email has long been a concern to legal professionals, but in recent surveys the majority of legal organizations indicate that they send confidential or privileged communications/documents to clients via email. The issue of security can be handled in a number of ways, including requiring clients to provide oral or written consent to having confidential information sent via email, adding a confidentiality statement at the end of each email message, using encryption software, or just not using email to send confidential documents.

Email Software

Sending and receiving email requires email software. Email software performs a variety of functions, including storing names and email addresses in an address book, retrieving messages, forwarding messages, storing sent messages, and attaching files to messages. Most law offices use the Microsoft Outlook program for email.

Spam **Spam** refers to unwanted or unsolicited email messages. It is the electronic version of junk mail. Spam has become quite common; although many laws have been passed to stop this veritable flood of unwanted messaging, it continues with almost no reduction apparent. It is now standard practice to install spam filters (programs that limit the amount of spam that gets through) on both office and personal computers.

spam
Unwanted or unsolicited email messages that are sent to many recipients; the electronic equivalent of junk mail.

Phishing **Phishing** is a type of Internet fraud. In hopes of gaining personal information from users, such as passwords, Social Security numbers, and bank account information, "phishers" send fraudulent emails in which they impersonate legitimate senders. The phishing message may ask you to confirm or reenter personal or confidential information "for security purposes," may warn you that an attempt has been made to access an account, and may even pose as a government agency alerting you to security-compromising occurrences. Many times, the phishers create exact replicas of real sites that look legitimate and authentic; however, anyone who follows links in such an email will end up at a bogus, illegitimate site where any information entered will be stolen and used fraudulently. Email and Internet users should always be suspicious of messages that ask for personal information.

phishing
A type of Internet fraud; "phishers" send fraudulent emails, in which they impersonate legitimate senders, in hopes of gaining personal information from responders.

Email Record Retention and Destruction

Email has become a de facto standard for client communication. This has caused a number of issues and problems that at first were not anticipated.

For example, typical email mailbox sizes can be 500 MB or more—but email boxes were never intended to be a place for storage of client information. In years gone by, legal professionals would send client correspondence via letter and keep a copy in the client's file. Now, email is so prevalent that hard-copy correspondence is the exception rather than the rule. As a way to deal with this change, many legal organizations now have record management software that paralegals and attorneys can use to store electronic case-related information in a central networked environment that allows searching and provides other capabilities. In many firms, legal professionals are now required to "file" client emails, not in the folders in their email programs, but in the folders of the firm's record management program. When an email is filed in the records management program, a record is created that both the user and others in the firm can access. In addition, once an email is in the records management program, it becomes subject to the program's retention rules, so that it is deleted and destroyed at the proper time.

This latter capability addresses another problem with email left in email folders: These messages live on forever. Record retention policies are put in place to limit the amount of information retained based on the type of information. Some legal organizations have moved to automatic deletion of emails in mailboxes (not those stored in record management programs) after a certain number of days (typically 90 or 180 days). This helps manage the amount of storage the email systems continually use, to keep the performance of the email system fast and to reduce potential liability for retaining records that are not needed but may contain information harmful to the legal organization or its clients.

Email Encryption and Digital Signatures

Because email may pass through many network servers before it reaches its destination, it is subject to being read by system administrators, hackers, and others. It is often said that email is more like a postcard than a sealed letter. Some legal organizations use encryption software to protect confidential emails sent to others. Encryption software "locks" email so that it can be opened only by the intended recipient. There are two types of encryption program designs: one is called symmetric and the other asymmetric (also called public key).

With symmetric encryption, when the sender runs the email through the encryption program, a key is created that scrambles the file. The sender then sends the encrypted email to the recipient and separately transmits the decoding key, which is typically a password or a data file. Running the same encryption program, the recipient uses the decoding key to unscramble the message. Symmetric encryption is fast but not as safe as asymmetric encryption, because someone could intercept the key and decode the messages. Because of its speed, though, symmetric encryption is commonly used for e-commerce transactions.

Asymmetric encryption (also called public-key encryption) is more complex, but it is also more secure. Two related keys are required: a public key and a private key. The user makes a public key available to anyone who might send the user encrypted information. That public key can only encode data; it cannot decode it. The private key stays safe with the user. When people wish to send the user encrypted information, they encrypt it using the user's public key (but only the user can decrypt it with the user's private key). Thus, the person sending the user a message has a digital signature file that has been encrypted with the sender's private key. When the user receives the message, the user decrypts it with the private key. Asymmetric encryption is more complex, and the process takes longer, but it is safer.

Email Etiquette and Tips

The following points of email etiquette will help you communicate your messages effectively to readers:

- Be succinct and clear; use short paragraphs.
- Spell-check and reread your emails. It is especially important that you double-check the spelling of all names within an email.
- Be careful to treat email as business correspondence. These are formal documents requiring formal language (for example, do not use the letter "u" as a

substitute for the word "you"). Do not call the recipient by his or her first name unless you are sure it is appropriate to do so.

- Do not use ALL CAPS. Using all caps is equivalent to SHOUTING! Use all caps only when absolutely necessary.

- If you are unsure about a message someone has sent you, ask for clarification and do not assume that you have guessed correctly about the meaning.

- Be careful of Reply All. Sometimes users get an email with 20 other people copied on it. If the user selects Reply, only the sender of the original email will get a response, but selecting Reply All will send a reply to all 20 of the original recipients. Before you select Reply All, make sure you really want to send it to everyone on the original message.

- Check email at least daily.

- As a rule, do not use email to communicate with clients regarding sensitive information. For sensitive communications,, it is probably better not to use email at all, but if you have any doubts, always ask the client first. If you do send such information via email, be aware of privacy/confidentiality issues and take appropriate security measures.

- Double-check the email address in any message to make sure you entered the correct one.

- Limit each email message to one topic. It is difficult to decide where to file multiple-topic emails, and it is sometimes difficult to follow up on them. Multiple follow-up requests or actions could be buried in one email, but they are liable to be missed by a busy client or legal professional.

- Always password-protect word-processing and other documents sent to clients. By password-protecting documents, you add some degree of security to the attachment with minimal effort.

Problems with Email

Although email is inexpensive and convenient, it is not perfect. Keep the following considerations in mind when using email:

- Do not assume that an email was read just because you sent it.

- Email relies on computer technology that occasionally fails or is delayed.

- Be careful what you say in emails, as they can be forwarded to others.

- Remember that email is not necessarily confidential. Email security can be breached in many ways, including:
  - leaving confidential emails open on your computer screen for others to read over your shoulder.
  - leaving your office for lunch or for a break while signed into your email program.
  - printing emails that others can find (such as at a network printer).
  - using a password such as "password" or names of family members that would be easy for others to guess.

INTRODUCTION TO COMPUTER-ASSISTED LEGAL RESEARCH

Computer-assisted legal research (CALR) uses online, fee-based service providers (third-party vendors) such as Westlaw and LexisNexis. Users subscribe to the service and are given a password with which to access it. Unlike Internet-based legal research, fee-based CALR can be expensive. CALR services have thousands and thousands of different databases, so they offer an extremely large pool of information from which to draw. After a user connects to the CALR service, the user accesses a database in which to perform legal research. The user then searches the database using key words or phrases to find the legal information he or she is looking for.

Many legal organizations use a combination of CALR, Internet-based legal research, and manual legal research, because each has its advantages and disadvantages and each may be the best, depending on the specific situation involved.

MANUAL LEGAL RESEARCH

Traditionally, legal research was accomplished using manual methods. Manual legal research is performed in a law library, using books, periodicals, indexes, and digests. Usually, the first step in researching a specific legal issue is to find the appropriate subject heading that covers that issue in a legal index or digest.

When a relevant case or statute is located in an index or digest, the researcher must locate and retrieve the bound volume containing the information so that he or she can read the entire case or statute. Cases and statutes should also be cite checked. **Cite checking** refers to the process of ensuring that a specific citation is correct (no typos), confirming that the case or statute is still valid, and that the decision has not been overturned or the statute repealed or amended.

Manual legal research does offer some advantages over computer-based legal research. When conducting computer-based legal research, the user becomes the "indexer," and must decide what words or phrases the author might have used to describe a situation or case the user is looking for. This is important, since the user may not be an expert (and typically is not) in that particular subject matter, so the user is searching for something that he or she may not know much about. The user is also completely dependent on the computer software to perform the search. If the user is inexperienced with the particular program or service, or makes an assumption when the computer makes a different one, cases or material can be overlooked or left out of the results. When conducting manual research, users use manual indexes that have been written by people: typically attorneys, librarians, or experts in indexing. These expert indexers can create sophisticated, conceptually focused indexes that computer searching simply cannot replicate. In addition, manual indexes include not only the exact words of the text indexed, but also synonyms, cross-references, summaries, and other analysis that can help the user find what he or she is looking for. Particularly for legal researchers who are unfamiliar with a particular area of the law, manual research provides features that give insight into doctrine, concepts, and analysis that computer-assisted legal research does not.

CALR: ONLINE LEGAL DATABASES

CALR services search the words of the cases, statutes, and documents themselves. Once connected to a legal information service, the user must select a database and then enter a search query. A **search query** instructs the information service to search a specific database for the occurrence of certain words and combinations of words. The legal information service responds by retrieving all cases or documents that match or meet the conditions of the search query. For example, a search query could be formulated to find all occurrences of the words *automobile*, *rollover*, and *liability* in cases for the state of California. The CALR system would then retrieve a list of cases that fulfill the search query.

Because legal information services use the full text of a document, indexes and digests are not needed. Instead, a user simply enters common words that describe

---

cite checking
Doing research to verify that a case or statute is still valid and that the decision has not been overturned or the statute repealed.

---

search query
An instruction to an information service to search a specific database for the occurrence of certain words and combinations of words. Searches can be limited by restricting the query terms, by searching only in specific databases, and by searching only in certain parts of a document (such as the title, synopsis, headnote, etc.).

the issue, and the system retrieves all cases and documents that meet the request. Westlaw and LexisNexis are the exception to this general rule. Westlaw and LexisNexis users can either search the full text of documents (bypassing indexes or digests), or they can use headnotes (an indexing/digesting system). Because the information is stored electronically on large mainframes, the database can be searched and the documents quickly retrieved. The documents that are retrieved can be read online, sent offline to a printer, or downloaded to a user's computer and then cut and pasted into a word-processing document. **Online** means being connected to an information system and running up charges. **Offline** means not being connected to an information service and not accruing charges (except possibly a printing or downloading charge). Documents may also be sent via email or facsimile to a particular destination. Alternatively, a list of the appropriate cases or documents can be printed or downloaded so the user can go to a law library and examine the hard-copy book.

Cite checking can also be done using CALR. Many legal information systems can check the correctness of a citation and the validity of cases or statutes almost instantly.

CALR can also be more convenient than manual research. Nearly all legal information services are available 24 hours a day, unlike most law libraries. Also, the research can be done from a legal professional's own office. In addition, the information that is available online is almost always more current than information available in printed books or even supplements.

Although CALR is both fast and convenient, it is *not* free. Commercial legal information services charge both yearly subscription fees and fees based on the amount of time connected to their systems. Some legal information services also charge fees for every search done on their systems. Because CALR is so expensive, new or inexperienced users can run up large bills quickly. Therefore, it is particularly important that new users get good training and develop a thorough understanding of the CALR system they will be using. Legal organizations often bill this expense to their clients, either directly or by incorporating the cost of CALR into their hourly rates.

Some services, such as Westlaw and LexisNexis, now offer flat-rate billing options as an alternative to paying for "connect" time. For a flat monthly fee, the firm can have unlimited access to all or certain libraries or databases specified in the package. Regardless of billing method, an attorney or paralegal can access Westlaw or LexisNexis from anywhere.

FEE-BASED COMPUTER-ASSISTED LEGAL RESEARCH SERVICES

A number of companies currently provide CALR services to the legal community. Westlaw and LexisNexis are by far the largest, and offer users the most depth in terms of both legal and nonlegal electronic resources available. Other CALR providers include Loislaw (www.loislaw.com), National Law Library (www.itislaw.com), Fastcase (www.fastcase.com), and Versuslaw (www.versuslaw.com). However, Westlaw and LexisNexis continue to have the largest share of the market.

While users have several options for fee-based CALR, users should always plan some basic strategies before going online to do CALR, because of the cost involved. A research plan should include knowing which service to use, what database(s) to access, how to formulate queries in the language and syntax of the chosen service, and how to use related information to make search queries specific and narrow enough to yield the desired information quickly and accurately.

online
Connected to the Internet; in relation to fee-based CALR services, connected to the service and incurring charges.

offline
No longer connected to the Internet; in relation to fee-based CALR services, no longer connected to the information service and thus not accruing charges (except possibly for printing or downloading).

Know Which Databases You Want to Access

Always plan which databases you want to search. Most CALR providers have hundreds, if not thousands, of searchable databases. For instance, if you want to search for all cases on a certain topic within the state of New Mexico, you would tell the service to access the New Mexico case law database and begin the search. It is best to determine which database(s) you will need to use *before* you log on to your service provider, rather than waiting until the meter is running and costs are being incurred.

Know the Name of the Client for Which the Research Is Being Done

Find out the name of the client or case for which the search is being conducted. Your firm may charge clients for CALR expenses, so it is important to know what case the research is for.

Know the Facts and Issues of the Case

Before you undertake CALR, it is important that you have a good understanding of the facts of the case you are working on, and specifically what issue or question you need to answer by completing the research. It is remarkably easy to spend hours online, haphazardly looking through case after case and incurring costs, but not finding what you are looking for; it is important to stay focused on the goal of the research. Another reason users must have a good understanding of the factual and legal issues of the case is that often a search must be modified to be made more restrictive. (For example, you cannot skim through 800 cases returned in response to an overly broad query.) Thus, to effectively restrict a search, you must have a good understanding of the issues involved, so that you can effectively narrow the search down to only relevant information.

Know How You Want the Information Delivered

It is important to know what format the information should take when you have retrieved the cases or documents you were looking for. Westlaw and LexisNexis, for example, offer several different options for storing the information. You can send the information to a printer, save the document as a PDF file, have the document sent to an email address, download the information to a word-processing file, copy the information to the Clipboard, or have the document sent to a fax machine. Many users download such information to a word processor, because this gives them many options for searching and using the material. Once downloaded, users can read the information at their leisure, cut and paste the information into another document such as a brief or pleading, or print the information.

WESTLAW

This section contains general information about how to use Westlaw, its many features, how to navigate around the system, and how to use Westlaw as a research tool. Westlaw is a full-text computer-assisted legal research service provided by Thomson Reuters. According to Thomson Reuters, Westlaw is one of the largest law libraries in the world, with more than 40,000 separate databases available to its users. It contains case law from all federal and state courts, statutes from all 50 states, statutes, legislative history of acts of Congress, regulations, case dockets, public records, business and legal news, law reviews, treatises, and much more.

In February 2010, Westlaw introduced a new platform, called WestlawNext. WestlawNext has noticeably different screen views and simplified search methods (e.g., it eliminates the need to search specific databases). The rest of this section discusses both the traditional Westlaw platform and the differences between Westlaw-Next and "classic" Westlaw.

Accessing Westlaw

To access Westlaw via the Internet, you need a Web browser, an Internet account, and a Westlaw account. The web address for Westlaw is www.westlaw.com. To enter the Westlaw site, you enter your Westlaw user name, Westlaw password, and a Client ID. The Client ID lets users track their Westlaw usage and charge the costs back to specific clients.

Welcome to Westlaw Screen

When Westlaw is started, it typically brings up the "Welcome to Westlaw" page (see Exhibit 8–8). Current news and information about Westlaw are displayed in the main section of this screen. Note in Exhibit 8–8 that two tabs are displayed in the upper left of the screen: "Westlaw" and "Paralegal." The "Westlaw" tab is displayed in Exhibit 8–8. The tabs may be customized and are covered in more detail later in this chapter.

KeyCite is Westlaw's cite-checking feature. It allows users to determine whether cases are still good law or if they have been overturned or otherwise limited, and whether statutes are still on the books or have been repealed or amended. KeyCite also allows users to find every instance in which a case or statute has been cited or referenced by other cases. Exhibit 8–8 includes several references to KeyCite, including a KeyCite this citation: field (left center) and a link to KEYCITE (top center). KeyCite is covered in more detail later in this chapter.

As shown in Exhibit 8–8, the Find this document by citation: feature allows you to enter a citation and then be taken directly to it. For example, if you entered "220 FRD 212" (*Note:* It is not necessary to use *Bluebook* citation style when using this feature), the case would then be automatically displayed without your having to enter

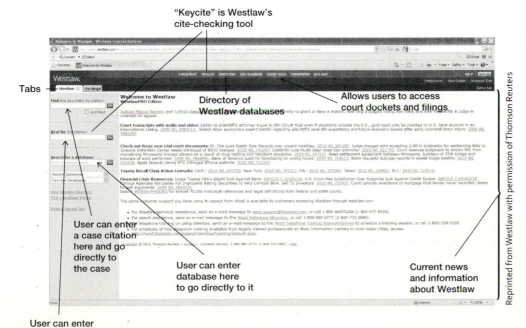

EXHIBIT 8–8

Welcome to Westlaw screen

EXHIBIT 8–9

Westlaw Tabs

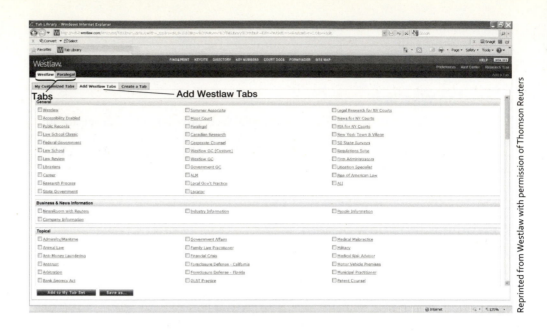

a database or enter search criteria. The DIRECTORY link at the top middle of the screen displays a directory of the many Westlaw databases. (Databases are covered later in this chapter.)

The Search for a database: feature (see Exhibit 8–8 at bottom left) allows you to enter a database identifier, such as "Allcases," and then go directly to the search screen where you can enter search criteria.

In the top middle of the screen is the link to KEY NUMBERS. The West Key Number System assigns key numbers and terms to legal issues. Thus, you can conduct legal research by using a topical list of legal issues that has been compiled by Westlaw's attorney-editors. The Key Numbers feature is covered in more detail later in this chapter.

Tabs and the Paralegal Tab in Westlaw

Tabs allow a user to directly access a number of Westlaw features, including various databases. In Exhibit 8–9, notice the two tabs near the top left of the screen: "Westlaw" and "Paralegal." In Exhibit 8–9, the user clicked "Add a Tab" near the top of the screen and then selected each of these tabs. Exhibit 8–9 shows that the user can select from "General," "Business & News Information," and "Topical" tabs. Tabs can also be created for different jurisdictions (e.g., Florida). Tabs are a great way of customizing Westlaw. For example, notice in Exhibit 8–10 that the Paralegal tab is selected.

Exhibit 8–10 demonstrates that many of the tools that paralegals commonly use are now at the user's fingertips. The user can quickly access cases and statutes, public records and information about people, information about companies, court documents, forms and checklists, and other information. The Paralegal tab is a timesaving feature that Westlaw has created specifically for busy paralegals. We will use the Paralegal tab as the primary starting point in Westlaw throughout the remainder of this section.

Find by Citation

As mentioned earlier, the **Find by Citation** feature allows a Westlaw user to immediately retrieve a specific case or statute by entering its citation (see the first screen in

---

Find by Citation

A Westlaw feature that allows a user to immediately retrieve a specific case or statute by entering its citation.

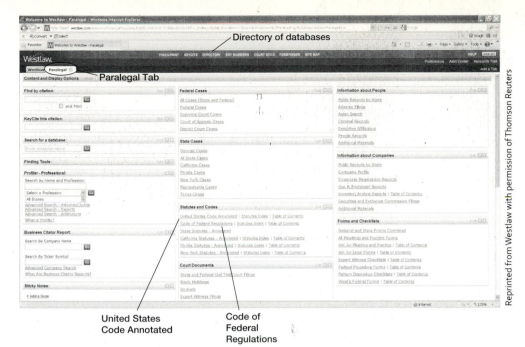

EXHIBIT 8–10

Paralegal Tab

Directory of databases

Paralegal Tab

United States
Code Annotated

Code of
Federal
Regulations

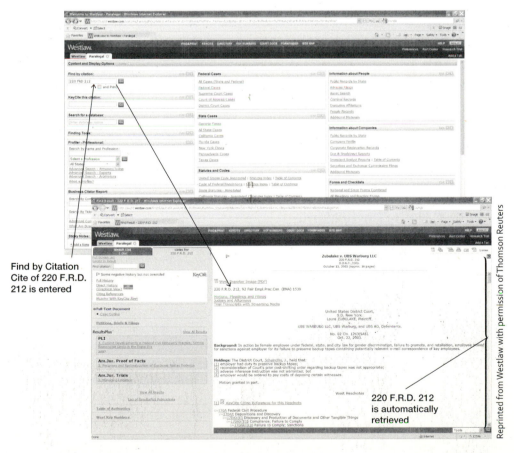

EXHIBIT 8–11

Find by Citation

Find by Citation
Cite of 220 F.R.D.
212 is entered

220 F.R.D. 212
is automatically
retrieved

Exhibit 8–11). This feature is convenient if you already have a case cite. Although it does not provide you with additional cases or documents, as it does when you execute a search query, the case itself can be used as a starting point for conducting further research. The Find by Citation feature is also extremely quick because you do not have to enter a database identifier or a search query. The first screen in Exhibit 8–11 shows

EXHIBIT 8–12

Find a Case by Party Name

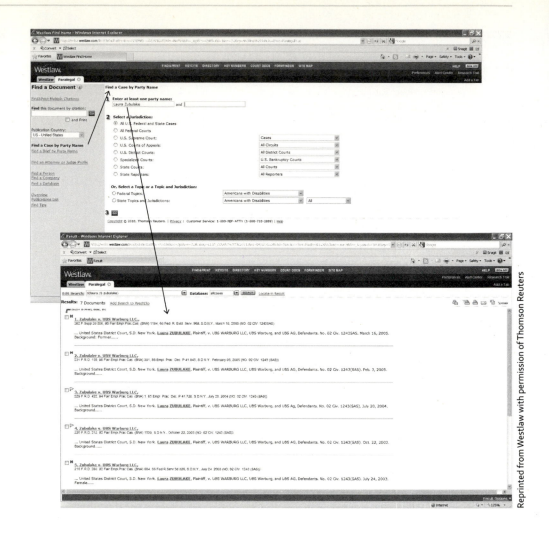

the citation as entered in the Find by Citation: field, and the second screen shows the case retrieved.

Find a Case by Party Name

Find a Case by Party Name A Westlaw feature that allows a user who knows the name of at least one party to retrieve a case without knowing the case citation or entering a search query.

Find a Case by Party Name (on the left side of the first screen of Exhibit 8–12) is a Westlaw feature that allows you to retrieve a case if you know the name of at least one party; you need not know the case citation or enter a search query. Notice in the first screen of Exhibit 8–12 that the user clicked Find a Case by Party Name, entered the party's name (Laura Zubulake), selected a jurisdiction (in this instance "All U.S. Federal and State Cases"), and clicked on Go. A list of possible cases was retrieved (see the second screen of Exhibit 8–12), including the actual case the user was looking for (*Zubulake v. UBS Warburg, LLC;* note that there are a number of cases with the same name). Although there are other ways to find a case by party name (discussed later in this chapter), the Find a Case by Party Name feature is convenient if you do not have a full citation for a case and do not know much about a case other than the name of one party.

Westlaw Databases

Westlaw has catalogued all of its information by subject matter and jurisdiction; Westlaw calls these divisions "databases." Westlaw offers users thousands of databases to search and query. Notice that in the Paralegal tab in Exhibit 8–10, many different kinds and types of resources are available. All of these resources are databases that

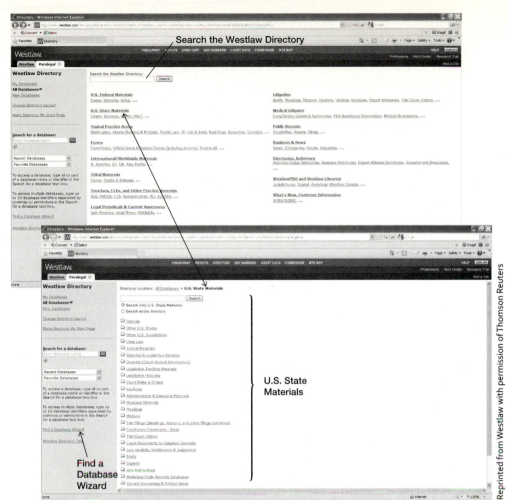

Reprinted from Westlaw with permission of Thomson Reuters

EXHIBIT 8–13

Westlaw Directory of databases

a user can search. For example, in Exhibit 8–10, under "Federal Cases," users can access the All Cases (State and Federal) database, which literally contains all state and federal cases. Users could also access the United States Code Annotated, the Code of Federal Regulations, public records by state, and forms. The Paralegal tab in Exhibit 8–10 shows just a few of the myriad databases available in Westlaw.

In Exhibit 8–10, notice the word "DIRECTORY" in the top middle of the screen. This is a link to the directory database shown in the first screen of Exhibit 8–13. Exhibit 8–13 shows the broad scope of databases and other information sources that are available in Westlaw. These databases include a variety of federal and state materials. The second screen in Exhibit 8–13 shows the screen for U.S. State Materials. The U.S. State Materials pages allow you to access the statutes and laws of any state, review court dockets, conduct legislative history research, and access court rules. Notice in the first screen of Exhibit 8–13 that additional databases covering international law, topical legal areas, treatises, law reviews, business news, public records, and other subjects are also available on Westlaw. (Students should note that schools often have special educational licenses; therefore, it is possible that not all Westlaw databases will be available.)

Users can also enter the name of a potential database in the Search for a database: field (see the first screen of Exhibit 8–13). For example, if you entered "New York Times" in the Search for a database: field, Westlaw would display several databases that were related to the *New York Times.* Users can also find a database using the Find a Database Wizard (see the second screen in Exhibit 8–13, bottom left). With this

EXHIBIT 8–14

Computer-assisted legal research query plan and form

COMPUTER-ASSISTED LEGAL RESEARCH QUERY FORM

Date: *June 1*   **Research's Initials:** *TPB*   **Client/Case:** *Jones v. Unitas*

Estimate Time on Service: *15 min.*

Service to be Used: (Westlaw) Lexis/Nexis LoisLaw Fastcase Versus Law Internet CD/ROM

Database(s) to be searched:

All federal and Georgia

Type of Search: Natural Language   (Terms and Connectors)

Issues/Question: *What is the liability of a property owner if a trespassing child is injured in the property owner's swimming pool?*

Search Term 1	Connector 1	Search Term 2	Connector 2	Search Term 3	Connector 3
negligence	*&*	*trespass!*	*/s*	*child*	*&*

Synonym(s)

_____   _____   _____

Search Term 4	Connector 4	Search Term 5	Connector 5	Search Term 6	Connector 6
"swimming pool"	__	_____	_____	_____	_____

Query: *negligence & trespass! /s child & "swimming pool"*

© Cengage Learning 2012

feature, you answers a series of questions, such as "What are you trying to find?," and select a category from a multiple-choice list. Westlaw then guides you to the appropriate database.

Creating and Refining Search Queries in Westlaw

Before going online on Westlaw or any CALR system, it is helpful to plan out a query strategy in advance. This limits the time spent online, all of which incurs charges. You must decide what you want to accomplished and how to accomplish it. Formulating a good search query takes some practice and some time. Exhibit 8–14 shows an example of a query formulation for Westlaw, in the context of a search/query form.

Identify the Keywords to Be Searched and Any Synonyms   Before you log in to the CALR system, always identify the keywords that describe the issue. You should also identify synonyms or alternate spellings of keywords. Computers cannot think for themselves; users must do this for them. Thus, if your search only asks for all cases that have the word *physician* in them, the system will not retrieve a relevant case that uses the word *doctor*. Failing to include an adequate number of synonyms in a query can make the query incomplete or too narrow, so relevant cases or materials will be missed.

The query in Exhibit 8–14 deals with whether a property owner may be liable in negligence for injuries sustained by a trespassing child in the property owner's swimming pool. The keywords that describe the legal issue are *negligence, trespassing, child,* and *"swimming pool."*

Identify the Type of Search to Be Performed   Westlaw offers two different kinds of searching. The first kind is plain-English searching, which Westlaw calls "Natural Language." The second kind of searching, which Westlaw calls "Terms and Connectors," is a Boolean logic search method that uses operators such as *and,* to connect terms or ideas, and *or,* when two or more terms or concepts are needed to describe an idea.

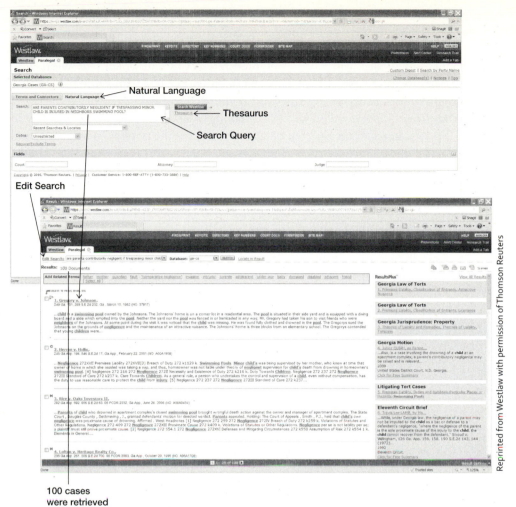

EXHIBIT 8–15

Westlaw Natural Language search

Natural Language searching in Westlaw uses plain English, without the need for complex connectors or syntax. The advantage of Natural Language is that it is easier to use; the disadvantage is that the search may not be as precise as a Terms and Connectors search. Using Natural Language, searches can be entered in the form of a sentence or question. For example, the question in the Issue/Question: field of the form in Exhibit 8–14 can be entered directly into Westlaw Natural Language (see Exhibit 8–15). In Exhibit 8–15, the user first selected the database called Georgia Cases (GA_CS) and then selected the Natural Language search tab (Exhibit 8–15, first screen). The user then entered the search query and clicked "Search Westlaw." Westlaw analyzed the statistical relevance of the terms and retrieved the documents that most closely matched the search requests (see the second screen of Exhibit 8–15). By default, a Natural Language search yields 100 results, although you can adjust the settings to allow more or fewer results. The results are presented beginning with the one that most closely matches the query terms.

Terms and connectors searching uses Boolean logic and operators/connectors to connect terms to describe an idea. The query at the bottom of Exhibit 8–14 shows a Terms and Connectors search in final form.

Once you have identified the keywords for the search, specified any synonyms, and informed the system that you will be using Terms and Connectors, you must next signify the relationships between the terms, using connectors. **Connectors** show a relationship between the keywords in a search query. For example, in Exhibit 8–14, notice the words and symbols in the "Connector" fields. These include the connector

Natural Language

A query/search technique that uses plain English, without the need for complex connectors or syntax, to search for documents.

Terms and Connectors

A search technique that uses Boolean logic and operators/connectors to connect query terms.

connectors

Characters that define or show a relationship between the keywords in a search query.

"/s," which in Westlaw means to search for two or more words within the same sentence; "/p," which in Westlaw means to search for two or more words within the same paragraph; "&," which in Westlaw means to search for two or more words within a document; and a space, which Westlaw interprets as OR and which tells Westlaw to find documents that have either one word or the other (e.g., find documents that use either the word *mortgage* OR the word *contract*). The final query in Exhibit 8–14 reads: "*negligence & trespass! /s child & "swimming pool"*. The query tells Westlaw to search for documents in the selected databases that have the phrases "negligence" and *trespass!* (e.g., *trespasser* or *trespassing*) within the same sentence as the word "child," and which also contain the term "swimming pool" somewhere in the document.

Several different types of connectors are available in Westlaw (see Exhibit 8–16). The broader the connector, such as "OR" as opposed to "AND," the more expansive the search and the more documents will be retrieved. Conversely, the more narrow the connector, such as "/3" (within three words), the smaller the number of documents that will be retrieved. Depending on the results of a query, you can edit your query and use more expansive or more narrow connectors as necessary. Notice, in the

EXHIBIT 8–16

Westlaw connectors and expanders

Connector	Definition	Search Query	Documents Found
Space bar	OR	mortgage contract	All documents that have either the word *mortgage* or the word *contract* anywhere in them
&	AND	mortgage & contract	All documents that contain both the word *mortgage* and the word *contract* anywhere in them
/p	Paragraph	mortgage /p contract	All documents that contain the both the word *mortgage* and the word *contract* in the same paragraph
/s	Sentence	mortgage /s contract	All documents that contain both the word *mortgage* and the word *contract* in the same sentence
/n	Words	mortgage /3 contract	All documents that contain both the word *mortgage* and the word *contract* within three words of each other
" "	Phrase	"personal jurisdiction"	All documents where the exact phrase *"personal jurisdiction"* occurs
+s	Precedes within the same sentence	personal +s jurisdiction	All documents where *personal* precedes *jurisdiction* in the same sentence
+n	Precedes within a number of words	personal +3 jurisdiction	All documents where *personal* precedes *jurisdiction* within three words
%	BUT NOT	R.I.C.O. % "Puerto Rico"	All documents with the word *RICO* (i.e. Racketeer Influenced and Corrupt Organization Act) but not *Puerto Rico*

Expander	Definition	Search Query	Documents Found
!	Root Expander	medic!	All documents that have the words medicine, medical, medicate, or medication
*	Universal character	kn*w	All documents that have the word know or knew in them

Reprinted from Westlaw with permission of Thomson Reuters

top left of the second screen of Exhibit 8–15, that the user has an option called Edit Search.

Unlike a Natural Language search, there is no default number of results for a Terms and Connectors search; the search will list all of the relevant results. Another difference is that the results are presented in chronological order, beginning with the most recent result.

With the same search terms, it is possible to get noticeably different results, presented in a different order, depending on whether you used Natural Language or Terms and Connectors. Thus, it is advisable to use both methods when conducting a query search.

Identify Any Expanders That Might Be Necessary When writing a search query, you must also take into account variations of your chosen keywords. For example, in Exhibit 8–14, the root word *negligence* might appear in some materials in a variant form, such as *negligent*. You can include a root expander in the query so that variations of a word will not be missed when the system is searching for relevant cases. A **root expander** enables Westlaw to retrieve multiple words with the same root. The exclamation mark (!) in Exhibit 8–14 is a root expander that tells Westlaw to find all words with the root of *neglig*. Thus, the words *negligence* and *negligent* will searched for in the database.

Another type of expander is a **universal character**, which represents one letter or number and enables an information system to retrieve words with minor variations. The asterisk (*) is used as a universal character in Westlaw. For example, the query "kn*w" would retrieve cases containing the terms *know* and *knew*. A universal character can be placed anywhere in a word, and more than one universal character can be used in or at the end of a word (e.g., "test**" would retrieve *test, tests,* and *tested* but not *testify*). Exhibit 8–15 lists common Westlaw expanders.

root expander
A character that enables a legal information system to retrieve multiple words with the same root.

universal character
A character that represents one letter or number; enables a legal information service to retrieve words with minor variations.

Additional Westlaw Searching Tips Exhibit 8–17 gives a number of additional search tips for using Westlaw. Another helpful feature for Westlaw query design

Tip Number/Description	Explanation
1. The more terms in the query, the fewer cases retrieved	A common problem for new Westlaw users is that their searches tend to retrieve hundreds of cases, too many to look through. Adding more terms to the query limits the number of cases retrieved.
2. Use singular terms	Westlaw automatically adds plurals (e.g., "*child*" returns "*child's*" and "*children*"). If a user searches the plural (e.g., "*children*") only the plural is searched for.
3. Use quotes cautiously	Using quotes only search as for exact phrases, so "*statute of limitations*" will not search for *limitations of action* or *limitation period*.
4. Use hyphens	When you do not know how a phrase might appear in a document, use hyphens. *Non-resident* retrieves "*non-resident*," "*non resident*," and "*nonresident*."
5. Use periods in acronyms	When you do not know if an acronym might appear with periods or not, use periods. *F.B.I.* will retrieve "*F.B.I.*," "*FBI*," and "*F B I*".

EXHIBIT 8–17
Westlaw search tips

EXHIBIT 8–18

Using the Thesaurus

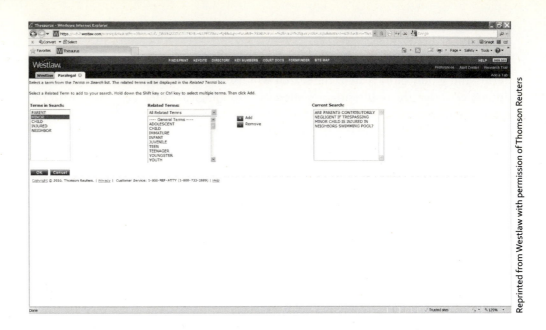

is the Thesaurus tool. In Exhibit 8–15 (first screen), notice the word "Thesaurus" just under "Search Westlaw." Exhibit 8–18 shows the "Thesaurus" feature in Westlaw. In Exhibit 8–18, the search word "MINOR" is highlighted, and Westlaw provides synonyms, such as "ADOLESCENT," "CHILD," and "JUVENILE." The Thesaurus tool can be very helpful when formulating search queries.

Exhibit 8–19 shows the Terms and Connectors search formulated in Exhibit 8–14 and the results of that search. Notice in the first screen of Exhibit 8–19 that one of the fields in the search screen is Dates: and that "Unrestricted" is currently shown. Users have many date options in Westlaw, including limiting searches to documents published in the past 30, 60, or 90 days; the past three years; after a user-defined date (e.g., after 1/1/2010); or before a user-defined date (e.g., before 1/1/2009).

Notice in the first screen of Exhibit 8–19 that one of the options is Fields:. Users can limit searches to certain fields or parts of a document, including the title of the case/document, the synopsis, headnotes, judge, attorneys, and so on. For example, if you wanted to search for the title of a case, you could either use the Find a Case by Party Name feature discussed previously, or select the down arrow next to Field: in the Terms and Connectors query pane and select Title. You could then enter a case name such as *Gregory & Johnson*. The completed search query would be ti(Gregory & Johnson).

Working with Retrieved Cases in Westlaw and Expanding a Search

The second screen of Exhibit 8–19 shows that 11 cases were initially retrieved. Only a brief summary of each case, showing some of the search terms found, is initially displayed. To see the full text of a case, you would click on the name of the case (in this instance, *Gregory v. Johnson*). Exhibit 8–20 (first screen) shows the first page of the *Gregory v. Johnson* case.

The Synopsis   Notice in Exhibit 8–20 (first screen) that the background and holdings of the case are displayed. This is called the synopsis of the case. The synopsis of a case is written by Westlaw research attorneys to summarize and help users understand the case. This is something that many CALR services (other than Westlaw and Lexis-Nexis) do not offer. By reading the synopsis, you can evaluate the case and determine whether it is on point.

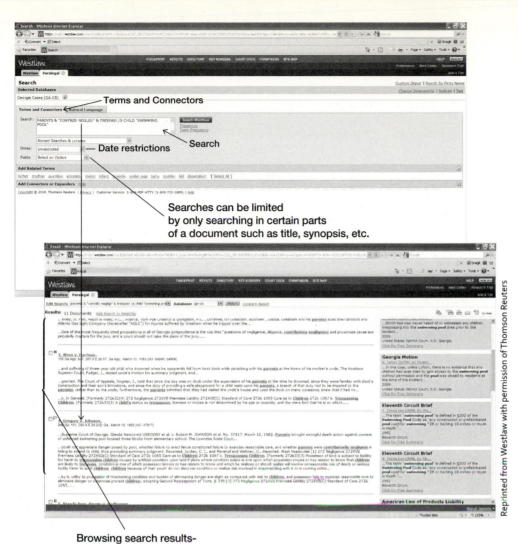

EXHIBIT 8–19
Terms and Connectors search in Westlaw

Terms and Connectors

Search

Date restrictions

Searches can be limited by only searching in certain parts of a document such as title, synopsis, etc.

Browsing search results–11 documents retrieved

Searching Terms and Moving to Additional Cases Exhibit 8–20 (first screen) shows the search terms in the synopsis as highlighted. Search terms are always highlighted in the document so that you can clearly see the terms you are searching for. Notice in Exhibit 8–20 (at the bottom of the first screen), that the words "Doc 4 of 11" appear and there is a left arrow and a right arrow on either side. This shows that you are currently viewing the fourth case that was retrieved. To go to the next document, you would click the right arrow; to go to the previous case, you would click the left arrow. Notice also in Exhibit 8–20 (at the bottom of the first screen), that the word "Term" is shown with a left arrow and right arrow on either side. To go to your next search term, you would click the right arrow next to "Term." In this manner, you can view all of the search terms in the document to evaluate whether the document is on point or not.

If the documents are not relevant, or if too many or too few documents are identified, you should modify the query. Sometimes when cases are retrieved in Westlaw, another option appears next to "Term," called "Best." In Westlaw, "Best" means that this portion of the case has the greatest concentration of your search terms. Sometimes it is more efficient to use the "Best" option and go straight to the place in the case with the most search terms, rather than painstakingly going through the case looking at each highlighted search term.

EXHIBIT 8–20

A retrieved case in Westlaw

Locate in Result

A Westlaw command that allows a user to search the retrieved documents for particular terms, whether or not those terms appeared in the user's original search.

ResultsPlus

A Westlaw feature that automatically includes other documents related to a user's search, such as legal texts, treatises, and law review articles; no additional search is needed to retrieve these supplementary materials.

Distribution Options After you have determined that the documents retrieved are relevant, you have several distribution options to select from (see Exhibit 8–20, top right of the first screen). Options include "West Reporter Image" (which creates a PDF file of the case), "Quick Print" (which quickly prints the case), "Print" (which prints the case with additional options), "email" (which emails the case to an address supplied by the user), and "Download" (which either opens the case or saves it as a word-processing document).

Locate in Result Notice, in Exhibit 8–20 (top left of the first screen), the option entitled "Locate in Result." The **Locate in Result** command allows a user to search the retrieved documents for particular terms, whether or not those terms appeared in the user's original search. For instance, if the search in the example had retrieved 75 cases, you could search the retrieved cases for another term to further cull the cases retrieved. This can be particularly helpful when you retrieve more cases than you can easily skim through.

ResultsPlus Exhibit 8–20 (lower left of the first screen) also shows a section that says "ResultsPlus." **ResultsPlus** is a Westlaw feature that automatically includes other documents, such as legal texts, treatises, law review articles, and the like, that have a high statistical likelihood of matching the concepts in a user's search (no additional search is needed to get these). In Exhibit 8–20, a section of the Restatement on Torts related to the liability of property owners when a trespassing child is injured is suggested as being a possible source of additional information. ResultsPlus suggestions can be extremely helpful and can assist you in expanding or furthering a research project.

Headnotes and Key Numbers   The second screen of Exhibit 8–20 shows West **Headnotes and Key Numbers**. Headnotes summarize each major issue in a case. Most cases include a number of Headnotes. Each Headnote is classified under one or more Topics and Key Numbers in the West Key System. Headnotes and Key Numbers digest the case and break down legal issues into smaller issues that can be more easily tracked and organized. Each Topic and Key Number represents a particular point of law. They allow users to expand their research while still staying on point. In Exhibit 8–20, notice that the Headnote speaks to the issue of the liability of property owners when trespassing children are injured by an artificial condition (e.g., a swimming pool).

Also in Exhibit 8–20, notice the Key Number 272k1067. This is a Key Number related to the issue at hand. Suppose, for example, that this is the specific legal issue you need to research. You could select this Key Number (272k1067) to search for other cases with the same Key Number or Headnote (see Exhibit 8–21). In the first screen of Exhibit 8–21, Westlaw has automatically entered the Key Number 272k1067. In Exhibit 8–21, the user has selected "Most Recent Cases," so the most recent cases are sorted first; and then has selected the database to search, which is "State: Georgia." When the user clicked "Search," the second screen of Exhibit 8–21 was displayed, showing the user 20 cases with the specific Headnote (272k1067) that is directly on point. The user can now click each case and read it. Headnotes and Key Numbers are a great way to find resources on point.

KeyCite   **KeyCite** is Westlaw's citation research tool. It allows users to determine if the case, statute, or other document is good law and allows users to expand their research by finding other sources that have cited the reference.

KeyCite: Determining if a Case/Statute Is Good Law   KeyCite allows Westlaw users to determine whether a case has been overruled or still is good law, or if a

> ### Headnotes and Key Numbers
> Westlaw feature that classifies each legal issue in a case and allows users to search and retrieve other cases with similar Headnotes and Key Numbers.

> ### KeyCite
> Westlaw feature that allows users to determine if a case, statute, or other document is good law and enables users to expand their research by finding other sources that have cited the reference.

EXHIBIT 8–21
Searching for similar Headnotes/Key Numbers in Westlaw

EXHIBIT 8–21

(*continued*)

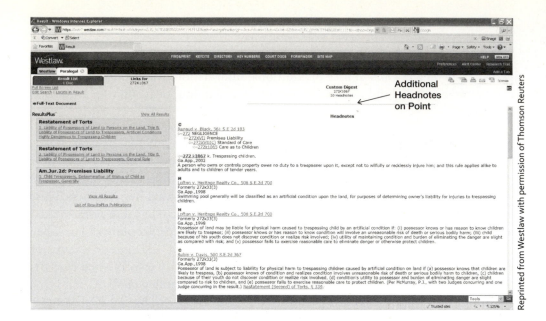

statute has been found unconstitutional or has been repealed. In Exhibit 8–22 (first screen), the cite "249 Ga 151" has been entered in the KeyCite this citation: field. The second screen shows the KeyCite results as displayed. KeyCite uses a colored flag system to help you easily determine whether a case or statute is good law (see Exhibit 8–23). A red flag means that the case is no longer good law for at least one of the points of law it contains. A yellow flag means that the case had had some negative treatment, but has not been reversed or overruled. Notice that in the KeyCite listing in Exhibit 8–22 (second screen) for the *Gregory v. Johnson* case (this is a court of appeals decision that was reversed by the citing case), a red flag appears next to the title of the case, indicating that the case is no longer good law for at least one of the issues it discusses. Also, notice in the first screen of Exhibit 8–20 that a yellow KeyCite flag is displayed at the beginning of the case. Westlaw has integrated KeyCite into the full text of documents. Notice also in Exhibit 8–20 that from the case itself (in the middle left of the first screen), the user can access full KeyCite information for the case, including a full history of the case.

Sometimes it takes years for a case to work its way through the court system. KeyCite Alert is a Westlaw feature that notifies a user (typically through email) when the status of a case changes in KeyCite. Exhibit 8–22 (second screen, left-hand side) shows the Monitor With KeyCite Alert option.

KeyCite: Finding Other Sources That Have Cited the Reference KeyCite allows a user to track all of the times a document has been cited by other references. Notice in Exhibit 8–24 (first screen) on the left side of the screen the words "Citing References." The second screen in Exhibit 8–24 shows the "Citing References" information in KeyCite for the case of *Hashemi v. Campaigner Publications, Inc.* Notice in the second screen of Exhibit 8–24 that the *Hashemi* case has been cited by 223 documents. Notice in Exhibit 8–24 (second screen) that over the first entry listed (*Sharpe v. Van Hauen*), there are two stars. These are depth-of-treatment stars (see Exhibit 8–23) which mean that the *Sharpe* case briefly discussed the *Hashemi* case. If the *Sharpe* case had simply cited the *Hashemi* case, the *Sharpe* case would have only one star. Notice also in Exhibit 8–24 that the fifth case listed (*Buchanan v. Bowman)* has quotation marks toward the end of the listing. This means that the *Hashemi* case was actually quoted in the *Buchanan* case.

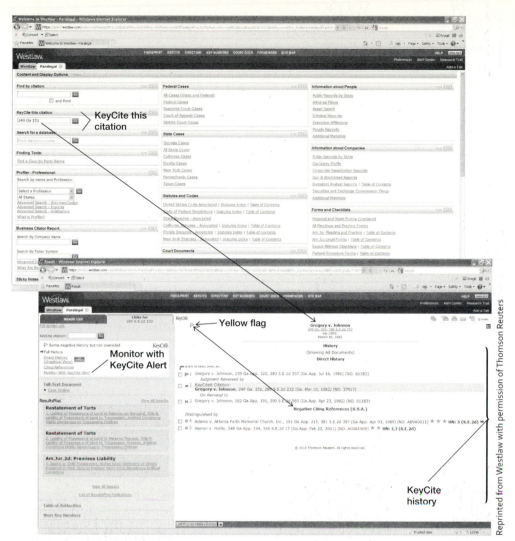

EXHIBIT 8–22

Using KeyCite

Court Dockets/Documents

Westlaw has the capability to search many (but not all) federal and state court dockets. This is sometimes helpful if you are trying to keep track of a piece of litigation or if you are trying to find information about a person or company. The dockets retrieved usually show the type of action, case number, judge, courthouse, and the status of the case (open or closed).

Public Records Search

Westlaw allows users to search a number of state public records. Although its databases are not comprehensive or exhaustive, such searches are straightforward and can be quite productive. Westlaw public record searches can be used to find the whereabouts of people and to otherwise find information about people, such as assets, property ownership, and related records. Westlaw can also access a variety of public records about businesses, including company profiles, corporate registration records, and SEC filings, among other records.

WestlawNext

In early 2010, Westlaw introduced a new version of Westlaw, WestlawNext. This version enables users to search more efficiently and effectively. WestlawNext streamlines

EXHIBIT 8–23

KeyCite symbols

KeyCite Symbol	Explanation
▶ RED FLAG	• In cases and administrative decisions, a red flag warns that the case or administrative decision is no longer good law for at least one of the points of law it contains. In statutes and regulations, a red flag warns that the statute or regulation has been amended by a recent session law or rule, repealed, superseded, held unconstitutional, or preempted in whole or in part.
▷ YELLOW FLAG	• In cases and administrative decisions, a yellow flag warns that the case or administrative decision has had some negative treatment, but has not been reversed or overruled. In statutes and regulations, a yellow flag warns that a statute has been renumbered or transferred by a recent session law; that an uncodified session law or proposed legislation affecting the statute is available (statutes merely referenced, i.e., mentioned, are marked with a green C); that the regulation has been reinstated, corrected or confirmed; that the statute or regulation was limited on constitutional or preemption grounds or its validity was otherwise called into doubt; or that a prior version of the statute or regulation received negative treatment from a court.
H BLUE H	• In cases and administrative decisions, a blue H indicates that there is direct history but it is not known to be negative.
C GREEN C	• A green C indicates that the case/administrative decision has citing references but no direct history or negative citing references. It also indicates that a statute/regulation has citing references, but no updating documents.
★★★★	• Depth of treatment stars indicate how extensively a cited case or administrative decision has been discussed by the citing case. The more stars, the more extensive the coverage. One star, for example, means that the case was only cited.
" QUOTATION MARKS	• Quotation marks indicate that the citing case or administrative decision directly quotes the cited case.

the research process by eliminating the traditional Westlaw tabs and databases. The first screen of Exhibit 8–25 shows the welcome screen for WestlawNext. Notice that there is only one place to enter a search query, whether it be for a cite check or a detailed search for a specific case or statute. You only have to choose a jurisdiction (see Exhibit 8–25, second screen) and enter your query.

In Exhibit 8–25, the user is looking for cases in Georgia in which a trespassing child was injured in a neighbor's swimming pool. The user selected both All Federal and the state of Georgia as the jurisdictions (see Exhibit 8–25, second screen) and entered the search query. The results of the search are shown in the third screen of Exhibit 8–25. In traditional Westlaw, one would typically see only cases or statutes, depending on the database selected. In Exhibit 8–25 (third screen), an Overview of all of the search results is presented. On this screen you can see summaries of selected cases, statutes, regulations, and so on, and (on the left side of the screen) links to the complete search results appear. Finally, the fourth screen of Exhibit 8–25 shows how a case looks in WestlawNext. Notice that the KeyCite results are available at the top of the screen and may be accessed by clicking on the desired search.

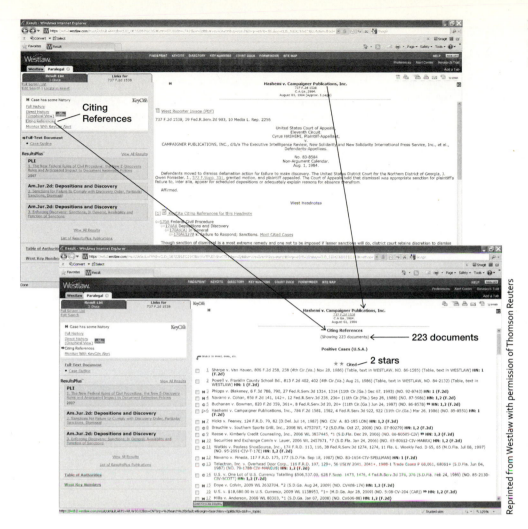

EXHIBIT 8–24

Citing references for a case in KeyCite

Westlaw Training

Becoming proficient at manual legal research requires one to understand the resources available and how to use them effectively. Similarly, learning to use CALR services, such as Westlaw, takes time. Westlaw is an extremely powerful research tool

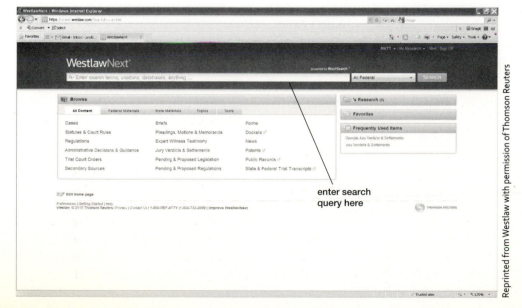

EXHIBIT 8–25

WestlawNext

EXHIBIT 8–25

(*continued*)

Jurisdictions selected

All search results

Overview (13)   Cases found

Statutes found

KeyCite results

and has an enormous number of features, databases, commands, and complexities. To learn to use all of these vast resources takes some time. Westlaw provides a number of excellent tools to assist users in learning how to use its service. At west. thomson.com/organization/paralegals, users can access many different training programs, including free user's guides in PDF format such as the *Westlaw Guide for Paralegals*. Westlaw also offers many web-based training videos. Each one takes approximately five minutes to complete and includes full sound and step-by-step instruction. Users of this website do not need a valid Westlaw password to access the web-based training. At this website, users have the opportunity to take a short training course and, upon successful completion, print out an official certificate from Westlaw.

Many other types of training are also available. For example, Westlaw offers toll-free assistance by Westlaw research attorneys who can advise users on search strategies.

LEXIS/NEXIS

LexisNexis is a comprehensive, full-text, CALR service provider. It was the first on-line full-text legal information service and is one of the world's largest. This section covers LexisNexis's databases, search/query structure, and other features.

Accessing LexisNexis

LexisNexis can be accessed via the Internet. To do so, you need a web browser, an Internet account, and a LexisNexis account. The web address for accessing LexisNexis is www.lexis.com. To enter the LexisNexis site, you enter your ID and password (see Exhibit 8–26).

LexisNexis Research System Tabs

LexisNexis gives users a number of research options, which are shown as tabs across the top of the screen. They include *MyLexis*, Search, Research Tasks, Get a Document, *Shepard's*, Alerts, Total Litigator, Transactional Advisor, and Counsel Selector.

EXHIBIT 8–26

LexisNexis sign-in screen

EXHIBIT 8–27

MyLexis tab

MyLexis The *MyLexis* tab is a customizable page that allows the user to conduct a "Quick Search," as well as providing the user access to as many as 12 search tools. Exhibit 8–27 shows a list of the search tools available on the *MyLexis* tab.

Search There are four subtabs under the Search tab (see Exhibit 8–28). The first is the [Search] by Source subtab. The by Source subtab provides access to the same "Quick Search" tool available in the *MyLexis* tab, and also allows you to search for useful databases. The second is the [Search] by Topic or Headnote subtab, which allows you to search within a specified topic. The third is [Search] by Guided Search Form, which provides a roadmap for a search. The fourth is the [Search] by Dot Command, which allows you to search by the library and file names of the desired search category.

EXHIBIT 8–28

Search tab

Access to common
legal databases

EXHIBIT 8–29

Research Tasks tab

Research Tasks   Users can access databases and begin searches using the Research Tasks tab. Exhibit 8–29 shows the Research Tasks page. Research Tasks are arranged by subject matter (see the first screen of Exhibit 8–29). For example, the second screen of Exhibit 8–29 shows the Tax resources that are displayed when the user selected "Tax." Notice that, in the second screen of Exhibit 8–29, under "Select sources to search within:," LexisNexis lists a number of tax-related databases that the user can search in, either individually or collectively. Also, notice that Exhibit 8–29 shows many other tax-related resources the user can access from this one screen. The Research Tasks feature is convenient because it allows you to (1) access a number of related LexisNexis databases, (2) run a search query from the same screen, and (3) access other subject-matter–related sources.

Get a Document   The Get a Document tab allows users to retrieve individual documents from LexisNexis quickly, by entering either the citation, the names of the parties, or the docket number. The first subtab is **Get by Citation**. The Get by Citation subtab allows you to immediately retrieve a specific case or statute by entering its citation. In Exhibit 8–30 (first screen), the user has entered "451 F.Supp.2d 16." LexisNexis automatically retrieved the case without the user having to enter a database or search criteria (see the second screen of Exhibit 8–30). Get by Citation is comparable to Westlaw's Find by Citation.

Get by Citation

A LexisNexis feature that allows a user to immediately retrieve a specific case or statute by entering its citation.

EXHIBIT 8–30

Get a Document tab

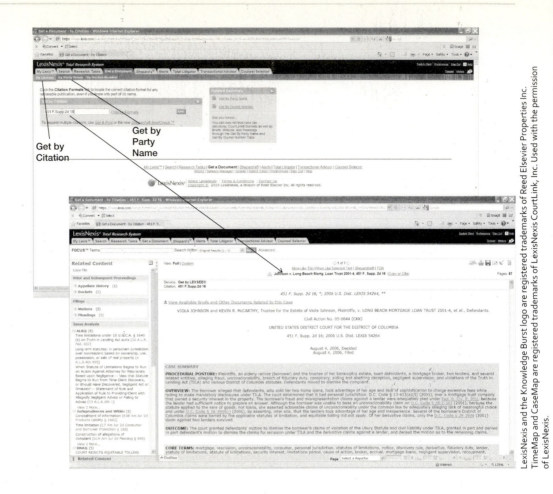

Get by Party Name

A LexisNexis feature that allows a user to retrieve a case by entering the name(s) of a party (or parties).

The second subtab is **Get by Party Name**. The Get by Party Name feature allows a LexisNexis user to retrieve a document such as a case by entering the name(s) of a party or parties. You enter a party name, select the jurisdiction, and then select "search." The document is then automatically retrieved without your having to enter a full search query. Get by Party Name is a quick and efficient way to find a case if you just have a party's name. Get by Party Name is similar to Westlaw's Find a Case by Party Name.

The third subtab is [Get] by Docket Number, which allows you to retrieve a case by entering the docket number of that case.

Alerts

If you want to be sure to stay current on a specific legal issue, you can set up an alert. Alerts use searches that you have saved and run them automatically at intervals you specify. These results can be stored for viewing online or delivered by email.

Total Litigator

The Total Litigator tab provides an effective method to find, manage, and utilize information obtained throughout the litigation process. This tab collects a variety of litigation resources in a single place.

Transactional Advisor

The Transactional Advisor tab provides a collection of research links and tools specifically designed to retrieve the forms, latest news, and other information associated with transactional law.

Counsel Selector

Counsel Selector is a link to www.martindale.com, which is an online attorney directory. When an attorney in one city needs the assistance of an attorney in another city or state, martindale.com is an easy and convenient tool for finding counsel.

LexisNexis Databases

The database coverage of LexisNexis is extremely broad. It includes case law, statutes, news, business, medical-related information, public records, and much more. Lexis-Nexis allows users to conduct research in a number of different ways.

Search Tab Notice in Exhibit 8–28 that the user is in the Search tab (near the top left of the screen). Under Option 2 – Look for a Source, the user is in the Legal subtab (see Exhibit 8–28). From the Legal subtab, the user can access many common databases, such as Federal & State Cases, Combined; Federal Court Cases, Combined; United States Code Service, individual state resources (not shown in Exhibit 8–28), and others. Next to the databases, there are open boxes. This is where you select which databases to search in. You can select multiples boxes/databases at one time and can search in multiple databases with one query.

Notice also in Exhibit 8–28 that there are other subtabs, including News & Business, Public Records, and Find A Source. Users can configure these subtabs according to their needs. With subtabs, you can quickly access a large variety of LexisNexis databases. You can also browse for databases using the Find A Source subtab (see Exhibit 8–31). In Exhibit 8–31 (third screen), the user selected "U" from the alphabetical list, indicating that he wished to see all of the databases in LexisNexis that start with the letter "U."

Natural Language The advantage of using Natural Language is ease of use. The disadvantage is that the search may not be as precise as a Terms and Connectors search. The Natural Language feature in LexisNexis works like the Natural Language feature in Westlaw, allowing searches to be entered in the form of a sentence or question. For example, the query "Can a Federal court get personal jurisdiction over a non-resident company where the only contact is assignment of a mortgage?" can be entered directly into LexisNexis Natural Language (see Exhibit 8–32). In this example, the user selected the "DC Federal & State Cases, Combined" database, and then selected Natural Language in the search screen (see Exhibit 8–32, first screen). The user then entered the search query and entered some terms in the Restrict using Mandatory Terms field, including "personal jurisdiction." This means that any case retrieved must contain these terms. The user then clicked "Search." LexisNexis analyzed the statistical relevance of the terms and retrieved the documents that most closely matched the search requests. Notice in the second screen of Exhibit 8–32 that the *Johnson v. Long Beach Mortgage* case was retrieved (third in the list).

EXHIBIT 8–31

Search by Source tab

LexisNexis and the Knowledge Burst logo are registered trademarks of Reed Elsevier Properties Inc. TimeMap and CaseMap are registered trademarks of LexisNexis CourtLink, Inc. Used with the permission of LexisNexis.

EXHIBIT 8–32

LexisNexis Natural Language screen

Terms and Connectors Exhibit 8–33 shows selected connectors and expanders in LexisNexis. LexisNexis automatically searches for plurals of words and most possessive nouns. LexisNexis uses the exclamation mark (!) as a root expander and the asterisk (*) as a universal character, just as Westlaw does.

LexisNexis includes several types of connectors that for the most part are similar to those in Westlaw. Connectors in LexisNexis that are the same as Westlaw include OR, /p, /s, and /n. Connectors in LexisNexis that are similar, but not identical, to those in Westlaw are AND (which in Westlaw is represented as "&") and AND NOT (which in Westlaw is represented as %). In LexisNexis, some connectors can be entered in more than one way; for example, "/p" can also be entered as "w/p." The final query in Exhibit 8–34 reads "'personal jurisdiction' /s non-resident /s compan! /p

Connector	Definition	Search Query	Documents Found
OR	OR	mortgage OR contract	All documents that have either the word *mortgage* or the word *contract* anywhere in them
AND	AND	mortgage AND contract	All documents that contain both the word *mortgage* and the word *contract* anywhere in them
w/p or /p	Paragraph	mortgage w/p contract; or mortgage /p contract	All documents that contain both the word *mortgage* and the word *contract* in the same paragraph
w/s or /s	Sentence	mortgage w/s contract; or mortgage /s contract	All documents that contain both the word *mortgage* and the word *contract* in the same sentence
w/n or /n	Words	mortgage w/3 contract; or mortgage /3 contract	All documents that contain both the word *mortgage* and the word *contract* within three words of each other
" "	Phrase	"personal jurisdiction"	All documents in which the exact phrase *"personal jurisdiction"* occurs
Pre/n	Precedes by n words	personal Pre/3 jurisdiction	All documents where *personal* precedes *jurisdiction* within three words
AND NOT	AND NOT	R.I.C.O. AND NOT PUERTO RICO	All documents with the word *RICO* (i.e., Racketeer Influenced and Corrupt Organizations Act) but not *Puerto Rico*
Expander	**Definition**	**Search Query**	**Documents Found**
!	Root expander	medic!	All documents that have the words *medicine, medical, medicate,* or *medication*
*	Universal character	kn*w	All documents that have the word *know* or *knew* in them

EXHIBIT 8–33
LexisNexis connectors and expanders

mortgage OR contract AND long-arm." The query tells LexisNexis to search for documents in the selected database (DC Federal & State Cases, Combined) that have the phrase *personal jurisdiction* within the same sentence as the word *non-resident,* within the same sentence as *compan! (company or companies),* and within the same paragraph as *mortgage* or *contract,* and which also contain the word *long-arm* somewhere in the document. Notice in Exhibit 8–34 (second screen) that the *Johnson v. Long Beach Mortgage* case was retrieved.

Easy Search   Easy Search is a type of search in LexisNexis that returns only the most relevant documents and, according to LexisNexis, is optimized for short search queries that contain only two or three terms. For example, you could enter "personal jurisdiction non-resident" in Easy Search and LexisNexis would retrieve some leading cases on that subject.

Suggest Terms for My Search   The Suggest Terms for My Search feature in LexisNexis shows synonyms for terms in the search query. This is a helpful tool for refining searches. The LexisNexis Suggest Terms for my Search feature is similar to Westlaw's Thesaurus feature.

Working with Retrieved Cases in LexisNexis

LexisNexis gives you a number of different options for viewing and working with retrieved documents. After you have executed a search in LexisNexis, the system can display the retrieved documents in one of four formats. LexisNexis also provides features that help you work with the documents retrieved.

Display Formats   The four main display formats available in LexisNexis are Cite, KWIC, Full, and Custom.

EXHIBIT 8–34

LexisNexis Terms and Connectors search

Cite The Cite format shows a bibliographic list of the citations retrieved. Cite can either display the search terms or hide the search terms (see Exhibit 8–35, where the hits are shown). In the second screen of Exhibit 8–32, to the right of the View: field, notice that Cite is selected in the upper left corner of the screen. A list of the case cites is displayed, including an overview and core terms for each. In Exhibit 8–32, the search-term hits are hidden.

When you click Show Hits, the search terms as they appear in the case are included in the list (see Exhibit 8–35). You can either display or hide the hits. If you have the Show Hits option turned on, a lot of information is provided about each

EXHIBIT 8–35

LexisNexis display format:
Cite/Show Hits

case, but it is difficult to quickly search through a large numbers of retrieved cases. If you have Hide Hits turned on (see Exhibit 8–32, second screen), you can see more cases, but with less detail. Both options are helpful, depending on what you are trying to accomplish at the time.

KWIC The KWIC option, by default, shows a 25-word window of text around your search terms. KWIC is helpful when you want to see the context in which your search terms appear, but do not want to read the full text of the case.

Full The Full view shows you the full text of the document (see Exhibit 8–34, second screen).

Custom Using the Custom view, you can configure the display format to meet your individual needs.

Case Summaries LexisNexis includes a Case Summary section for each case (see Exhibit 8–34, second screen). The Case Summary includes the procedural posture of the case, an overview of the case, the outcome or disposition of the case, and the "Core Terms" used in the case. The Case Summary section makes it easy to understand the context of a case and its result. LexisNexis's Case Summary feature is similar to Westlaw's Synopsis feature.

Navigation Frame The Navigation Frame appears at the bottom of a retrieved document (see Exhibit 8–34, second screen). The Explore feature allows you to navigate within the document, moving to the top of the document, viewing the dissent, moving to the place in the document where the attorneys are listed, and so forth. The Page feature allows you to navigate to a specific hard-copy reporter page. The Doc feature takes you to the next or previous document. Alternatively, you can click in the Doc box, enter a document number, and go to the specific document. The Term feature allows you to go to the next/previous search term. Viewing the search terms is helpful when you are trying to evaluate whether a document is on point.

Headnotes

Headnotes in LexisNexis summarize each major issue in a case. Most cases include several Headnotes. When you find a Headnote on point, you can select the More Like This Headnote link next to that specific Headnote. In the More Like This Headnote screen that is then displayed, you can search similar Headnotes in LexisNexis by jurisdiction. Headnotes are a great way to expand your research while staying on point.

Shepard's Citations

Shepard's Citations is LexisNexis's citation research tool. It allows you to determine if a case, statute, or other document is good law and helps you expand your research by finding other sources that have cited the case. To access *Shepard's Citations*, select the *Shepard's* tab (see Exhibit 8–36, first screen). There are actually four separate cite-checking tools on the *Shepard's* tab. They appear as subtabs and include *Shepard's*, Table of Authorities, Auto-Cite, and LEXCITE (see Exhibit 8–36).

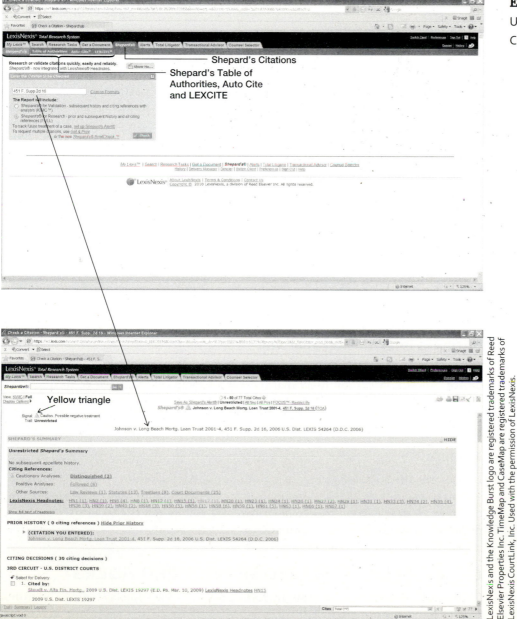

EXHIBIT 8–36

Using LexisNexis Shepard's Citations

EXHIBIT 8–37

LexisNexis *Shepard's* Signal™ Indicators

Shepard's Signal ™ Indicators	Explanation
●	• Warning: Negative treatment is indicated
Q	• Questioned: Validity questioned by citing references
▲	• Caution: Possible negative treatment
◆	• Positive treatment is indicated
A	• Citing references with analysis available
I	• Citation information available

Notice in the first screen of Exhibit 8–36 that the user has selected the *Shepard's* subtab, entered a cite (451 F. Supp.2d 16), selected the FULL format for the resulting report, and then selected "Check." The system returns both the history of the case and citing references (see Exhibit 8–36, second screen). Notice the yellow triangle at the top of the second screen in Exhibit 8–36. The yellow triangle means that the case has had some negative treatment, but has not yet been reversed or overruled. Notice that in the case itself (see Exhibit 8–34, second screen), a yellow triangle is displayed near the title of the case. *Shepard's* uses colored shapes so the user can easily determine whether a case or statute is good law (see Exhibit 8–37).

Public Records Searches

Using LexisNexis, you can access many different public records databases. Notice in Exhibit 8–38 that there is a subtab (on the Search tab) called "Public Records." Exhibit 8–38 shows the databases available through the Public Records subtab.

Business Information Searches

Using LexisNexis, you can access a large number of news and business information sources. Notice in Exhibit 8–39 that there is a subtab called "News & Business" on the Search tab. Exhibit 8–39 shows the databases and topics available through the News & Business subtab.

Training

LexisNexis offers a wide variety of training options, including e-learning modules, webinars, training guides, and seminars. See www.lexis.com. Many of the e-learning modules are available online free of charge, and you do not need a LexisNexis ID or password to access the e-learning modules.

OTHER CALR FEE-BASED SERVICE PROVIDERS

Other CALR service providers include Loislaw (www.loislaw.com), National Law Library (www.itislaw.com), Fastcase (www.fastcase.com), and Versuslaw

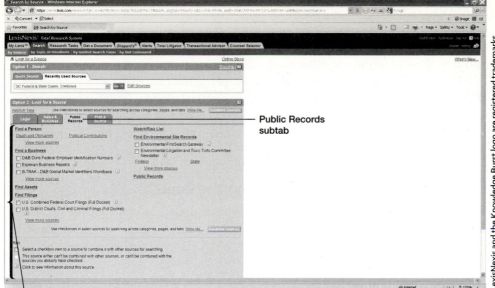

EXHIBIT 8–38

LexisNexis Public Records tab

Public Records subtab

Public Records databases

LexisNexis and the Knowledge Burst logo are registered trademarks of Reed Elsevier Properties Inc. TimeMap and CaseMap are registered trademarks of LexisNexis CourtLink, Inc. Used with the permission of LexisNexis.

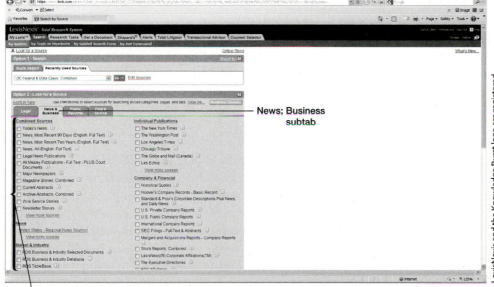

EXHIBIT 8–39

LexisNexis News & Business tab

News; Business subtab

News; Business databases

LexisNexis and the Knowledge Burst logo are registered trademarks of Reed Elsevier Properties Inc. TimeMap and CaseMap are registered trademarks of LexisNexis CourtLink, Inc. Used with the permission of LexisNexis.

(www.versuslaw.com). These service providers compete against Westlaw and Lexis-Nexis on the basis of price. Their services offer less breadth of electronic information, and fewer features and functions. For some firms, this is fine. For example, if a law firm has only a few legal professionals and they practice in specific areas such as divorce, criminal, or estate law, a subscription to one of these service providers that only includes case law and statutes for the firm's state might suffice.

INCREASED PRODUCTIVITY ON CALR SYSTEMS

Every minute on an online legal database system is costly, unless the organization has negotiated a flat-rate monthly billing option. However, you can follow some general guidelines and take several precautions to increase your productivity and reduce CALR costs.

Do Not Read Cases Online

In most instances, do not stay online to read the cases you have found. If you have the book in which the case appears, simply get the cite, terminate the CALR session, and read the text of the case from the book offline.

If you do not have access to the book, print the case offline or download it. With many CALR providers, you are incurring several charges whenever you are connected, including an access service charge (if you used this method to connect to the service) and a database charge. If you read a case online, you are still incurring both types of charges.

Do Not Make Typos When Entering the Search

A typo in a search command can cost you several dollars as you wait for the CALR service to run the (inappropriate) search. Double-check your search command for typos before executing it.

Always Plan the Search

Always carefully plan out your search before going online, and always have several alternative searches ready. This can save your firm hundreds of dollars a month in online charges.

Call the CALR's Research Attorneys

If you need to do a particularly difficult search, try calling one of the research attorneys provided by many CALR systems. For Westlaw and LexisNexis, the call is toll-free. The research attorneys are experts at CALR and can help you prepare a successful search. They will even run a search online for you to make sure the search query is correct.

CD-ROM LEGAL DATABASES

CD-ROM legal database
A CD-ROM disk containing a (searchable) legal database, such as a state case law reporter.

A **CD-ROM legal database** is a database like the ones found on Westlaw or LexisNexis, but is packaged compactly on one or more CD-ROMs. For example, the complete set of *Federal Reporters*, which contain federal appellate court decisions from 1880 to the present, takes up more than 150 linear feet of shelf space in a law library—and this does not count the indexes necessary to use the reporters effectively. The same *Federal Reporters* are available on 12 CD-ROM disks, which take up only a few inches of shelf space, and come with a search engine that allows you to search for needed material. Many CD-ROM publishers also offer connections to the Internet or an online service so that research can be updated. These CDs can be loaded into one computer on a network, so that other computers logged into the same network can have also access them.

ETHICAL CONSIDERATIONS

Use of the Internet and email raise several ethical considerations. These include the reliability of Internet information that you might use to support a client's case; problems regarding marketing on the Internet, including use of unsolicited email (spam) to market a law firm; confidentiality issues surrounding use of email for correspondence with clients and others; and competence in legal research.

Reliability of Information on the Internet

As mentioned earlier in this chapter, the reliability of information on the Internet is not guaranteed. Anyone can host a website, send emails, post information on listservs and discussion groups, and generally communicate freely on the Internet with little if any oversight; therefore, users cannot assume that any information is necessarily accurate. There is a tremendous amount of information on the Internet that is opinion, hearsay, innuendo, mistaken, and flat-out untruth. As an Internet user, you should adopt a *caveat emptor* ("Let the buyer beware") philosophy. Whenever possible, you should attempt to verify information found on the Internet and develop cross-checks to make sure the information is accurate. This is particularly true when using new sites that you have never visited before. It is not unlike using *Shepard's* to check the accuracy of cases that you cite to make sure they are still valid and current law. If you cannot corroborate or verify a piece of information, or have any doubts about the source, it is probably best not to use it.

Although no ethical rule deals specifically with Internet research, attorneys do have a duty to perform work in a competent manner. Thus, when performing factual or legal research on the Internet for a client's case, legal professionals must do so in a competent and thorough manner. This, of course, includes a duty not to cite or otherwise use inaccurate information.

Marketing on the Internet

Many law firms market their services to clients using the Internet. Because of the potential for abuse, most states heavily regulate the legal ethics area of attorney advertising and marketing. According to typical ethical restrictions, lawyers cannot use false or misleading information; create unjustified expectations, such as by publishing recent jury verdicts they received; and cannot directly solicit potential with whom they do not or have not had a relationship (ambulance chasing).

States are currently creating new ethics rules that apply specifically to all electronic communication. These rules cover all forms of Internet marketing: law-firm web pages, use of banner ads and links, use of Internet chat rooms to solicit clients, and use of email to solicit prospective clients, among others.

Marketing on the Internet—Spam

As indicated previously, spam is unsolicited emails sent to others. In an infamous case in Tennessee, a lawyer spammed email listservs and discussion groups with a promotion for his immigration practice. His spam was reportedly received by thousands of people in many countries and resulted in many complaints to the Tennessee disciplinary authority. The attorney was charged with several ethical violations, including: (1) failing to label his email as advertising; (2) failing to submit a copy of the email to the state bar disciplinary authorities; and (3) referring to himself as an "immigration lawyer," in violation of a rule governing specialization; among other ethical breaches. The Tennessee Supreme Court suspended the attorney's license for one year as a result of the spamming.

Email Confidentiality

As discussed earlier, confidentiality is an important issue when legal professionals use email to communicate with clients. Practical considerations for using email ethically include:

- Having a policy for the legal organization regarding the use of email and how it will be used to communicate with clients.
- Consulting clients about what type of information they want communicated via email, how often the client receives or responds to email, and other information about the particulars of the client's specific email system or habits.

- Sending a test email to a client to ensure that the right email address is being used.
- Adding a confidentiality statement to all client emails. This is similar to the statements that appear on many fax cover pages, declaring that the information is intended solely for the recipient and any third party who receives it should immediately forward it or destroy it.
- Not using email at all for particularly sensitive information.

Ethical Considerations in CALR

Other ethical considerations and duties also apply to computer-assisted legal research, such as taking the time to perform competent legal research, citing quotes appropriately, and not plagiarizing.

Performing Competent Legal Research

Performing competent legal research is a fundamental aspect of representing a client in a competent and ethical manner. A client comes to an attorney to be advised on both the factual and legal nature of the client's legal matter. Because the U.S. system of law is based on legal precedent, it is absolutely essential that an attorney understand the legal aspects of a client's matter. This includes performing the legal research to know how to appropriately represent and advise the client. Sometimes wading through mountains of case law, statutes, legislative history, indexes, legal encyclopedias, treatises, law review articles, regulations, court rules, and other materials to support a client's position is like finding a needle in a haystack. It takes skill, thoroughness, and exhaustive preparation to find the right information and to zealously represent the client's interests. Although a client can assist with presenting the facts of a case, the client cannot help regarding the preparation of legal arguments and authorities. This responsibility lies with the attorney and paralegal.

If attorneys fail to present competent legal arguments based on competent legal research, not only have the attorneys failed to perform their ethical duty, but they may also have committed legal malpractice. Courts have generally recognized that an attorney has a duty to perform competent legal research. For example, the court in *Gosnell v. Rentokil,* 175 F.R.D. 508, 510 n.1 (N.D. Ill. 1997), considered the question of whether an attorney had a duty to Shepardize a case (e.g., to confirm that the case the attorney was citing was still good law). In *Gosnell* the court stated:

> It is really inexcusable for any lawyer to fail, as a matter of routine, to Shepardize all cited cases (a process that has been made much simpler today than it was in the past, given the facility for doing so under Westlaw or Lexis). Shepardization would of course have revealed that the "precedent" no longer qualified as such.

Simply put, it is imperative to perform thorough legal research to adequately protect the rights and interests of your client.

Plagiarizing

Plagiarizing is the act of using another person's writing or ideas and passing it off as one's own. It is important for all legal professionals to avoid plagiarizing when performing legal research and writing. This problem can be avoided easily simply by citing the authority that has been used, and making it clear where quotations begin and end.

It is dishonest to take credit for the work of another. In addition to ethical considerations, plagiarism can also be a violation of copyright and intellectual property rights. Thus, it is extremely important to appropriately cite and give credit to the author when another person's work is used.

SUMMARY

The Internet or the information superhighway connects hundreds of millions of computers and thousands of networks around the world. Services available on the Internet include email, listservs, newsgroups, instant messaging, File Transfer Protocol, World Wide Web, blogs, RSS, and podcasts.

Several different types of search engines are available on the Web, including individual search engines that compile their own searchable databases, subject-oriented search engines that organize information into topical menus of subjects, and metasearch engines that send a search to multiple search engines. The terms invisible web or deep web refer to the approximately 50 percent of the World Wide Web that lies within databases, is password protected, or is otherwise not accessible through search engines. To access those sites, the user must go to them directly.

The Internet can be used to perform legal research, but it is not at all like using Westlaw or LexisNexis, because the legal information there is not contained in one central depository. Legal research on the Internet is most efficient when you know exactly what you are looking for, such as a specific case or statute. The Internet is better suited to factual research than legal research. The Internet can be used for performing general research, public record searches, finding people or information about people, accessing news information, conducting business research, and finding expert witnesses, among many other things. Many legal organizations maintain web pages on the Internet. They represent a 24/7 opportunity for marketing the legal organization.

Effectively all paralegals use email on a daily basis in their jobs. Email is a de facto standard for communication throughout the legal community and between legal professionals and clients. Spam, phishing, and loss of confidentiality represent the downside of email use.

Persons doing computer-assisted legal research use computers to research and retrieve legal information. Two of the largest fee-based CALR service providers are Westlaw and LexisNexis. Less expensive choices, such as Loislaw and Versuslaw, are also available.

Westlaw maintains more than 40,000 databases and offers an array of features. Find by Citation is a Westlaw feature that allows a user to enter a cite and be taken directly to the cite without entering a search query or database. Westlaw's Natural Language search system uses plain English instead of complex connector strings to search for documents. Westlaw's Terms and Connectors search system uses Boolean logic and operators/connectors to combine terms into a search query. Common Westlaw connectors include /s, /p, &, and /n. Root expanders like ! enable Westlaw to retrieve words with the same root. The Locate in Result Westlaw feature allows users to search a retrieved document for particular terms, whether or not the terms appeared in the original search. Headnotes and Key Numbers in Westlaw summarize every major issue in a case and allow users to find additional cases on the same topic. KeySearch is a Westlaw tool that allows users to find documents using a topical legal index, without having to formulate a search query. KeyCite is a Westlaw citation tool that can be used to check if a case is still good law or to list all the times a source has been referred to in other documents. Westlaw also has many nonlegal databases that allow users to search public records, news, and business-related information.

LexisNexis is a large CALR service provider that, like Westlaw, has captured a large part of the CALR market. LexisNexis offers databases and features similar to those of Westlaw. Some LexisNexis features include Get by Citation, Get by Party Name, Natural Language, and *Shepard's Citations*. The terms and connectors used in LexisNexis are very similar, but not identical, to the Westlaw terms and connectors. LexisNexis, like Westlaw, includes value-added features, including case summaries and Headnotes.

CD-ROM legal databases allow users to search for case law using CD-ROMS. CD-ROMS take up much less shelf space than physical books, but are not as up-to-date as online CALR services. CD-ROM legal databases use search engines similar to those of Westlaw or LexisNexis.

Ethical considerations and duties apply both to law-firm use of the Internet/email and to legal research. It is important that research be conducted competently and that legal professionals avoid plagiarizing other people's work when using research results.

KEY TERMS

blog
bookmark
CD-ROM legal database
cite checking
computer-assisted legal research (CALR)
connectors
electronic mail (email)
File Transfer Protocol (FTP)
Find a Case by Party Name
Find by Citation
Get by Citation
Get by Party Name
Headnotes and Key Numbers

individual search engine
instant messaging (IM)
Internet Service Provider (ISP)
invisible web
KeyCite
library gateway
listserv
Locate in Result
metasearch engine
Natural Language
offline
online
phishing
podcast

portal
ResultsPlus
root expander
RSS
search query
spam
specialty search engine
subject directory
subject-specific database
Terms and Connectors
uniform resource locator (URL)
universal character
web browser
World Wide Web

INTERNET SITES

Internet sites for this chapter include:

ORGANIZATION	PRODUCT/SERVICE	WORLD WIDE WEB ADDRESS
GENERAL LEGAL SITES ON THE INTERNET		
ABA Legal Technology Resource Center	In-depth information on law-related Internet, intranet, and extranet sites	www.abanet.org/tech/trc
FindLaw	Legal research portal/search engine	www.findlaw.com
Hieros Gamos	Legal research portal/search engine	www.hg.org
Internet Legal Resource Guide	Legal research portal/search engine	www.ilrg.com
Law and Politics Internet Guide	Legal research portal/search engine	www.lpig.org
Legal Information Institute at Cornell Law School	Large collection of links to law-related resources	www.law.cornell.edu
Virtual Chase	Large collection of law-related resources	www.virtualchase.com
WashLaw at Washburn University Law School	Large collection of links to law-related resources	www.washlaw.edu
COMPUTER-ASSISTED LEGAL RESEARCH INTERNET SITES		
Fastcase, Inc.	Fastcase, CALR provider	www.fastcase.com
ITIS, Inc.	National Law Library, CALR provider	www.itislaw.com
Loislaw.com, Inc.	Loislaw, CALR provider	www.loislaw.com
Reed Elsevier Inc.	LexisNexis, CALR provider	www.lexisnexis.com
Reed Elsevier Inc.	LexisNexis training	www.lexisnexis.com
Thomson/West	Westlaw, CALR provider	www.westlaw.com
Thomson/West	Westlaw training	west.thomson.com/westlaw
VersusLaw, Inc.	VersusLaw, CALR provider	www.versuslaw.com

TEST YOUR KNOWLEDGE

1. To connect to the Internet, a user needs an ISP. What does ISP stand for?

2. What is another name for an electronic mailing list that allows people on the list to send email to and receive email from everyone on the list?

3. What are the differences between individual, specialty, and metasearch engines?

4. What tool can users access to better control their searches in search engines such as Google?

5. If a user wanted to search for *bikes* but not *motorcycles* in a search engine such as Google, how would the search query best be formulated?

6. True or False: The Internet is better suited to factual research than to legal research.

7. Name three categories of factual information related to a case that a paralegal might search for on the Internet.

8. A useful tool in an Internet browser that allows a user to search the contents of a web page is called _____.

9. In Westlaw, what is the name of the plain-English search feature?

10. When using Terms and Connectors in Westlaw, a space between two search terms means what?

11. What do the /s, /p, and /n connectors signify in Westlaw?

12. What is the root expander character in Westlaw?

13. What is the universal character in Westlaw?

14. If you write a Terms and Connectors search query in Westlaw and retrieve a large number of cases, what action can you take to reduce the number of cases retrieved?

15. In Westlaw, what does the Locate in Results feature do?

16. What does Westlaw's KeyCite feature do?

17. True or False: Westlaw has Headnotes but LexisNexis does not.

18. What feature in LexisNexis allows a user to search retrieved cases for additional search terms, whether or not those terms were in the original search?

19. True or False: Westlaw's Synopsis and LexisNexis's Case Summary are comparable features.

20. What is the LexisNexis case citation tool called?

21. True or False: /p, /s, /n, and quotation marks all work the same in Westlaw and LexisNexis.

ON THE WEB EXERCISES

1. Using a general search engine such as Google or Yahoo, find three law-related blogs. Write a two-page paper summarizing the content found on the three blogs.

2. Using a general search engine such as Google or Yahoo, find one article related to accessing the "invisible" or "deep" web. Write a two-page paper summarizing the article.

3. Visit any five websites listed in Exhibit 8–4. Print out the title page of each site and write a two-page paper comparing and contrasting the five sites.

4. Using a general search engine such as Google or Yahoo, find one article related to accessing public records on the Web. Write a two-page paper summarizing the article.

5. Visit any five websites listed in Exhibit 8–6. Print out the title page of each site and write a two-page paper comparing and contrasting the five sites.

6. Using the Google Maps feature at www.google.com, print out a satellite or street level picture of where you currently live. If it is not available, print out one of a place with which you are familiar.

7. Locate and print out the *Model Code of Ethics and Professional Responsibility* for the National Federation of Paralegal Associations.

8. Find a list of websites of local paralegal organizations that are associated with the National Association of Legal Assistants.

9. Use at least three different search engines to find the website for the Association of Trial Lawyers of America. Compare the results of each search. Which search engine did you like best, and why?

10. Find an email address for any member of Congress from your state. Write a short description of how you went about finding the email address.

11. Find a list of law-related listservs and subscribe to at least one.

12. Using the Internet, find a list of Web resources for immigration law.

13. Find regulations implementing the Family and Medical Leave Act by searching in the *Code of Federal Regulations* as published online by the U.S. government.

14. Use SEC EDGAR filings and other information to research recent developments regarding Microsoft Corporation. Use at least five different sources of information. Prepare a one-page summary of the information you gathered.

15. Go to www.west.thomson.com/support/user-guide/westlaw and review at least one Westlaw training guide. Write a two-page memo summarizing what you learned.

16. Go to www.lexis.com and take at least one free e-learning module. Write a two-page memo summarizing what you learned.

17. Visit the websites of two other CALR service providers (not Westlaw or LexisNexis) and compare their products and pricing, if it is available. Which of the services did you like best, and why? Write a two-page memo summarizing your research.

QUESTIONS AND EXERCISES

1. Interview an attorney, paralegal, or secretary in a legal organization regarding their use of the Internet and email. How has it changed over time?

2. As a new paralegal in a solo practitioner's office, you notice that the office has been slow to embrace technology. The office does not have a high-speed Internet connection and the attorney does not see the need to get one because the Internet is barely used in the office. The office mainly handles personal injury, divorce, and collection cases. Write a one-page memo to the attorney regarding the advantages of using the World Wide Web for this office.

3. You are a paralegal working on a personal injury case in which your firm's client had her hand cut off in an accident on the job. The defendant admits liability and is trying to settle the case for an amount that the attorney thinks is too low. The attorney asks you to formulate a search query in Westlaw or LexisNexis in the hope that you can determine what amount of damages juries have awarded for this type of accident or case.

4. The attorney you work for wants you to perform CALR on the following issue. The attorney is representing a client who worked for a governmental agency. The client was fired from the agency because the client was arrested for driving under the influence of alcohol while off duty. The criminal charges were dropped and the client was not formally prosecuted. The attorney asks you to formulate a search query plan, using a CALR service. What is your query?

ETHICS QUESTION

A new client has received a letter from the Internal Revenue Service informing him that unless he pays the IRS $314.23, he will be sued. The client insists that no taxes are owed and wants your firm to research the tax code, regulations, and case law to find legal authority to support his position. You estimate that it will take more than five hours to complete this research. Your firm bills $90 an hour for your services. What ethical issues, if any, are raised by this scenario?

 Go to the Workbook to complete the Hands-On Exercises.

 Access an interactive eBook, chapter-specific interactive learning tools, including flash cards, quizzes, and more in your Paralegal CourseMate, accessed through CengageBrain.com.

CHAPTER 9

The Electronic Courthouse, Automated Courtroom, and Presentation Graphics

CHAPTER OBJECTIVES

After completing this chapter, you should be able to do the following:

1. Explain what the "electronic courthouse" is.
2. Describe how an automated courtroom works.
3. Describe what presentation software does.
4. Explain how presentation software can be used in the legal environment.

The courthouses of the past, with paper files and manual systems, have changed. Electronic courthouses, which allow electronic filing of court documents and access to court records, dockets, files, and other data via the Internet, are a reality in many jurisdictions. Courtrooms have changed as well. In many jurisdictions, automated courtrooms have evidence display systems, which include computers and monitors for the judge, attorneys, court reporter, jurors, and the public. In these automated courtrooms, presentation graphics and trial presentation software are used to present evidence to the court and jurors electronically, using computers and monitors. The presentations can include text, photographs, video, animation, sound, clip art, re-creations of scenes or actions, and much more.

THE ELECTRONIC COURTHOUSE

The notion of the local courthouse as a place to which legal professionals must mail documents, or where they must hand-file documents and access court records and court files using manual methods, is rapidly disappearing. In many jurisdictions, legal professionals can now instantly file motions, briefs, and other documents electronically, and can instantly access court dockets and court records using the Internet. With electronic filing, courts accept electronic versions of legal documents via the Internet or other electronic means instead of requiring a hard copy of the document to be physically presented.

The federal district and bankruptcy courts have been on the cutting edge of this technology for several years. As of this writing, the Case Management/Electronic Case Filing (CM/ECF) system is used in more than 98 percent of the federal courts: 93 district courts, 93 bankruptcy courts, the Court of International Trade, the Court of Federal Claims, and 10 of the United States Courts of Appeals. To date, more than

27 million cases have been put on the CM/ECF system. More than 250,000 legal professionals have filed documents using the Internet and CM/ECF. The plan is for all United States courts to convert to use of CM/ECF in the near future.

Filing documents using the system is easy. The user logs onto a court's website with a court-issued password, enters some general information about the case and the document to be filed, and then submits the document to be filed in Portable Document Format (PDF). Once the PDF file is received, a notice of receipt is generated and sent to the user. Other parties to the action then automatically receive an email notifying them of the filing. The CM/ECF system also gives courts the option to make filed documents accessible to the public over the Internet.

Another federal system, the Public Access to Court Electronic Records (PACER) program, allows the public to access court-related information (see Exhibit 9–1). PACER is an electronic public access service that allows users to obtain a variety of docket and case-related information regarding federal courts using the Internet. Links to all courts are provided from the PACER website. To access PACER, a user must register with the PACER Service Center, have an Internet connection, and log into the system. There is also a small charge for the service. PACER allows users to request information about an individual or case, including:

- Party and participant listings, including attorneys and judges
- General case-related data, including the nature of the lawsuit, the cause(s) of action alleged, and the amount of damages requested
- A chronology of events/docket items in the case
- The case status
- Judgment(s) and appeals

Using PACER, a person can also access the United States Case/Party Index, which allows one to search for party names throughout much of the federal court system.

Although the federal court system is rapidly nearing the end of its electronic courthouse implementation project, it may take some years for all the states to catch up. Some states have completed the move to electronic systems, but many are still moving through the implementation stage. Traditional roadblocks to these types of systems include cost, standardization issues, security, and obtaining the hardware and software needed to support electronic filing. Like the federal court system, many state courts have selected Portable Document Format (PDF) as their standard for filing documents electronically.

EXHIBIT 9–1

Public Access to Court
Electronic Records (PACER)

Source: http://www.pacer.gov

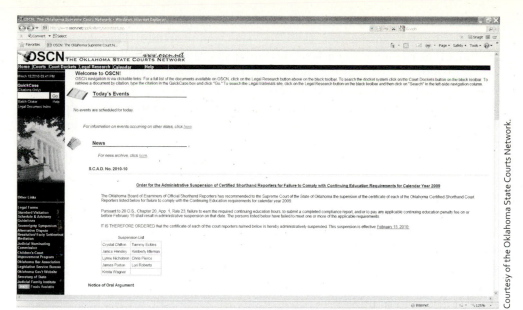

EXHIBIT 9–2

Internet Access to the Oklahoma State Courts Network

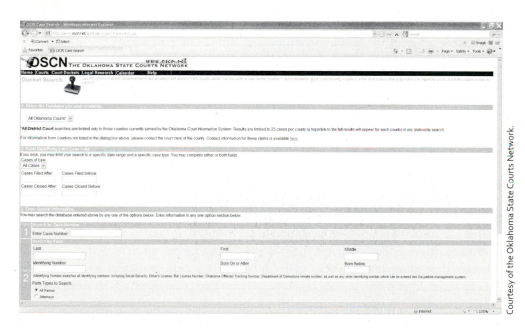

The Oklahoma State Courts Network (www.oscn.net) is a good example of state implementation of this technology. The Oklahoma State Courts Network allows users to access court dockets statewide, including the Oklahoma Supreme Court, the Court of Criminal Appeals, the Court of Civil Appeals, and 77 district courts (see Exhibit 9–2).

Electronic services such as Westlaw and LexisNexis also have access to some court dockets and can electronically track document filings in cases and access court records. Some of these services even automatically alert the legal professional (electronically) to new filings in cases, at intervals such as once a week or twice a week. Although a legal organization must pay the vendor for these services (as opposed to getting them free when states or courts implement the program), many legal organizations find it worth the cost.

THE AUTOMATED COURTROOM

In addition to automating access to the courthouse, many courts are also automating their courtrooms. Most automated courtrooms include evidence display systems, videoconferencing, and real-time court reporting.

evidence display system
Technology that provides networked computer monitors to a judge, jury, court reporter, clerk, attorneys, and the public.

document camera
An overhead projector that uses a camera to display hard-copy documents that have not been imaged.

An **evidence display system** typically provides networked computer monitors to the judge, jurors, court reporter, clerk, attorneys, and the public. The master controls are located at the judge's bench so that he or she can control all monitors, sound systems, and/or cameras in the courtroom. The attorneys and/or judge can use the evidence display system to display properly admitted evidence such as images, photographs, video images, animations, and others. Most systems also include a **document camera**, an overhead projector that uses a camera to display hard-copy documents that have not been imaged.

Many evidence display systems also support videoconferencing. With this capability, if a judge approves the use, a witness could testify at a trial without being physically present in the courtroom.

Another extremely useful courtroom technology is real-time court reporting. With this system, a witness's testimony, as transcribed by a court reporter, becomes available within a few seconds after utterance of the testimony. The testimony can be displayed on the courtroom monitors or transmitted to the judge, jurors, or attorneys on a real-time basis.

It is now routine for trial attorneys to present opening statements and closing arguments, cross-examine witnesses, and display evidence using electronic means such as presentation graphics software or trial presentation software. These presentations are made in front of the jury using automated courtroom equipment.

The automated courtroom thus offers many advantages over a manual one. Electronic presentations and evidence can be viewed by everyone in the courtroom simultaneously (so that everyone can see the same thing at the same time). Electronic presentation of evidence can simplify complex subjects and add to the ability of judges, jurors, and others to comprehend and understand the issues and facts in a case. For years, educators have known that people remember far more of what they see than of what they merely hear. Combining these two sensory modes enhances both comprehension and understanding of the material presented.

The automated courtroom is also more convenient than manual methods and actually saves court time. For example, if an attorney images all of her exhibits to be admitted for trial, they can then be electronically displayed; there is no need to rely on or shuffle through hard-copy documents, which can be lost or damaged. Computer software that automatically tracks trial exhibits, in addition to displaying them using the evidence display system, can also save time for everyone involved. In some courts, criminal defendants who are too hostile to appear in court can view the proceedings offsite via a live video/audio feed. Using presentation graphics and trial presentation programs, legal professionals are able to get the most out of automated courtroom equipment.

OVERVIEW OF PRESENTATION AND TRIAL PRESENTATION SOFTWARE

Presentation software allows users to create visually interesting electronic presentations. Many legal professionals use generic presentation graphics programs, such as Microsoft PowerPoint, to create presentations for trials, such as exhibits, graphs, and charts, as well as presentations for internal training purposes or public seminars. Using presentation software, one can combine a number of elements to create visually interesting presentations, including text, color, video, animation, clip art, graphs, charts, and sound. A user builds a presentation by organizing evidence, transcripts, images, photographs, and other materials into individual slides; the software then gives the user the options of showing all the slides at one time, or controlling the timing of presentation with a remote control. Most presentation programs can also create outlines and speaker's notes.

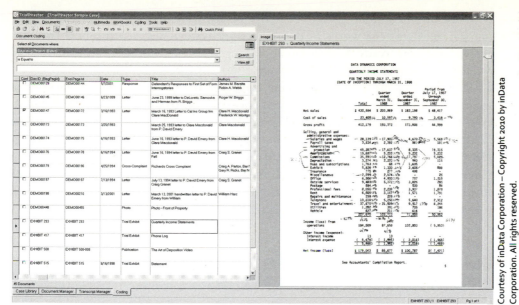

EXHIBIT 9–3

Some trial presentation programs can manage documents.

In addition to generic presentation programs, there are **trial presentation programs** that have been specifically designed to meet the needs of practicing attorneys, particularly those who try cases to juries and courts. TrialDirector and Sanction are examples of trial presentation programs designed specifically for the legal market.

Trial presentation programs can do much more than just display electronic slides. Some trial presentation programs can manage documents, including maintaining document abstracts and tracking: who admitted the document (plaintiff or defendant); the Bates number of the document; the date the document was admitted into evidence; the witness who was on the stand when the document was admitted; the status of the document, including whether introduction of the document was objected to; and other information (see Exhibit 9–3). Even in relatively small cases, managing and tracking all the documents in a trial can be difficult and time-consuming. Trial presentation programs can automate that process in addition to displaying electronic documents.

Trial presentation programs can manage complex tasks, such as combining video/audio, graphs, and documents into a single slide or presenting these materials individually (see Exhibit 9–4). Trial presentation software also can synchronize the

trial presentation programs
Presentation graphics programs specifically designed to meet the needs of trial attorneys.

EXHIBIT 9–4

Trial presentation software can manage both video and documentary material.

playback of video/audio with a transcript of prior testimony, so that a factfinder can not only read the words of the transcript, but can also see and hear the witness speaking the words. Trial presentation programs can also display presentations in applications such as Microsoft PowerPoint.

Notably, trial presentation programs can access data nonsequentially. PowerPoint works well when everything is linear and goes straight from beginning to end. However, most trials do not proceed this way. Attorneys need to be able to produce a particular document on a moment's notice. Trial presentation programs can access data quickly and conveniently, unlike PowerPoint. In addition, most trial presentation programs have the ability to search the trial database and access data quickly and efficiently. Generally speaking, trial presentation programs are quite powerful and are generally better suited to most trial purposes than generic presentation programs.

CREATING LEGAL PRESENTATIONS WITH MICROSOFT POWERPOINT

It is quite easy to create legal presentations with general presentation software like Microsoft PowerPoint. In this chapter, we walk through the process of creating an opening statement for a case using the interface of Microsoft PowerPoint 2007.

The Screen and Views

Exhibit 9–5 shows the title page for the opening statement presentation. Notice that, as in any Microsoft Office 2007 program, the ribbon bar, Office Button, title bar, and Quick Access toolbar are displayed. In Exhibit 9–5, the slide counter in the lower left of the screen shows that the user is on the first of six slides. This helpful feature lets you know at all times where you are in the presentation.

EXHIBIT 9–5

PowerPoint 2007 slide

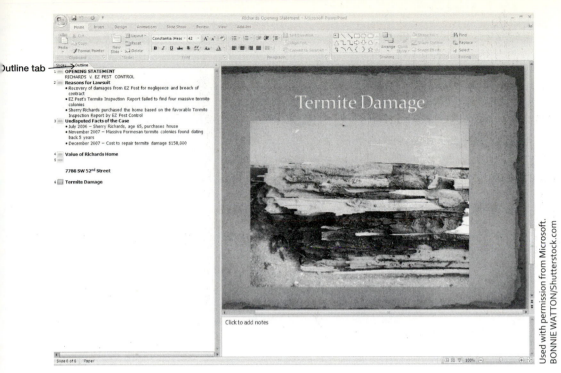

Outline tab

Used with permission from Microsoft. BONNIE WATTON/Shutterstock.com

EXHIBIT 9–6

Microsoft PowerPoint Normal view—Outline display mode

Three icons are displayed at the lower right of the screen. These three icons represent the different ways the user can view or see this presentation: Normal view, Slide Sorter view, and Slide Show view.

Normal View The Normal view for this particular program is shown in Exhibit 9–6. The **normal view** shows the slide that is being created. On the left side of the screen is the text for all the slides in this presentation. Notice in Exhibit 9–5 that the Slides tab is selected. In Normal view, you can select either Slides or the Outline display mode (see the upper left of Exhibit 9–6). Exhibit 9–6 shows the second slide of the presentation; this time the slide is shown in Normal view and the Outline tab in the upper left of the window is selected. The outline portion of the screen, as the name implies, shows an outline of the presentation. Notice in Exhibit 9–6 that the outline portion of the screen shows some of the same information contained in the current slide but without any graphic elements. Also, Exhibit 9–5 shows a section of the screen (under the slide) where you can enter speaker's notes about that particular slide. These can be printed out for reference purposes when you are ready to give the presentation. Speaker's notes can be created for each slide of the presentation.

Slide Sorter View The **slide sorter view** shows the slides in the presentation, but in a greatly reduced format. The slide sorter view is typically used to review and/or change the order of slides. For example, to move slide 8 in front of slide 3, you would simply click on slide 8 and drag it in front of slide 3. The program will automatically renumber the slides, but you must manually recheck and change cross-references on other slides when you do this. Slide Sorter view gives you a big picture of the presentation and allows you to easily organize or reorganize the presentation.

Slide Show View The **slide show view** is used during a presentation or when you are developing a presentation and want to learn how the audience will actually see the

normal view
PowerPoint screen that shows the slide that is being created, an outline of the total presentation, and speaker's notes for the slide currently displayed.

slide sorter view
PowerPoint screen that shows the slides in the presentation, but in a greatly reduced format; typically used to review and/or change the order of slides.

slide show view
PowerPoint screen used during a presentation or when the user wants to preview how the audience will actually see the slide. Only the current slide is shown on the screen. The program interface, menus, outline view, and speaker's notes are not shown.

EXHIBIT 9–7

Options for adding a new slide

slide. The only thing shown on the screen is the slide itself. The program interface, outline, and speaker's notes are not shown.

Backgrounds, Adding Slides, and Formatting a Presentation

background

The design on which the other elements of the presentation (words, clip art, etc.) are placed.

The first step in creating a presentation is to select the background. The **background** is the design on which the other elements of the presentation (words, clip art, etc.) will be placed. It is similar to the canvas of a painting. PowerPoint comes with several predesigned backgrounds that you can choose from. You can also create your own backgrounds or select backgrounds from Microsoft Office Online.

The next step in creating a presentation is to add slides. PowerPoint 2007 has a New Slide command found on the Home ribbon (see Exhibit 9–7). The New Slide command gives you a menu of different formats for creating a slide (see Exhibit 9–7). These automatic formats make it easy to select a format and then quickly begin entering the information.

Photographs, Clip Art, Word Art

clip art

Predrawn art.

PowerPoint allows you to include clip art, photographs, and word art in presentations. **Clip art** is predrawn art. Be careful when considering the use of clip art in trial and legal presentations; some clip art actually diminishes the professional appearance of the presentation. Make sure that what you choose is appropriate, well executed, and (most importantly) enhances the impact or comprehensibility of your presentation; never throw in images just for the sake of having a picture.

Notice that the presentation in Exhibit 9–8 includes several clear, high-impact photographs. High-quality photographs can enhance the professionalism of a presentation and create strong visual impact. Word art may also be useful for highlighting material, or for creating a consistent visual theme throughout a presentation. **Word art** features allow you to add special formatting to text, including three-dimensional (3-D) designs.

word art

Feature that allows users to add special formatting to text.

Graphs/Charts

PowerPoint allows you to create graphs and charts, either as stand-alone elements (such as a graph for a case) or as part of a presentation. Notice in Exhibit 9–9 that

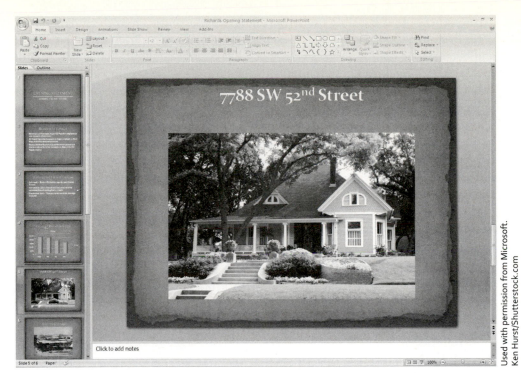

EXHIBIT 9–8

Photographs in PowerPoint

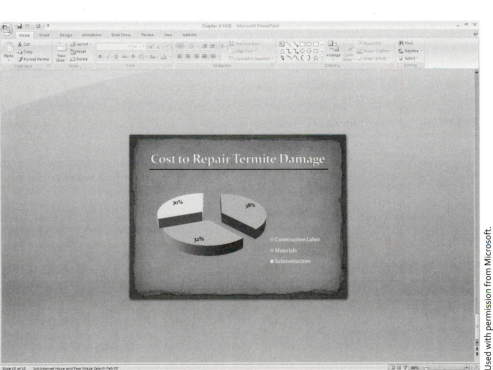

EXHIBIT 9–9

Graph in PowerPoint

the graph has the same background as the rest of the presentation and that it is in 3-D. PowerPoint provides a wide variety of graph and chart formats to choose from, including column charts, bar graphs, and pie charts.

Multimedia, Transition, and Animation Effects

Multimedia effects, such as sound files and video clips, can also be added to presentations, so that sound and video will run whenever the slide is displayed. This can add interest and excitement to a presentation. (It also engages more sensory modalities, so that factfinders are more likely to comprehend and remember the material.)

slide transition
Effects that control how the program proceeds from one slide to another.

Another option is a **slide transition** effect, which controls how the program proceeds from one slide to another. For example, you could move from slide 2 to slide 3 and make slide 3 appear on the screen much like horizontal blinds being drawn, with each piece sliding onto the screen individually until the slide is complete. Animation refers to other effects, such as how bullet points appear on the screen. You could make bullet points and text "fly" onto the screen individually, either automatically or when the mouse button is pushed. Animation is similar to slide transitions, but it happens within a slide instead of between slides. Again, be careful in using transition and animation effects so as to not diminish the professionalism (or comprehensibility) of the presentation. Always remember that the reason for using any effect is to enhance the impact, interest, and comprehensibility of your presentation, not to show off technological capabilities.

Displaying a Presentation

PowerPoint allows a presentation to be output in many different formats. These include slide show presentations; printing the presentation in black and white or color; printing it as overhead transparency slides; or exporting it into web-based learning software. In addition, you can print the slides, an outline, speaker's notes, or a combination of these items.

CREATING PRESENTATIONS WITH TRIALDIRECTOR

Trial presentation software such as TrialDirector allows you to integrate images of physical evidence, excerpts of video depositions, and slides from PowerPoint into your presentation.

Overview of TrialDirector

Exhibit 9–10 shows a sample screen from TrialDirector. On the left side of the screen is the Case Library. The Case Library consists of:

- Case Explorer. This lists all of the items in a case in three categories: Documents (Imaged Documents, Photo Documents, and Native File Documents), Transcripts, and Multimedia.
- Workbooks Explorer. Workbooks are electronic files that you can use to organize items as needed. Three workbooks are provided when a new case is opened (Search Results, Trial Exhibits, and Witnesses). Additional workbooks can be created for specific purposes requiring presentation of visual information (opening argument, closing argument, examination of specific witnesses, etc.).

On the right side of the screen is the Desktop Workspace. This is where you can see the items contained in the Case Explorer and Workbooks. By clicking on a document in the Case Library, you can see it in the Desktop Workspace. Individual items can be placed in a Workbook by clicking on the item, dragging it, and dropping it in the desired Workbook.

At the bottom of the screen are the Quick Access tabs, which allow you to change from the Case Library to the Document Manager, the Transcript Manager, or the Coding database.

The Document Manager organizes electronic exhibits, including scanned images, excerpts of video depositions, and presentations created in Adobe Acrobat or Microsoft PowerPoint. These documents can then be prepared for presentation at trial using annotation tools that include a highlighter, arrow, note, and stamp tools. Excerpts of video depositions (called clips) can be included, which lets you integrate key portions to be presented at trial.

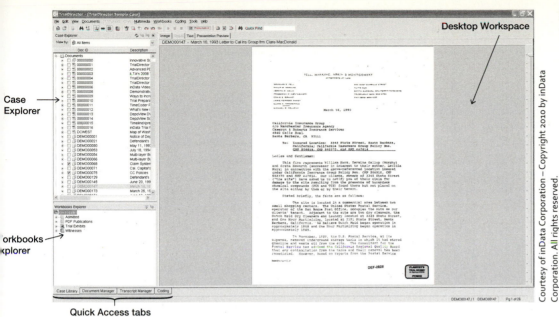

EXHIBIT 9–10
TrialDirector screen

The Transcript Manager allows you to show all or part of a video deposition and have the text/transcript of the deposition scrolling on the screen simultaneously.

The Coding database is a searchable repository of information about the specific items contained within the Case Library. For example, the Coding database may include the document ID, the date of the document, the author of the document, the specific issues related to the document, and so on. This information can be input directly, using TrialDirector, or it may be imported from another program (such as Summation). When you are in the Coding tab, you can choose either Column view (which displays multiple records) or Form view (which displays a single record).

Presentation mode is the tool that displays the specific item(s) for the court to see. With a video projector, you may use the Presentation mode to display images of evidence, video clips from depositions, and slides made to inform and persuade the factfinder.

Image Annotations

Images of documents and other items may be annotated (or "marked-up") to emphasize specific portions for the jury or to communicate an idea to a colleague. Examples of annotations include:

- Highlighting
- Arrows pointing to specific items
- Boxes and circles
- Redactions
- Handwritten notes
- Sticky notes
- Labels
- Stamps
- Callouts

Some of these items can be assigned varying colors and widths.

These annotations are accessed through the Annotation toolbar, as shown in Exhibit 9–11; there you can see examples of highlighting, arrows, and circles. Exhibit 9–12 shows examples of handwritten notes and sticky notes. Finally, in Exhibit 9–13, the user has applied stamps and a label to the photograph. When

EXHIBIT 9–11

Annotations on a
TrialDirector slide

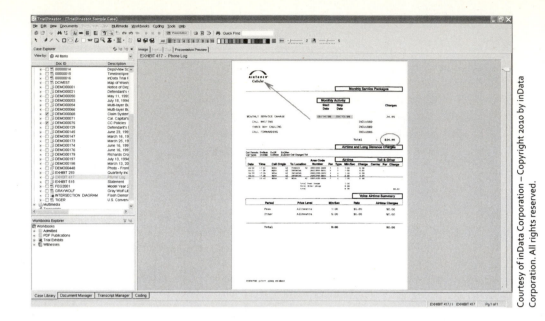

EXHIBIT 9–12

Notes on a TrialDirector slide

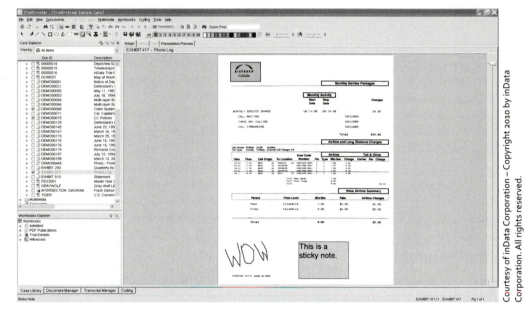

EXHIBIT 9–13

Photograph with stamps and
labels in TrialDirector

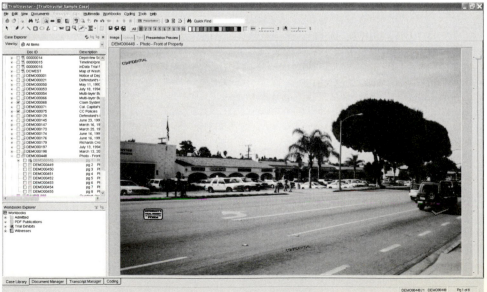

adding these annotations, the user does not destroy or spoliate the original item; rather, a new image is created that incorporates the annotations.

Workbooks

Workbooks in TrialDirector are created and used by legal professionals to store and organize the evidence needed at trial. Common examples of workbooks include those created to organize the images required for:

- Examination (and cross-examination) of individual witnesses
- Proving (or disputing) specific claims for damages
- Display at trial
- Opening and closing statements

The items held within the workbooks are not removed from the Case Explorer; rather, they are newly created image files (essentially, they are copies of the documents held within the Case Explorer). Individual workbooks are maintained and accessed through the Workbook Explorer.

Working with Depositions

Trial presentation programs typically offer the ability to store, organize, edit, and display depositions. The deposition may be displayed alone or accompanied by a scrolling transcript. In addition, it is possible to display specific images at precise times during presentation of the deposition. This allows the jurors to see and hear the witness talk about a piece of evidence while also allowing them to see an image of the actual evidence.

In addition, other types of videos may be presented to the jury, such as videos displaying the effects of a person's negligence or malpractice, damage done by a storm, or videos showing the site where the cause of action occurred (e.g., the intersection where an automobile collision occurred).

Coding

Trial presentation software gives you the opportunity to add information to individual images, which should make it easier for you to organize them prior to trial and to find them during trial.

In TrialDirector, this is accomplished by "coding" images. The Coding tab enables you to add related information to an image, such as:

- Whether an image is privileged
- Whether an image is confidential
- Page numbers
- Date
- Type of document
- Title of document
- Author(s) of document
- Recipients of document
- Source of the image

Coding may also take the form of assigning issue codes to portions of deposition testimony and images of the physical evidence of the case. This facilitates the organization and retrieval of information while preparing for trial and during the trial.

The coding information may be imported from a litigation support program (such as Summation), or the information may be input directly in TrialDirector through the Coding tab.

Presentation

The essence of any presentation software, be it one designed specifically for trial or a more generic one such as PowerPoint, is the ability to present information to a group of persons in a manner that engages them and keeps their attention. It should also be relatively simple to use, especially if it is to be used in court in front of a jury. Closing argument is not a good time to discover that the presentation software will not "present."

The Presentation mode in TrialDirector allows you to move images around the screen, integrating still images, video clips, and deposition clips into a single, seamless presentation. It is possible to prepare a script for a presentation in advance of trial, so that you do not have to fuss with the computer in the presence of the judge and jury. (See the following section for notes about rehearsing your presentations.)

COURTROOM PRESENTATION TIPS

In some legal organizations, the creation of presentations for trials falls to paralegals. Creating and designing trial presentations is different from creating other presentations. In addition, often a paralegal actually operates the computer and presentation/equipment during trial, to allow the attorney(s) to concentrate on litigation. This section offers a variety of tips and tricks related to preparing and showing courtroom presentations.

Test All Computer Equipment in Advance and Have Staff Support

It is impossible to overstate the importance of having the technology used at trial to actually work when it is supposed to. If the courtroom is equipped with its own technology, such as a projector and screen, then users only have to ensure that they have the proper cables and other hardware to interface with the court's equipment. If the court is not properly or adequately equipped, then users will have supply and set up all of the necessary equipment, such as a portable projector, screen, and speakers. Other necessary equipment might include a laptop computer, cables, extension cords, and a printer/scanner/copier.

It is crucial that you test and retest *all* of the hardware and software—in the configuration in which you plan to use it—to make sure that it works. Leave nothing to chance, and have backup equipment available if at all possible. Little things, such as testing electrical outlets, are critical; just because they are there doesn't mean they work. Never add or include new or untested equipment at the last minute; leave yourself enough time to work out any possible kinks. Thoroughly check out the courtroom in advance of the trial, if possible, so that you understand the complete layout of the room and what problems could potentially arise.

Possible complications include incompatible computer platforms, insufficient electrical connections, slow or spotty Internet or wireless connections, awkward or obstructed lines of sight for the factfinders, poor lighting, display monitors that are too small or poorly placed, and inadequate sound systems, among many, many others. The more of these obstacles you can predict and plan for (or work around), the better off your team will be.

Always Rehearse

Always rehearse, many times, before putting on a presentation to a judge or jury. This is particularly critical if a support person (such as a paralegal) will be running the hardware and/or software. It takes time to prepare trial presentations and to work out all the kinks and problems. In addition, even if the technology works, in the end it really comes down to the presenter and how well that person presents the information to the judge or jury. For the presentation to be effective, everything must work together and flow well—and that takes time and practice.

Don't Keep Judges or Juries Waiting—Bring Powerful Technology

Always make sure the software you are using can run adequately on the computer hardware you are using. Judges and juries get extremely impatient when a user's computer constantly shows the Windows "hourglass" icon. The new class of trial presentation software, in particular, has hefty computing needs in terms of both active and storage memory. Always use a computer with more than enough horsepower to get the job done. (Of course, you will have thoroughly tested your setup and presentation(s) before you get to trial, so you should know well ahead of time if there are problems in this area.)

Always Have a Backup Plan

Always have a backup plan—*always*, every time. It is a sad fact that hard disks crash, CDs and DVDs get scratched, software freezes, computers get unplugged, cables wear out, bright lights wash out computer screens, operator errors occur, and information gets accidentally deleted. It is critical that you always have a backup plan in case the technology fails. Something—anything—is better than nothing. A presentation that is printed out and can be copied and handed to the judge or jurors is better than no presentation at all.

Keep It Simple—Don't Overload Slides with Too Much Information

Presentations should be professional, clean, and simple. A common mistake is to put too many bullet points on a single slide. This makes the slide difficult to read. In addition, the font size of slide text should be relatively large, because some jurors may have trouble reading small fonts. Ambient lighting, such as from overhead fixtures or glare from courtroom windows, can wreak havoc with visibility, especially if the display monitors are undersized or poorly placed. Know ahead of time what you will be dealing with and prepare the presentation accordingly.

Use Color Conservatively

It is fine to include some color, but presentation designs should be conservative and professional—no loud, extravagant colors, and not too many colors. Color should be used to enhance the presentation, not distract the viewers.

Use Animation, Sound, and Clip Art Cautiously

Use animation, sound clips, and clip art cautiously in trial presentations. Because they often have a cartoonish quality, they tend to diminish the quality and professionalism of a presentation. It is easy for these elements to come off as cheap, cheesy, or just in poor taste. The acid test for any element is whether it enhances the comprehensibility, interest, and overall impact of the presentation.

Use Images, Maps, Video, and Charts/Graphs When Possible

Include graphical elements, such as images (photographs), maps, video, and charts/graphs, in a presentation whenever possible. They add excitement and diversity to text and many times make it easier for jurors to understand the concept you are trying to convey.

Video testimony is particularly important. For example, if a witness states something in open court that is different from his or her testimony given in a video deposition, the ability to play the video deposition in front of the jury and impeach the witness's current testimony is priceless.

Scan Key Documents and Use Markup Tools

Scan the key documents in a case, so that you can include them as part of a complete presentation. If documents are in electronic form, you can use presentation software to mark or highlight important passages for easy identification by the factfinder.

Include Timelines

Timelines are critical in just about every case that goes to trial. They explain what happened, in chronological order. Attorneys often present things out of sequence for specific reasons, and witnesses often jump around in their testimony or are unclear regarding dates and times. Hence, timelines are crucial for bringing everything in a case together for a jury.

Allow Extra Time to Pass Security Checkpoints

If you have ever tried to take a laptop computer onto an airplane, you may have an idea of what it will take to get through courthouse security with computers, projectors, speakers, and other equipment. Be sure to give yourself enough time to physically get the equipment into the courthouse and set up in the courtroom.

ETHICAL CONSIDERATIONS

Ethical considerations regarding trial and presentation software and graphics revolve around competency and rules of evidence. It is important, when putting together anything that will be used in a client's case, to make sure that it is well thought out and competently executed. It is certainly not unusual for a paralegal to be asked to create a chart, graph, table, exhibit, or even a full presentation for trial. It is extremely important that these be prepared with a high degree of accuracy and competency.

In addition, anything that is presented at trial or to a factfinder will be subject to the rules of evidence and could be objected to by the opposing party. Charts, graphs, and tables may be viewed as **demonstrative evidence**. Examples of demonstrative evidence include maps, diagrams, models, charts, and illustrations. The admissibility of demonstrative evidence is largely controlled by the rules of evidence and the judge sitting on the case. Arguments between attorneys regarding a piece of demonstrative evidence often concern whether it fairly and reasonably depicts the subject matter it covers. Thus, the heart of admissibility of demonstrative evidence depends on the accuracy, quality, and competency of the exhibit itself.

demonstrative evidence
All evidence other than testimony.

SUMMARY

Electronic courthouses, where legal professionals file documents electronically and have instant access to court information, are becoming a reality. Automated courtrooms with computers and monitors for all participants are also a reality.

Presentation software allows users to create visually interesting electronic presentations. Presentation graphics programs are used in legal organizations for creating internal training programs, public seminars, and presentations for clients, and developing trial presentations. Some of these programs are generic business presentation programs. A trial presentation program is specifically designed to meet the needs of practicing attorneys, particularly those who try cases to juries and courts.

Most presentation graphics programs have several views and display presentations to work with. Creating new presentations entails creating a background design; adding slides; adding and formatting text; adding photographs, clip art, and word art; adding graphs and charts; and creating multimedia effects and transition/animation effects.

Designing and presenting trial presentations to judges and juries takes a great deal of preparation and thought. Tips for doing this well include testing computer equipment in advance, always having a backup plan, and always rehearsing presentations. To create professional, effective presentations, keep slides simple and uncluttered; use color conservatively; use animation, sound, and clip art cautiously; use images, maps, video, and charts/graphs as much as possible; scan key documents; use markup tools; and include timelines.

KEY TERMS

background	evidence display system	slide transition
clip art	normal view	trial presentation programs
demonstrative evidence	slide show view	word art
document camera	slide sorter view	

INTERNET SITES

Internet sites for this chapter include:

ORGANIZATION	SOFTWARE PRODUCT	WORLD WIDE WEB ADDRESS
Adobe Acrobat	PDF file creation program	www.adobe.com
Case Management/Electronic Case Files	The federal courts' case management and electronic case files system	www.uscourts.gov
Corel Corp.	Presentations X3 presentation program	www.corel.com
Doar	Trial presentation services vendor	www.doar.com
Idea, Inc.	Trial Pro	www.trialpro.com
InData Software	TrialDirector trial presentation software	www.indatacorp.com
LexisNexis	TimeMap (timeline creation software)	www.casemap.com
Microsoft Corp.	PowerPoint presentation software	www.microsoft.com
Public Access to Court Electronic Records	PACER (electronic public access to federal court information)	pacer.psc.uscourts.gov
Verdict Systems	Sanction trial presentation software	www.verdictsystems.com

TEST YOUR KNOWLEDGE

1. True or False: Only a few courts, cases, or attorneys participate in the federal courts' Case Management/Electronic Case Filing system.
2. What standard do most courts use for submission of electronic documents?
3. What is a document camera?
4. True or False: Trial presentation programs and generic presentation programs such as Microsoft PowerPoint have the same features.
5. Why should you be careful when using clip art and sound files in trial presentations?
6. Name four things to remember when using presentation programs in the courtroom.

ON THE WEB EXERCISES

1. Use a general search engine, such as Google or Yahoo!, to find several articles regarding use of computer presentation programs in the courtroom or before a jury. Write a two-page paper summarizing your research.
2. Use the Internet sites listed in this chapter and/or a general search engine (such as Google or Yahoo!) to find two trial presentation programs. Compare the prices, features, support, and training available. Download trial versions of the programs if you can. Write a two-page memo summarizing your research and findings. Identify the program that you think is best and explain why.

QUESTIONS AND EXERCISES

1. Contact an attorney, paralegal, or court staff member in your area and interview that person regarding his or her experiences using technology in the courtroom, electronic filing, or accessing electronic court records. Write a two-page memo summarizing your interview.

ETHICS QUESTION

You are working with trial presentation software to prepare a brief video clip of an opposing party's deposition. As you are creating the clip, you notice that if you stop the clip one second sooner, the opposing witness appears to be scowling. You would like to present the opposing witness in a less than flattering light. What ethical issues, if any, arise from this scenario?

 Go to the Workbook to complete the Hands-On Exercises.

 Access an interactive eBook, chapter-specific interactive learning tools, including flash cards, quizzes, and more in your Paralegal CourseMate, accessed through CengageBrain.com.

GLOSSARY

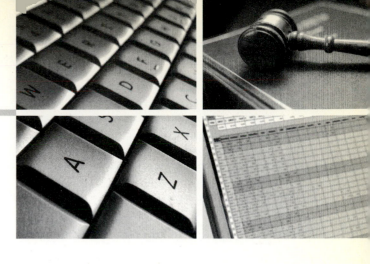

absolute cell reference   A cell address in a spreadsheet program formula that does not change when it is copied to a new location.

access rights   Network security measure that limits a user's access to only those directories and programs that the user is authorized to use.

access time   The amount of time it takes to transfer data between a storage device and RAM.

accessible data   Data that have not been deleted and can be accessed without the use of special tools and/or software.

activity hourly rate   A fee based on hourly rates that vary depending on the type of service or activity performed and the degree of difficulty of the activity.

aged accounts receivable report   A report showing all cases that have outstanding balances due and how much these balances are past due.

analytical litigation support programs   A type of software that helps legal professionals analyze a case from a number of different perspectives and draw conclusions about cause-and-effect relationships between facts and evidence in a case.

antivirus and antispyware utilities   Programs that attempt to prevent virus and spyware programs from getting into the computer system; most also function to locate and remove any viruses or spyware that do manage to get into the computer.

application service provider (ASP)   A company that provides software or a service application through the Internet directly to the user's computer.

application software   Instructions (programs) that tell the computer to perform a specific function or task, such as word processing.

arithmetic operators   Symbols that tell a spreadsheet how to compute values. Examples include addition signs, subtraction signs, and multiplication signs.

attorney or paralegal hourly rate   A fee based on the attorney's or paralegal's level of expertise and experience in a particular area.

automatic page numbering   Word-processor feature that automatically numbers the pages of a document for the user; also renumbers pages as material is moved, added, or deleted.

auxiliary storage device   A device that stores information so that it can be retrieved for later use. Auxiliary storage devices retain data after power to the computer has been turned off. Auxiliary storage devices include flash drives, hard disk drives, and others.

background   The design on which the other elements of the presentation (words, clip art, etc.) are placed.

backing up   Making a copy of a user's computer files.

backup utility   Program that creates a copy of a user's hard disk or other storage device. The backup copy can be restored if the hard disk is damaged or lost.

bar code scanner   Device that reads the special lines of bar codes. Can be used to track documents in litigation, or physical objects such as office furniture and equipment.

bar/column graph   A graph consisting of a sequence of bars that illustrate numerical values.

Bates stamp   Marks a page with a sequential number and then automatically advances to the next number.

billable hour   Sixty minutes of legal services.

billing   The process of issuing invoices (bills) to collect monies for legal services performed and for expenses incurred.

blended hourly rate fee   A single hourly rate that is set by taking into account the mix of attorneys working on the matter.

blog   A website with information contained in posts (writings resembling diary or journal entries) that are arranged in reverse chronological order.

bookmark   A tool that enables a user to quickly and easily go back to a website or web page.

Boolean logic search   A computer search that allows a search request to include or exclude words, or use other search criteria, so that the search is either refined or broadened.

cable modem   A data modem that is designed to work over cable TV lines.

calendaring   A generic term used to describe the function of recording appointments for any type of business; includes personal information management.

case management   A legal term that usually encompasses functions such as docket control, deadlines, things to do, contact information by case, case notes, document assembly, document tracking by case, integrated billing, and email.

case retainer   A fee that is billed at the beginning of a matter, is not refundable to the client, and is usually paid at the beginning of the case as an incentive for the office to take the case.

case type productivity report   A report showing which types of cases (e.g., criminal, personal injury, bankruptcy, etc.) are the most profitable.

cash advance   Unearned monies that are paid before services are rendered, to cover the attorney's future fees and expenses.

CD-ROM legal database   A CD-ROM disk containing a (searchable) legal database, such as a state case law reporter.

cell   An intersection between a row and a column in a spreadsheet.

cell address   The row and column location of a cell, usually expressed with column identifier first and row identifier second.

283

cell pointer   The cursor in a spreadsheet program.

cell width   The number of characters that can be placed in any given cell in a spreadsheet program.

central processing unit (CPU)   The part of a computer that contains the processor chip and main memory. The CPU organizes and manipulates information, in addition to coordinating with peripheral devices.

centralized word-processing system   A system in which all the word-processing documents for an organization are input or typed in a single location or by one department (i.e., a word processing department).

cite checking   Doing research to verify that a case or statute is still valid and that the decision has not been overturned or the statute repealed.

clawback   The ability to have privileged material that has been produced inadvertently returned with no waiver of privilege.

client hourly rate   A fee based on a single hourly charge for the client, regardless of which attorney works on the case and what she or he does on the case.

client/server network   A network that uses a server (or servers) to enhance the function and meet the needs of the other computers on the network.

clip art   Predrawn art.

column   An area that extends down a page vertically.

comment   Word-processor feature that allows a user to annotate and create notes in a document without changing the text of the document.

compare documents   Word-processor feature that allows a user to compare and contrast two documents, either side by side or by blacklining (usually through the creation of a third document showing differences).

compression utility   Program that reorganizes a file so that the file takes up less room when it is saved. Many large files that are downloaded from the Internet are routinely compressed to reduce the time needed for the download.

computer   An electronic device that accepts input data, processes data, outputs data, and stores data electronically; types include desktop, laptop, handheld, tablet, and file server.

computer-aided transcription (CAT)   A process that automatically deciphers a court reporter's notes and converts them into a computer-readable format.

computer-assisted legal research (CALR)   Research method in which computers are used to find and retrieve legal information.

central processing unit (CPU)   The part of a computer that contains the processor chip and main memory. The CPU organizes and manipulates information, in addition to coordinating with peripheral devices.

computer virus   A destructive computer program that may be designed to delete data, corrupt files, or do other damage; may also be self-replicating, using an "infected" computer to transmit itself to other computers.

connectors   Characters that define or show a relationship between the keywords in a search query.

contingency fee   A fee collected if the attorney successfully represents the client; typically a percentage of the total recovery.

data filtering   The process of searching and culling the data to find relevant information and reduce the overall size of the dataset.

data value   One item of information; the smallest piece of information in a table.

database   A collection of related data items. Databases are created because the information contained in them must be accessed, organized, and used.

database management system (DBMS)   Application software that manages a database by storing, searching, sorting, and organizing data.

decentralized word-processing system   A system in which individuals or separate departments in an organization perform their own word processing.

de-duplication (de-duping)   The process of marking or deleting records that are duplicates.

deleted data   Data that at one time were active on a computer, but which have since been deleted.

demonstrative evidence   All evidence other than testimony.

disaster recovery plan   A prewritten plan of action to be followed if a disaster befalls the legal organization.

discovery   The pretrial stage of litigation where parties disclose to each other information about their case.

docket control   A legal-specific term that refers to entering, organizing, tracking, and controlling all the appointments, deadlines, and due dates for a legal organization.

document abstract litigation support system   Software that allows users to enter document abstracts or summaries into a computer and then search and retrieve the information contained in those abstracts or summaries.

document assembly software   Powerful computer program that creates standardized templates and forms.

document camera   An overhead projector that uses a camera to display hard-copy documents that have not been imaged.

document imaging   A system in which documents are scanned into a computer and the documents' actual images (similar to photographs) are retained in the computer.

document management software   Program that organizes, controls, distributes, and allows for extensive searching of electronic documents, typically in a networked environment.

double indenting   Word-processor feature (also found in other types of programs) that indents text an equal distance from the left and right margins.

DSL (Digital Subscriber Line)   A type of digital phone line that allows both data and voice to be transmitted on the same line, simultaneously if desired. Transmission speed is fairly fast.

earned retainer   The money the law office or attorney has earned and is entitled to deposit in the office's or attorney's own bank account.

electronic billing   Client billing that uses a standard electronic format, using such means as the Internet, and conforms to standard billing codes.

electronic discovery (e-discovery)   The process of producing and receiving litigation documents in electronic format.

electronic filing   Supplying electronic versions of legal documents to a court, via the Internet or other electronic means, when the court does not require the hard copy of the document.

electronic mail (email)   Computerized communication function that enables users to send and receive messages almost instantly.

electronically stored information (ESI)   The term used by the Federal Rules of Civil Procedure to refer to all electronic data, including writings, drawings, graphs, charts, photographs, sound recordings, images, and other data compilations stored in any medium from which information can be obtained or translated.

encryption   Process of running a message through an encoder that uses an encrypting key to alter the characters in the message. Unless the person wanting to read the message has the encryption key needed to decode it, the message appears unreadable.

endnote   Material that is printed at the end of a chapter or document; marked in text by a numbered referent.

evidence display system   Technology that provides networked computer monitors to a judge, jury, court reporter, clerk, attorneys, and the public.

expense slip   A record of each expense item a firm incurs on behalf of the client.

extranet   A secure web-based site that allows clients to access information about their cases and collaborate with the legal professionals who are providing legal services to them.

field   A column in a table that contains a category of information.

File Transfer Protocol (FTP)   A tool or standard for transferring electronic files over the Internet.

Find a Case by Party Name   A Westlaw feature that allows a user who knows the name of at least one party to retrieve a case without knowing the case citation or entering a search query.

Find by Citation   A Westlaw feature that allows a user to immediately retrieve a specific case or statute by entering its citation.

firewall   Security measure that allows users from inside an organization to access the Internet but keeps outside users from entering the computer or LAN.

flat fee   A fee for specific legal services that is billed as a fixed amount.

footer   Text that appears at the bottom of each page of a document.

footnote   Material that is printed at the bottom of a page; marked in text by a numbered referent.

form   Setup that allows a user to view, enter, and edit data in a custom format designed by the user.

formulas   Expressions used in spreadsheet programs to automatically perform calculations on other values.

full-text retrieval litigation support system   Software that enables a user to search (and retrieve information from) the full text of documents stored in the system.

function command   A predefined calculation used in a spreadsheet program to speed up the process of entering complex formulas.

Get by Citation   A LexisNexis feature that allows a user to immediately retrieve a specific case or statute by entering its citation.

Get by Party Name   A LexisNexis feature that allows a user to retrieve a case by entering the name(s) of a party (or parties).

gigahertz (GHz)   Measure of the clock speed of a computer.

hard disk drive   A reliable and fast auxiliary storage device that stores data on a rigid magnetic disk; may be built into the computer (internal) or a freestanding peripheral device (external).

hardware   The physical equipment of a computer system, as opposed to programs or software.

harvesting data   The process of collecting ESI from the client's information systems.

header   A title or heading that appears at the top of each page of a document.

Headnotes and Key Numbers   Westlaw feature that classifies each legal issue in a case and allows users to search and retrieve other cases with similar Headnotes and Key Numbers.

hourly rate fee   A fee for legal services that is billed to the client by the hour at an agreed upon rate.

image format   A file structure that shows an image of a document as if it were being viewed in the original application, without the need to use or even have the original application.

imaging   Scanning a document into a computer so the user can see an exact picture of the document on the computer.

inaccessible data   Data that can be accessed only with the use of special tools and/or software.

individual search engine   Search engine that compiles its own searchable database.

in-house computerized litigation support system   A litigation support system set up by the firm's or attorney's own staff on their own computer(s).

input   Data or information that is entered or transferred into a computer (including by keyboard, mouse, scanner, voice, etc.).

input device   Devices used to enter information into a computer; include the mouse, keyboards, scanners, voice recognition devices, digital cameras, and others.

instant messaging (IM)   Communication function that allows users to converse in real time with other users who are using the same IM program. As soon as a user connects to the Internet, the user will know which of his or her colleagues are signed on and be able to send them messages.

Internet   One of the world's largest computer networks; actually a "network of networks." It allows hundreds of millions of users around the world to share information.

Internet service provider (ISP)   Supplies users with Internet services such as the World Wide Web, email, listservs, newsgroups, and others.

intranet   An internal network designed to provide and disseminate information to internal staff; most mimic the look and feel of the World Wide Web.

invisible web   Term for the large portion of the World Wide Web that is not accessible to search engine spiders. This includes PDF files, password-protected sites, some databases, documents behind firewalls, and other data/sites.

KeyCite   Westlaw feature that allows users to determine if a case, statute, or other document is good law and enables users to expand their research by finding other sources that have cited the reference.

landscape   A method of printing that arranges data across the width of a page.

legacy data   Data created with obsolete computer media and programs.

legal malpractice   An attorney's breach of an ordinary standard of care that a reasonable attorney would have adhered to under the same circumstances.

library gateway   A collection of databases and information sites arranged by subject.

license agreement   Contract setting out the user's rights and restrictions on how a piece of software can be used.

line graph   A graph that plots numerical values as a time line.

listserv   An electronic mailing list that allows people on the list to send messages to and receive messages from everyone on the list via email.

litigation hold   An order suspending destruction or disposal of all relevant hard-copy and electronically stored information, instituted when a party reasonably anticipates litigation.

litigation support service provider   A company that, for a fee, sets up a litigation support system and enters all documents necessary for a case.

litigation support software   Program that assists attorneys and paralegals in organizing, storing, retrieving, and summarizing the information that is gathered during the litigation of a lawsuit.

local area network (LAN)   A multiuser system linking computers that are in close proximity for the purpose of communication.

Locate in Result   A Westlaw command that allows a user to search the retrieved documents for particular terms, whether or not those terms appeared in the user's original search.

macro   Word-processor feature that records the user's keystrokes, saves those keystrokes, and then allows the user to play those keystrokes back.

magnetic tape system   Storage device that records data on magnetic tape.

main memory   The part of the CPU that stores information that the computer is processing. Main memory consists of read-only memory and random-access memory.

management reports   Reports used to help managers analyze whether the office is operating in an efficient, effective, and profitable manner.

memory chips   Parts of a computer that store or hold information.

merging   The process of combining a form with a list of variables to automatically produce a document; sometimes called document generation.

metadata   Electronically stored information that may identify the origin, date, author, usage, comments, or other information about a file; "data about data."

metasearch engine   Search engine that does not crawl the Web or compile its own database, but instead sends the user's search request to a number of different individual search engines and then eliminates duplicates and sorts the sites retrieved.

modem   A device that allows computers in different locations to communicate using a telephone line.

monitor   Screen that displays computer output.

mouse   An input device used to move the cursor on the monitor. The cursor moves in the same direction as the mouse is moved.

native format   A file structure as defined by the original application in which the file was created.

Natural Language   A query/search technique that uses plain English, without the need for complex connectors or syntax, to search for documents.

network operating system   System that handles communication tasks between the computers on a network.

normal view   PowerPoint screen that shows the slide that is being created, an outline of the total presentation, and speaker's notes for the slide currently displayed.

objective/bibliographical coding   System in which only basic information about documents (document number, document name, date, author, recipient, and so forth) is recorded in a document abstract database. The coder makes no subjective characterizations about the document.

offline   No longer connected to the Internet; in relation to fee-based CALR services, no longer connected to the information service and thus not accruing charges (except possibly for printing or downloading).

online   Connected to the Internet; in relation to fee-based CALR services, connected to the service and incurring charges.

operating account   Bank account used by a law firm for the deposit of earned fees and payment of law firm expenses.

operating system software (program)   A set of instructions that tell the computer how to operate its own circuitry and manage its components; also controls how the computer communicates with input, output, and auxiliary storage devices. Allows the user to manage the computer.

optical character recognition (OCR)   A technology that allows the text of documents to be read or scanned into a computer so the text of the document can be searched or brought into a word processor to be edited.

optical storage devices   Devices that use laser beams to write data onto small plastic disks. Optical storage devices can record hundreds of megabytes of data on a single disk.

output   Information or computer results that are produced or transmitted from a computer to a user as a result of the computer's operations (including to monitor, printer, etc.).

output device   Peripheral device that provides a user with the data a computer has generated, accessed, or manipulated.

paperless office   Firm in which all hard-copy documents are converted into electronic form(s) for storage, processing, and distribution.

password   Code entered into a computer system or software that acts as a key, allowing the user to access the system and the information it contains.

peer-to-peer network   A computer network in which each computer acts as both a server and a client.

peripheral devices   Pieces of equipment that are connected to a computer to perform specific functions, such as storing information (auxiliary storage devices), inputting information (input devices), outputting information (output devices), and communicating with other computers (communication devices).

personal information manager (PIM) System that consolidates a number of different tasks into one computer program. Most PIMs handle or provide functions for calendaring, things to do, a contact database that tracks names and addresses of people, note-taking, email, and other tasks.

phishing A type of Internet fraud; "phishers" send fraudulent emails, in which they impersonate legitimate senders, in hopes of gaining personal information from responders.

pie chart A chart that represents each value as a piece or percentage of a whole (a total "pie").

Pleading Wizard Feature in some word processors that helps legal professionals quickly and easily create a legal pleading by providing a standard form or forms having users answer questions about the pleading to be created.

podcast An audio or video recording that is posted on the Internet and made available for users to download so they can listen or watch it on a computer or mobile computing device.

Portable Document Format (PDF) A file format developed by Adobe Systems, Inc., for sharing files independently of the application that created the file or the computer's operating system.

portal A "jumping-off" spot for many things on the Web, offering searching, hierarchical directories, news, sports, shopping, entertainment, and much more.

portrait A method of printing that arranges data down the length of a page.

power-on password Password that the computer immediately prompts the user to enter after the machine has been turned on, but before the computer has completely booted the operating system software. If the user does not know the password, the system will not start and the computer will be unusable.

pre-billing report A rough draft compilation of billings.

primary file A file that contains the information that remains the same (the constant) in a document that is used more than once; usually referred to as a form or template in a merge document.

processor chip The part of the computer that performs the actual arithmetic computations and logic functions.

project management software Application program that allows the user to track the sequence and timing of the separate activities of a larger project or task.

proximity search A computer search that scans a database for words that are in a given proximity to one another.

pure retainer A fee that obligates the office to be available to represent the client throughout the agreed upon time period.

query Statement that extracts data from a table based on criteria designed by the user. A query allows a user to search for and sort only the information the user is looking for at that time.

random-access memory (RAM) A part of main memory that is temporary and volatile in nature; it is erased every time the computer's power is turned off. Application programs and data are loaded into RAM when the computer is processing the data.

read-only memory (ROM) A part of main memory that contains permanent information a computer uses to operate itself. ROM can be read, but cannot be written to.

real-time transcription System through which an attorney or paralegal connects a computer with the appropriate software to the court reporter's transcription machine, so that within seconds of the testimony being spoken, a rough-draft version of the transcript appears on the computer screen.

record A collection of fields that is treated as a unit; essentially, one row in a table.

recurring entry A calendar entry that must be done regularly or often.

relative cell reference A cell address in a spreadsheet program formula that automatically changes to reflect its new location when it is copied.

removable drive A small portable device that stores a large amount of data; often used to transfer information between computers.

report Function that extracts and prints data from a table or query as designed by the user. Whereas forms are designed to be used on the screen, reports are designed to be printed.

ResultsPlus A Westlaw feature that automatically includes other documents related to a user's search, such as legal texts, treatises, and law review articles; no additional search is needed to retrieve these supplementary materials.

retainer for general representation A retainer typically used when a client such as a corporation or school board requires continuing legal services throughout the year.

root expander A character that enables a legal information system to retrieve multiple words with the same root.

row An area that extends across a page horizontally.

RSS A group of formats that are used to publish and distribute news feeds, blogs, and podcasts.

rule-based entry A method of entering events in a case management system so that entering one event automatically triggers creation of a list of subsequent calendaring events, based on a rule that was programmed into the application.

safe harbor A provision of the FRCP providing that parties who act in good faith but inadvertently destroy ESI as a routine part of their information systems handling are not subject to sanctions for that destruction.

sampling data The process of testing data to determine if it is appropriate for production.

search query An instruction to an information service to search a specific database for the occurrence of certain words and combinations of words. Searches can be limited by restricting the query terms, by searching only in specific databases, and by searching only in certain parts of a document (such as the title, synopsis, headnote, etc.).

secondary file The file that contains the information that varies (the variable) in a merge document.

single-user system A computer that can accommodate only one person at a time and is not linked to other systems or computers.

single-word search A computer search that scans a database for matches to a single word.

slide show view   PowerPoint screen used during a presentation or when the user wants to preview how the audience will actually see the slide. Only the current slide is shown on the screen. The program interface, menus, outline view, and speaker's notes are not shown.

slide sorter view   PowerPoint screen that shows the slides in the presentation, but in a greatly reduced format; typically used to review and/or change the order of slides.

slide transition   Effects that control how the program proceeds from one slide to another.

soft deletions   Information that has been deleted and is not available to the user, but which nonetheless has not been overwritten; can often be fully restored, with complete integrity, by forensic experts.

software   Computer programs that instruct the computer hardware how to function and perform tasks.

sound card   A device that enhances the sounds that come out of a computer and/or enables speakers attached to a computer to function. Nearly all computers now come with a sound card.

spam   Unwanted or unsolicited email messages that are sent to many recipients; the electronic equivalent of junk mail.

specialty search engine   Search engine that searches only in specific topical areas or sites.

speech recognition   The ability of a computer to understand spoken words.

spoliation   The destruction of relevant documents (or other materials) in litigation.

spreadsheet   A computerized version of an accountant's worksheet or ledger page.

spreadsheet software   Programs that calculate and manipulate numbers using labels, values, and formulas.

spyware   A general term for software that tracks a user's movement on the Internet for advertising and marketing purposes, collects personal information about the user, or changes the configuration of the user's computer without the user's consent.

stacked column graph   A graph that depicts values as separate sections in a single or stacked column.

statute of limitations   A law that sets a limit on the length of time a party has to file a suit. If a case is filed after the statute of limitations has run (expired), the claim is barred and is dismissed as a matter of law.

storage   Retention of electronic information for future use (using storage devices such as hard disks, CD-ROMs, DVDs, flash drives, and other media).

storage capacity   The maximum amount of data that can be stored on a device.

style   A named set of formatting characteristics that users can apply to text.

subject directory   A site maintained by a staff of people who select sites to include in the directory.

subjective coding   Entering information in a document abstract program about what the document means, including what case issues the document is relevant to or notes about the document.

subject-specific database   A database devoted to a single subject or area.

super wildcard search   A computer search that scans a database for derivatives of a word, using variations both in front of and in back of the root word.

table   A collection of related information stored in rows and columns.

table of authorities   Automated word-processor feature that allows the program to generate an accurate list of case and statute citations (authorities), along with the page number(s) on which each cite appears.

Terms and Connectors   A search technique that uses Boolean logic and operators/connectors to connect query terms.

text   Descriptive data, such as headings and titles, used for reference purposes in a spreadsheet.

TIFF (Tagged Image File Format)   A vendor-neutral file structure that produces image format documents.

timekeeper   Anyone who bills for time, including partners, associates, and paralegals.

timekeeper productivity report   A report showing how much billable and nonbillable time is being spent by each timekeeper.

timekeeping   Tracking time for the purpose of billing clients.

timeslip   A slip of paper or computer record that records information about the legal services legal professionals provide to each client.

track changes   Word-processor feature that allows reviewers to make or recommend changes to a document; these changes can later be either accepted or rejected by the original author.

trial presentation programs   Presentation graphics programs specifically designed to meet the needs of trial attorneys.

trust or escrow account   A bank account, separate and apart from a law office's or attorney's operating bank account, where unearned client funds are deposited.

unearned retainer   Money that is paid up front by the client as an advance against the attorney's future fees and expenses. Until the money is actually earned by the attorney or law office, it actually belongs to the client.

uniform resource locator (URL)   The address of a web page.

universal character   A character that represents one letter or number; enables a legal information service to retrieve words with minor variations.

utility software   Instructions that help users with the housekeeping and maintenance tasks a computer requires; helps manage either the hardware or software aspects of a computer.

value billing   A type of fee agreement that is based not on the time required to perform the work, but on the basis of the perceived value of the services to the client.

values   Numbers that are entered into a spreadsheet program for the purpose of making calculations.

videoconferencing   A private broadcast between two or more remote locations, with live image transmission, display, and sound. Uses data communications to conduct long-distance, face-to-face meetings.

video adapter card   Piece of hardware that acts as an interface between the monitor and the computer.

Voice over Internet Protocol (VoIP)   Functionality that allows users to make telephone calls using a broadband Internet connection instead of a regular phone line.

web browser   The interface or program that allows the user to see web pages.

"what if" analysis   A feature of spreadsheets that allows the user to build a spreadsheet and then change the data to reflect alternative planning assumptions or scenarios.

wide area network (WAN)   A multiuser system linking computers that may be located thousands of miles apart.

wildcard search   A computer search that scans a database for derivatives of a word.

Windows   A graphical operating system developed by Microsoft for IBM-compatible computers. Various versions of Windows include Windows XP, Windows Vista, and Windows 7.

wireless modem   Modems that many mobile phones and handheld computers now use to connect to the Internet.

wireless networking   System that allows computers on the network to communicate with each other using wireless antennas coordinated through a wired access point.

word art   Feature that allows users to add special formatting to text.

word-processing software   Program used to edit, manipulate, and revise text to create documents.

World Wide Web   An Internet system, navigation tool, and graphical/multimedia interface that retrieves information using links to other web pages. To access the Web, a user needs a web browser program.

INDEX

Up to $500 Tuition Reimbursement for You Plus, Up to a $500 Credit for Your Firm

Paralegals trained on Abacus are among the most valuable legal professionals in today's job market. Technology makes a difference and successful attorneys know the importance of proven products and skilled staff. Technology is also worth money to paralegals and their firms.

Special Offer for Students & Instructors

This course is the launch pad for your career and qualifies you and your law firm for valuable benefits:

1. **We'll send you a check for $50 for each user (first time purchase) of AbacusLaw. You can put it towards tuition for this course or your ongoing legal education.**

2. **By hiring you for its staff, your firm can receive a discount of $50 for each first time AbacusLaw user, up to $500.**

3. **New Abacus users get unlimited access to online training.**

With AbacusLaw, law firms avoid duplicate data entry, save time on administrative tasks and reduce errors. Calendars, contacts, cases, conflict checking, time, billing and accounting are all integrated in one quick-to-learn, easy-to-use program.

Abacus calendaring lets you use court rules to ensure complete and accurate scheduling. Color displays show conflicts and events by type or by attorney. It's one of the many powerful, easy-to-use features of AbacusLaw.

ABACUS ™
Award Winning Legal Software

You're eligible for the tuition check and your firm can take advantage of the hiring bonus offer if you are currently a legal assistant/paralegal student or instructor, starting today and for a full year after completing this course. For details, call us at **800-726-3339** or visit **www.abacuslaw.com**. You'll be glad you did.

Reliably create and distribute PDF documents and forms

Ideal for people who prepare and share PDF documents, Acrobat 9 is the world's leading PDF writer and contains the capabilities needed to combine multiple files in a single PDF. Easily create fillable PDF forms. And apply basic document security features.

- **Combine and organize content in a single PDF file**
  Combine documents, e-mails, images, spreadsheets, and web pages in a single PDF file that preserves the formatting of the originals.

- **Quickly create and distribute forms**
  Use the new Form Wizard to create forms from paper or electronic documents that can be filled in and returned electronically.

- **Share documents more securely**
  Easy-to-use security features enable you to password-protect PDF files. Set permissions to control printing, copying, or changes. And apply digital signatures to ensure authenticity.

Learn more at http://www.adobe.com/acrobat

TOWERING
COLLECTIONS
OF **PAPER**
AND **ELECTRONIC**
DOCUMENTS?

Cut Them Down To Size With LAW PreDiscovery™

Only LA W PreDisco very has the power and flexibility to help you manage even the most daunting data collections—quickly and efficiently. W hether you're dealing with hard copy or hard drives, use LAW PreDiscovery to reduce initial processing costs!

On average, LAW PreDiscovery **pays for itself within two months.**
To see how much you could save, check out our exclusive **ROI calculator** at **lexisnexis.com/cutdiscovery**

 LexisNexis®

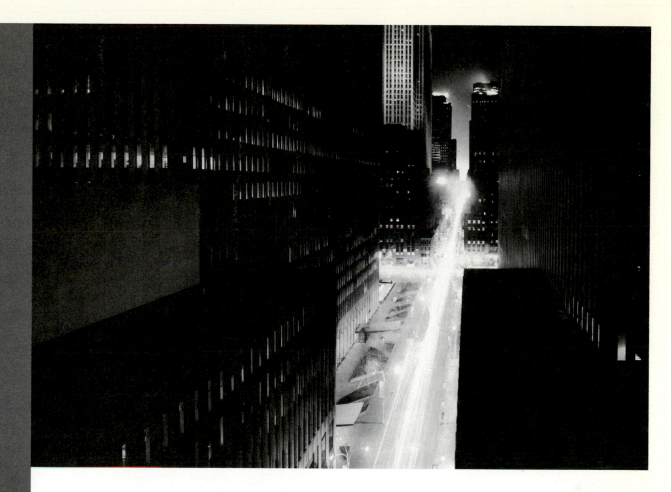

You told us the shortest distance between your email and our research is a straight line.

Introducing Lexis® *for* Microsoft® Office. Focus on delivering work for your clients, not switching between programs. Now, when you're creating a Word document or working in Outlook,® you can pull content directly from Lexis® with intuitive simplicity. We've teamed with Microsoft® to bring this innovation to our customers' existing work flow processes. It's just one example of intuitive tools created for legal minds, by legal minds. Another LexisNexis® innovation that enables better outcomes.

 LexisNexis®   For more information, go to www.lexisnexis.com/office

AD Summation

PUTTING LITIGATORS IN COMMAND

AD Summation is an award-winning suite of litigation support solutions that allows you to manage massive volumes of information for legal review and case data management. When you command every aspect of your case, you win.

ALL THE TOOLS YOU NEED, FROM ONE RELIABLE SOURCE

Managing massive volumes of information efficiently and accurately is the key to winning complex cases. AD Summation leads the industry in providing the solution to organize, find and distill large volumes of disparate information – in one easy-to-use application. All the key evidence you need is at hand during every phase of your case.

A SOLUTION FOR EVERY SITUATION

Only AD Summation offers a complete and comprehensive solution that works for every situation and every member of your legal team – whether the case you're working on is big or small, in-house or hosted.

AD SUMMATION IBLAZE

Power and portability are yours with our premium, award-winning litigation support solution. Designed for the desktop or laptop, this solution helps you efficiently manage case information, such as transcripts and documents, with the benefits of full-text imaging, PDF support, OCR on-the-fly, electronic evidence support and comprehensive production tools.

AD SUMMATION ENTERPRISE

The award-winning technology and time-tested functionality of iBlaze is combined with the power of a scalable database, in this robust solution designed for scale in an enterprise environment. Big cases require powerful support, and AD Summation Enterprise lets you master the massive amounts of information generated by today's complex cases.

CASEVANTAGE

For over a decade AD Summation has offered an award-winning, database-driven litigation support software platform that provides secure Internet access to case data and eDiscovery tools using nothing more than a standard Web browser. Thanks to its intuitive Web-based interface, AD Summation CaseVantage is the ideal legal review software platform for working with distributed teams and outside parties. Simple to learn and use, CaseVantage allows the case administrator to set up new users in minutes, using simple screens to define user properties and preferences including key contacts, permissions, contract-specific billing information and client-specific data storage locations.

AD SUMMATION LITIGATION SERVICES

Ideal for large cases that involve multi-party and multi-district litigation, AD Summation Litigation Services is a subscription-based hosting service that lets you collaborate securely and successfully on a reliable, neutral website.

CONTACT US TODAY

800.574.5199 / +1.801.377.5410
sales@accessdata.com

AccessData
A Pioneer in Digital Investigations Since 1987

AccessData Group is the maker of Summation and has pioneered digital investigations and litigation support for more than 20 years. AccessData's solutions are best of breed in litigation hold, forensic collection, data processing, advanced analysis, reporting, legal review and case data management. With AccessData Group you can address the entire EDRM, leveraging time-tested, court-validated technology with the same advanced analytics relied on by government agencies and law enforcement. Yet, AccessData solutions are by far the easiest to use, so our customers are able leverage our robust solutions without having to pay for training or additional services to get up and running.

inData **TrialDirector**® 6

Trial Presentation Software

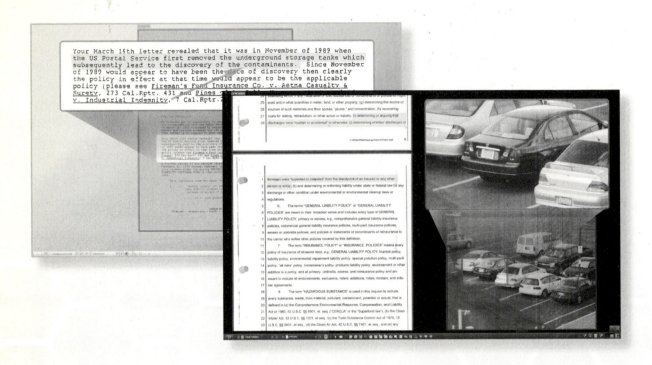

POWERFUL NEW FEATURES INCLUDE:

New Pack-N-Go

Use this handy wizard to pack up your entire case, then simply unpack it on your laptop for trial.

New Presentation Mode

TrialDirector's new presentation engine has been completely re-designed for a more dynamic presentation.

New Clip Editing

With TrialDirector 6, clip creation and editing is easier, faster, and more intuitive than ever.

Grid View - it's Back!

The Grid View is back and better than ever! New enhancements make exhibit navigation a breeze.

For a complete list of additional features and free evaluation software, visit www.trialdirector.com or call 800-828-8292.

inData®

Compatible with Windows 7